1 The early dribbling game of organised football with seven forwards and sometimes even as many as eight used.
2 Scotland's successful withdrawal to a stronger midfield in the 1870s.
3 The 2-3-5 of the 1880s and a defensive drift.
4 The 'WM' formation of the 1930s with a defensive centre back introduced.
5 The 4-2-4 formation developed from Hungary and Brazil in the 1950s and an extra central defender.
6 Italy's ultra defensive 'Catenaccio' system from the 1960s with a 'libero' (free back) or sweeper at the back of four defenders.
7 The 4-3-3 'wingless wonders' style popular after England's 1966 World Cup success. Only by comparison with **6** is it a more adventurous system. The Open Arrow compares it differently with **5**.
8 The 4-4-2 system with its heavily populated midfield area from the 1970s.

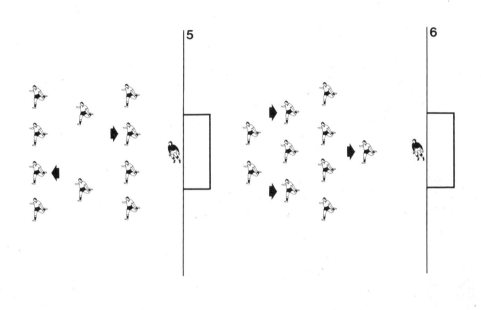

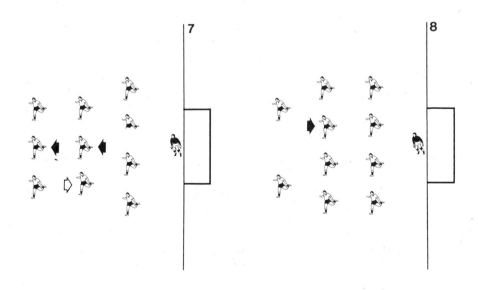

THE **GUINNESS** BOOK OF
SOCCER
FACTS AND FEATS

Jack Rollin

GUINNESS SUPERLATIVES LIMITED
2 CECIL COURT, LONDON ROAD, ENFIELD, MIDDLESEX

© Jack Rollin and Guinness Superlatives Ltd 1978

Editorial: Stan Greenberg and Alex E Reid
Design: David L Roberts
Photo Research: Beverley Waites
Artwork: Pat Gibbon, Jan Sem and David L Roberts

Published in Great Britain by
Guinness Superlatives Ltd
2 Cecil Court, London Road, Enfield, Middlesex

ISBN 0 900424 45 1

'Guinness' is a registered trade mark of
Arthur Guinness Son & Co Ltd

Colour separation by
Newsele Litho Ltd, London and Milan

Printed in Great Britain by
Ebenezer Baylis & Son Ltd, Leicester
and bound by
The Newdigate Press Ltd, Dorking

ACKNOWLEDGEMENTS
The author wishes to acknowledge the following
sources: Maurice Golesworthy, The Encyclopaedia of
Association Football; C. R. Williamson; Rothmans Football Yearbooks; FIFA News; World Soccer; also the
following assistance: Peter Dunk and Margaret
Millership.
The author and publishers wish to acknowledge the
following for black and white photographs: Brian
Bramley, Aldershot News p.93, 94, 95; Coloursport p.9,
11(l), 14(u), 27, 91(lr), 111, 115, 116, 127, 161, 173, 175(lr),
199, 201; Keystone Press p.10(l); Popperfoto p.9(l), 11(r),
13(l), 26, 128, 175(ll); Press Association p.91(ll), 196,
218(l); Radio Times Hulton Picture Library p.10(r), 28,
175(u); Syndication International p.6(u), 7, 12, 13(u),
14(l), 91(u), 129, 218(u), 235.

CONTENTS

INTRODUCTION

This is not a history book or even one which specifically concerns itself with soccer records. But it does attempt to present some of the achievements in the game from a rather different angle than usual.

Soccer has never been well served in its statistics, a thin line often dividing fact from fiction. Indeed, though organised football has been in existence for more than a century, the retention of accurate records has yet to be perpetuated.

There is no official source of actual goalscorers. In this country the Football Association and the Football League are concerned with match results and scores only. Individual clubs keep their own records but by no means all of them.

In the days before the turn of the century in particular, contemporary reports often made scant reference to actual goalscorers and, carried to an absurdity, this practice was partly responsible on one occasion for there being confusion over the final score in an international match involving two of the home countries.

Moreover there is a tendency by clubs to eliminate own goals in order, understandably, to boost the performances of their own players. There has never been an attempt to decide what does or does not constitute an own goal. Similarly if two players are concerned in the scoring of a particular goal and a deflection occurs off one of them there is no ruling to solve this problem either.

There also remains a reluctance to recognise the status of the substitute. Many consider them to be superfluous as far as records are concerned even though they have been in regular Football League usage alone for 13 seasons.

Perhaps in our insular thoughts we still consider them to be 'not quite cricket'. In cricket a sub is never named, can only field and never bats. Yet in football he becomes an integral part of the team immediately he steps on to the field.

Elsewhere in the world the substitute when used is given full recognition, just as paradoxically this country awards him international status.

Here, too, is another area of some confusion. Though international appearances by players are referred to as 'caps', from the practice in England at least of awarding an actual cap to the player concerned, the individual receives one each for matches against foreign teams but in the British International Championship he has one only for the three matches involved in a given series. 'Caps' do not exist abroad.

Then again, in South America, it is widely practised that international fixtures fulfilled by the national team against even club sides are regarded as full fixtures and their players are listed as having made international appearances in them.

There is no doubt that the oldest club in the world is Sheffield F.C. probably formed in 1855, the year given as its foundation. Only the minute book for 1857 is in existence though one for 1855 was apparently lost.

The first F.A. Cup Final produced a player who participated under an assumed name and though this does reflect the casual informality associated with its early years, it provides more evidence that to discuss, in any serious terms, the origins of the game, whether in China, Japan or in Rome, would be akin to mythology.

If Cambridge University produced one of the first set of rules it was Oxford who initially showed how the game should be played. They appeared in six F.A. Cup semi-finals, four finals and even won it in 1874.

Also the term 'soccer' is said to have arisen out of the habit prevalent at Oxford University of adding 'er' to certain words like togs (toggers), swots or mugs (swotters or muggers). Towards the end of the 19th century the game was always referred to as Association Football to differentiate between it and Rugby football, but it was at Oxford that they took the 'soc' out of Association and then turned this into 'soccer'.

The word is often attributed to one of Oxford University's most famous internationals, Charles Wreford Brown. When asked one day whether he was going to play rugger he replied 'No – soccer'.

The keeping of a record of football statistics is like struggling with a gigantic jigsaw which you know is not complete, some of the pieces being merely mislaid, others lost forever.

MILESTONES

1848 The first rules drawn up at Cambridge University.

1855* Sheffield, the oldest soccer club still in existence, founded.

1862 Notts County, the oldest Football League club, founded.

1863 Football Association formed in London on 26 October.

1865 Tape to be stretched across the goals 8 ft. from the ground.

1866 Offside rule altered to allow a player to be onside when three of opposing team are nearer their own goal-line.
Fair catch rule omitted.

1867 Queen's Park, the oldest Scottish club, founded.

1869 Kick-out rule altered and goal-kicks introduced.

1871 Start of the F.A. Cup. Goalkeepers first mentioned in laws.

1872 First official international, between Scotland and England at Glasgow.
The Wanderers win the F.A. Cup final.
Corner kick introduced.

1873 Scottish F.A. formed and the start of the Scottish Cup.

1874 Umpires first mentioned in laws.
Shinguards introduced.

1875 The cross-bar replaces tape on the goal-posts.

1876 F.A. of Wales formed.
The first international between Scotland and Wales.

1877 The London Association and the Sheffield Association agree to use the same rules.
A player may be charged by an opponent if he is facing his own goal.

*The date of Sheffield's foundation was given as 1855 in the Sheffield City Almanack (1902). And in the issue of the *Sheffield Telegraph* dated 29 September 1954 an article quoted H. B. Willey, a previous Secretary of the club, as follows: 'I used to have the Minute Book for 1855 but it was borrowed and never returned.'

1878 Referees use a whistle for the first time.

1879 First international between England and Wales.
Cliftonville, the oldest Irish club, founded.

1880 Irish F.A. formed and the start of the Irish Cup.

1882 Ireland's first internationals with Wales and England.
International Football Association Board set up.
Two-handed throw-in introduced.

1883 First international between Scotland and Ireland.
The first British International Championship.

1885 Professionalism legalised in England.
Arbroath beat Bon Accord 36–0 in Scottish Cup; still a record score for an official first-class match.

1886 International caps first awarded.

1888 Football League formed.

1889 Preston North End achieve the League and F.A. Cup 'double'.

1890 Irish League formed.
First hat-trick in the F.A. Cup Final, by Blackburn's William Townley.
Goal nets invented.

1891 Scottish League formed.
Referees and linesmen replace umpires.
Introduction of the penalty kick.

1892 Penalty taker must not play the ball twice.
Extra time allowed for taking a penalty.
Goal nets used in F.A. Cup Final for the first time.
Division Two of the Football League formed.

1893 Scotland adopts professionalism.

1894 First F.A. Amateur Cup final.
Division Two of Scottish League formed.
Referee given complete control of the game. Unnecessary for players in future to appeal to him for a decision.
Goalkeeper can only be charged when playing the ball or obstructing an opponent.

1895 F.A. Cup stolen from a Birmingham shop window. It was never recovered.

Goalposts and cross-bars must not exceed 5 in. in width.

Player taking throw-in must stand on touch-line.

1897 Aston Villa win both the League and the F.A. Cup.

The Corinthians tour South America.

The word 'intentional' introduced into the law on handling.

1898 Players' Union first formed.

1899 Promotion and relegation first used in the Football League, replacing Test Matches.

1901 Tottenham Hotspur win the F.A. Cup while members of the Southern League.

1902 Terracing collapses during the Scotland-England match at Ibrox Park, killing 25.

1904 FIFA formed in Paris, on 21 May.

1905 First £1,000 transfer. Alf Common moves from Sunderland to Middlesbrough.

First international in South America, between Argentina and Uruguay.

England joins FIFA.

1907 Amateur F.A. formed. Players' Union

Alf Common, transferred in football's first four figure deal. (Syndication International)

The wrecked terracing at Ibrox in 1902 after the tragedy. In 1971 there was an even greater disaster at the ground at the end of a Rangers v Celtic match when the fatalities numbered 66.

(now PFA) re-formed.

1908 England play in Vienna, their first international against a foreign side.
The first Olympic soccer tournament, in London, won by the United Kingdom.

1910 Scotland, Wales and Ireland join FIFA.

1912 Goalkeeper not permitted to handle ball outside his own penalty area.

1913 Defending players not to approach within ten yards of ball at a free-kick.

1914 Defending players not to approach within ten yards of ball at corner kick.

1916 The South American Championship first held.

1920 Division Three (Southern Section) of the Football League formed.
Players cannot be offside at a throw-in.

1921 Division Three (Northern Section) formed.

1922 Promotion and relegation introduced in the Scottish League.

1923 First F.A. Cup final at Wembley: Bolton beat West Ham before a record crowd.

The Daily Mirror's front page record of the first Wembley final. (Syndication International)

1924 A goal may be scored direct from a corner kick.

1925 Offside law changed to require two instead of three defenders between attacker and goal.
Player taking throw-in must have both feet on touch-line.

1926 Huddersfield Town achieve the first hat-trick of League Championships.

1927 Cardiff City take the F.A. Cup out of England for the first time.
Mitropa Cup begins.
J. C. Clegg, President of the F.A., knighted.

1928 British associations leave FIFA over broken-time payments to amateurs.
First £10,000 transfer: David Jack goes from Bolton to Arsenal.
Dixie Dean scores 60 goals for Everton in Division One, a Football League record.

1929 England lose 4–3 to Spain in Madrid, their first defeat on the continent.
Goalkeeper compelled to stand still on his goal-line at penalty-kick.

1930 Uruguay win the first World Cup, in Montevideo, Uruguay.
F. J. Wall, secretary of the F.A., knighted.

1931 Goalkeeper permitted to carry ball four steps instead of two.
Instead of free-kick after a foul throw-in it reverts to opposing side.
Scotland lose 5–0 to Austria in Vienna, their first defeat on the continent.

1933 Numbers worn for the first time in the F.A. Cup final.

1934 Italy win the second World Cup, in Rome, Italy.

1935 Arsenal equal Huddersfield's hat-trick of League Championships.
Arsenal centre-forward Ted Drake scores seven goals against Aston Villa at Villa Park, a Division One record.

1936 Defending players not permitted to tap the ball into goalkeeper's hands from a goal-kick.
Luton centre-forward Joe Payne scores 10 goals against Bristol Rovers, a Football League record.
Dixie Dean overhauls Steve Bloomer's 352 goals in the Football League.

The victorious Cardiff City side with the F.A. Cup in 1927. Captain Fred Keenor holds the trophy.

Stanley Rous pictured in January 1949.

Joe Payne who scored 10 for Luton Town on his first appearance as a centre-forward. (Coloursport)

1937   A record crowd of 149,547 watch the Scotland v. England match at Hampden Park.

Defending players not permitted to tap the ball into goalkeeper's hands from free-kick inside penalty area.

Weight of ball increased from 13–15 oz. to 14–16 oz.

Arc of circle ten yards radius from penalty spot to be drawn outside penalty area.

1938   Italy retain the World Cup, in Paris, France.

Laws of the game rewritten.

Scotland's Jimmy McGrory retires, having scored 550 goals in first-class football, a British record.

1946   British associations rejoin FIFA.

The Burnden Park tragedy: 33 killed and over 400 injured during an F.A. Cup tie between Bolton and Stoke.

1949   Aircraft carrying Italian champions Torino crashes at Superga near Turin, killing all on board.

England beaten 2–0 by Republic of Ireland at Goodison Park, so losing their unbeaten home record against sides outside the home countries.

Rangers win the first 'treble' – Scottish League, Scottish Cup and League Cup.

S. F. Rous, secretary of the F.A., knighted.

1950   Uruguay win the fourth World Cup, in Rio de Janeiro, Brazil.

England, entering for the first time, lose 1–0 to USA.

Scotland's unbeaten home record against foreign opposition ends in a 1–0 defeat by Austria at Hampden Park.

1951   Obstruction included as an offence punishable by indirect free-kick.

Studs may project three-quarters of an inch instead of half an inch.

1952   Billy Wright overhauls Bob Crompton's record of 42 caps.

Newcastle United retain the F.A. Cup, the first club to do so in the 20th century.

England lose their unbeaten home record

against continental opposition, going down 6–3 to Hungary at Wembley.

1954　West Germany win the fifth World Cup in Berne, Switzerland.

England suffer their heaviest international defeat, beaten 7–1 by Hungary at Budapest.

The Union of European Football Associations (UEFA) formed.

Ball not to be changed during the game unless authorised by the referee.

West Germany's captain Fritz Walter with the Jules Rimet trophy presented after the 1954 World Cup.

Duncan Edwards the Manchester United wing-half who died as a result of the injuries he received in the Munich air disaster in 1958. He had been England's youngest cap in 1955. (Press Association)

the Munich air disaster on 6 February.

Brazil win the sixth World Cup, in Stockholm, Sweden.

Sunderland, continuously in Division One, relegated.

Football League re-organisation: Division Three and Division Four started.

1959　Billy Wright plays his 100th game for England, against Scotland, and retires at the end of the season with a world record 105 appearances.

1960　USSR win the first European Nations Cup, in Paris, France.

Real Madrid win the European Cup for the fifth consecutive time.

1961　Sir Stanley Rous becomes President of FIFA.

Tottenham Hotspur win the League and Cup, the first 'double' of the 20th century.

The Professional Football Association (PFA) succeed in achieving the abolition of the maximum wage.

Fiorentina win the first European Cup-Winners Cup.

1955　European Cup of the Champions and Inter-Cities Fairs Cup started.

1956　Real Madrid win the European Cup.

First floodlit match in the Football League: Portsmouth v. Newcastle United on 22 February.

1957　George Young retires with a record 53 Scottish caps.

John Charles of Leeds United becomes the first British player to be transferred to a foreign club (Juventus, Italy).

1958　Manchester United lose eight players in

Billy Wright, the first England player to make 100 appearances for his country. (Coloursport)

Arthur Rowley reached a record 434 League goals with four different clubs. (Popperfoto)

1962   Brazil retain the World Cup, in Santiago, Chile.

Denis Law is transferred from Torino to Manchester United, the first transfer over £100,000 paid by a British club.

1963   The centenary of the F.A. England beat the Rest of the World 2–1, at Wembley.

The Football League's 'retain and transfer' system declared illegal.

Tottenham Hotspur win the European Cup-Winners' Cup, the first British success in Europe.

1964   Spain win the European Nations' Cup, in Madrid, Spain.

More than 300 killed and 500 injured in rioting during an Olympic qualifying game between Peru and Argentina at Lima, Peru.

Jimmy Dickinson (Portsmouth) becomes the first player to make 700 Football League appearances.

1965   Stanley Matthews becomes the first footballer to be knighted.

Arthur Rowley retires having scored a record 434 Football League goals.

The Football League agree to substitutes for one injured player.

1966   England win the eighth World Cup, at Wembley.

The Football League allow substitutes for any reason.

1967   Alf Ramsey, England's team manager, knighted.

Celtic become the first Scottish club to win the European Cup.

1968   Italy win the European Football Championship, in Rome, Italy.

A world record transfer: Pietro Anastasi moves from Varese to Juventus for £440,000.

Manchester United win the European Cup: Matt Busby knighted.

Leeds United become the first British club to win the Fairs Cup.

1969   Leeds win the Football League Championship with a record 67 points.

1970   Brazil win the ninth World Cup, in Mexico City and win the Jules Rimet Trophy outright.

Bobby Charlton wins his 106th England cap in the quarter-finals to overhaul Billy Wright's record.

Bobby Charlton with some of his England caps. He made 106 appearances. (Syndication International)

The first £200,000 transfer in Britain: Martin Peters moves from West Ham to Tottenham Hotspur.

1971 Britain's worst-ever crowd disaster: 66 killed at a match between Rangers and Celtic at Ibrox Park.
Arsenal achieve the League and Cup 'double'.
Barcelona win the Fairs Cup outright (to be replaced by the UEFA Cup) after beating the holders Leeds United 2–1.

1972 Tottenham Hotspur defeat Wolverhampton Wanderers in the first all-British European final, the UEFA Cup.
West Germany win the European Football Championship, in Brussels, Belgium.

1973 Ajax win the European Cup for the third consecutive time.
Bobby Moore makes his 108th appearance for England, a new record.
Johann Cruyff becomes the first £1 million transfer, moving from Ajax to Barcelona for £922,300.

1974 Joao Havelange of Brazil replaces Sir Stanley Rous as President of FIFA.
West Germany win the tenth World Cup in Munich, West Germany.
Denis Law makes his 55th appearance for Scotland, a new record.

Denis Law who made a record 55th appearance for Scotland against Zaire in 1974. (Coloursport)

Terry Paine leading Hereford United out for his 806th
League appearance against his previous club
Southampton. He made his 824th and last in May 1977
(Syndication International)

1975 Leeds United banned from competing in
      Europe for any of two seasons in the next
      four, after their fans rioted at the Euro-
      pean Cup final in Paris.

Terry   Paine   overhauls   Jimmy
Dickinson's record of 764 League games.

1976 Bayern Munich win the European Cup
      for the third consecutive time.
      Czechoslovakia win the European
      Football Championship in Belgrade,
      Yugoslavia, beating West Germany.

Six Bayern Munich players with three European Cup trophies. From left to right: Gerd Muller, Franz Roth, Georg
Schwarzenbeck, Johnny Hansen, Josef Maier and Franz Beckenbauer. (Popperfoto)

Pat Jennings makes his 60th appearance for Northern Ireland, a new record.

The Football League finally abandon 'goal average', introducing 'goal difference'.

Liverpool win their ninth League title, overhauling Arsenal's record.

1977   Liverpool win their 10th League title as well as the European Cup.

Kevin Keegan transferred from Liverpool to SV Hamburg for £500,000, the highest fee involving a British club.

Kenny Dalglish transferred from Celtic to Liverpool for £440,000, a record fee between British clubs.

First World Youth Cup, held in Tunisia and won by USSR.

1978   Liverpool retain the European Cup.

Nottingham Forest the only Football League club not a limited company win their first Championship title. Forest also win the League Cup.

Ipswich Town become the 40th different team to win the F.A. Cup.

Kenny Dalglish makes his 56th appearance for Scotland to overhaul Denis Law's record.

Kevin Keegan wearing his Hamburg shirt with its Hitachi-sponsored emblem. (Coloursport)

The eleventh World Cup was held in Argentina (see p.235 for full details).

Louis Edwards, Manchester United Chairman (left), Gordon McQueen and United Manager Dave Sexton at the near £500,000 signing of the Scottish international centre-half.

WORLD SOCCER

FIFA

The Federation Internationale de Football Association was founded at a meeting on 21 May 1904 and is the official governing body of the game throughout the world. Belgium, Denmark, France, Holland, Spain, Sweden and Switzerland were represented.

England joined in 1905 followed by Scotland, Ireland and Wales in 1910. All four home countries ceased membership on two occasions from 1920 to 1924 because they opposed association with the former wartime enemies Austria, Germany and Hungary. They left again in 1928 over the definition of amateurism and the question of broken time payments but returned finally in 1946.

FIFA consists of the National Associations which are affiliated to and recognised by it as the bodies which control Association Football in their respective countries.

It is divided into six continental Confederations: Africa, America (North and Central and Caribbean and known as Concacaf), America South, Asia, Europe and Oceania. The present headquarters are in Zurich, Switzerland.

Written into the statutes of FIFA had originally been the idea of organising an international cup competition but this World Cup as it became known did not take place until 1930 (see p.235).

In 1913 FIFA was given representation on the International Football Association Board which had been formed in 1886 by the four Associations of England, Scotland, Ireland and Wales to provide a uniform a code of rules. The Board meets at least once a year to discuss alterations to the Laws of the Game.

The Presidents of FIFA have been: Robert Guerin (France), 22 May 1904 to 4 June 1906; D. B. Woolfall (England), 4 June 1906 to 24 October 1918; Jules Rimet (France), 1 March 1921 to 21 June 1954; Rololphe William Seeldrayers (Belgium), 21 June 1954 to 7 October 1955; Arthur Drewry (England), 9 June 1956 to 25 March 1961; Sir Stanley Rous (England), 28 September 1961 to 11 June 1974; Dr Joao Havelange (Brazil) from 11 June 1974.

The growth of FIFA members: 1904 7; 1914 24; 1923 31; 1930 41; 1938 51; 1950 73; 1954 85; 1968 135; 1977 146.

Jules Rimet, the man who gave his name to the original World Cup trophy as FIFA's President.

FIFA COUNTRIES

Information correct up to FIFA survey 1974 except for countries admitted since then. Where no National Stadium details are given there is no specific venue used as such.

Country	FA founded	Affiliated to FIFA	Confederation	Season
AFGHANISTAN	1922	1948		
ALBANIA	1932	1932		Sept–June
ALGERIA	1962	1963	1964	Sept–June
ANTIGUA	1967	1970		Aug–Dec
ARGENTINA	1893	1912	1916	Mar–Dec
AUSTRALIA	1961	1963	1966	Mar–Oct
AUSTRIA	1904	1905	1954	Feb–June & Aug–Dec
BAHAMAS	1967	1968		Oct–May
BAHRAIN	1951	1966	1970	Oct–June
BANGLADESH	1972	1974	1974	Apr–Dec
BARBADOS	1910	1968	1968	Feb–May
BELGIUM	1895	1904	1954	Aug–May
BENIN (DAHOMEY) PEOPLE'S REPUBLIC	1968	1969	1969	Nov–June
BERMUDA	1928	1962	1966	Oct–Apr
BOLIVIA	1925	1926	1926	Apr–Dec
BOTSWANA		1976		
BRAZIL	1914	1923	1916	Jan–June & Aug–Dec
BRUNEI	1959	1969	1970	Sept–Mar
BULGARIA	1923	1924	1954	Mar–June & Aug–Dec
BURMA	1947	1947	1958	May–Feb
BURUNDI	1948	1972	1972	
CAMEROON	1960	1962	1963	Oct–Aug
CANADA	1912	1948		May–Nov
CENTRAL AFRICAN REPUBLIC	1937	1963	1965	Oct–July
CHILE	1895	1912	1916	Apr–Dec
CHINA (REPUBLIC)	1936	1954	1955	Jan–Dec
COLOMBIA	1925	1931	1940	Feb–Dec
CONGO	1962	1964	1966	Feb–Oct
COSTA RICA	1921	1927	1962	Mar–Oct
CUBA	1924	1932	1961	July–Nov
CYPRUS	1934	1948	1962	Oct–June
CZECHOSLOVAKIA	1901	1906	1954	Mar–June & Aug–Nov
DENMARK	1889	1904	1954	Apr–Nov
DOMINICAN REPUBLIC	1953	1958	1964	Mar–Sept
ECUADOR	1925	1926	1930	May–Dec
EGYPT	1921	1923	1956	Sept–June
ENGLAND	1863	1905–20; 1924–28; 1946	1954	Aug–June
ETHIOPIA	1943	1953	1957	Sept–June
FIJI	1936	1963	1963	Mar–Sept
FINLAND	1907	1908	1954	Apr–Oct
FRANCE	1919	1904	1954	Aug–June
GABON	1962	1963	1967	Oct–July
GAMBIA	1952	1966	1962	Oct–July
GERMANY (EAST)	1948	1952	1954	Aug–June
GERMANY (WEST)	1900	1904–45; 1950	1954	Aug–June
GHANA	1957	1958	1958	Jan–Oct
GREECE	1926	1927	1954	Sept–June
GRENADA	1924	1976		July–Dec
GUATEMALA		1933	1961	May–Oct
GUINEA	1959	1961	1962	Oct–June
GUYANA	1902	1968	1969	Mar–Dec
HAITI	1912	1934	1957	Oct–June
HONDURAS	1951	1951	1951	Feb–Oct
HONG KONG	1914	1954	1954	Sept–June
HUNGARY	1901	1907	1954	Mar–June & Aug–Nov
ICELAND	1947	1929	1954	May–Oct
INDIA	1937	1948	1954	Jan–Dec
INDONESIA	1930	1952	1954	Jan–Dec
IRAN	1920	1945	1958	Apr–Feb
IRAQ	1948	1951	1971	Oct–May
IRELAND (NORTHERN)	1880	1911–20; 1924–28; 1946	1954	Aug–May
IRELAND (REPUBLIC)	1921	1923	1954	Aug–May
ISRAEL	1928	1929	1956	Sept–June
ITALY	1898	1905	1954	Sept–June

FIFA COUNTRIES

Clubs	Teams	Players	Referees	National colours Shirts/shorts	National Stadium venue	Capacity
30	150	3,300	230	White/white		25,000
33	130	4,070	350	Red/black	Qemal Stafa, Tirana	24,000
723	2,637	39,033	787	Green/white	Stade Olympique d'Alger	80,000
42	42	644	31	Gold/black	Antigua Recreation Ground, St John's	30,000
2,647	13,303	224,166	2,525	Blue, white/black		
1,100	11,857	165,000	1,850	Green/white	Olympic Park, Melbourne	48,500
1,819	5,767	249,032	1,835	Red/white	Wiener Stadion, Prater, Vienna	73,243
27	27	476	8	Blue/white		
36	60	2,714	45	White/red	ISA Town Stadium	16,000
1,162	50	25,684	375	Orange/white	Dacca Stadium, Dacca	55,000
43	66	950	34	Royal blue/gold	Barbados, Waterfords, St Michael	12,000
2,901	7,449	150,430	4,585	White/white	Heysel Stadium, Brussels	70,000
31	19	5,165	61	Green	Quartier Akpakpa, Cotonou	7,000
33	46	1,257	27	Blue/white	Prospect, Devonshire	10,000
305	320	11,789	202	Green/white	Hernando Siles, La Paz	35,000
				Sky blue/white		
5,024	15,320	82,400	1,173	Yellow/blue	Mario Filho (Maracana), Rio	220,000
22	25	83	14	White/white		
2,307	5,312	109,722	2,243	White/green	Vassil Levsky Stadium, Sofia	60,000
550	550	14,000	1,312	Red/white	Aungsan Memorial Stadium, Rangoon	45,000
132	53	3,930	125	White/white	FFB Bujumbura	6,000
200	209	7,961	448	Green/red	Ahmadou Ahidjo, Yaounde	50,000
1,000	3,000	90,872	391	Red/red		
256	283	7,200	92	Blue/white	Barthelemy Boganda, Bangui	35,000
4,350	12,750	282,696	4,227	Red/blue	Comuna de Nunoa, Santiago	77,127
24	200	4,600	210	Red/white	Taipei	22,000
3,685	3,685	74,172	1,382	Orange/grey	El Campin, Bogota	57,000
141	130	4,230	70	Red/red	Stadium of the Revolution, Brazzaville	50,000
431	421	12,429	126	Red/blue	Explanada de la Sabana, San Jose	30,000
70	714	12,900	160	White/blue	Juan Abrantes, Havana	18,000
43	42	11,850	93	Sky blue/white	GSO Nicosia	12,000
6,776	26,847	348,000	5,060	Red/white	Strahov, Prague	60,000
1,390	7,400	208,000	1,800	Red/white	Idraetspark, Copenhagen	50,000
72	382	5,531	25	Blue/white	Olympic Stadium, Santo Domingo	22,000
170	200	5,750	100	Yellow/blue	Estadio Modelo, Guayaquil	48,772
168	168	8,000	358	Red/white	Nasser Stadium, Nasr Town, Cairo	100,000
36,904	36,904	1,108,000	9,503	White/navy blue	Empire Stadium, Wembley	100,000
160	320	13,425	955	Green/yellow	Haile Selasse First Stadium, Addis Abeba	30,000
18	20	15,000	120	White/black		
734	1,667	32,863	1,700	White/blue	Olympia Stadion, Helsinki	50,000
14,533	52,000	852,722	11,233	Blue/white	Parc de Princes, Paris	50,000
275	275	8,086	128	Green/yellow	Stade RP Lefebvre, Libreville	7,000
39	39	850	27	White/white	Box-Bar Stadium, Bathurst	6,000
4,730	22,515	486,109	16,205	White/blue	Central Stadium, Leipzig	100,000
16,641	94,903	2,952,280	34,100	White/black		
300	220	4,000	300	Yellow/yellow	Sports Stadium, Accra	30,000
1,616	1,572	81,800	1,615	White/blue	Karaiskaki, Athens	42,000
15	15	200	15	Green/red		
1,611	1,521	30,440	202	Blue/white	Mateo Flores, Guatemala	50,000
300	78	6,711	126	Red/yellow	Stadium of 28 September, Conakry	40,000
103	125	1,605	62	Green/black	Sports Club, Georgetown	5,800
40	13	750	29	Red/black	Stade Sylviocator, Port-au-Prince	15,000
365	365	10,510	393	Blue/white	Norte a Sur	22,000
66	97	2,350	120	Red/white	Government Stadium, Sookungoo	28,000
2,924	5,125	153,514	4,721	Red/white	Nepstadion, Budapest	80,000
65	396	11,456	232	Blue/white	Laugardalsvollur, Reykjavik	15,100
1,857	1,857	40,854	2,770	Light blue/white	New Delhi	40,000
1,900	370	69,000	306	Red/white	Senajan, Djakarta	110,000
422	1,986	43,300	163	Green/white	Aria Mehre, Tehran	100,000
141	48	1,120	311	White/white	Sha'ab Stadium, Baghdad	50,000
740	740	14,800	328	Green/white	Windsor Park, Belfast	58,000
1,745	2,800	50,328	395	Green/white		
544	548	20,000	500	White/blue	Ramat-gan	55,000
15,269	15,602	634,730	13,106	Blue/white	Olympic Stadium, Rome	90,000

FIFA COUNTRIES

Country	FA founded	Affiliated to FIFA	Confederation	Season
IVORY COAST	1960	1960	1960	Nov–Aug
JAMAICA	1910	1962	1963	Aug–Apr
JAPAN	1921	1929–45; 1950	1954	Mar–Jan
JORDAN	1949	1958	1970	June–Dec
KENYA		1960	1968	June–Mar
KHMER	1933	1953	1957	Nov–Oct
KOREA (NORTH)	1945	1958	1974	Mar–Nov
KOREA (SOUTH)	1928	1948	1954	Mar–Nov
KUWAIT	1952	1962	1964	Oct–May
LAOS	1951	1952	1968	Oct–May
LEBANON	1933	1935	1964	Oct–June
LESOTHO	1932	1964	1964	Nov–Oct
LIBERIA		1962		
LIBYA	1963	1963	1965	Sept–Apr
LIECHTENSTEIN	1933	1974	1974	Aug–July
LUXEMBOURG	1908	1910	1954	Aug–June
MACAO	1939	1976	1976	Oct–June
MADAGASCAR	1961	1964	1963	Nov–Oct
MALAWI	1966	1967		Mar–Oct
MALAYSIA	1933	1956	1954	Feb–Sept
MALI	1960	1962	1963	Oct–June
MALTA	1900	1959	1960	Sept–May
MAURITANIA	1961	1964	1968	Nov–July
MAURITIUS	1952	1962	1963	Sept–June
MEXICO	1927	1929	1961	July–Oct
MOROCCO	1955	1956	1951	Sept–June
NEPAL	1951	1970	1971	Apr–Nov
NETHERLANDS (HOLLAND)	1889	1904	1954	Aug–June
NETHERLANDS ANTILLES	1921	1932	1961	Aug–Feb
NEW ZEALAND	1891	1948	1966	Mar–Oct
NICARAGUA	1968		1968	June–Sept
NIGER	1967	1967	1967	Jan–June & Sept–Dec
NIGERIA	1945	1959	1959	Jan–Dec
NORWAY	1902	1908	1954	Apr–Nov
PAKISTAN	1948	1948	1950	Mar–Oct
PANAMA		1938		
PAPUA-NEW GUINEA	1962	1963	1963	Feb–Nov
PARAGUAY	1906	1921	1921	May–Dec
PERU	1922	1922	1926	Apr–Dec
PHILIPPINES	1907	1928	1954	July–Apr
POLAND	1919	1923	1955	Mar–June & Aug–Nov
PORTUGAL	1914	1926	1954	Sept–July
PUERTO RICO	1940	1960	1962	Mar–June
QATAR	1960	1970	1972	Oct–May
RHODESIA	1965	1965		Feb–Oct
RUMANIA	1908	1930	1955	Aug–July
RWANDA		1976		
EL SALVADOR	1935	1938	1962	Jan–Nov
SAUDI ARABIA	1959	1959	1972	Sept–May
SCOTLAND	1873	1910–20; 1924–28; 1946	1954	July–Apr
SENEGAL	1960	1964	1963	Oct–July
SIERRA LEONE	1967	1967	1967	May–Dec
SINGAPORE	1892	1952	1952	Mar–Dec
SOMALIA	1951	1961	1968	Sept–Feb
SPAIN	1913	1904	1954	Sept–June
SRI LANKA	1939	1950	1958	Sept–Mar
SUDAN	1936	1948	1956	July–June
SURINAM	1920	1929		Mar–Dec
SWAZILAND		1976		
SWEDEN	1904	1904	1954	Apr–Oct
SWITZERLAND	1895	1904	1954	July–June
SYRIA	1936	1937	1970	Sept–June
TANZANIA	1930	1964	1960	Sept–Aug

FIFA COUNTRIES

Clubs	Teams	Players	Referees	National colours Shirts/shorts	National Stadium venue	Capacity
78	105	3,255	60	Orange/white	Stade Houphouet-Boigny, Abidjan	27,456
146	35	20,124	48	Green/black	Independence Park, Kingston	40,000
16,317	13,788	260,000	2,068	Blue/white	Tokyo	72,000
22	34	1,000	27	White/black	Amman International Stadium, Amman	30,000
190	180	6,840	143	White/white	City Stadium, Nairobi	18,000
30	32	650	42	Blue/white	CSN Phnom-Penh	170,000
45	64		257	Red/white	Moranbong Stadium, Pyongyang	60,000
476	113	2,047	50	Red/blue	Seoul Municipal Stadium	30,000
13	25	900	52	Blue/white	Shuweikh Secondary School Stadium, Kuwait	25,000
93	152	2,812	86	Red/white	Vientiane	5,000
92	128	2,720	70	Red/white	Cite Sportive, Beyrouth	60,000
56	66	1,400	50	White/blue Red, white/white	Lesotho Stadium, Maseru	10,700
69	123	2,088	82	Blue/white	Tripoli Sports City Stadium, Gurgi	70,000
7	60	1,200	11	Blue, red/red	Landessportplatz, Vaduz	10,000
203	484	12,047	302	Red/white	Stade Municipal, Luxembourg	15,100
120	70	2,000		Green/white	Campo Desportivo	12,000
528	310	11,041	207	White/white	Stade Municipal de Mahamasina, Tananarive	13,600
58	52	744	31	Red/red	Kamuzu Stadium, Blantyre	52,970
315	28	7,839	295	Black, gold/white	Merdeka Stadium, Kuala Lumpar	29,000
123	155	4,600	47	Green/yellow	Stade Omnisport, Bamako	30,000
238	362	8,164	80	Red/white	Gzira Stadium	30,000
59	64	1,930	43	Green/yellow	Nouakchott	6,000
40	40	8,500	28	Red/white	King George V Stadium, Curepipe	39,000
56	58,000	1,331,850	3,356	Green/white	Aztec Stadium, Mexico City	108,499
285	792	10,300	1,000	Red/white	Stade d'Honneur, Casablanca	40,000
33	45	700	21	Red/white	Dasarath Rangashala, Tripureswar, Kathmandu	25,000
6,509	36,667	856,515	11,742	Orange/white	Olympic Stadion, Amsterdam	67,000
103	112	4,300	70	White/white	Rif Stadium, Otrabanda, Willemstad	6,000
312	725	10,485	305	White/black		
31	8	160	14	Blue/blue	Managua	30,000
45			100	White/white	Niamey	7,082
326	723	80,190	809	Green/white	Surulere, Lagos	50,000
2,850	5,100	84,000	2,000	Red/white	Ullevaal Stadion, Oslo	24,500
576	43	13,000	295	Green/white Red, blue/blue	Karachi	35,000
320	368	5,700	140	Green/white	Konedobu, Port Moresby	22,000
742		110,000	600	Red, white/blue	Paraguayan Football League Stadium	50,000
6,158	6,958	139,360	2,316	White/white	Lima	45,000
350	390	7,000	49	Blue/white	Rizal Memorial Stadium, Manila	30,000
3,137	11,223	364,348	5,912	White/red	Tenth Anniversary Stadium, Warsaw	87,000
880	224	40,815	1,150	Red/white	Stade National, Lisbon	51,000
21	515	6,818	71	White, red/blue	County Club	8,000
11	14	1,200	36	Maroon, white/white	Doha Athletic Stadium, Doha	8,000
605	420	11,684	250	White/black	Rufaro Stadium, Salisbury	32,000
5,214	5,214	99,451	4,537	Yellow/blue Green/black	Stade 23 August, Bucharest	95,000
592	592	12,806	365	Blue/blue	Florblanca, San Salvador	30,000
104	162	8,200	160	Green/white	Malaz Ground, Riyadh	25,000
3,874	7,426	117,000	1,080	Dark blue/white	Hampden Park, Glasgow	134,000
65	118	3,168	134	Green/yellow	Dempa Diop, Dakar	13,000
	104	8,120	640	Green/yellow	Brookfields Stadium, Freetown	15,000
79	110	1,710	66	Red/white	Jalan Besar Stadium, Singapore	20,000
16	29	816	37	Sky blue/white	Cons Stadium, Mogadiscio	15,000
4,671	4,671	148,700	4,601	Red/blue		
575	98	17,375	315	Maroon/white	Sugathadasa Stadium, Colombo	25,000
750	771	36,840	555	White/white	Khartoum Stadium, Khartoum	30,000
174	69	3,810	50	Green/white Blue, gold/white	Surinam Stadion, Paramaribo	20,000
3,003	6,011	122,701	3,660	Yellow/blue	Fotbollstadion, Solna	52,000
1,286	5,350	116,300	2,630	Red/white	Wankdorf Stadium, Berne	60,000
105		16,660	214	White/white	Stade Al-Abbassiyne, Damascus	45,000
	51		76	Green/black	Dar-es-Salaam	3,000

FIFA COUNTRIES

Country	FA founded	Affiliated to FIFA	Confederation	Season
THAILAND	1916	1925	1957	Nov–Apr
TOGO	1960	1962	1963	Oct–July
TRINIDAD & TOBAGO	1906	1963	1964	June–Dec
TUNISIA		1960	1960	Sept–June
TURKEY	1923	1923	1962	Sept–June
UGANDA	1924	1959	1959	Jan–Nov
UNITED ARAB EMIRATES	1971	1972	1974	7 months
UPPER VOLTA	1960	1964	1964	Oct–June
URUGUAY	1900	1923	1916	Mar–Dec
USA	1913	1913		Sept–Apr (NASL: Apr–Aug)
USSR	1912	1946	1954	Apr–Nov
VENEZUELA	1926	1952	1952	Mar–Dec
VIETNAM (PEOPLE'S REPUBLIC)	1962	1964		Nov–May
VIETNAM (SOUTH)	1923	1948	1954	Aug–July
WALES	1876	1910–20; 1924–28; 1946	1954	Aug–May
YEMEN	1940	1967		Sept–May
YUGOSLAVIA	1919	1919	1955	Mar–Dec
ZAIRE	1919	·1964	1963	June–Mar
ZAMBIA	1929	1964	1964	Mar–Nov

WORLD'S OLDEST CLUBS

Although the actual date of Sheffield F.C. being founded lies between 1855 and 1857 they are still the oldest club in the world.

It may well have been that Sheffield were in being in 1855 but may not have been in regular competition until later. And this also applies to many other clubs throughout the world who were formed but did not play Association Football immediately upon their inauguration.

In Denmark, for example, BK Copenhagen were formed in 1876 but did not take up soccer until another three years had elapsed. A similar argument might be made out for others in this list showing the oldest club for particular countries:

Argentina	Buenos Aires F.C.	1865	Malta	Floriana St. George's	1900
Austria	First Vienna	1884	Norway	Christiania	1885
Belgium	U.S. Gantoise	1874	Peru	Union Cricket	1893
Brazil	Flamengo	1895	Poland	Cracovia F.C.	1906
Bulgaria	Sofia F.K.	1909	Portugal	Lisbon F.C.	1875
Czechoslovakia	Slavia Prague	1882	Rumania	Petrolul Ploesti	1905
Denmark	BK Copenhagen	1876	Scotland	Queen's Park F.C.	1867
England	Sheffield F.C.	c.1855	South Africa	Durham F.C.	1882
Finland	Kamraterna	1893	Spain	Athletic Bilbao	1898
France	Havre A.C.	1872	Sweden	Orgryte	1875
Germany	T.G.S. Ulm	1866	Switzerland	Saint-Gall	1879
Greece	Panathinaikos	1908	Turkey	Galatasaray	1905
Holland	Haarlem F.C.	1879	Uruguay	Albion F.C.	1882
Hungary	Ujpest Dozsa	1885	USA	Harvard University	1860
Ireland	Cliftonville	1879	USSR	Morozowstky	1887
Italy	Genoa F.C.	1893	Wales	Druids F.C.	1870
Luxembourg	Jeunesse Esch	1902	Yugoslavia	Brask	1893

Clubs	Teams	Players	Referees	National colours Shirts/shorts	National Stadium venue	Capacity
115	116	5,000	127	Crimson red/white	Suphachalasai Stadium, Bangkok	39,924
144	144	4,340	85	Red/white	Stade General Etienne Eyadema, Lome	20,000
132	132	3,590	147	Red/black	Queen's Park Oval, Port of Spain	20,000
145	500	14,500	600	Red/white	Stade Olympique, El Menzah, Tunis	50,000
1,432	1,540	43,229	1,821	White/white	19 Mayis Stadium, Ankara	35,000
400	720	1,582	178	Yellow/black	Nakivubo Stadium, Kampala	50,000
20	40	1,162	45	Red	Abu Dhabi Stadium, Abu Dhabi	60,000
55	60	3,510	72	White/white	Stade Municipal de Ougadougou	4,000
970	970	101,550	140	Blue/black	Centenary Stadium, Montevideo	75,000
1,202	520	42,685	1,100	White/blue		
50,163	180	4,300,000	94,000	Red/white	Lenin Stadium, Moscow	104,000
600	1,053	21,670	318	Red/black		
55	800	16,000	181	Red/white	Stade Hang Day, Hanoi	40,000
58	58	1,148	70	Yellow/white	Cong Hoa Stadium, Saigon	22,060
1,200	2,000	38,600	850	Red/white	Ninian Park, Cardiff	58,000
	36	1,700	40	Light blue/white	Stadium of the Martyr, Crater, Aden	4,500
7,455	4,029	122,372	5,530	Blue/white		
2,011	2,047	49,170	1,303	Green/yellow	Stade Tata Raphael, Kinshasa	60,000
20	280	4,100	290	Green/orange	Independence Stadium, Lusaka	30,000

WORLD FOOTBALL COMPETITIONS

Competition	Commenced	Organisation
African Champion Clubs Cup	1964	On European Cup lines and held annually, except 1965. Most successful clubs: TP Mazembe (Zaire) 1967, 1968; Hafia, Conakry (Guinea) 1972, 1975.
African Nations Cup	1957	For national teams and held every two years. Most successful country: Egypt 1957, 1959; Ghana 1963, 1965; Zaire 1968, 1974.
African Cup Winners Cup	1975	On European Cup Winners Cup lines and held annually.
Anglo-Italian Cup	1970	Club tournament between English and Italian League clubs held annually except in 1974 and 1975 before becoming the Anglo-Italian Semi-Professional Inter-League Cup in 1976.
Anglo-Italian League Cup Winners Cup	1969	Held annually for the winners of the League Cup and the Italian Cup except for 1972 to 1974 and 1977.
Anglo-Italian Semi-Professional Cup	1975	Held annually on a tournament basis between English non-league clubs and Italian semi-professional teams.
Asian Champion Clubs Cup	1967	Held only four times with Israeli clubs being the most successful.
Asian Cup	1956	Held every four years for national teams. Iran have won it in 1968, 1972 and 1976.
Asian Games	1951	Succeeded Far Eastern Championship of 1913 to 1934 and West Asian Games. China most successful nation pre-war.
Asian Youth Tournament	1959	Open for national youth teams in the area and held annually in principle.
Atlantic Cup	1956	Contested between Argentina, Brazil and Uruguay until Paraguay joined in in 1975. Brazil have won all three: 1956, 1960, 1975.
Balkan Championship	1929	Held annually in pre-war until 1936. Revived twice briefly since. Rumania and Bulgaria have won three tournaments each.
Balkan Club Cup	1962	Originally for the runners-up of Balkan countries League teams but increased in entries and organised on European Cup lines.
Balkan Cup for Under-23's	1968	Held annually for national teams in the area at Under-23 level.
Baltic Cup	1928	Held annually until 1938 except for two years with Latvia, Estonia and Lithuania as the contestants.
Barassi Cup	1968	Held annually between winners of English and Italian amateur cup competitions except for 1974 and 1977.
Carlos Dittborn Cup	1962	Held irregularly between Chile and Argentina national teams.

WORLD FOOTBALL COMPETITIONS Continued

Competition	Commenced	Organisation
Concacaf Champion Club Cup	1967	Held in principle every year with Mexican clubs being the most successful.
Concacaf Championship	1941	Held in principle every two years for national teams with Costa Rica the most successful country.
Dr. Gero Cup	1927	Often known as the International Cup for national teams in Europe and held irregularly as a forerunner of the European Nations Cup.
European Nations Cup for Amateurs	1963	After two unofficial tournaments three have been held since 1967 for national teams at this level.
European Under-23 Championship	1972	Held every two years for national teams at this level but for the 1976–78 competition the age limit became Under-21. Eastern European teams have been the most successful.
Inter-American Cup	1969	Played between the winners of the South American Cup (Libertadores Cup) and the Concacaf Cup. Not held since 1974 but Independiente (Argentina) have won it three times.
International Summer Cup (formerly Rappan Cup and Intertoto Cup)	1962	Held annually for club sides on the continent purely for the purpose of summer pools and since 1967 has not even provided a winner from its various groups.
Latin Cup	1949	Another forerunner of the European Cup held annually up to 1957 for Latin European countries club teams.
Lipton Cup	1905	Held at irregular intervals between national teams of Argentina and Uruguay.
Mediterranean Cup	1949	Held at irregular intervals as a tournament for national teams in the area.
Mitropa Cup	1927	Oldest club competition in Europe and is still held annually after several revivals for Central European clubs. Often appeared under other titles.
Newton Cup	1906	Held at irregular intervals between the national teams of Argentina and Uruguay.
O'Higgins Cup	1955	Held at irregular intervals between the national teams of Brazil and Chile.
Oswaldo Cruz Cup	1950	Held at irregular intervals between the national teams of Brazil and Paraguay.
Pan American Championship	1952	Held every four years usually for amateur national teams in South America and Concacaf.
Rio Branco Cup	1931	Held at irregular intervals between the national teams of Brazil and Uruguay.
Roca Cup	1914	Held at irregular intervals between the national teams of Argentina and Brazil.
Rosa Chevalier Boutell Cup	1923	Held at irregular intervals between the national teams of Argentina and Paraguay.
Scandinavian Championship	1924	Held over four years between teams in Scandinavia. Sweden has been the most successful country.
Super Cup	1972	Played annually between the winners of the European Champions Cup and Cup Winners Cup except 1974.
World Military Championships	1950	Held in principle every year for armed forces teams and usually for those who still have a form of national service.
World University Championships	1967	Student level national teams for tournament held every two years since the first series. Rumania have won it twice 1972, 1974.

Football touraments are held at such events as the Pan Arabic Games, Mediterranean Games, South East Asian Games etc., as well as in many countries on an annual basis too numerous to mention at either club or national level.

Some of the competitions referred to in the table above have been discontinued or replaced by other cups. In addition the 1975 Atlantic Cup was also used to determine the winners of individual competitions. Oswaldo Cruz Cup, Roca Cup, Rio Branco Cup and Coronel Bogado Cup (Argentina v Paraguay). Other played in South America include the Pinto Duran Cup (Uruguay v Chile) and Artigas Cup (Paraguay v Uruguay).

N.B. Other competitions mentioned elsewhere.

BRITISH SOCCER

The Football Association

The Football Association was formed on 26 October 1863 at a meeting at the Freemason's Tavern, Great Queen Street, London. Apart from interested individuals who attended, the following clubs were represented: Barnes, Blackheath, Charterhouse, Perceval House (Blackheath), Kensington School, War Office, Crystal Palace, Blackheath Proprietary School, The Crusaders, Forest (Epping Forest) and No Names (Kilburn).

It is the governing body of the game in England and the oldest of its kind in the world.

The F.A. Cup

The institution of a Football Association Challenge Cup was first discussed at a meeting in the offices of the *Sportsman* on 20 July 1871 and approved on 16 October 1871.

The competition commences every year in September with a preliminary round of 48 ties. The remainder of the entries come in at the first qualifying round. Twenty non-league clubs are excused until the fourth qualifying round. At the First Round proper at which stage the 48 clubs of

Divisions Three and Four enter with the previous season's F.A. Trophy finalists and two other selected non-league teams. The 24 who emerge after the Second Round proper join with the League clubs from Divisions One and Two who have been exempted until then and it continues as a strict elimination contest. The aggregate attendance for the 1976–77 season was reported at 3,177,693 for all matches at which crowd figures were returned.

The record for F.A. Cup wins is the seven by Aston Villa in 1887, 1895, 1897, 1905, 1913, 1920 and 1957.

F.A. CUP WINNERS HIGHLIGHTS: 1871–1978

Wanderers: 1871–72, 1872–73, 1875–76, 1876–77, 1877–78
The Wanderers were one of only 15 initial entries in 1871–72, three of whom later scratched. Originally formed by ex-public school and university players in 1860 as Forest F.C., they beat the 7-4 on favourites Royal Engineers 1–0 in the first final. Only 2,000 turned up at Kennington Oval to see the game, with an admission price of one shilling thought to be responsible for the poor attendance. Goalscorer M. P. Betts, an Old Harrovian, played under the assumed name of A. H. Chequer because he had once played for Harrow Chequers.

Since the Challenge Cup was exactly that, Wanderers were able to gain a bye to the final and choose their own venue the following year. Hence the 1873 final was played at Lillie Bridge. But this rule was then dropped. The Wanderers won this silver cup worth £20 on three more consecutive occasions to keep it. But they gave it back to the F.A. on the understanding that it was not to be won outright by any other club. C. H. R. (Charles) Wollaston appeared in all five of their finals.

Oxford University: 1873–74
Though it was at Cambridge that the game's rules were once written, it was Oxford who became the only University side to win the F.A. Cup. The Dark Blues were one of the strongest sides at the time, and included four England internationals.

Royal Engineers: 1874–75
The only Army team to win the cup, they were also concerned in the first drawn F.A. Cup Final. After being held 1–1 by Old Etonians, the Engineers won 2–0. They were composed of commissioned officers and included Scottish international Capt. Renny-Tailyour, capped at both soccer and rugby.

Old Etonians: 1878–79, 1881–82
After two earlier appearances in the final, the public school Old Boys showed that the Eton Wall Game was not their sole sporting claim. They included the Hon. A. F. Kinnaird, already a veteran cup finalist of six occasions and later to become Lord Kinnaird F.A. President. This was after he won five winners' medals in nine finals. At the end of the game in 1882 when they had defeated Blackburn Rovers, the red-bearded Kinnaird jumped for joy and stood on his head. In 1911 he was presented with the Cup itself for his services to the game.

Clapham Rovers: 1879–80
The previous beaten finalists had a team built round half-back N. C. (Norman) Bailey, who won 21 caps for England, and R. H. (Reginald) Birkett who also played for his country at rugby football.

Old Carthusians: 1880–81
This was the first cup winning side to show any real team work in the days of individualism and their 3–0 win equalled the record score in a final up to then.

Blackburn Olympic: 1882–83
The Cup went north for the first time. The winning team was driven on a wagonette by six horses accompanied by a brass band through cheering crowds in Blackburn.

Blackburn Rovers: 1883–84, 1884–85, 1885–86, 1889–90, 1890–91, 1927–28
The Cup remained in Blackburn for another three years. Scotland's Queen's Park provided the 1884 opposition. The following year the same team took the field with a similar outcome. Their appearance produced the first five-figure attendance – 12,500. Blackburn fans travelled 'Oop for t'Coop' and the phrase stuck. They released flights of pigeons and set a pattern for northern

invasions of the south – contemporarily described as a 'northern horde of uncouth garb and strange oaths'! The occasion of the final was born, and professionalism was soon accepted.

But they made hard work of the hat-trick never since achieved. Having watched the Boat Race in freezing conditions they were in poor shape for the afternoon's game and drew. For the first time the final went out of London to be decided at Derby where skipper and centre-forward James Brown clinched the game with a dribble half the length of the field. Yet Rovers came near to matching this hat-trick in the 1890s; James Forrest collecting two more medals to make a total of five in teams which put six past Sheffield Wednesday – William Townley getting three – and three past Notts County. Their last success again came against all the odds. Huddersfield were favourites but a goal after 30 seconds by John Roscamp put them well on the way to equal Villa's record of six wins at the time.

Aston Villa: 1886–87, 1894–95, 1896–97, 1904–05, 1912–13, 1919–20, 1956–57
The most successful F.A. Cup winning team of all time holding the record of seven wins, they were the first winners from the Midlands. And the 1887 final was the first to be decided between sides from the same city. Villa repeated their success over Albion in 1895 in the first final at Crystal Palace. Many of the 42,560 crowd missed the only goal scored in the opening seconds. Afterwards the club put the cup on show in a Birmingham shop and it was stolen, never recovered and the club were fined £25.

The 1897 triumph was the completion of their League and Cup 'double', all five final goals coming in twenty-five minutes of the first half with the lead changing hands three times. In 1905 Harry Hampton was their hero with both goals against Newcastle United. Eight years later they met Sunderland. Villa were lying second to their opponents in the League – the first time that the two top League sides had met in the final. Appropriately a world record crowd of 120,081 turned up. Clem Stephenson told Sunderland's Charlie Buchan early on that 'I dreamt we should win 1–0 with a goal headed by Barber'. They did and it equalled Wanderers' five wins.

The Claret and Blues won again in 1920 with 10 internationals in their side though the only goal luckily rebounded off the back of Kirton's neck. Villa's seventh win in 1957 was marred by a controversial collision between Peter McParland and Manchester United's goal-keeper Ray Wood who was carried off on a stretcher.

West Bromwich Albion: 1887–88, 1891–92, 1930–31, 1953–54, 1967–68
It was third time lucky for Albion in their third successive final and they achieved it with an all-English eleven – the first time the winners had been drawn from one country. Their wage bill was £10 a week yet they beat proud Preston North End, the club who had beaten Hyde United 26–0 on the way to the final. The gates were closed at The Oval for the first time ever at a football match with 17,000 inside. Sixty-six years later Albion beat Preston in the last minute by the odd goal in five.

Albion also gained revenge on Villa in 1892, the last final played at The Oval, and one graced with a crossbar and goalnets for the first time. In 1931 Albion won the Cup and made it back to Division One in the same season. Their last win came by a single goal in 1968 scored by Jeff Astle after Everton had pressed them most of the time.

Preston North End: 1888–89, 1937–38
To Preston went the honour of the first League and Cup double. They won the League title without losing a match and the Cup without conceding a goal. Preston had to wait half a century for their second win when George Mutch converted the first Wembley penalty in off the bar to win the match sixty seconds from the end of extra time against Huddersfield to avenge a similar defeat by the same opposition sixteen years earlier. For Huddersfield's Joe Hulme the 1938 Cup Final was his fifth at Wembley.

Wolverhampton Wanderers: 1892–93, 1907–08, 1948–49, 1959–60
Out of London for the first time and played at Fallowfield, Manchester, the final was watched by a crowd of 45,000. The gates were shut and thousands were locked out. Those inside spilled on to the pitch and from the experience of this game enclosures and crash barriers emerged. In 1908 despite Newcastle having 90% of the play, Wolves, then in Division Two, won 3–1, the Rev. Kenneth Hunt, the last amateur to gain an F.A. Cup Winners medal, opening the scoring for them. Another goal came from William Ewart

Hedley whose wife had just presented him with triplets.

Their 1949 Cup winning side contained four internationals in attack, Billy Wright in the half-back line, and England's goalkeeper Bert Williams. In 1960 Wolves won against a Blackburn Rovers side which had Dave Whelan carried off with a broken leg.

Notts County: 1893–94
Notts County became the first Division Two team to win the Cup – a one-sided affair in which James Logan scored a hat-trick for the winners and it was the only final ever held originally (excluding replays) at Everton.

Sheffield Wednesday: 1895–96, 1906–07, 1934–35
The new Cup was fashioned and went to Yorkshire for the first time with two opportunist goals from outside left Fred Spiksley, one of which went in and out so fast that the Wolves goalkeeper thought it still in play. They won again in 1907 by the odd goal in three – a Battle of the Roses against Everton, the winning goal coming only four minutes from the end. Two goals in the last five minutes by Ellis Rimmer gave Wednesday their third cup. Rimmer had been given a lucky horseshoe at half-time.

Nottingham Forest: 1897–98, 1958–59
Midland rivals Derby County were beaten in their first final despite the presence of Steve Bloomer in their side. Forest overcame an even greater handicap during their only other Cup success when sixty-one years later they lost Roy Dwight with a broken leg but held out to win. Dwight watched the second half on TV from a hospital bed. Forest manager Billy Walker had been in charge of Sheffield Wednesday's 1935 side and skippered Aston Villa in 1920.

Sheffield United: 1898–99, 1901–02, 1914–15, 1924–25
Three years after their neighbours, United brought the cup back to Sheffield with 'Nudger' Needham also shackling Bloomer. In 1902 they beat Southampton after a replay. The 1915 final held at Old Trafford was known as the 'Khaki Cup Final' as the crowd was composed mostly of servicemen with, World War I in progress. Ten years later they took advantage of one Cardiff

City error to win. Thomas Doyle and Harold Johnson won medals as their fathers had done respectively in 1899 and 1902.

Bury: 1899–1900, 1902–03
Aptly named the Shakers, they beat Southampton by four clear goals in 1900 and the ill-fated Derby for a final record score of 6–0 in 1903. This remains the biggest winning margin in a final. And their run that season was achieved without having a goal scored against them.

Tottenham Hotspur: 1900–01, 1920–21, 1960–61, 1961–62, 1966–67
Spurs were members of the Southern League in 1901 and since the formation of the Football League in 1888 no other non-League side has won the cup. It was an unforgettable occasion with a world record crowd of 110,820 basking on a sun-lit afternoon with some climbing trees for a vantage point at the Crystal Palace. But they had to go to Bolton for a replay before Spurs won 3–1 against Sheffield United to take the cup back south after 20 years. In 1921 a classical side containing Arthur Grimsdell, Fanny Walden and Jimmy Dimmock the scorer triumphed. Forty years on and a 'double' success for another out-standing side. The Danny Blanchflower – Dave Mackay – John White inspired side did it again in the Cup the following year. In 1967's all-London final, it was another victory for Spurs against Chelsea with Mackay winning his third cup winners' medal.

Manchester City: 1903–04, 1933–34, 1955–56, 1968–69
They won the first all-Lancashire final with the attacking centre-half much the vogue and wing-halves playing wide on the touchlines; individual dribbling and ball control were at their height. The goal which beat Bolton was scored by Billy Meredith arguably the most outstanding Welsh footballer of all time. Losing 1–0 to Portsmouth seventeen minutes from the end of the 1934 final, City were grateful for Fred Tilson's half-time comment that 'he would get two'. He did just that. In goal, teenage Frank Swift fainted at the end. The 'Revie Plan' was instrumental in City

Bert Trautmann (left) the Manchester City goalkeeper holding the broken neck he sustained against Birmingham City and clutching the F.A. Cup trophy with Don Revie.

taking the Cup in 1956 – Don Revie's deep-lying scheming and Bert Trautmann bravely playing out the dying minutes with a broken neck. One goal by Neil Young was sufficient to beat Leicester in 1969 in the 'Cabbage Patch' final – so called because of the state the Wembley pitch was in that day following an earlier Horse of the Year show.

Everton: 1905–06, 1932–33, 1965–66
The best player on view in the 1906 final was named John Sharp and it was from his cross that Alec Young scored fifteen minutes from the end. With Dixie Dean in harness they won in 1933 again when the players were numbered for the first time in the final – but from 1 to 22. A tremendous revival highlighted 1966. After being two down to Sheffield Wednesday, they won 3–2 with Mike Trebilcock scoring twice. But the losers became the first beaten side to do a lap of honour at Wembley.

Manchester United: 1908–09, 1947–48, 1962–63, 1976–77
United's first cup win came in a game in which neither they nor Bristol City had played in a final before. Billy Meredith was now on United's wing and United supporters brought with them stone jars of strong ale and sandwiches an inch thick. Their 1948 victory by 4–2 was arguably the finest ever final at Wembley. Their pedigree had shown in beating six Division One sides on the way. The front line of Jimmy Delaney, Johnny Morris, Jack Rowley, Stan Pearson and Charlie Mitten was in great form. Johnny Carey steadied them with his 'keep playing football' speech.

In 1963 Pat Crerand and Albert Quixall probed the openings and David Herd and Denis Law supplied the goals. For manager, Matt Busby, it was a present after the trials the post-Munich era had produced. Their fourth success against Liverpool in a meeting of the country's two best supported teams in 1977 prevented what their opponents were hoping would be a 'treble' of League, F.A. Cup and European Cup achievements.

Newcastle United: 1909–10, 1923–24, 1931–32, 1950–51, 1951–52, 1954–55
For the fourth time in six seasons they appeared in the final – this time to succeed over Barnsley but only after a last-minute header by Jock

Bill McCracken the Newcastle United and Irish international full-back.

Rutherford forced a replay during which the crowd broke on to the field at Everton. The quality of United's football with players like Peter McWilliam, Colin Veitch and Bill McCracken had always deserted them in the finals down south, but not here. In 1924 they had to bring into the side an inexperienced second team goalkeeper who played a blinder. Controversy in 1932 with the 'over the goal line' equaliser against Arsenal when Jimmy Richardson crossed for Jack Allen to level the scores and put United on the way to winning.

A Jackie Milburn duo finished Blackpool in 1951, one of them a solo effort after a 40 yard run. But it took them 84 minutes to score the next year against a ten-man Arsenal team who lost Walley Barnes after a quarter of an hour. Then George Robledo, their Chilean-born centre-forward, headed a goal. Three years later injury to another back, Jimmy Meadows of Manchester City, helped to put the Cup on Tyneside for the sixth time, though a Jackie Milburn goal in 45 seconds contributed. Milburn, Bobby Cowell and Bobby Mitchell won their third winning medals and Newcastle had made it five wins – a record at Wembley.

Bradford City: 1910–11
With no copyright existing at the time, replicas of the Cup made it necessary for a change of design. With this third F.A. Cup trophy made in Bradford it was appropriately won by a team from that city – but it has never returned. City fielded a side with a record number of eight Scotsmen.

Barnsley: 1911–12
A Division Two club, they reached the final after a marathon twelve-match run including replays. Extra time was needed in the replay before they won through. Typical of their spirit was the defender who took a boot off for attention to his foot but raced back without it to clear a dangerous attack. After that match extra time was enforced during the final.

Burnley: 1913–14
Defences were on top in this second all-Lancashire final with Liverpool and it fell to Burnley's captain Tommy Boyle to become the first man to receive the F.A. Cup from a reigning monarch as the match was attended by King George V.

Huddersfield Town: 1921–22
The first time that a Cup Final was decided by a penalty kick. Preston players complained bitterly that the infringement had occurred outside the area. But Billy Smith who had been brought down took the kick and he scored despite the antics of the goalkeeper who was still allowed to move before the kick was taken in those days. It was the last final at Stamford Bridge.

Bolton Wanderers: 1922–23, 1925–26, 1928–29, 1957–58
Wembley's first final had an official attendance of 126,047 but between 160,000 and 200,000 probably gained admission and swarmed all over the pitch. Owing to the man on the white horse – PC Scorey and 'Billy' – and the good sense of the crowd a disaster was averted. The game was eventually played with the pitch ringed with spectators. David Jack was the first man to score at Wembley. Since then finals have been all-ticket. Bolton won it again in 1926 and 1929. Five Bolton players won their third winners' medals. In 1958 the sympathy of the country was with Manchester United after Munich, but Wanderers won again.

Cardiff City: 1926–27
The only side to take the F.A. Cup out of England, Cardiff won it through a tragic error by the Arsenal goalkeeper Dan Lewis – a Welsh international. Cardiff had one Englishman, four Irishmen, three Scots and three Welshmen in their team. It was the first Cup Final to be broadcast.

Arsenal: 1929–30, 1935–36, 1949–50, 1970–71
Masterminded by manager Herbert Chapman in 1930 and with a deep-lying inside-forward in

The first Wembley Cup Final and chaos on the pitch.

The Graf Zeppelin flies above Wembley at the 1930 F.A. Cup Final.

Alex James, a short-legged artist in long shorts, Bob John at wing-half and Cliff Bastin on the wing, they won in style. Above, the Graf Zeppelin flew. 'Policeman' Herbie Roberts at centre-half, 'Iron Man' Wilf Copping at wing-half and flying winger Joe Hulme appearing in his fourth final, featured in 1936 though the real hero was scorer Ted Drake who played with an injured knee heavily bandaged.

Two goals by Reg Lewis were enough in 1950 while in 1971 it was the great 'double' year for the Gunners who beat Liverpool as they had twenty-one years before; substitute Eddie Kelly scoring the equaliser which turned the game Arsenal's way, five days after clinching the championship.

Sunderland: 1936–37, 1972–73
The TV cameras were at the final for the first time and inspired by local lad Raich Carter, Sunderland gradually pulled round after conceding a goal, to win 3–1. The Cup went to Wearside for the second time on Wembley's 50th anniversary when as a Division Two side they overcame Leeds United after goalkeeper Jimmy Montgomery produced a vital 70th minute double save.

Portsmouth: 1938–39
When the Wolves autograph book came into the Pompey dressing room before the game the signatures were shaky and unrecognisable. It gave Portsmouth confidence and with Jack Tinn's 'lucky spats' and the 'Pompey Chimes'

ringing out on the terraces, Wolves were beaten 4–1. One of the scorers was Bert Barlow, signed that season from Wolves.

Derby County: 1945–46
Derby's Cup luck changed at last. Before the final Derby captain Jack Nicholas went to a gypsy encampment where a curse put on them in 1895 was ceremoniously removed. Carter, of previous Sunderland fame, combined with Peter Doherty to defeat Charlton whose Bert Turner scored for both sides. And the ball burst during the game.

Charlton Athletic: 1946–47
The ball burst again this year. And with only six minutes remaining Burnley's formidable defence was holding out until Chris Duffy volleyed a goal. After scoring he raced the length of the field before he was caught by his delighted colleagues.

Blackpool: 1952–53
It was Stanley Matthews' final but only after an injury-hit Bolton crashed in the last twenty minutes after leading 3–1. Stan Mortensen scored a hat-trick – the equaliser from a free kick at which his colleague Ernie Taylor said 'bet you sixpence you don't score'. Then a jinking Matthews run and cross to Bill Perry sealed it.

West Ham United: 1963–64, 1974–75
John Sissons, the youngest Cup Final scorer at the age of 18, walked off with a sympathetic arm round Preston's Howard Kendall. Kendall, at 17

years and 345 days, had been the youngest cup finalist. Geoff Hurst scored a goal on the ground where he was to make World Cup history two years later. Two goals by Alan Taylor who had been playing for Fourth Division Rochdale six months before gave them their second win during a match in which neither trainer had to be called upon.

Liverpool: 1964–65, 1973–74

Bill Shankly led his team to success. He had been a player in the 1937 and 1938 finals. Liverpool were handicapped by a shoulder injury to Gerry Byrne but it was a defence-dominated final which went to extra time. Three second-half goals gave them victory in 1974 which paid little heed to Newcastle's Wembley tradition.

Chelsea: 1969–70

For the first time the game was not settled at Wembley. It needed a replay at Old Trafford. Twice Chelsea were behind yet equalised and in the replay were behind again before finally getting the winner from David Webb, who had been turned almost inside out in the original game at Wembley by Eddie Gray of Leeds United.

Leeds United: 1971–72

The Centenary Year final and Leeds beat the League and Cup holders of 1971 with a goal made for Allan Clarke by Mick Jones who dislocated his elbow in the last minute and had to collect his medal in great pain.

Southampton: 1975–76

Third time lucky for Southampton, the sixth Second Division side to succeed, and for whom Bobby Stokes scored seven minutes from the end.

Ipswich Town: 1977–78

The 40th different team to win the trophy the only goal coming from Roger Osborne in the 76th minute. It was his last kick in the match because he had to be substituted through exhaustion!

F.A. CUP POT-POURRI

Since the formation of the Football League in 1888 all but seven F.A. Cup winners have been drawn from Division One clubs. Six were teams from Division Two: Notts County (1894), Wolverhampton Wanderers (1908), Barnsley (1912), West Bromwich Albion (1931), Sunderland (1973) and Southampton (1976). The seventh was Tottenham Hotspur who were a Southern League club when they won the Cup in 1901.

Tottenham actually fulfilled 74 first team fixtures that season though not all of them of a competitive nature. They fielded their seniors in two regular leagues, the First Division of the Southern League in which they played 28 matches, with another 16 matches being played in the Western League. In addition they appeared in eight F.A. Cup matches including three replays, one of which was the final against Sheffield United. Their complete record that season was Played 74; Won 42; Lost 15; Drawn 17; Goals for 179; Goals against 92. Their highest scoring game was a friendly on 8 January 1901 against a German touring side which Spurs won 9–6. And the entire season was completed between 1 September and 30 April.

The first Scottish club to become members of the Football Association in London was Queen's Park in November 1870. The famous Scottish amateur club twice reached the F.A. Cup Final in 1884 and 1885, losing to Blackburn Rovers on each occasion before the Scottish F.A. (founded in March 1873) made a rule banning their clubs from membership of any other association after May 1887.

The first Welsh team to enter the F.A. Cup competition was the Druids in 1876. Nicknamed the 'Ancient Britons' this Welsh club from Ruabon, near Wrexham, was for many years one of the most powerful in Wales and their reputation spread further afield. They were finalists in eight of the first nine Welsh Cup Finals, winning five of them, and in all carried off this trophy eight times before the club was finally disbanded in 1927.

In 1876 they scratched from the F.A. Cup after being drawn to meet the Shropshire Wanderers, but the following year they defeated the same club 1–0 and received a bye in the second round before going down 8–0 to the strong and talented Royal Engineers.

The Druids eventually lost status because they were unable to hold on to their best players, but at their peak it was remarkable how many really accomplished footballers they managed to unearth in their own locality. One group alone, the

Davies family of Cefn, provided them with five brothers, four of whom went on to play for Wales. Indeed, allowing for the difficulty arising out of some players appearing for more than one club, it is a matter of fact that none of the first 37 Welsh international teams (that is up to 1891) ever took the field without a Druid or a former player of that club included in it.

There have been several examples of outstanding sportsmanship often overlooked in the years since the advent of professionalism. One of the finest concerned the Old Etonians F.C., who were among the pioneering amateur teams of the late 19th century.

Between 1874 and 1884 the Old Etonians appeared in six F.A. Cup Finals, winning twice in 1879 and 1882. In the earlier of those two successful campaigns they came up against one of the new breed of footballing sides – Darwen, composed neither of the old boys of public schools nor sons of middle-class gentry, but of working-class lads, some of whom were, even as early as that 1878–79 season, being paid by the club for their services.

The original game between these two contrasting teams was drawn 5–5 and there was no decisive result in the replay which again ended level at 2–2 after extra time.

With the Lancashire cotton workers apparently having such an excellent chance of becoming the first Northern side to reach the F.A. Cup semi-finals, the sum of £175 was raised so that the Darwen team could indulge in some special training at Blackpool. Among the subscribers to that fund was the Old Etonians club itself who donated £5. The F.A. contributed another £10. For such an amount of money in those days it was possible to kit out a whole team, including football boots, for not much more than the price of the modern football jersey.

The sea air and special training did not save Darwen from a 6–2 defeat in their third meeting with the Old Etonians at the Oval, and after beating Nottingham Forest in the semi-finals the Old Boys club accounted for Clapham Rovers 1–0 before a 5,000 crowd in the Final.

In the formative days of professional football, clubs did not train as regularly or as diligently as they do now, so it is interesting to recall that in the 'Athletic News' dated 3 January 1888, before their First Round F.A. Cup tie with Aston Villa, reference was made to the Preston North End club, 'who have not trained previously this season . . . but are now at the Palace Hotel, Southport, undergoing cold water treatment, shooting seagulls, and playing football.' Villa were at their favourite training quarters at Holte Fleet, 'a quaint country spot on the banks of the River Severn, and within a few miles of Worcester.'

Preston won this particular encounter 3–1 and went through to the final where they were surprisingly beaten 2–1 by West Bromwich Albion. Interest was such in this final that it is the first game on record for which it is known that the gates had to be closed before the kick-off. The attendance was a new record at that time of 19,000.

It is often mentioned that Preston were so confident of victory at the Oval in that final that they wanted to be photographed with the Cup *before* the game. This incident had been referred to in many histories of the game but about 40 years later John Goodall, who was Preston's centre-forward on that occasion, finally gave it the lie.

There have been several instances of an F.A. Cup Final team including a pair of brothers, the most recent in 1977 when Manchester United fielded the brothers Brian and Jimmy Greenhoff, but there has been only one Cup Final with two pairs of brothers on the field. That was in 1876 when the Wanderers beat the Old Etonians 3–0 in a replay after a goalless draw.

The winning team on that occasion included the brothers Frank and Hubert Heron (Hubert went on to win three winners' medals in Wanderers' hat-trick of victories), while the Old Etonians lined up with the brothers the Hon. Edward and Hon. Alfred Lyttelton, two great all-round sportsmen of their day. The Hon. Alfred Lyttelton also played cricket for England v. Australia.

An F.A. Cup semi-final was played in Scotland in 1885, the only semi-final in this competition ever played outside England. It was a replayed tie between the leading Scottish amateur club Queen's Park and Nottingham Forest, who had drawn their first game 1–1 at Derby.

The replay was played on the ground of Merchiston Castle School, Edinburgh, and Queen's Park were clear winners 3–0. That victory took the Scottish club to the F.A. Cup

Final for the second year in succession. In 1884 they had lost 2–1 to Blackburn Rovers and this following year they were beaten again 2–0 by the same English club.

The first signs of real Cup tie fever were seen at Perry Barr, the former Aston Villa ground, in January 1888 when the Villa (F.A. Cup holders) were drawn at home to Preston North End, another of the country's most powerful teams. A crowd of 27,000 packed the ground and during the game they encroached onto the pitch and play was held up while mounted police and Hussars from the Great Brook Street barracks cleared the playing area.

There was argument among officials present as to whether or not the game should be declared a 'friendly' and naturally enough, considering the final score 3–1 in their favour, Preston North End were not much in favour of the decision to declare the cup-tie abandoned. A subsequent meeting of the F.A. Council behind closed doors and with the Press excluded decided that because of Villa's failure to control the crowd, the game should be awarded to Preston.

In 1888–89 Sunderland were drawn to meet Sunderland Albion, another local side formed only that year by a number of prominent members of the original Sunderland club who had broken away following disagreement over the policy of importing Scottish professionals. This policy had landed them in trouble with the F.A.

The new club set out to break the senior club and excitement in the locality was intense when they were drawn to meet each other in successive weeks in both the Durham Cup and the F.A. Cup. However, Sunderland withdrew, and their Chairman's explanation was that the excitement of Cup ties made scientific football impossible and now that these ties had served their purpose in helping to popularise the game they should be dropped. The local citizens took that remarkable statement with a pinch of salt, and in fact Sunderland were back in both Cup competitions the following season.

Instead of a Cup-tie a friendly was arranged with Sunderland beating the Albion 2–0 and the receipts were handed over to charity. A return match played a few weeks later also went in Sunderland's favour, this time by 3–2. This may have been the turning point for the Albion, for

while the older Sunderland club continued to prosper, Albion struggled on until August 1892 when they went into voluntary liquidation.

In February 1911 Northampton Town (then of the Southern League) shook First Division Newcastle United (the Cup holders) by holding them to a 1–1 draw in a Second Round (modern Fourth Round equivalent) tie at St. James's Park. A crowd of 42,000 saw Sandy Higgins put Newcastle ahead, but the visitors equalised from the kick-off with an individual goal by Frank Bradshaw and then held on to force a replay.

Although they were then one of the most successful sides in the country, Newcastle obviously did not relish a trip to Northampton and for a little matter of £900 they persuaded their opponents to return to Newcastle for the replay. The gate at this game scarcely covered Newcastle's outlay and they only just scraped through with a solitary goal by their leading scorer, Albert Shepherd, from the penalty spot. Shepherd had missed the first game when he had to drop out at the last minute owing to the death of his four-year-old son.

Chelsea made one of the finest fight-backs ever seen in a First Round Cup tie with Swindon in 1914–15. The two sides had fought a 1–1 draw at Stamford Bridge and Swindon had agreed to switch the replay to the same ground. This time the Southern League side established a two-goal lead and it was not until five minutes from the end that Chelsea managed to secure an equaliser. In extra time, however, the Division One club really took firm control and turned what had earlier seemed to be a likely defeat into a remarkable 5–2 victory.

Among the feats of small clubs performing 'giant-killing' acts Darlington are seldom mentioned. Yet, in 1919–20 season, this North Eastern club achieved what was for 55 years a unique event when they defeated a Division One side on the senior club's home ground while they themselves were still a non-league team.

Darlington's victims were Sheffield Wednesday. The Yorkshire club were held to a goalless draw at Darlington, but in the replay of this First Round tie (modern Third Round equivalent) at Hillsborough, Wednesday were beaten 2–0.

The 'giant-killing' act that first gained fame for Charlton Athletic took place during the 1922–23 season when, as a comparatively unknown Division Three (Southern Section) side, they beat three Division One teams in the F.A. Cup competition.

Their first victims were Manchester City, beaten 2–1 at Maine Road (the City's first defeat in six games), next came Preston North End, who were defeated 2–0 at The Valley, and three weeks later, in the Third Round (modern equivalent Fifth Round), West Bromwich Albion came to Charlton and lost 1–0 before a crowd of over 31,000.

Charlton were again drawn at home in the Fourth Round against another Division One side, Bolton Wanderers, and the likelihood of the club appearing in its first Wembley Cup Final increased.

Unfortunately Charlton were to wait another 23 years before playing at Wembley, for on 10 March 1923 a crowd of over 41,000 (an attendance record not beaten at The Valley until 13 years later when The Athletic were fighting their way into Division One) saw David Jack score Bolton's winning goal. Bolton themselves went on to reach the Final seven weeks later, the first Cup Final to be held at Wembley, and defeated Charlton's London neighbours West Ham United 2–0.

A change in the rules enabled Cardiff City to reach the F.A. Cup Final for the first time in their history in 1925. It had been in the previous close season that the International Board had decided that in future a goal could be scored direct from a corner-kick. This change in the Laws enabled Willie Davies of Cardiff City to score one of the most dramatic goals since the Welsh club had been formed.

It was in the Fourth Round (modern equivalent Six Round) tie with Leicester City and with less than a minute remaining for play the teams were level at one goal each. Davies took a corner-kick which curled right in under the bar. Even he did not realise it was a goal until he was engulfed by congratulatory players and supporters. And this goal from a corner-kick had enabled Cardiff City to win through to the semi-finals with eight seconds to spare.

Orient's record defeat is 8–0 at home to Aston Villa in an F.A. Cup tie on 30 January 1929, but it is not generally appreciated that only four days earlier these two teams had fought a goalless

draw. The draw was remarkable because a Division Three side had held one of the country's leading teams on the Division One side's home ground (Aston Villa were fifth at the time), and the second result was astonishing because it produced such a contrasting score from the first match.

The draw for the F.A. Cup has frequently thrown up some strange coincidences. Recent years have repeated instances of the same clubs having been paired together on more than one occasion and in the 1960s Leicester City and Manchester City actually came into conflict four seasons in succession.

In the 1965–66 season it was a fifth round tie which needed a replay after a 2–2 draw and which Manchester City eventually won 1–0; the following season in the third round they were again successful 2–1, but in 1967–68 in the fourth round despite being drawn at home for the third consecutive time City were held to a 0–0 draw with Leicester winning the replay 4–3. Manchester City won the 1968–69 Final beating Leicester 1–0.

Brighton and Hove Albion and Watford had also been drawn together in consecutive seasons forty years previously. In the 1924–25 season in a first round tie the original game ended in a 1–1 draw with Brighton winning the replay 4–3 on their own ground. The following season there was another first round replay also after a 1–1 draw, this time at Brighton, with Watford taking home advantage in the replay to win 2–0. Watford were again successful in 1926–27 by the only goal of the match in a second round match on their own ground.

Probably even more remarkable is the fact that neighbouring Burnley and Preston North End, two of the Football League's twelve 1888 original clubs, have gone into the competition in all its subsequent seasons and have never met.

Walton and Hersham's 4–0 against Brighton and Hove on 28 November 1973, following a 0–0 home draw in a first round tie became the biggest-ever F.A. Cup away victory by an amateur team against Football League opponents.

Of 40 F.A. Cup first round ties played on 19 November 1955, 24 were played on the grounds of Football League clubs. Yet the biggest crowd at any of these 40 games was 20,609 at the match between Peterborough United (Midland League) and Ipswich Town.

Of the 40 similarly played first round ties on 15 November 1969, 21 were played on the grounds of Football League clubs, and the highest attendance was 12,622 at that between Northern Premier League club Wigan Athletic and Port Vale.

Of 20 F.A. Cup second round ties played on 17 December 1977 the biggest crowd was 13,871 at that between Northern Premier League club Wigan Athletic and Sheffield Wednesday.

The quickest goal scored in the F.A. Cup by a player who was making his debut in first-class football was one by Albert Taylor, an Irish outside-left, with Luton Town against Blackburn Rovers on 10 January 1953. He scored in the first 45 seconds.

In the 1963–64 season Oxford United became the only Football League club ever drawn at home six times in succession in one season against Folkestone, Kettering, Chesterfield, Brentford, Blackburn Rovers and Preston North End.

Preston North End visited Manchester City in the F.A. Cup's fifth round and Manchester United in the sixth during the 1947–48 season, both games being played at Maine Road, which the two clubs shared at the time. It was the only example in history of a team playing successive away ties in different rounds in the same season on the same ground.

There has been only one known instance of two teams meeting twice in the F.A. Cup on successive days. In the fourth round in the 1954–55 season Aston Villa and Doncaster Rovers fought the last of four drawn games – on a Monday. The fifth round was due on the following Saturday, and they were ordered to meet again on the Tuesday. Doncaster eventually won 3–1 at The Hawthorns, West Bromwich, after a total playing time of nine hours.

In 1963 Manchester City, Norwich City and Sheffield United all played ties in the third (6 March), fourth (12 March) and fifth (16 March) round of the F.A. Cup within an 11-day spell – an unparalleled sequence in the competition's history. The congestion had been caused through the effects of a severe winter which produced an unprecedented list of postponements.

Of 34 ties in the F.A. Cup first round on 24 November 1928, only one between Gillingham and Torquay United finished level. It was the smallest proportion of draws in the history of a full day's programme of F.A. Cup matches.

Chesterfield's opponents in the F.A. Cup's first two rounds in the 1960–61 season were Doncaster Rovers and Oldham Athletic, and so they were again a year later! The mathematicians at Manchester University assessed the odds against such a double coming up as 3,081 to one.

The 1950–51 season was the only one since the 1914–18 war in which no non-League club reached the F.A. Cup's third round. Of the 25 non-League clubs which figured in the competition proper 19 were knocked out in the first round and the other six in the second.

Southend United are the only team to have scored nine goals or more three times in F.A. Cup-ties since the last war and four times since the 1914–18 war. The matches involved were: 10–1 v. Golders Green in 1934–35; 9–2 v. Barnet in 1946–47, plus 9–0 and 10–1 v. King's Lynn and Brentwood respectively both in 1968–69.

The only instance in history of two players of the same club both scoring hat-tricks in successive F.A. Cup rounds in the competition proper also arose in the 1968–69 season. For Southend Billy Best and Gary Moore each scored three times in the 9–0 defeat of King's Lynn; Best scored five and Moore four in the 10–1 defeat of Brentwood.

Harry Brooks scored five goals in each of two successive F.A. Cup matches for Aldershot during the 1945–46 season. On 24 November he scored five in a second leg tie against Reading and on 8 December he repeated his effort in the first leg of the second round tie against Newport (Isle of Wight).

Never, before or since, did ground advantage count for so little in an F.A. Cup as in the fifth round in February 1935. Of the eight teams drawn at home only Everton (3–1 v. Derby County) were successful.

Charlton Athletic are the only club to have

figured in a Wembley F.A. Cup final after having lost a game in the competition in the same season. They reached Wembley in 1945–46, but they had lost at Fulham by 2–1 in the third round after having beaten them at home 3–1 when ties that season were on a home and away basis.

Jimmy Scoular, destined to become a Scottish international half-back and Newcastle United's F.A. Cup winning captain, was the first player in history ever known to turn out for two clubs in the competition in the same season. In 1945–46 he played for Gosport against Salisbury City in a preliminary round match and for Portsmouth against Birmingham in the third.

No other player during the last 65 years ever appeared in an F.A. Cup winning team after so few Football League appearances as Barry Stobart. When he figured at inside-right in Wolves' winning side against Blackburn Rovers on 7 May 1960, he had played in only four Division One matches.

At an F.A. Cup-tie at Newcastle on 10 February 1953 between United and Swansea Town there was a 63,480 crowd, with receipts of nearly £10,000, but the game was abandoned through fog after only eight minutes and, of course, there was no money refunded to spectators.

Two ties in the F.A. Cup's fifth round on 18 February 1961 drew an aggregate of 123,261 spectators in Birmingham – 69,672 at the Aston Villa v Tottenham Hotspur game and 53,589 at Birmingham City v Leicester City. The aggregate was an all-time record for the biggest crowds ever seen in any provincial city or town on the same day.

Though Peterborough United and Reading have not reached Division Two in the post-war period they have been consistent in reaching the third round of the F.A. Cup more times than any other clubs. Reading have achieved the feat on 17 occasions while Peterborough have done it 16 times.

The only example in history of a team meeting opponents from the same county as itself in each of four consecutive rounds in the F.A. Cup competition proper was when Bradford Park Avenue faced other Yorkshire sides – York City, Bradford City, Sheffield Wednesday and Leeds

United – in the first four of season 1951–52. The run was ended at Leeds when United won 2–0.

Middlesbrough's post-war F.A. Cup record is by far the worst of all 22 clubs in Division One during 1977–78. In 32 seasons they have never proceeded beyond the sixth round. In fact throughout their entire history they have been unable to progress further. Yet during a period in their history when they reverted to amateur status they twice won the F.A. Amateur Cup in 1895 and 1898. Blyth Spartans became the first non-league club to reach the fifth round of the F.A. Cup since the Football League was expanded to 86 clubs in 1921 when they achieved this feat in 1977–78.

No other Football League club since the war has won so many successive F.A. Cup-ties against non-League teams as Reading. They had won 14 such post-war ties before they lost 1–0 away to Brentwood in the first round in season 1969–70.

In the 1947–48 season Manchester United were drawn in turn against six Division One clubs in the F.A. Cup, a unique event in the history of the competition. The sequence was: third round Aston Villa (A) won 6–4; fourth round Liverpool (H) won 3–0; fifth round Charlton Athletic (H) 2–0; sixth round Preston North End (H) 4–1; semi-final Derby County (at Hillsborough) won 3–1 and final Blackpool (at Wembley) won 4–2.

The first round tie with Villa was worth recalling with its ten goals on a dismal afternoon of rain and on a muddy pitch. Villa scored from the kick-off without a United player touching the ball. But within six minutes United had equalised and after another 11 minutes were in front. At half-time they led 5–1.

Villa however produced a spirited come-back to score three times in succession but in the closing minutes United made the match safe with a sixth goal from a corner-kick.

That season, too, United's Old Trafford ground was still out of commission because of war damage and their 'home' matches were played at Goodison Park against Liverpool; at Huddersfield against the Cup holders Charlton and at Maine Road against Preston.

The Sunderland side that won the F.A. Cup in

1973 dispersed to other clubs so quickly that by the beginning of the 1977–78 season only one remained at Roker Park – Scottish forward Bobby Kerr – and he was on the transfer list at his own request.

One of the best defensive records in F.A. Cup history belongs to Bradford City, a club that has not made such an impression in this competition in recent years but won the Cup as long ago as 1911. It was at that time that they enjoyed a run of 12 consecutive Cup ties without conceding a goal. After beating Norwich City 2–1 in the Second Round (present Fourth Round) in February 1911 they kept their goal intact throughout more than 19 hours of Cup football before going down 3–2 to Barnsley in the third replay of a Fourth Round (present Sixth Round)

tie in March 1912.

This run included the two games in the Cup Final of 1911 when they first drew 0–0 with Newcastle United, the Cup holders, and then won the replay 1–0 at Old Trafford when the Newcastle goalkeeper failed to hold an easy header from Jock Spiers, one of the few occasions that City were on the target while their defence had to withstand incessant attacks from the Newcastle team.

Incidentally, that Bradford City side included only two Englishmen and the trophy they carried off that season was the new F.A. Cup made by a Bradford firm, Messrs Fattorini and Sons. It was a remarkable coincidence that a Bradford team should have won the new Cup in its first season considering that no side from Bradford ever appeared in the Final either before or since.

The Football League

The Football League was originally constituted with 12 clubs: Accrington, Aston Villa, Blackburn Rovers, Bolton Wanderers, Burnley, Derby County, Everton, Notts County, Preston North End, Stoke, West Bromwich Albion and Wolverhampton Wanderers. It was formed following an earlier meeting a month previously on 17 April 1888 at The Royal Hotel, Manchester.

Three other clubs – Sheffield Wednesday, Nottingham Forest and Halliwell – applied for membership but could not be accepted because of the difficulty of arranging fixtures.

The prime mover behind the League idea had been a Scot, William McGregor, living in Birmingham and an official of Aston Villa. He wrote to the leading clubs in an effort to regularise the fixtures which had hitherto been on a haphazard basis despite the growth of professionalism in the years immediately preceeding.

A Division Two was added in 1892 consisting of 12 clubs by which time the Division One complement had grown to 16. Subsequent addition brought the total of both divisions up to 22 each in 1919–20.

A Division Three was added in 1920 and this was split into two sections, Northern and Southern, the following year. By 1923 each section comprised 22 clubs and in 1950 they became 24.

In 1958–59 these sections were reorganised to form a national Division Three and Division Four with four up and four down promotion and relegation between them.

Growth of the Football League:		
Season	Clubs	Divisions
1888–89	12	1
1891–92	14	1
1892–93	28	2
1893–94	31	2
1894–95	32	2
1898–99	36	2
1905–06	40	2
1919–20	44	2
1920–21	66	3
1921–22	86	4
1923–24	88	4
1950–51	92	4

Promotion and relegation for the bottom two clubs and the top two of Division One and Two was introduced in 1898–99. Previously the issues had been decided by a series of Test Matches which had been brought in when the League had been increased to two divisions in 1892–93.

On the formation of the regional Division Three only one from each was promoted but in 1973 the existing four up and four down for the lower two divisions was added to when the League accepted three up and three down between the first three divisions.

The first Football League games were played on Saturday, 8 September 1888, and the most successful start was made by Bolton Wanderers who were three goals up against Derby County within six minutes of the kick-off at Pike's Lane (Bolton's home ground at that time). But Derby made a remarkable fight-back and were leading 4–3 at the interval before finishing as 6–3 winners.

RESIGNATIONS AND WITHDRAWALS

Since the Football League was founded in 1888 only 25 clubs have either resigned or failed to gain re-election. In the case of Leeds City in 1919 they were wound up in October 1919 for alleged irregularities and their fixtures were taken over by Port Vale.

Resigned

Accrington Stanley (1893 and 1962)
Glossop North End (1919)

*New Brighton (1901)
Stalybridge Celtic (1923)
Wigan Borough (1931)

Not re-elected

Aberdare Athletic (1927)
Ashington (1929)
Barrow (1972)
Bootle (1893)
Bradford Park Avenue (1970)
Burton United (1907)
Burton Wanderers (1897)
Darwen (1899)
Durham City (1928)
Gainsborough Trinity (1912)
Gateshead (1960)
Loughborough Town (1900)
Merthyr Tydfil (1930)
Middlesbrough Ironopolis (1894)
Nelson (1931)
*New Brighton (1951)
Northwich Victoria (1894)
Southport (1978)
**Thames (1932)
Workington (1977)

*Same club
**Did not apply

All that remained of Accrington Stanley's one-time glory as members of the Football League.

FOOTBALL LEAGUE

Ground	Capacity & Record	Shirts/shorts	League career	Honours (domestic) League	Cup
ALDERSHOT (1926)					
Recreation Ground High Street Aldershot GU11 1TW 117×76 yd	20,000 19,138 v Carlisle FA Cup 4th Rd replay, 28 January 1970	Red, blue, white trim/ white	1932–58 Div. 3(S) 1958–73 Div. 4 1973–76 Div. 3 1976– Div. 4	Highest placing 8th Div. 3 1974	FA Cup 5th Rd 1932–3 League Cup never past 2nd Rd
ARSENAL (1886)					
Arsenal Stadium Highbury London N5 110×71 yd.	60,000 73,295 v Sunderland Div. 1 9 March 1935	Red, white sleeves/ white	1893–1904 Div. 2 1904–13 Div. 1 1913–15 Div. 2 1919– Div. 1	Div. 1 Champions 1931, 1933, 1934, 1935, 1938, 1948, 1953, 1971 Runners-up 1926, 1932, 1973, Div. 2 runners-up 1904	FA Cup winners 1930, 1936, 1950, 1971 Runners-up 1927, 1932, 1952, 1972, 1978 League Cup runners-up 1968, 1969
ASTON VILLA (1874)					
Villa Park Trinity Road Birmingham B6 6HE 115×75 yd	53,000 76,588 v Derby Co FA Cup 6th Rd 2 March 1946	Claret, blue sleeves/white	1888 (founder members of League) 1936–38 Div. 2 1938–59 Div. 1 1959–60 Div. 2 1960–67 Div. 1 1967–70 Div. 2 1970–72 Div. 3 1972–75 Div. 2 1975– Div. 1	Div. 1 Champions 1894, 1896, 1897, 1899, 1900, 1910, Runners-up 1889, 1903, 1908, 1911, 1913, 1914, 1931, 1933 Div. 2 Champions 1938, 1960 Runners-up 1975 Div. 3 Champions 1972	FA Cup winners 1887, 1895, 1897, 1905, 1913, 1920, 1957 (a record) Runners-up 1892, 1924 League Cup winners 1961, 1975, 1977 Runners-up 1963, 1971
BARNSLEY (1887)					
Oakwell Ground Grove Street Barnsley 111×75 yd	38,500 40,255 v Stoke City FA Cup 5th Rd 15 February 1936	Red/white	1898 elected to Div. 2 1932–34 Div. 3(N) 1934–38 Div. 2 1938–39 Div. 3(N) 1946–53 Div. 2 1953–55 Div. 3(N) 1955–59 Div. 2 1959–65 Div. 3 1965–68 Div. 4 1968–72 Div. 3 1972– Div. 4	Div. 3(N) Champions 1934, 1939, 1955 Runners-up 1954 Div. 4 runners-up 1968	FA Cup winners 1912 Runners-up 1910 League Cup never past 3rd Rd
BIRMINGHAM CITY (1875)					
St Andrews Birmingham B9 4NH 115×75 yd	51,000 66,844 v Everton FA Cup 5th Rd 11 February 1939	Blue, white trim/white, blue trim	1892–94 Div. 2 1894–96 Div. 1 1896–1901 Div. 2 1901–02 Div. 1 1902–03 Div. 2 1903–08 Div. 1 1908–21 Div. 2 1921–39 Div. 1 1946–48 Div. 2 1948–50 Div. 1 1950–55 Div. 2 1955–65 Div. 1 1965–72 Div. 2 1972– Div. 1	Div. 2 Champions 1893, 1921, 1948, 1955 Runners-up 1894, 1901, 1903, 1972	FA Cup runners-up 1931, 1956 League Cup winners 1963

CLUB DIRECTORY

Most League Points	Goals	Record win	Player with highest number of goals Aggregate	Individual	Most League appearances	Most capped player

ALDERSHOT

| 56, Div. 4 1972–73 | 83, Div. 4 1963–64 | 8–1 v Gateshead Div. 4 13 September 1958 | Jack Howarth 171, 1965–71, 1972–77 | Jack Howarth 25 Div. 3 1973–74 | Len Walker 450, 1964–76 | None |

ARSENAL

| 66, Div. 1 1930–31 | 127, Div. 1 1930–31 | 12–0 v Loughborough T. Div. 2 12 March 1900 | Cliff Bastin 150, 1930–47 | Ted Drake 42 Div. 1 1934–35 | George Armstrong 500, 1960–77 | Terry Neill 44, N. Ireland 1961–70 |

ASTON VILLA

| 70, Div. 3 1971–72 | 128, Div. 1 1930–31 | 13–0 v Wednesbury Old Athletic FA Cup 1st Rd 1886 | Harry Hampton 213, 1904–20 Billy Walker 213, 1919–34 | Pongo Waring 49 Div. 1 1930–31 | Charlie Aitken 560, 1961–76 | Peter McParland 33, N Ireland 1954–61 |

BARNSLEY

| 67, Div. 3(N) 1938–39 | 118, Div. 3(N) 1933–34 | 9–0 v Loughborough T Div. 2 28 January 1899 Accrington Stanley Div. 3(N) 3 February 1934 | Ernest Hine 123, 1921–26, 1934–38 | Cecil McCormack 33 Div. 2 1950–51 | Barry Murphy 514, 1962–78 | Eddie McMorran 9, N Ireland 1950–52 |

BIRMINGHAM CITY

| 59, Div. 2 1947–48 | 103, Div. 2 1893–94 | 12–0 v Walsall Town Swifts Div. 2 17 December 1892 Doncaster Rovers Div. 2 11 April 1903 | Joe Bradford 249, 1920–35 | Joe Bradford 29 Div. 1 1927–28 | Gil Merrick 486, 1946–60 | Harry Hibbs 25, England 1929–36 |

Ground	Capacity & Record	Shirts/shorts	League career	Honours (domestic) League	Cup
BLACKBURN ROVERS (1875)					
Ewood Park Blackburn BB2 4JF 166×72 yd	47,500 61,783 v Bolton W FA Cup 6th Rd 2 March 1929	Blue-white halves/white	1888 (founder members of League) 1936–39 Div. 2 1946–47 Div. 1 1947–57 Div. 2 1957–66 Div. 1 1966–71 Div. 2 1971–75 Div. 3 1975– Div. 2	Div. 1 Champions 1912, 1914 Div. 2 Champions 1939 Runners-up 1958 Div. 3 Champions 1975	FA Cup winners 1884, 1885, 1886, 1890, 1891, 1928 Runners-up 1882, 1960 League Cup semi-finalists 1962
BLACKPOOL (1887)					
Bloomfield Road Blackpool FY1 6JJ 111×73 yd	38,000 39,118 v Manchester U Div. 1 19 April 1952	Tangerine, white trim/ white	1896 elected to Div. 2 1899 failed re-election 1900 re-elected 1900–30 Div. 2 1930–33 Div. 1 1933–37 Div. 2 1937–67 Div. 1 1967–70 Div. 2 1970–71 Div. 1 1971–78 Div. 2 1978– Div. 3	Div. 1 runners-up 1956 Div. 2 Champions 1930 Runners-up 1937, 1970	FA Cup winners 1953 Runners-up 1948, 1951 League Cup semi-finalists 1962
BOLTON WANDERERS (1874)					
Burnden Park Bolton BL3 2QR 113×76 yd	51,000 69,912 v Manchester C FA Cup 5th Rd 18 February 1933	White/navy blue	1888 (founder members of League) 1899–1900 Div. 2 1900–03 Div. 1 1903–05 Div. 2 1905–08 Div. 1 1908–09 Div. 2 1909–10 Div. 1 1910–11 Div. 2 1911–33 Div. 1 1933–35 Div. 2 1935–64 Div. 1 1964–71 Div. 2 1971–73 Div. 3 1973–78 Div. 2 1978– Div. 1	Div. 2 Champions 1909, 1978 Runners-up 1900, 1905, 1911, 1935 Div. 3 Champions 1973	FA Cup winners 1923, 1926, 1929, 1958 Runners-up 1894, 1904, 1953 League Cup semi-finalists 1977
AFC BOURNEMOUTH (1899)					
Dean Court Ground Bournemouth Dorset 115×75 yd	22,000 28,799 v Manchester U FA Cup 6th Rd 2 March 1957	Red, white trim/white	1923 elected to Div. 3(S) 1970–71 Div. 4 1971–75 Div. 3 1975– Div. 4	Div. 3(S) runners-up 1948 Div. 4 runners-up 1971	FA Cup never past 6th Rd League Cup never past 4th Rd
BRADFORD CITY (1903)					
Valley Parade Ground Bradford BD8 7DY 110×70 yd	23,469 39,146 v Burnley FA Cup 4th Rd 11 March 1911	Amber with maroon panel and trim/ maroon	1903 elected to Div. 2 1908–22 Div. 1 1922–27 Div. 2 1927–29 Div. 3(N) 1929–37 Div. 2 1937–61 Div. 3 1961–69 Div. 4 1969–72 Div. 3 1972–77 Div. 4	Div. 2 Champions 1908 Div. 3(N) Champions 1929 ———————— 1977–78 Div. 3 1978– Div. 4	FA Cup winners 1911 League Cup never past 5th Rd

Most League Points	Goals	Record win	Player with highest number of goals		Most League appearances	Most capped player
			Aggregate	Individual		

BLACKBURN ROVERS

Most League Points	Goals	Record win	Aggregate	Individual	Most League appearances	Most capped player
60, Div. 3 1974–75	114, Div. 2 1954–55	11–0 v Rossendale United FA Cup 1884–85	Tommy Briggs 140, 1952–58	Ted Harper 43 Div. 1 1925–26	Ronnie Clayton 580, 1950–69	Bob Crompton 41, England 1902–14

BLACKPOOL

58, Div. 2 1929–30 & 1967–68	98, Div. 2 1929–30	10–0 v Lanerossi Vicenza Anglo-Italian tournament 10 June 1972	Jimmy Hampson 247, 1927–38	Jimmy Hampson 45 Div. 2 1929–30	Jimmy Armfield 568, 1952–71	Jimmy Armfield 43, England 1959–66

BOLTON WANDERERS

61, Div. 3 1972–73	96, Div. 2 1934–35	13–0 v Sheffield United FA Cup 2nd Rd 1 February 1890	Nat Lofthouse 255, 1946–61	Joe Smith 38 Div. 1 1920–21	Eddie Hopkinson 519, 1956–70	Nat Lofthouse 33, England 1951–58

AFC BOURNEMOUTH

62, Div. 3 1971–72	88, Div 3(S) 1956–57	11–0 v Margate FA Cup 1st Rd 20 November 1971	Ron Eyre 202, 1924–33	Ted MacDougall 42 Div. 4 1970–71	Ray Bumstead 412, 1958–70	Tommy Godwin 4, Eire 1956–58

BRADFORD CITY

63, Div. 3(N) 1928–29	128, Div. 3(N) 1928–29	11–1 v Rotherham United Div. 3(N) 25 August 1928	Frank O'Rourke 88, 1906–13	David Layne 34 Div. 4 1961–62	Ian Cooper 443, 1965–77	Harry Hampton 9, N Ireland 1911–14

Ground	Capacity & Record	Shirts/shorts	League career	Honours (domestic) League	Cup
BRENTFORD (1889)					
Griffin Park Braemar Road Brentford Middlesex TW8 0NT 114×75 yd	37,000 39,626 v Preston NE FA Cup 6th Rd 5 March 1938	Red-white striples/black	1920 (founder member of Div. 3) 1921–33 Div. 3(S) 1933–35 Div. 2 1935–47 Div. 1 1947–54 Div. 2 1954–62 Div. 3 1962–63 Div. 4 1963–66 Div. 3 1966–72 Div. 4 1972–73 Div. 3 1973–78 Div. 4 1978– Div. 3	Div 2. Champions 1935 Div. 3(S) Champions 1933 Runners-up 1930, 1958 Div. 4 Champions 1963	FA Cup never past 6th Rd League Cup never past 3rd Rd
BRIGHTON & HOVE ALBION (1900)					
The Goldstone Ground Old Shoreham Road Hove, Sussex BN3 7DE 112×75 yd	36,000 36,747 v Fulham Div. 2 27 December 1958	Blue-white stripes/blue	1920 (founder member of Div. 3) 1921–58 Div. 3(S) 1958–62 Div. 2 1962–63 Div. 3 1963–65 Div. 4 1965–72 Div. 3 1972–73 Div. 2 1973–77 Div. 3 1977– Div. 2	Div. 3(S) Champions 1958 Runners-up 1954, 1956 Div. 3 runners-up 1972, 1977 Div. 4 Champions 1965	FA Cup never past 5th Rd League Cup never past 4th Rd
BRISTOL CITY (1894)					
Ashton Gate Bristol BS3 2EJ 115×75 yd	37,000 43,335 v Preston NE FA Cup 5th Rd 16 February 1935	Red/white	1901 elected to Div. 2 1906–11 Div. 1 1911–22 Div. 2 1922–23 Div. 3(S) 1923–24 Div. 2 1924–27 Div. 3(S) 1927–32 Div. 2 1932–55 Div. 3(S) 1955–60 Div. 2 1960–65 Div. 3 1965–76 Div. 2 1976– Div. 1	Div. 1 runners-up 1907 Div. 2 Champions 1906 Runners-up 1976 Div. 3(S) Champions 1923, 1927, 1955 Runners-up 1938 Div. 3 runners-up 1965	FA Cup runners-up 1909 League Cup semi-finalists 1971
BRISTOL ROVERS (1883)					
Bristol Stadium Eastville Bristol BS5 6NN 110×70 yd	39,333 38,472 v Preston NE FA Cup 4th Rd 30 January 1960	Blue-white quarters/white	1920 (founder members of Div. 3) 1921–53 Div. 3(S) 1953–62 Div. 2 1962–74 Div. 3 1974– Div. 2	Div. 3(S) Champions 1953 Div. 3 runners-up 1974	FA Cup never past 6th Rd League Cup never past 5th Rd
BURNLEY (1882)					
Turf Moor Burnley BB10 4BX 115×73 yd	38,000 54,775 v Huddersfield T FA Cup 3rd Rd 23 February 1924	Claret/white	1888 (founder member of League) 1897–98 Div. 2 1898–1900 Div. 1 1900–13 Div. 2 1913–30 Div. 1 1930–47 Div. 2 1947–71 Div. 1 1971–73 Div. 2 1973–76 Div. 1 1976– Div. 2	Div. 1 Champions 1921, 1960 Runners-up 1920, 1962 Div. 2 Champions 1898, 1973 Runners-up 1913, 1947	FA Cup winners 1914 Runners-up 1947, 1962 League Cup semi-finalists 1961, 1969

Most League Points	Goals	Record win	Player with highest number of goals		Most League appearances	Most capped player
			Aggregate	Individual		
						BRENTFORD
62, Div. 3(S) 1932–33 Div. 4 1962–63	98, Div. 4 1962–63	9–0 v Wrexham Div. 3 15 October 1963	Jim Towers 153, 1954–61	Jack Holliday 36 Div. 3(S) 1932–33	Ken Coote 514, 1949–64	Idris Hopkins 12, Wales 1934–39
						BRIGHTON & HOVE ALBION
65, Div. 3(S) 1955–56 Div. 3 1971–72	112, Div. 3(S) 1955–56	10–1 v Wisbech FA Cup 1st Rd 13 November 1965	Tommy Cook 113, 1922–29	Peter Ward 32 Div. 3 1976–77	Tug Wilson 509, 1922–36	Jack Jenkins 8, Wales 1924–26
						BRISTOL CITY
70, Div. 3(S) 1954–55	104, Div. 3(S) 1926–27	11–0 v Chichester FA Cup 1st Rd 5 November 1960	John Atyeo 315, 1951–66	Don Clark 36 Div. 3(S) 1946–47	John Atyeo 597, 1951–66	Billy Wedlock 26, England 1907–14
						BRISTOL ROVERS
64, Div. 3(S) 1952–53	92, Div. 3(S) 1952–53	7–0 Swansea T Div. 2 2 October 1954 Brighton & HA Div. 3(S) 29 November 1952 Shrewsbury T Div. 3, 21 March 1964	Geoff Bradford 245, 1949–64	Geoff Bradford 33 Div. 3(S) 1952–53	Harry Bamford 487, 1946–58	Matt O'Mahoney 6, Eire 1, N Ireland 1938–39
						BURNLEY
62, Div. 2 1972–73	102, Div. 1 1960–61	9–0 v Darwen Div. 1 9 January 1892 Crystal Palace FA Cup 2nd Rd replay 1908–09 New Brighton FA Cup 4th Rd 26 January 1957	George Beel 178, 1923–32	George Beel 35 Div. 1 1927–28	Jerry Dawson 530, 1906–29	Jimmy McIlroy 52, N Ireland 1951–63

Ground	Capacity & Record	Shirts/shorts	League career	Honours (domestic) League	Cup
BURY (1885)					
Gigg Lane Bury BL9 9HR 112×72 yd	35,000 35,000 v Bolton W FA Cup 3rd Rd 9 January 1960	White/royal blue	1894 elected to Div. 2 1895–1912 Div. 1 1912–24 Div. 2 1924–29 Div. 1 1929–57 Div. 2 1957–61 Div. 3 1961–67 Div. 2 1967–68 Div. 3 1968–69 Div. 2 1969–71 Div. 3 1971–74 Div. 4 1974– Div. 3	Div. 2 Champions 1895 Runners-up 1924 Div. 3 Champions 1961 Runners-up 1968	FA Cup winners 1900, 1903 League Cup semi-finalists 1963
CAMBRIDGE UNITED (1919)					
Abbey Stadium Newmarket Road Cambridge 115×75 yd	12,000 14,000 v Chelsea Friendly 1 May 1970	Black-amber stripes/black	1970 elected to Div. 4 1973–74 Div. 3 1974–77 Div. 4 1977–78 Div. 3 1978– Div. 2	Div. 4 Champions 1977 Div. 3 runners-up 1978	FA Cup never past 3rd Rd League Cup never past 2nd Rd
CARDIFF CITY (1899)					
Ninian Park Cardiff CF1 8SX 112×76 yd	46,000 57,800 v Arsenal Div. 1 22 April 1953	Blue with yellow and white trim/ blue	1920 elected to Div. 2 1921–29 Div. 1 1929–31 Div. 2 1931–47 Div. 3(S) 1947–52 Div. 2 1952–57 Div. 1 1957–60 Div. 2 1960–62 Div. 1 1962–75 Div. 2 1975–76 Div. 3 1976– Div. 2	Div. 1 runners-up 1924 Div. 2 runners-up 1921, 1952, 1960 Div. 3(S) Champions 1947 Div. 3 runners-up 1976	FA Cup winners 1927 Runners-up 1925 League Cup semi-finalists 1966
CARLISLE UNITED (1904)					
Brunton Park Carlisle CA1 1LL 117×78 yd	28,000 27,500 v Birmingham C FA Cup 3rd Rd 5 January 1957 and Middlesbrough FA Cup 5th Rd 7 February 1970	Blue/white	1928 elected to Div. 3(N) 1958–62 Div. 4 1962–63 Div. 3 1963–64 Div. 4 1964–65 Div. 3 1965–74 Div. 2 1974–75 Div. 1 1975–77 Div. 2 1977– Div. 3	Promoted to Div. 1 1974 Div. 3 Champions 1965 Div. 4 runners-up 1964	FA Cup never past 6th Rd League Cup semi-finalists 1970
CHARLTON ATHLETIC (1905)					
The Valley Floyd Road Charlton London SE7 8AW 114×78 yd	66,000 75,031 v Aston Villa FA Cup 5th Rd 12 February 1938	Red/white	1921 elected to Div. 3(S) 1929–33 Div. 2 1933–35 Div. 3(S) 1935–36 Div. 2 1936–57 Div. 1 1957–72 Div. 2 1972–75 Div. 3 1975– Div. 2	Div. 1 runners-up 1937 Div. 2 runners-up 1936 Div. 3(S) Champions 1929, 1935	FA Cup winners 1947 Runners-up 1946 League Cup never past 4th Rd

Most League Points	Goals	Record win	Player with highest number of goals Aggregate	Player with highest number of goals Individual	Most League appearances	Most capped player
						BURY
68, Div. 3 1960–61	108, Div. 3 1960–61	12–1 v Stockton FA Cup 1st Rd replay 1896–97	Norman Bullock 124, 1920–35	Norman Bullock 31 Div. 1 1925–26	Norman Bullock 506, 1920–35	Bill Gorman 11, Eire 1936–38
						CAMBRIDGE UNITED
65, Div. 4 1976–77	87, Div. 4 1976–77	6–0 v Darlington Div. 4 18 September 1971	Brian Greenhalgh 47, 1971–74	Alan Biley 21 Div. 3 1977–78	Terry Eades 248, 1970–71	None
						CARDIFF CITY
66, Div. 3(S) 1946–47	93, Div. 3(S) 1946–47	9–2 v Thames Div. 3(S) 6 February 1932	Len Davies 127, 1921–29	Stan Richards 31 Div 3(S) 1946–47	Tom Farquharson 445, 1922–35	Alf Sherwood 39, Wales 1946–56
						CARLISLE UNITED
62, Div. 3(N) 1950–51	113, Div. 4 1963–64	8–0 v Hartlepools United Div. 3(N) 1 September 1928 Scunthorpe United Div. 3(N) 25 December 1952	Jimmy McConnell 126, 1928–32	Jimmy McConnell 42 Div. 3(N) 1928–29	Alan Ross 465, 1963–78	Eric Welsh 4, N Ireland 1966–67
						CHARLTON ATHLETIC
61, Div. 3(S) 1934–35	107, Div. 2 1957–58	8–1 Middlesbrough Div. 1 12 September 1953	Stuart Leary 153, 1953–62	Ralph Allen 32 Div. 3(S) 1934–35	Sam Bartram 583, 1934–56	John Hewie 19, Scotland 1956–60

Ground	Capacity & Record	Shirts/shorts	League career	Honours (domestic) League	Cup

CHELSEA (1905)

| Stamford Bridge London SW6 114×71 yd | 60,000 82,905 v Arsenal Div. 1 12 October 1935 | Blue/blue | 1905 elected to Div. 2 1907–10 Div. 1 1910–12 Div. 2 1912–24 Div. 1 1924–30 Div. 2 1930–62 Div. 1 1962–63 Div. 2 1963–75 Div. 1 1975–77 Div. 2 1977– Div. 1 | Div. 1 Champions 1955 Div. 2 runners-up 1907, 1912, 1930, 1963, 1977 | FA Cup winners 1970 Runners-up 1915, 1967 League Cup winners 1965 Runners-up 1972 |

CHESTER (1884)

| The Stadium Sealand Road Chester CH1 4LW 114×76 yd | 20,000 20,500 v Chelsea FA Cup 3rd Rd replay 16 January 1952 | Blue-white stripes/blue | 1931 elected to Div. 3(N) 1958–75 Div. 4 1975– Div. 3 | Div. 3(N) runners-up 1936 | FA Cup never past 5th Rd League Cup semi-finalists 1975 |

CHESTERFIELD (1866)

| Recreation Ground Chesterfield 114×72 yd | 28,500 30,968 v Newcastle U Div. 2 7 April 1939 | Blue/white | 1899 elected to Div. 2 1909 failed re-election 1921 elected to Div. 3(N) 1931–33 Div. 2 1933–36 Div. 3(N) 1936–51 Div. 2 1951–58 Div. 3(N) 1958–61 Div. 3 1961–70 Div. 4 1970– Div. 3 | Div. 3(N) Champions 1931, 1936 Runners-up 1934 Div. 4 Champions 1970 | FA Cup never past 5th Rd League Cup never past 4th Rd |

COLCHESTER UNITED (1937)

| Layer Road Ground Colchester 110×71 yd | 16,150 19,072 v Reading FA Cup 1st Rd 27 November 1948 | Blue-white stripes/blue | 1950 elected to Div. 3(S) 1958–61 Div. 3 1961–62 Div. 4 1962–65 Div. 3 1965–66 Div. 4 1966–68 Div. 3 1968–74 Div. 4 1974–76 Div. 3 1976–77 Div. 4 1977– Div. 3 | Div. 4 runners-up 1962 | FA Cup never past 6th Rd League Cup never past 5th Rd |

COVENTRY CITY (1883)

| Highfield Road Coventry 110×75 yd | 48,000 51,457 v Wolverhampton W Div. 2 29 April 1967 | Sky blue/ sky blue | 1919 elected to Div. 2 1925–26 Div. 3(N) 1926–36 Div. 3(S) 1936–52 Div. 2 1952–58 Div. 3(S) 1958–59 Div. 4 1959–64 Div. 3 1964–67 Div. 2 1967– Div. 1 | Div. 2 Champions 1967 Div. 3 Champions 1964 Div. 3(S) Champions 1936 Runners-up 1934 Div. 4 runners-up 1959 | FA Cup never past 6th Rd League Cup never past 5th Rd |

Most League Points	Goals	Record win	Player with highest number of goals		Most League appearances	Most capped player
			Aggregate	Individual		
						CHELSEA
57, Div. 2 1906–07	98, Div. 1 1960–61	13–0 v Jeunesse Hautcharage Cup-Winners' Cup 1st Rd 29 September 1971	Bobby Tambling 164, 1958–70	Jimmy Greaves 41 Div. 1 1960–61	Peter Bonetti 584, 1960–78	Eddie McCreadie 23, Scotland 1965–69
						CHESTER
56, Div. 3(N) 1946–47 Div. 4 1964–65	119, Div. 4 1964–65	12–0 v York City Div. 3(N) 1 February 1936	Gary Talbot 83, 1963–67, 1968–70	Dick Yates 36 Div. 3(N) 1946–47	Ray Gill 408, 1951–62	Bill Lewis 9, Wales 1894–96
						CHESTERFIELD
64, Div. 4 1969–70	102, Div. 3(N) 1930–31	10–0 v Glossop North End Div. 2 17 January 1903	Herbert Munday 112, 1899–1909	Jimmy Cookson 44 Div. 3(N) 1925–26	Dave Blakey 613, 1948–67	Walter McMillen 4, N Ireland 1937–38
						COLCHESTER UNITED
60, Div. 4 1973–74	104, Div. 4 1961–62	9–1 v Bradford City Div. 4 30 September 1961	Martyn King 131, 1959–65	Bobby Hunt 37 Div. 4 1961–62	Peter Wright 421, 1952–64	None
						COVENTRY CITY
60, Div. 4 1958–59 Div. 3 1963–64	108, Div. 3(S) 1931–32	9–0 v Bristol City Div. 3(S) 28 April 1934	Clarrie Bourton 171, 1931–37	Clarrie Bourton 49 Div. 3(S) 1931–32	George Curtis 486, 1956–70	Dave Clements 21, N Ireland 1965–71

Ground	Capacity & Record	Shirts/shorts	League career	Honours (domestic) League	Cup
CREWE ALEXANDRA (1877)					
Football Ground Gresty Road Crewe 113×75 yd	17,000 20,000 v Tottenham H FA Cup 4th Rd 30 January 1960	Red/white	1892 (founder member of Div. 2) 1896 failed re-election 1921 re-elected to Div. 3(N) 1958–63 Div. 4 1963–64 Div. 3 1964–68 Div. 4 1968–69 Div. 3 1969– Div. 4	Highest position 10th Div. 2 1893	FA Cup semi-finalists 1888 League Cup never past 3rd Rd
CRYSTAL PALACE (1905)					
Selhurst Park London SE25 6PU 110×75 yd	51,000 49,498 v Chelsea Div. 1 27 December 1969	White with red diagonal band/white	1920 (founder member of Div. 3) 1921–25 Div. 2 1925–58 Div. 3(S) 1958–61 Div. 4 1961–64 Div. 3 1964–69 Div. 2 1969–73 Div. 1 1973–74 Div. 2 1974–77 Div. 3 1977– Div. 2	Div. 2 runners-up 1969 Div. 3 runners-up 1964 Div. 3(S) Champions 1921 Runners-up 1929, 1931, 1939 Div. 4 runners-up 1961	FA Cup semi-finalists 1976 League Cup never past 5th Rd
DARLINGTON (1883)					
Feethams Ground Darlington 110×74 yd	20,000 21,023 v Bolton W League Cup 3rd Rd 14 November 1960	White with red trim/black	1921 (founder member of Div. 3(N) 1925–27 Div. 2 1927–58 Div. 3(N) 1958–66 Div. 4 1966–67 Div. 3 1967– Div. 4	Div. 3(N) Champions 1925 Runners-up 1922 Div. 4 runners-up 1966	FA Cup never past 5th Rd League Cup never past 5th Rd
DERBY COUNTY (1884)					
Baseball Ground Shaftesbury Crescent Derby DE3 8NB 110×71 yd	38,500 41,826 v Tottenham H Div. 1 20 September 1969	White/blue	1888 (founder member of League) 1907–12 Div. 2 1912–14 Div. 1 1914–15 Div. 2 1915–21 Div. 1 1921–26 Div. 2 1926–53 Div. 1 1953–55 Div. 2 1955–57 Div. 3(N) 1957–69 Div. 2 1969– Div. 1	Div. 1 Champions 1972, 1975 Runners-up 1896, 1930, 1936 Div. 2 Champions 1912, 1915, 1969 Runners-up 1926 Div. 3(N) Champions 1957 Runners-up 1956	FA Cup winners 1946 Runners-up 1898, 1899, 1903 League Cup semi-finalists 1968
DONCASTER ROVERS (1879)					
Belle Vue Ground Doncaster 118×79 yd	30,000 37,149 v Hull City Div. 3(N) 2 October 1948	Red/white	1901 elected to Div. 2 1903 failed re-election 1904 re-elected 1905 failed re-election 1923 re-elected to Div. 3(N) 1935–37 Div. 2 1937–47 Div. 3(N) 1947–48 Div. 2 1948–50 Div. 3(N)	Div. 3(N) Champions 1935, 1947, 1950 Runners-up 1938, 1939 Div. 4 Champions 1966, 1969	FA Cup never past 5th Rd League Cup never past 5th Rd
				1950–58 Div. 2 1958–59 Div. 3 1959–66 Div. 4 1966–67 Div. 3	1967–69 Div. 4 1969–71 Div. 3 1971– Div. 4	

Most League Points	Goals	Record win	Player with highest number of goals		Most League appearances	Most capped player
			Aggregate	Individual		
						CREWE ALEXANDRA
59, Div. 4 1962–63	95, Div. 3(N) 1931–32	8–0 v Rotherham United Div. 3(N) 1 October 1932	Bert Swindells 126, 1928–37	Terry Harkin 34 Div. 4 1964–65	Tommy Lowry 436, 1966–77	Bill Lewis 12, Wales 1890–92
						CRYSTAL PALACE
64, Div. 4 1960–61	110, Div. 4 1960–61	9–0 v Barrow Div. 4 10 October 1959	Peter Simpson 154, 1930–36	Peter Simpson 46 Div. 3(S) 1930–31	Terry Long 432, 1956–69	Ian Evans 13, Wales 1975–77
						DARLINGTON
59, Div. 4 1965–66	108, Div. 3(N) 1929–30	9–2 v Lincoln City Div. 3(N) 7 January 1928	David Brown 74, 1923–26	David Brown 39 Div. 3(N) 1924–25	Ron Greener 442, 1955–68	None
						DERBY COUNTY
63, Div. 2 1968–69 Div. 3(N) 1955–56, 1956–57	111, Div. 3(N) 1956–57	12–0 v Finn Harps UEFA Cup 3rd Rd First leg 15 September 1976	Steve Bloomer 291, 1892–1906, 1910–14	Jack Bowers 37 Div. 1 1930–31 Ray Straw 37 Div. 3(N) 1956–57	Jack Parry 478, 1949–66	Roy McFarland 28, England 1971–76
						DONCASTER ROVERS
72, Div. 3(N) 1946–47	123, Div. 3(N) 1946–47	10–0 v Darlington Div. 4 25 January 1964	Tom Kettley 180, 1923–29	Clarrie Jordan 42 Div. 3(N) 1946–47	Fred Emery 406, 1925–36	Len Graham 14, N Ireland 1951–58

Ground	Capacity & Record	Shirts/shorts	League career	Honours (domestic) League	Cup

EVERTON (1878)

| Goodison Park Liverpool L4 4EL 112×78 yd | 58,000 78,299 v Liverpool Div. 1 18 September 1948 | Blue/white | 1888 (founder member of League) 1930–31 Div. 2 1931–51 Div. 1 1951–54 Div. 2 1954– Div. 1 | Div. 1 Champions 1891, 1915, 1928, 1932, 1939, 1963, 1970 Runners-up 1890, 1895, 1902, 1905, 1909, 1912 Div. 2 Champions 1931 Runners-up 1954 | FA Cup winners 1906, 1933, 1966 Runners-up 1893 1897, 1907, 1968 League Cup runners-up 1977 |

EXETER CITY (1904)

| St James Park Exeter 114×73 yd | 18,500 20,984 v Sunderland FA Cup 6th Rd replay 4 March 1931 | White/white | 1920 elected to Div. 3 1921–58 Div. 3(S) 1958–64 Div. 4 1964–66 Div. 3 1966–77 Div. 4 1977– Div. 3 | Div. 3(S) runners-up 1933 Div. 4 runners-up 1977 | FA Cup never past 6th Rd League Cup never past 3rd Rd |

FULHAM (1880)

| Craven Cottage Stevenage Road Fulham London SW6 110×75 yd | 42,000 49,335 v Millwall Div. 2 8 October 1938 | White/black | 1907 elected to Div. 2 1928–32 Div. 3(S) 1932–49 Div. 2 1949–52 Div. 1 1952–59 Div. 2 1959–68 Div. 1 1968–69 Div. 2 1969–71 Div. 3 1971– Div. 2 | Div. 2 Champions 1949 Runners-up 1959 Div. 3(S) Champions 1932 Div. 3 runners-up 1971 | FA Cup runners-up 1975 League Cup never past 5th Rd |

GILLINGHAM (1893)

| Priestfield Stadium Gillingham 114×75 yd | 22,000 23,002 v QPR FA Cup 3rd Rd 10 January 1948 | Blue/white | 1920 (founder member of Div. 3) 1921 Div. 3(S) 1938 failed re-election 1950 re-elected to Div. 3(S) 1958–64 Div. 4 1964–71 Div. 3 1971–74 Div. 4 1974– Div. 3 | Div. 4 Champions 1964 Runners-up 1974 | FA Cup never past 5th Rd League Cup never past 4th Rd |

GRIMSBY TOWN (1878)

| Blundell Park Cleethorpes South Humberside DN35 7PY 111×74 yd | 28,000 31,657 v Wolverhampton W FA Cup 5th Rd 20 February 1937 | Black-white stripes/black | 1892 (founder member of Div. 2) 1901–03 Div. 1 1903–10 Div. 2 1910 failed re-election 1911 re-elected to Div. 2 1920–21 Div. 3 1921–26 Div. 3(N) 1926–29 Div. 2 1929–32 Div. 1 1932–34 Div. 2 1934–48 Div. 1 1948–51 Div. 2 1951–56 Div. 3(N) | Div. 2 Champions 1901, 1934 Runners-up 1929 Div. 3(N) Champions 1926, 1956 Runners-up 1952 Div. 3 runners-up 1962 Div. 4 Champions 1972 _____ 1956–59 Div. 2 1959–62 Div. 3 1962–64 Div. 2 1964–68 Div. 3 | FA Cup semi-finalists 1936, 1939 League Cup never past 5th Rd _____ 1968–72 Div. 4 1972–77 Div. 3 1977– Div. 4 |

Most League Points	Goals	Record win	Player with highest number of goals		Most League appearances	Most capped player
			Aggregate	Individual		
						EVERTON
66, Div. 1 1969–70	121, Div. 2 1930–31	11–2 v Derby County FA Cup 1st Rd 1889–90	Dixie Dean 349, 1925–37	Dixie Dean 60 Div. 1 1927–28	Ted Sagar 465, 1929–53	Alan Ball 39, England 1966–71
						EXETER CITY
62, Div. 4 1976–77	88, Div. 3(S) 1932–33	8–1 v Coventry City Div. 3(S) 4 December 1926 Aldershot Div. 3(S) 4 May 1935	Alan Banks 105, 1963–66, 1967–73	Fred Whitlow 34 Div. 3(S) 1932–33	Arnold Mitchell 495, 1952–66	Dermot Curtis 1, Eire 1963
						FULHAM
60, Div. 2 1958–59 Div. 3 1970–71	111, Div. 3(S) 1931–32	10–1 v Ipswich Town Div. 1 26 December 1963	Johnny Haynes 159, 1952–70	Frank Newton 41 Div. 3(S) 1931–32	Johnny Haynes 598, 1952–70	Johnny Haynes 56, England 1954–62
						GILLINGHAM
62, Div. 4 1973–74	90, Div. 4 1973–74	10–1 v Gorleston FA Cup 1st Rd 16 November 1957	Brian Yeo 135, 1963–75	Ernie Morgan 31 Div. 3(S) 1954–55 Brian Yeo 31 Div. 4 1973–74	John Simpson 571, 1957–72	Fred Fox 1, England 1925 Damien Richardson 1, Eire 1973
						GRIMSBY TOWN
68, Div. 3(N) 1955–56	103, Div. 2 1933–34	9–2 v Darwen Div. 2 15 April 1899	Pat Glover 182, 1930–39	Pat Glover 42 Div. 2 1933–34	Keith Jobling 448, 1953–69	Pat Glover 7, Wales 1931–39

Ground	Capacity & Record	Shirts/shorts	League career	Honours (domestic) League	Cup
HALIFAX TOWN (1911)					
Shay Ground Halifax HX1 2YS 110×70 yd	25,000 36,885 v Tottenham H FA Cup 5th Rd 14 February 1953	Royal blue with white trim/ white	1921 (founder member of Div. 3(N)) 1958–63 Div. 3 1963–69 Div. 4 1969–76 Div. 3 1976– Div. 4	Div. 3(N) runners-up 1935 Div. 4 runners-up 1969	FA Cup never past 5th Rd League Cup never past 4th Rd
HARTLEPOOL UNITED (1908)					
The Victoria Ground Hartlepool 113×77 yd	16,500 17,426 v Manchester U FA Cup 3rd Rd 5 January 1957	Blue/white	1921 (founder member of Div. 3(N)) 1958–68 Div. 4 1968–69 Div. 3 1969– Div. 4	Div. 3(N) runners-up 1957	FA Cup never past 4th Rd League Cup never past 4th Rd
HEREFORD UNITED (1924)					
Edgar Street Hereford 111×80 yd	17,500 18,114 v Sheffield W FA Cup 3rd Rd 4 January 1958	White with black and red trim/ black	1972 elected to Div. 4 1973–76 Div. 3 1976–77 Div. 2 1977–78 Div. 3 1978– Div. 4	Div. 3 Champions 1976 Div. 4 runners-up 1973	FA Cup never past 4th Rd League Cup never past 3rd Rd
HUDDERSFIELD TOWN (1908)					
Leeds Road Huddersfield HD1 6PE 115×75 yd	48,000 67,037 v Arsenal FA Cup 6th Rd 27 February 1932	Blue-white stripes/white	1910 elected to Div. 2 1920–52 Div. 1 1952–53 Div. 2 1953–56 Div. 1 1956–70 Div. 2 1970–72 Div. 1 1972–73 Div. 2 1973–75 Div. 3 1975– Div. 4	Div. 1 Champions 1924, 1925, 1926 Runners-up 1927, 1928, 1934 Div. 2 Champions 1970 Runners-up 1920, 1953	FA Cup winners 1922 Runners-up 1920, 1928, 1930, 1938 League Cup semi-finalists 1968
HULL CITY (1904)					
Boothferry Park Hull HU4 6EU 112×75 yd	42,000 55,019 v Manchester U FA Cup 6th Rd 26 February 1949	Black-amber stripes/white	1905 elected to Div. 2 1930–33 Div. 3(N) 1933–36 Div. 2 1936–49 Div. 3(N) 1949–56 Div. 2 1956–58 Div. 3(N) 1958–59 Div. 3 1959–60 Div. 2 1960–66 Div. 3 1966–78 Div. 2 1978– Div. 3	Div. 3(N) Champions 1933, 1949 Div. 3 Champions 1966 Runners-up 1959	FA Cup semi-finalists 1930 League Cup never past 4th Rd
IPSWICH TOWN (1887)					
Portman Road Ipswich Suffolk IP1 2DA 112×72 yd	38,000 38,010 v Leeds United FA Cup 6th Rd 8 March 1975	Blue/white	1938 elected to Div. 3(S) 1954–55 Div. 2 1955–57 Div. 3(S) 1957–61 Div. 2 1961–64 Div. 1 1964–68 Div. 2 1968– Div. 1	Div. 1 Champions 1962 Div. 2 Champions 1961, 1968 Div. 3(S) Champions 1954, 1957	FA Cup winners 1978 League Cup never past 5th Rd

Most League Points	Goals	Record win	Player with highest number of goals Aggregate	Individual	Most League appearances	Most capped player
						HALIFAX TOWN
57, Div. 4 1968–69	83, Div. 3(N) 1957–58	7–0 v Bishop Auckland FA Cup 2nd Rd replay 10 January 1967	Ernest Dixon 129, 1922–30	Albert Valentine 34 Div. 3(N) 1934–35	John Pickering 367, 1965–74	None
						HARTLEPOOL UNITED
60, Div. 4 1967–68	90, Div. 3(N) 1956–57	10–1 v Barrow Div. 4 4 April 1959	Ken Johnson 98, 1949–64	William Robinson 28 Div. 3(N) 1927–28	Wattie Moore 448, 1948–64	Ambrose Fogarty 1, Eire 1964
						HEREFORD UNITED
63, Div. 3 1975–76	86, Div. 3 1975–76	11–0 v Thynnes FA Cup 1947–48	Dixie McNeil 85, 1974–77	Dixie McNeil 35 Div. 3 1975–76	Billy Tucker 137, 1972–77	Brian Evans 1, Wales 1973
						HUDDERSFIELD TOWN
64, Div. 2 1919–20	97, Div. 2 1919–20	10–1 v Blackpool Div. 1 13 December 1930	George Brown 142, 1921–29	Sam Taylor 35 Div. 2 1919–20 George Brown 35 Div. 1 1925–26	Billy Smith 520, 1914–34	Jimmy Nicholson 31, N Ireland 1965–71
						HULL CITY
69, Div. 3 1965–66	109, Div. 3 1965–66	11–1 v Carlisle United Div. 3(N) 14 January 1939	Chris Chilton 195, 1960–71	Bill McNaughton 39 Div. 3(N) 1932–33	Andy Davidson 511, 1947–67	Terry Neill 15, N Ireland 1970–73
						IPSWICH TOWN
64, Div. 3(S) 1953–54 1955–56	106, Div. 3(S) 1955–56	10–0 v Floriana (Malta) European Cup 1st Rd 25 September 1962	Ray Crawford 203, 1958–63, 1966–69	Ted Phillips 41 Div. 3(S) 1956–57	Tom Parker 428, 1946–57	Allan Hunter 40, N Ireland 1972–78

Ground	Capacity & Record	Shirts/shorts	League career	Honours (domestic) League	Cup
LEEDS UNITED (1919)					
Elland Road Leeds LS11 0ES 117×76 yd	50,000 57,892 v Sunderland FA Cup 5th Rd replay 15 March 1967	White/white	1920 elected to Div. 2 1924–27 Div. 1 1927–28 Div. 2 1928–31 Div. 1 1931–32 Div. 2 1932–47 Div. 1 1947–56 Div. 2 1956–60 Div. 1 1960–64 Div. 2 1964– Div. 1	Div. 1 Champions 1969, 1974 Runners-up 1965, 1966, 1970, 1971, 1972 Div. 2 Champions 1924, 1964 Runners-up 1928, 1932, 1956	FA Cup winners 1972 Runners-up 1965, 1970, 1973 League Cup winners 1968
LEICESTER CITY (1884)					
City Stadium Filbert Street Leicester 112×75 yd	34,000 47,298 v Tottenham H FA Cup 5th Rd 18 February 1928	Blue/white	1894 elected to Div. 2 1908–09 Div. 1 1909–25 Div. 2 1925–35 Div. 1 1935–37 Div. 2 1937–39 Div. 1 1946–54 Div. 2 1954–55 Div. 1 1955–57 Div. 2 1957–69 Div. 1 1969–71 Div. 2 1971–78 Div. 1 1978– Div. 2	Div. 1 runners-up 1929 Div. 2 Champions 1925, 1937, 1954, 1957, 1971 Runners-up 1908	FA Cup runners-up 1949, 1961, 1963, 1969 League Cup winners 1964 Runners-up 1965
LINCOLN CITY (1883)					
Sincil Bank Lincoln 110×75 yd	25,300 23,196 v Derby Co League Cup 4th Rd 15 November 1967	Red-white stripes/black	1892 (founder member of Div. 2) 1908 failed re-election 1909 re-elected 1911 failed re-election 1912 re-elected 1920 failed re-election 1921 re-elected 1921–32 Div. 3(N) 1932–34 Div. 2 1934–48 Div. 3(N) 1948–49 Div. 2 1949–52 Div. 3(N) 1952–61 Div. 2 1961–62 Div. 3 1962–76 Div. 4 1976– Div. 3	Div. 3(N) Champions 1932, 1948, 1952 Runners-up 1928, 1931, 1937 Div. 4 Champions 1976	FA Cup never past 5th Rd (equivalent) League Cup never past 4th Rd
LIVERPOOL (1892)					
Anfield Road Liverpool 4 110×75 yd	56,318 61,905 v Wolverhampton W FA Cup 4th Rd 2 February 1952	Red/red	1893 elected to Div. 2 1894–95 Div. 1 1895–96 Div. 2 1896–1904 Div. 1 1904–05 Div. 2 1905–54 Div. 1 1954–62 Div. 2 1962– Div. 1	Div. 1 Champions 1901, 1906, 1922, 1923, 1947, 1964, 1966, 1973, 1976, 1977 Runners-up 1899, 1910, 1969, 1974, 1975, 1978 Div. 2 Champions 1894, 1896, 1905, 1962	FA Cup winners 1965, 1974 Runners-up 1914, 1950, 1971, 1977 League Cup runners-up 1978

Most League Points	Goals	Record win	Player with highest number of goals		Most League appearances	Most capped player
			Aggregate	Individual		
						LEEDS UNITED
67, Div. 1 1968–69	98, Div. 2 1927–28	10–0 v Lyn Oslo (Norway) European Cup 1st Rd First leg 17 September 1969	John Charles 154, 1948–57, 1962	John Charles 42 Div. 2 1953–54	Jack Charlton 629, 1953–73	Billy Bremner 54, Scotland 1965–75
						LEICESTER CITY
61, Div. 2 1956–57	109, Div. 2 1956–57	10–0 v Portsmouth Div. 1 20 October 1928	Arthur Chandler 262, 1923–35	Arthur Rowley 44 Div. 2 1956–57	Adam Black 530, 1919–35	Gordon Banks 37, England 1963–66
						LINCOLN CITY
74, Div. 4 1975–76	121, Div. 3(N) 1951–52	11–1 v Crewe Alexandra Div. 3(N) 29 September 1951	Andy Graver 144, 1950–55, 1958–61	Allan Hall 42 Div. 3(N) 1931–32	Tony Emery 402, 1946–59	David Pugh 3, Wales, 1900–01 Con Moulson 3, Eire 1936–37 George Moulson 3, Eire 1948
						LIVERPOOL
62, Div. 2 1961–62	106, Div. 2 1895–96	11–0 v Strömsgodset (Norway) Cup-Winners' Cup 17 September 1974	Roger Hunt 245, 1959–69	Roger Hunt 41 Div. 2 1961–62	Ian Callaghan 640, 1960–78	Emlyn Hughes 54, England 1970–78

Ground	Capacity & Record	Shirts/shorts	League career	Honours (domestic) League	Cup
LUTON TOWN (1885)					
70–72 Kenilworth Road Luton 112×72 yd	25,000 30,069 v Blackpool FA Cup 6th Rd replay 4 March 1959	Orange with navy blue and white trim/navy blue	1897 elected to Div. 2 1900 failed re-election 1920 elected to Div. 3 1921–37 Div. 3(S) 1937–55 Div. 2 1955–60 Div. 1 1960–63 Div. 2 1963–65 Div. 3 1965–68 Div. 4 1968–70 Div. 3 1970–74 Div. 2 1974–75 Div. 1 1975– Div. 2	Div. 2 runners-up 1955, 1974 Div. 3 runners-up 1970 Div. 4 Champions 1968 Div. 3(S) Champions 1937 Runners-up 1936	FA Cup runners-up 1959 League Cup never past 4th Rd
MANCHESTER CITY (1887)					
Maine Road Moss Side Manchester M14 7WN 119×79 yd	52,500 84,569 v Stoke City FA Cup 6th Rd 3 March 1934	Sky blue/ sky blue	1892 elected to Div. 2 as Ardwick FC 1894 elected to Div. 2 as Manchester C 1899–1902 Div. 1 1902–03 Div. 2 1903–09 Div. 1 1909–10 Div. 2 1910–26 Div. 1 1926–28 Div. 2 1928–38 Div. 1 1938–47 Div. 2 1947–50 Div. 1 1950–51 Div. 2 1951–63 Div. 1 1963–66 Div. 2 1966– Div. 1	Div. 1 Champions 1937, 1968 Runners-up 1904, 1921, 1977 Div. 2 Champions 1899, 1903, 1910, 1928, 1947, 1966 Runners-up 1896, 1951	FA Cup winners 1904, 1934, 1956, 1969 Runners-up 1926, 1933, 1955 League Cup winners 1970, 1976 Runners-up 1974
MANCHESTER UNITED (1878)					
Old Trafford Manchester M16 0RA 116×76 yd	60,500 70,504 v Aston Villa Div. 1 27 December 1920	Red/white	1892 elected to Div. 1 as Newton Heath. Changed name 1902 1894–1906 Div. 2 1906–22 Div. 1 1922–25 Div. 2 1925–31 Div. 1 1931–36 Div. 2 1936–37 Div. 1 1937–38 Div. 2 1938–74 Div. 1 1974–75 Div. 2 1975– Div. 1	Div. 1 Champions 1908, 1911, 1952, 1956, 1957, 1965, 1967 Runners-up 1947, 1948, 1949, 1951, 1959, 1964, 1968 Div. 2 Champions 1936, 1975 Runners-up 1897, 1906, 1925, 1938	FA Cup winners 1909, 1948, 1963, 1977 Runners-up 1957, 1958, 1976 League Cup semi-finalists 1970, 1971, 1975
MANSFIELD TOWN (1905)					
Field Mill Ground Quarry Lane Mansfield 115×72 yd	23,500 24,467 v Nottingham F FA Cup 3rd Rd 10 January 1953	Amber/blue	1931 elected to Div. 3(S) 1932–37 Div. 3(N) 1937–47 Div. 3(S) 1947–58 Div. 3(N) 1958–60 Div. 3 1960–63 Div. 4 1963–72 Div. 3 1972–75 Div. 4	Div. 3 Champions 1977 Div. 4 Champions 1975 Div. 3(N) Runners-up 1951 1975–77 Div. 3 1977–78 Div. 2 1978– Div. 3	FA Cup never past 6th Rd League Cup never past 5th Rd

Most League Points	Goals	Record win	Player with highest number of goals		Most League appearances	Most capped player
			Aggregate	Individual		
						LUTON TOWN
66, Div. 4 1967–68	103, Div. 3(S) 1936–37	12–0 v Bristol Rovers Div. 3(S) 13 April 1936	Gordon Turner 243, 1949–64	Joe Payne 55 Div. 3(S) 1936–37	Bob Morton 494, 1948–64	George Cummins 19, Eire 1953–61
						MANCHESTER CITY
62, Div. 2 1946–47	108, Div. 2 1926–27	11–3 v Lincoln City Div. 2 23 March 1895	Tommy Johnson 158, 1919–30	Tommy Johnson 38 Div. 1 1928–29	Alan Oakes 565, 1959–76	Colin Bell 48, England 1968–75
						MANCHESTER UNITED
64, Div. 1 1956–57	103, Div. 1 1956–57, 1958–59	10–0 v Anderlecht (Belgium) European Cup Prelim Rd 26 September 1956	Bobby Charlton 198, 1956–73	Dennis Viollet 32 Div. 1 1959–60	Bobby Charlton 606, 1956–73	Bobby Charlton 106, England 1958–70
						MANSFIELD TOWN
68, Div. 4 1974–75	108, Div. 4 1962–63	9–2 v Rotherham United Div. 3(N) 27 December 1932 Hounslow Town replay 5 November 1962	Harry Johnson 104, 1931–36	Ted Harston 55 Div. 3(N) 1936–37	Don Bradley 417, 1949–62	None

Ground	Capacity & Record	Shirts/shorts	League career	Honours (domestic) League	Cup

MIDDLESBROUGH (1876)

Ground	Capacity & Record	Shirts/shorts	League career	Honours (domestic) League	Cup
Ayresome Park Middlesbrough Teesside 115×75 yd	42,000 53,596 v Newcastle U Div. 1 27 December 1949	Red with white trim/red	1899 elected to Div. 2 1902–24 Div. 1 1924–27 Div. 2 1927–28 Div. 1 1928–29 Div. 2 1929–54 Div. 1 1954–66 Div. 2 1966–67 Div. 3 1967–74 Div. 2 1974– Div. 1	Div. 2 Champions 1927, 1929, 1974 Runners-up 1902 Div. 3 runners-up 1967	FA Cup never past 6th Rd League Cup semi-finalists 1976

MILLWALL (1885)

Ground	Capacity & Record	Shirts/shorts	League career	Honours (domestic) League	Cup
The Den Cold Blow Lane London SE14 5RH 112×74 yd	40,000 48,672 v Derby Co FA Cup 5th Rd 20 February 1937	Blue/white	1920 (founder members of Div. 3) 1921 Div. 3(S) 1928–34 Div. 2 1934–38 Div. 3(S) 1938–48 Div. 2 1948–58 Div. 3(S) 1958–62 Div. 4 1962–64 Div. 3 1964–65 Div. 4 1965–66 Div. 3 1966–75 Div. 2 1975–76 Div. 3 1976– Div. 2	Div. 3(S) Champions 1928, 1938 Div. 3 runners-up 1966 Div. 4 Champions 1962 Runners-up 1965	FA Cup semi-finalists 1900, 1903, 1937 League Cup never past 5th Rd

NEWCASTLE UNITED (1882)

Ground	Capacity & Record	Shirts/shorts	League career	Honours (domestic) League	Cup
St James' Park Newcastle-upon-Tyne NE1 4ST 115×75 yd	54,000 68,386 v Chelsea Div. 1 3 September 1930	Black-white stripes/black	1893 elected to Div. 2 1898–1934 Div. 1 1934–48 Div. 2 1948–61 Div. 1 1961–65 Div. 2 1965–78 Div. 1 1978– Div. 2	Div. 1 Champions 1905, 1907, 1909, 1927 Div. 2 Champions 1965 Runners-up 1898, 1948	FA Cup winners 1910, 1924, 1932, 1951, 1952, 1955 Runners-up 1905, 1906, 1908, 1911, 1974 League Cup runners-up 1976

NEWPORT COUNTY (1912)

Ground	Capacity & Record	Shirts/shorts	League career	Honours (domestic) League	Cup
Somerton Park Newport Mon 112×78 yd	22,060 24,268 v Cardiff City Div. 3(S) 16 October 1937	Sky blue-white stripes/sky blue	1920 (founder member of Div. 3) 1921 Div. 3(S) 1931 dropped out of League 1932 re-elected 1932–39 Div. 3(S) 1946–47 Div. 2 1947–58 Div. 3(S) 1958–62 Div. 3 1962– Div. 4	Div. 3(S) Champions 1939	FA Cup never past 5th Rd League Cup never past 3rd Rd

NORTHAMPTON TOWN (1897)

Ground	Capacity & Record	Shirts/shorts	League career	Honours (domestic) League	Cup
County Ground Abington Avenue Northampton NN1 4PS 120×75 yd	20,000 24,523 v Fulham Div. 1 23 April 1966	White with claret trim/ white	1920 (founder member of Div. 3) 1921 Div. 3(S) 1958–61 Div. 4 1961–63 Div. 3 1963–65 Div. 2 1965–66 Div. 1 1966–67 Div. 2 1967–68 Div. 3 1968–76 Div. 4 1976–77 Div. 3 1977– Div. 4	Div. 2 runners-up 1965 Div. 3 Champions 1963 Div. 3(S) runners-up 1928, 1950 Div. 4 runners-up 1976	FA Cup never past 5th Rd League Cup never past 5th Rd

Most League Points	Goals	Record win	Player with highest number of goals		Most League appearances	Most capped player
			Aggregate	Individual		

Most League Points	Goals	Record win	Aggregate	Individual	Most League appearances	Most capped player
65, Div. 2 1973–74	122, Div. 2 1926–27	9–0 v Brighton & HA Div. 2 23 August 1958	George Camsell 326, 1925–39	George Camsell 59 Div. 2 1926–27	Tim Williamson 563, 1902–23	Wilf Mannion 26, England 1946–51

MILLWALL

| 65, Div. 3(S) 1927–28 Div. 3 1965–66 | 127, Div. 3(S) 1927–28 | 9–1 v Torquay United Div. 3(S) 29 August 1927 Coventry City Div. 3(S) 19 November 1927 | Derek Possee 79, 1967–73 | Richard Parker 37 Div. 3(S) 1926–27 | Barry Kitchener 449, 1967–78 | Eamonn Dunphy 22, Eire 1966–71 |

NEWCASTLE UNITED

| 57, Div. 2 1964–65 | 98, Div. 1 1951–52 | 13–0 v Newport County Div. 2 5 October 1946 | Jackie Milburn 178, 1946–57 | Hughie Gallacher 36 Div. 1 1926–27 | Jim Lawrence 432, 1904–22 | Alf McMichael 40, N Ireland 1949–60 |

NEWPORT COUNTY

| 56, Div. 4 1972–73 | 85, Div. 4 1964–65 | 10–0 v Merthyr Town Div. 3(S) 10 April 1930 | Reg Parker 99, 1948–54 | Tudor Martin 34 Div. 3(S) 1929–30 | Ray Wilcox 530, 1946–60 | (All for Wales) Fred Cook 2 1925 Jack Nicholls 2 1924 Alf Sherwood 2 1956 Bill Thomas 2 1930 Harold Williams 2 1949 |

NORTHAMPTON TOWN

| 62, Div. 3(S) 1952–53 Div. 3 1962–63 | 109, Div. 3 1962–63 Div. 3(S) 1952–53 | 10–0 v Walsall Div. 3(S) 5 November 1927 | Jack English 135, 1947–60 | Cliff Holton 36 Div. 3 1961–62 | Tommy Fowler 521, 1946–61 | E Lloyd Davies 12, Wales 1908–14 |

Ground	Capacity & Record	Shirts/shorts	League career	Honours (domestic) League	Cup
NORWICH CITY (1905)					
Carrow Road Norwich NOR 22 114×74 yd	32,000 43,984 v Leicester City FA Cup 6th Rd 30 March 1963	Yellow/green	1920 (founder member of Div. 3) 1921 Div. 3(S) 1934–39 Div. 2 1946–60 Div. 3 1960–72 Div. 2 1972–74 Div. 1 1974–75 Div. 2 1975– Div. 1	Div. 2 Champions 1972 Div. 3(S) Champions 1934 Div. 3 runners-up 1960	FA Cup semi-finalists 1959 League Cup winners 1962 Runners-up 1973, 1975
NOTTINGHAM FOREST (1865)					
City Ground Nottingham NG2 5FJ 115×78 yd	49,000 49,945 v Manchester U Div. 1 28 October 1967	Red/white	1892 elected to Div. 1 1906 Div. 2 1907 Div. 1 1911–22 Div. 2 1922–25 Div. 1 1925–49 Div. 2 1949–51 Div. 3(S) 1951–57 Div. 2 1957–72 Div. 1	Div. 1 Champions 1978 Runners-up 1967 Div. 2 Champions 1907, 1922 Runners-up 1957 Div. 3(S) Champions 1951 1972–77 Div. 2 1977– Div. 1	FA Cup winners 1898, 1959 League Cup winners 1978
NOTTS COUNTY (1862)					
County Ground Meadow Lane Nottingham NG2 3HJ 117×76 yd	40,000 47,310 v York City FA Cup 6th Rd 12 March 1955	Black-white stripes/black	1888 (founder member of League) 1893–97 Div. 2 1897–1913 Div. 1 1913–14 Div. 2 1914–20 Div. 1 1920–23 Div. 2 1923–26 Div. 1 1926–30 Div. 2 1930–31 Div. 3(S) 1931–35 Div. 2 1935–50 Div. 3(S) 1950–58 Div. 2 1958–59 Div. 3	Div. 2 Champions 1897, 1914, 1923 Runners-up 1895 Div. 3(S) Champions 1931, 1950 Runners-up 1937 Div. 4 Champions 1971 Runners-up 1960 1959–60 Div. 4 1960–64 Div. 3 1964–71 Div. 4 1971–73 Div. 3 1973– Div. 2	FA Cup winners 1894 Runners-up 1891 League Cup never past 5th Rd
OLDHAM ATHLETIC (1894)					
Boundary Park Oldham 110×74 yd	30,000 47,671 v Sheffield W FA Cup 4th Rd 25 January 1930	Blue/white	1907 elected to Div. 2 1910–23 Div. 1 1923–35 Div. 2 1935–53 Div. 3(N) 1953–54 Div. 2 1954–58 Div. 3(N) 1958–63 Div. 4 1963–69 Div. 3 1969–71 Div. 4 1971–74 Div. 3 1974– Div. 2	Div. 1 runners-up 1915 Div. 2 runners-up 1910 Div. 3(N) Champions 1953 Div. 3 Champions 1974 Div. 4 runners-up 1963	FA Cup semi-finalists 1913 League Cup never past 2nd Rd
ORIENT (1881)					
Leyton Stadium Brisbane Road Leyton London E10 5NE 110×80 yd	34,000 34,345 v West Ham U FA Cup 4th Rd 25 January 1964	White with two red stripes/ white	1905 elected to Div. 2 1929–56 Div. 3(S) 1956–62 Div. 2 1962–63 Div. 1 1963–66 Div. 2 1966–70 Div. 3 1970– Div. 2	Div. 2 runners-up 1962 Div. 3 Champions 1970 Div. 3(S) Champions 1956 Runners-up 1955	FA Cup semi-finalists 1978 League Cup never past 5th Rd

Most League Points	Goals	Record win	Player with highest number of goals		Most League appearances	Most capped player
			Aggregate	Individual		
						NORWICH CITY
64, Div. 3(S) 1950–51	99, Div. 3(S) 1952–53	10–2 v Coventry City Div. 3(S) 15 March 1930	Johnny Gavin 122, 1945–54, 1955–58	Ralph Hunt 31 Div. 3(S) 1955–56	Ron Ashman 590, 1947–64	Ted MacDougall 7, Scotland 1975
						NOTTINGHAM FOREST
70, Div. 3(S) 1950–51	110, Div. 3(S) 1950–51	14–0 v Clapton FA Cup 1st Rd 1890–91	Grenville Morris 199, 1898–1913	Wally Ardron 36 Div. 3(S) 1950–51	Bob McKinlay 614, 1951–70	Liam O'Kane 20, N Ireland 1970–75
						NOTTS COUNTY
69, Div. 4 1970–71	107, Div. 4 1959–60	15–0 v Thornhill United FA Cup 1st Rd 24 October 1885	Les Bradd 125, 1967–78	Tom Keetley 39 Div. 3(S) 1930–31	Albert Iremonger 564, 1904–26	Bill Fallon 7, Eire 1934–38
						OLDHAM ATHLETIC
62, Div. 3 1973–74	95, Div. 4 1962–63	11–0 v Southport Div. 4 26 December 1962	Eric Gemmell 110, 1947–54	Tom Davis 33 Div. 3(N) 1936–37	Ian Wood 452, 1966–78	Albert Gray 9, Wales 1924–27
						ORIENT
66, Div. 3(S) 1955–56	106, Div. 3(S) 1955–56	9–2 v Aldershot Div. 3(S) 10 February 1934 Chester League Cup 3rd Rd 15 October 1962	Tom Johnston 121, 1956–58, 1959–61	Tom Johnston 35 Div. 2 1957–58	Peter Allen 430, 1965–78	Mal Lucas 4, Wales 1962

Ground	Capacity & Record	Shirts/shorts	League career	Honours (domestic) League	Cup
OXFORD UNITED (1896)					
Manor Ground Beech Road Headington Oxford 112×78 yd	18,000 22,730 v Preston NE FA Cup 6th Rd 29 February 1964	Yellow/blue	1962 elected to Div. 4 1965–68 Div. 3 1968–76 Div. 2 1976– Div. 3	Div. 3 Champions 1968	FA Cup never past 6th Rd League Cup never past 5th Rd
PETERBOROUGH UNITED (1923)					
London Road Ground Peterborough PE2 8AL 112×76 yd	30,000 30,096 v Swansea T FA Cup 5th Rd 20 February 1965	Blue-white stripes/blue	1960 elected to Div. 4 1961–68 Div. 3 1968 demoted for financial irregularities 1968–74 Div. 4 1974– Div. 3	Div. 4 Champions 1961, 1974	FA Cup never past 6th Rd League Cup semi-finalists 1966
PLYMOUTH ARGYLE (1886)					
Home Park Plymouth Devon 112×75 yd	40,000 43,596 v Aston Villa Div. 2 10 October 1936	White with green and black trim/white	1920 (founder member of Div. 3) 1921–30 Div. 3(S) 1930–50 Div. 2 1950–52 Div. 3(S) 1952–56 Div. 2 1956–58 Div. 3(S) 1958–59 Div. 3 1959–68 Div. 2 1968–75 Div. 3 1975–77 Div. 2 1977– Div. 3	Div. 3(S) Champions 1930, 1952 Runners-up 1922, 1923, 1924, 1925, 1926, 1927 Div. 3 Champions 1959 Runners-up 1975	FA Cup never past 5th Rd League Cup semi-finalists 1965, 1974
PORTSMOUTH (1898)					
Fratton Park Frogmore Road Portsmouth PO8 8RA 116×73 yd	46,000 51,385 v Derby Co FA Cup 6th Rd 26 February 1949	Blue/white	1920 (founder member of Div. 3) 1921–24 Div. 3(S) 1924–27 Div. 2 1927–59 Div. 1 1959–61 Div. 2 1961–62 Div. 3 1962–76 Div. 2 1976–78 Div. 3 1978– Div. 4	Div. 1 Champions 1949, 1950 Div. 2 runners-up 1927 Div. 3(S) Champions 1924 Div. 3 Champions 1962	FA Cup winners 1939 Runners-up 1929, 1934 League Cup never past 5th Rd
PORT VALE (1876)					
Vale Park Burslem Stoke-on-Trent 116×76 yd	50,000 50,000 v Aston Villa FA Cup 5th Rd 20 February 1960	White/black	1892 (founder member of Div. 2) 1896 failed re-election 1898 re-elected 1907 resigned 1919 returned in October and took over the fixtures of Leeds City 1929–30 Div. 3(N) 1930–36 Div. 2 1936–38 Div. 3(N) 1938–52 Div. 3(S) 1952–54 Div. 3(N) 1954–57 Div. 2 1957–58 Div. 3(S)	Div. 3(N) Champions 1930,1954 Runners-up 1953 Div. 4 Champions 1959 ──────── 1958–59 Div. 4 1959–65 Div. 3 1965–70 Div. 4 1970–78 Div. 3 1978– Div. 4	FA Cup semi-finalists 1954 League Cup never past 2nd Rd

Most League Points	Goals	Record win	Player with highest number of goals		Most League appearances	Most capped player
			Aggregate	Individual		
						OXFORD UNITED
61, Div. 4 1964–65	87, Div. 4 1964–65	7–1 v Barrow Div. 4 19 December 1964	Graham Atkinson 73, 1962–73	Colin Booth 23 Div. 4 1964–65	John Shuker 480, 1962–77	David Roberts 6, Wales 1973–74
						PETERBOROUGH UNITED
66, Div. 4 1960–61	134, Div. 4 1960–61	8–1 v Oldham Athletic Div. 4 26 November 1969	Jim Hall 120, 1967–75	Terry Bly 52 Div. 4 1960–61	Tommy Robson 385, 1968–78	Ollie Conmy 5, Eire 1965–69
						PLYMOUTH ARGYLE
68, Div. 3(S) 1929–30	107, Div. 3(S) 1925–26, 1951–52	8–1 v Millwall Div. 2 16 January 1932	Sammy Black 180, 1924–38	Jack Cock 32 Div. 3(S) 1925–26	Sammy Black 470, 1924–38	Moses Russell 20, Wales 1920–28
						PORTSMOUTH
65, Div. 3 1961–62	87, Div. 3(S) 1923–24 Div. 2 1926–27 Div. 3 1961–62	9–1 v Notts County Div. 2 9 April 1927	Peter Harris 194, 1946–60	Billy Haines 40 Div. 2 1926–27	Jimmy Dickinson 764, 1946–65	Jimmy Dickinson 48, England 1949–56
						PORT VALE
69, Div. 3(N) 1953–54	110, Div. 4 1958–59	9–1 v Chesterfield Div. 2 24 September 1932	Wilf Kirkham 154, 1923–29, 1931–33	Wilf Kirkham 38 Div. 2 1926–27	Roy Sproson 761, 1950–72	Sammy Morgan 7, N Ireland 1972–73

Ground	Capacity & Record	Shirts/shorts	League career	Honours (domestic) League	Cup

PRESTON NORTH END (1881)

Deepdale Preston PR1 6RU 112×78 yd	38,000 42,684 v Arsenal Div. 1 23 April 1938	White/white	1888 (founder member of League) 1901–04 Div. 2 1904–12 Div. 1 1912–13 Div. 2 1913–14 Div. 1 1914–15 Div. 2 1919–25 Div. 1 1925–34 Div. 2 1934–49 Div. 1 1949–51 Div. 2 1951–61 Div. 1 1961–70 Div. 2 1970–71 Div. 3 1971–74 Div. 2 1974–78 Div. 3 1978– Div. 2	Div. 1 Champions 1889, 1890 Runners-up 1891, 1892, 1893 1906, 1953, 1958 Div. 2 Champions 1904, 1913, 1951 Runners-up 1915, 1934 Div. 3 Champions 1971	FA Cup winners 1889, 1938 Runners-up 1888, 1922, 1937, 1954, 1964 League Cup never past 4th Rd

QUEEN'S PARK RANGERS (1885)

South Africa Road London W12 7PA 112×72 yd	30,000 35,353 v Leeds U Div. 1 28 April 1974	Black-white hoops/white	1920 (founder member of Div. 3) 1921–48 Div. 3(S) 1948–52 Div. 2 1952–58 Div. 3(S) 1958–67 Div. 3 1967–68 Div. 2 1968–69 Div. 1 1969–73 Div. 2 1973– Div. 1	Div. 1 runners-up 1976 Div. 2 runners-up 1968, 1973 Div. 3(S) Champions 1948 Runners-up 1947 Div. 3 Champions 1967	FA Cup never past 6th Rd or equivalent League Cup winners 1967

READING (1871)

Elm Park Norfolk Reading 112×77 yd	27,200 33,042 v Brentford FA Cup 5th Rd 19 February 1927	Blue-white hoops/white	1920 (founder member of Div. 3) 1921–26 Div. 3(S) 1926–31 Div. 2 1931–58 Div. 3(S) 1958–71 Div. 3 1971–76 Div. 4 1976–77 Div. 3 1977– Div. 4	Div. 3(S) Champions 1926 Runners-up 1932, 1935, 1949, 1952	FA Cup semi-finalists 1927 League Cup never past 4th Rd

ROCHDALE (1907)

Spotland Willbutts Lane Rochdale 113×75 yd	28,000 24,231 v Notts Co FA Cup 2nd Rd 10 December 1949	Blue/white	1921 elected to Div. 3(N) 1958–59 Div. 3 1959–69 Div. 4 1969–74 Div. 3 1974– Div. 4	Div. 3(N) runners-up 1924, 1927	FA Cup never past 4th Rd League Cup runners-up 1962

ROTHERHAM UNITED (1884)

Millmoor Ground Rotherham 115×76 yd	24,000 25,000 v Sheffield U Div. 2 13 December 1952 and Sheffield W Div. 2 26 January 1952	Red, white sleeves/white	1893 elected to Div. 2 1896 failed re-election 1919 re-elected to Div. 2 1923–51 Div. 3(N) 1951–68 Div. 2 1968–73 Div. 3 1973–75 Div. 4 1975– Div. 3	Div. 3(N) Champions 1951 Runners-up 1947, 1948, 1949	FA Cup never past 5th Rd League Cup runners-up 1961

Most League Points	Goals	Record win	Player with highest number of goals		Most League appearances	Most capped player
			Aggregate	Individual		
						PRESTON NORTH END
61, Div. 3 1970–71	100, Div. 2 1927–28 Div. 1 1957–58	26–0 v Hyde FA Cup 1st series 1st Rd 15 October 1887	Tom Finney 187, 1946–60	Ted Harper 37 Div. 2 1932–33	Alan Kelly 447, 1961–75	Tom Finney 76, England 1946–58
						QUEEN'S PARK RANGERS
67, Div. 3 1966–67	111, Div. 3 1961–62	9–2 v Tranmere Rovers Div. 3 3 December 1960	George Goddard 172, 1926–34	George Goddard 37 Div. 3(S) 1929–30	Tony Ingham 519, 1950–63	Don Givens 19, Eire 1973–77
						READING
61, Div. 3(S) 1951–52	112, Div. 3(S) 1951–52	10–2 v Crystal Palace Div. 3(S) 4 September 1946	Ronnie Blackman 156, 1947–54	Ronnie Blackman 39 Div. 3(S) 1951–52	Dick Spiers 453, 1955–70	Pat McConnell 8, N Ireland 1925–28
						ROCHDALE
62, Div. 3(N) 1923–24	105, Div. 3(N) 1926–27	8–1 v Chesterfield Div. 3(N) 18 December 1926	Albert Whitehurst 117, 1923–28	Albert Whitehurst 44 Div. 3(N) 1926–27	Graham Smith 317, 1966–74	None
						ROTHERHAM UNITED
71, Div. 3(N) 1950–51	114, Div. 3(N) 1946–47	8–0 v Oldham Athletic Div. 3(N) 26 May 1947	Gladstone Guest 130, 1946–56	Wally Ardron 38 Div. 3(N) 1946–47	Danny Williams 459, 1946–62	Harold Millership 6, Wales 1920–21

Ground	Capacity & Record	Shirts/shorts	League career	Honours (domestic) League	Cup

SCUNTHORPE UNITED (1904)

Ground	Capacity & Record	Shirts/shorts	League career	Honours (domestic) League	Cup
Old Show Ground Scunthorpe South Humberside 112×78 yd	27,000 23,935 v Portsmouth FA Cup 4th Rd 30 January 1954	Red/red	1950 elected to Div. 3(N) 1958–64 Div. 2 1964–68 Div. 3 1968–72 Div. 4 1972–73 Div. 3 1973– Div. 4	Div. 3(N) Champions 1958	FA Cup never past 5th Rd League Cup never past 3rd Rd

SHEFFIELD UNITED (1889)

| Bramall Lane Ground Sheffield S2 4SU 117×75 yd | 49,000 68,287 v Leeds U FA Cup 5th Rd 15 February 1936 | Red, white and thin black stripes/black | 1892 elected to Div. 2 1893–1934 Div. 1 1934–39 Div. 2 1946–49 Div. 1 1949–53 Div. 2 1953–56 Div. 1 1956–61 Div. 2 1961–68 Div. 1 1968–71 Div. 2 1971–76 Div. 1 | Div. 1 Champions 1898 Runners-up 1897, 1900 Div. 2 Champions 1953 Runners-up 1893 1939, 1961, 1971 —————— 1976– Div. 2 | FA Cup winners 1899, 1902, 1915, 1925 Runners-up 1901, 1936 League Cup never past 5th Rd |

SHEFFIELD WEDNESDAY (1867)

| Hillsborough Sheffield S6 1SW 115×75 yd | 55,000 72,841 v Manchester C FA Cup 5th Rd 17 February 1934 | Blue-white stripes/blue | 1892 elected to Div. 1 1899–1900 Div. 2 1900–20 Div. 1 1920–26 Div. 2 1926–37 Div. 1 1937–50 Div. 2 1950–51 Div. 1 1951–52 Div. 2 1952–55 Div. 1 1955–56 Div. 2 1956–58 Div. 1 1958–59 Div. 2 | Div. 1 Champions 1903, 1904, 1929, 1930 Runners-up 1961 Div. 2 Champions 1900, 1926, 1952, 1956, 1959 Runners-up 1950 —————— 1959–70 Div. 1 1970–75 Div. 2 1975– Div. 3 | FA Cup winners 1896, 1907, 1935 Runners-up 1890, 1966 League Cup never past 4th Rd |

SHREWSBURY TOWN (1886)

| Gay Meadow Shrewsbury 116×76 yd | 18,000 18,917 v Walsall Div. 3 26 April 1961 | Blue/blue | 1950 elected to Div. 3(N) 1951–58 Div. 3(S) 1958–59 Div. 4 1959–74 Div. 3 | Div. 4 runners-up 1975 —————— 1974–75 Div. 4 1975– Div. 3 | FA Cup never past 5th Rd League Cup semi-finalists 1961 |

SOUTHAMPTON (1885)

| The Dell Milton Road Southampton SO9 4XX 110×72 yd | 31,000 31,044 v Manchester U Div. 1 8 October 1969 | Red-white stripes/black | 1920 (founder member of Div. 3) 1921–22 Div. 3(S) 1922–53 Div. 2 1953–58 Div. 3(S) 1958–60 Div. 3 1960–66 Div. 2 1966–74 Div. 1 1974–78 Div. 2 | Div. 2 runners-up 1966, 1978 Div. 3(S) Champions 1922 Runners-up 1921 Div. 3 Champions 1960 —————— 1978– Div. 1 | FA Cup winners 1976 Runners-up 1900, 1902 League Cup never past 5th Rd |

SOUTHEND UNITED (1906)

| Roots Hall Ground Victoria Avenue Southend-on-Sea 110×74 yd | 35,000 28,059 v Birmingham C FA Cup 4th Rd 26 January 1957 | Blue/white | 1920 (founder member of Div. 3) 1921–58 Div. 3(S) 1958–66 Div. 3 1966–72 Div. 4 1972–76 Div. 3 1976– Div. 4 | Div. 4 runners-up 1972, 1978 | FA Cup never past 5th Rd League Cup never past 3rd Rd |

Most League Points	Goals	Record win	Player with highest number of goals		Most League appearances	Most capped player
			Aggregate	Individual		
						SCUNTHORPE UNITED
66, Div. 3(N) 1957–58	88, Div. 3(N) 1957–58	9–0 v Boston United FA Cup 1st Rd 21 November 1953	Barrie Thomas 92, 1959–62, 1964–66	Barrie Thomas 31 Div. 2 1961–62	Jack Brownsword 600, 1950–65	None
						SHEFFIELD UNITED
60, Div. 2 1952–53	102, Div. 1 1925–26	11–2 v Cardiff City Div. 1 1 January 1926	Harry Johnson 205, 1919–30	Jimmy Dunne 41 Div. 1 1930–31	Joe Shaw 629, 1948–66	Billy Gillespie 25, N Ireland 1913–30
						SHEFFIELD WEDNESDAY
62, Div. 2 1958–59	106, Div. 2 1958–59	12–0 v Halliwell FA Cup 1st Rd 17 January 1891	Andy Wilson 200, 1900–20	Derek Dooley 46 Div. 2 1951–52	Andy Wilson 502, 1900–20	Ron Springett 33, England 1959–66
						SHREWSBURY TOWN
62, Div. 4 1974–75	101, Div. 4 1958–59	7–0 v Swindon Town Div. 3(S) 1954–55	Arthur Rowley 152, 1958–65	Arthur Rowley 38 Div. 4 1958–59	Joe Wallace 329, 1954–63	Jimmy McLaughlin 5, N Ireland 1961–63
						SOUTHAMPTON
61, Div. 3(S) 1921–22 Div. 3 1959–60	112, Div. 3(S) 1957–58	11–0 v Northampton Town Southern League 28 December 1901	Terry Paine 160, 1956–74	Derek Reeves 39 Div. 3 1959–60	Terry Paine 713, 1956–74	Mike Channon 45, England 1972–77
						SOUTHEND UNITED
60, Div. 4 1971–72 Div. 4 1977–78	92, Div. 3(S) 1950–51	10–1 v Golders Green FA Cup 1st Rd 24 November 1934 Brentwood FA Cup 2nd Rd 7 December 1968	Roy Hollis 122, 1953–60	Jim Shankly 31 Div. 3(S) 1928–29 Sammy McCrory 31 Div. 3(S) 1957–58	Sandy Anderson 451, 1950–63	George Mackenzie 9, Eire 1937–39

Ground	Capacity & Record	Shirts/shorts	League career	Honours (domestic) League	Cup
SOUTHPORT (1881)					
Haig Avenue Southport PR8 6JZ 113×77 yd	21,000 20,010 v Newcastle U FA Cup 4th Rd replay 26 January 1932	Old gold/blue	1921 (founder member of Div. 3(N)) 1958–67 Div. 4 1967–70 Div. 3 1970–73 Div. 4 1973–74 Div. 3 1974–78 Div. 4	Div. 4 Champions 1973 Runners-up 1967 _____ (Not re-elected) Wigan Athletic elected in their place	FA Cup never past 6th Rd League Cup never past 2nd Rd
STOCKPORT COUNTY (1883)					
Edgely Park Stockport Cheshire SK3 9DD 110×75 yd	24,904 27,833 v Liverpool FA Cup 5th Rd 11 February 1950	White/blue	1900 elected to Div. 2 1904 failed re-election 1905 re-elected to Div. 2 1905–21 Div. 2 1921–22 Div. 3(N) 1922–26 Div. 2 1926–37 Div. 3(N) 1937–38 Div. 2 1938–58 Div. 3(N) 1958–59 Div. 3 1959–67 Div. 4 1967–70 Div. 3 1970– Div. 4	Div. 3(N) Champions 1922, 1937 Runners-up 1929, 1930 Div. 4 Champions 1967	FA Cup never past 5th Rd League Cup never past 4th Rd
STOKE CITY (1863)					
Victoria Ground Stoke-on-Trent 116×75 yd	48,000 51,380 v Arsenal Div. 1 29 March 1937	Red-white stripes/white	1888 (founder member of League) 1890 not re-elected 1891 re-elected 1907–08 Div. 2 1908 resigned for financial reasons 1919 re-elected to Div. 2 1922–23 Div. 1 1923–26 Div. 2 1926–27 Div. 3(N)	Div. 2 Champions 1933, 1963 Runners-up 1922 Div. 3(N) Champions 1927 _____ 1927–33 Div. 2 1933–53 Div. 1 1953–63 Div. 2 1963–77 Div. 1 1977– Div. 2	FA Cup semi-finalists 1899, 1971, 1972 League Cup winners 1972
SUNDERLAND (1879)					
Roker Park Sunderland 112×72 yd	53,500 75,118 v Derby Co FA Cup 6th Rd replay 8 March 1933	Red-white stripes/black	1890 elected to Div. 1 1958–64 Div. 2 1964–70 Div. 1 1970–76 Div. 2 1976–77 Div. 1 1977– Div. 2	Div. 1 Champions 1892, 1893, 1895, 1902, 1913, 1936 Runners-up 1894, 1898, 1901, 1923, 1935 Div. 2 Champions 1976 Runners-up 1964	FA Cup winners 1937, 1973 Runners-up 1913 League Cup semi-finalists 1963
SWANSEA CITY (1900)					
Vetch Field Swansea 110×70 yd	35,000 32,796 v Arsenal FA Cup 4th Rd 17 February 1968	White/white	1920 (founder member of Div. 3) 1921–25 Div. 3(S) 1925–47 Div. 2 1947–49 Div. 3(S) 1949–65 Div. 2 1965–67 Div. 3 1967–70 Div. 4 1970–73 Div. 3	Div. 3(S) Champions 1925, 1949 _____ 1973–78 Div. 4 1978– Div. 3	FA Cup semi-finalists 1926, 1964 League Cup never past 4th Rd

Most League Points	Goals	Record win	Player with highest number of goals Aggregate	Individual	Most League appearances	Most capped player

SOUTHPORT

| 62, Div. 4 1972–73 | 88, Div. 3(N) 1930–31 | 8–1 v Nelson Div. 3(N) 1 January 1931 | Alan Spence 98, 1962–69 | Archie Waterston 31 Div. 3(N) 1930–31 | Arthur Peat 401, 1962–72 | Terry Harkin 2, N Ireland 1968 |

STOCKPORT COUNTY

| 64, Div. 4 1966–67 | 115, Div. 3(N) 1933–34 | 13–0 v Halifax Town Div. 3(N) 6 January 1934 | Jackie Connor 132, 1951–56 | Alf Lythgoe 46 Div. 3(N) 1933–34 | Bob Murray 465, 1952–63 | Harry Hardy 1, England 1924 |

STOKE CITY

| 63, Div. 3(N) 1926–27 | 92, Div. 3(N) 1926–27 | 10–3 v West Bromwich Albion Div. 1 4 February 1937 | Freddie Steele 142, 1934–49 | Freddie Steele 33 Div. 1 1936–37 | Eric Skeels 506, 1958–76 | Gordon Banks 36, England 1967–72 |

SUNDERLAND

| 61, Div. 2 1963–64 | 109, Div. 1 1935–36 | 11–1 v Fairfield FA Cup 1st Rd 1894–95 | Charlie Buchan 209, 1911–25 | Dave Halliday 43 Div. 1 1928–29 | Jim Montgomery 537, 1962–77 | Billy Bingham 33, N Ireland 1951–58 Martin Harvey 33, N Ireland 1961–71 |

SWANSEA CITY

| 62, Div. 3(S) 1948–49 | 90, Div. 2 1956–57 | 8–0 v Hartlepool United Div. 4 1 April 1978 | Ivor Allchurch 166, 1949–58, 1965–68 | Cyril Pearce 35 Div. 2 1931–32 | Wilfred Milne 585, 1919–37 | Ivor Allchurch 42, Wales 1950–58 |

Ground	Capacity & Record	Shirts/shorts	League career	Honours (domestic) League	Cup
SWINDON TOWN (1881)					
County Ground Swindon Wiltshire 114×72 yd	28,000 32,000 v Arsenal FA Cup 3rd Rd 15 January 1972	Red/white	1920 (founder member of Div. 3) 1921–58 Div. 3(S) 1958–63 Div. 3 1963–65 Div. 2 1965–69 Div. 3 1969–74 Div. 2 1974– Div. 3	Div. 3 runners-up 1963, 1969	FA Cup semi-finalists 1910, 1912 League Cup winners 1969
TORQUAY UNITED (1898)					
Plainmoor Ground Torquay Devon TQ1 3PS 112×74 yd	22,000 21,908 v Huddersfield T FA Cup 4th Rd 29 January 1955	White with blue and yellow trim/ white	1927 elected to Div. 3(S) 1958–60 Div. 4 1960–62 Div. 3 1962–66 Div. 4 1966–72 Div. 3 1972– Div. 4	Div. 3(S) runners-up 1957	FA Cup never past 4th Rd League Cup never past 3rd Rd
TOTTENHAM HOTSPUR (1882)					
748 High Road Tottenham London N17 110×73 yd	52,000 75,038 v Sunderland FA Cup 6th Rd 5 March 1938	White/blue	1908 elected to Div. 2 1909–15 Div. 1 1919–20 Div. 2 1920–28 Div. 1 1928–33 Div. 2 1933–35 Div. 1 1935–50 Div. 2 1950–77 Div. 1 1977–78 Div. 2 1978– Div. 1	Div. 1 Champions 1951, 1961 Runners-up 1922, 1952, 1957, 1963 Div. 2 Champions 1920, 1950 Runners-up 1909, 1933	FA Cup winners 1901, 1921, 1961, 1962, 1967 League Cup winners 1971, 1973
TRANMERE ROVERS (1883)					
Prenton Park Prenton Road West Birkenhead 112×74 yd	25,000 24,242 v Stoke City FA Cup 4th Rd 5 February 1972	White/blue	1921 (founder member of Div. 3(N)) 1938–39 Div. 2 1939–58 Div. 3(N) 1958–61 Div. 3 1961–67 Div. 4 1967–75 Div. 3 1975–76 Div. 4 1976– Div. 3	Div. 3(N) Champions 1938	FA Cup never past 5th Rd League Cup never past 4th Rd
WALSALL (1888)					
Fellows Park Walsall 113×73 yd	24,100 25,453 v Newcastle U Div. 2 29 August 1961	Red/white	1892 elected to Div. 2 1895 failed re-election 1896–1901 Div. 2 1901 failed re-election 1921 (founder member of Div. 3(N)) 1927–31 Div. 3(S) 1931–36 Div. 3(N) 1936–58 Div. 3(S) 1958–60 Div. 4 1960–61 Div. 3 1961–63 Div. 2 1963– Div. 3	Div. 4 Champions 1960 Div. 3 runners-up 1961	FA Cup never past 5th Rd League Cup never past 4th Rd

Most League Points	Goals	Record win	Player with highest number of goals		Most League appearances	Most capped player
			Aggregate	Individual		
						SWINDON TOWN
64, Div. 3 1968–69	100, Div. 3(S) 1926–27	10–1 v Farnham United Breweries FA Cup 1st Rd 28 November 1925	Harry Morris 216, 1926–33	Harry Morris 47 Div. 3(S) 1926–27	John Trollope 738, 1960–78	Rod Thomas 30, Wales 1967–73
						TORQUAY UNITED
60, Div. 4 1959–60	89, Div. 3(S) 1956–57	9–0 v Swindon Town Div. 3(S) 8 March 1952	Sammy Collins 204, 1948–58	Sammy Collins 40 Div. 3(S) 1955–56	Dennis Lewis 443, 1947–59	None
						TOTTENHAM HOTSPUR
70, Div. 2 1919–20	115, Div. 1 1960–61	13–2 v Crewe Alexandra FA Cup 4th Rd replay 3 February 1960	Jimmy Greaves 220, 1961–70	Jimmy Greaves 37 Div. 1 1962–63	Pat Jennings 472, 1964–77	Pat Jennings 66, N Ireland 1964–77
						TRANMERE ROVERS
60, Div. 4 1964–65	111, Div. 3(N) 1930–31	13–4 v Oldham Athletic Div. 3(N) 26 December 1935	Bunny Bell 104, 1931–36	Bunny Bell 35 Div. 3(N) 1933–34	Harold Bell 595, 1946–64	Albert Gray 3, Wales 1931
						WALSALL
65, Div. 4 1959–60	102, Div. 4 1959–60	10–0 v Darwen Div. 2 4 March 1899	Tony Richards 184, 1954–63 Colin Taylor 184, 1958–73	Gilbert Alsop 40 Div. 3(N) 1933–34, 1934–35	Colin Taylor 459, 1958–63, 1964–68, 1969–73	Mick Kearns 11, Eire 1973–77

Ground	Capacity & Record	Shirts/shorts	League career	Honours (domestic) League	Cup
WATFORD (1891)					
Vicarage Road Watford WD1 8ER 113×73 yd	36,500 34,099 v Manchester U FA Cup 4th Rd 3 February 1969	Gold/black	1920 (founder member of Div. 3) 1921–58 Div. 3(S) 1958–60 Div. 4 1960–69 Div. 3 1969–72 Div. 2 1972–75 Div. 3	Div. 3 Champions 1969 Div. 4 Champions 1978 ———————— 1975–78 Div. 4 1978– Div. 3	FA Cup semi-finalists 1970 League Cup never past 3rd Rd
WEST BROMWICH ALBION (1879)					
The Hawthorns West Bromwich B71 4LF 115×75 yd	44,000 64,815 v Arsenal FA Cup 6th Rd 6 March 1937	Blue-white stripes/white	1888 (founder member of League) 1901–02 Div. 2 1902–04 Div. 1 1904–11 Div. 2 1911–27 Div. 1 1927–31 Div. 2 1931–38 Div. 1 1938–49 Div. 2 1949–73 Div. 1 1973–76 Div. 2 1976– Div. 1	Div. 1 Champions 1920 Runners-up 1925, 1954 Div. 2 Champions 1902, 1911 Runners-up 1931, 1949	FA Cup winners 1888, 1892, 1931, 1954, 1968 Runners-up 1886, 1887, 1895, 1912, 1935 League Cup winners 1966 Runners-up 1967, 1970
WEST HAM UNITED (1900)					
Boleyn Ground Green Street Upton Park London E13 110×72 yd	41,000 42,322 v Tottenham H Div. 1 17 October 1970	Claret with blue yoke/white	1919 elected to Div. 2 1923–32 Div. 1 1932–58 Div. 2 1958–78 Div. 1	Div. 2 Champions 1958 Runners-up 1923 ———————— 1978– Div. 2	FA Cup winners 1964, 1975 Runners-up 1923 League Cup runners-up 1966
WIMBLEDON (1889)					
Plough Lane Ground Durnsford Wimbledon London SW19	15,000 18,000 v HMS Victory FA Amateur Cup 1932–33	White/white	1977 elected to Div. 4	Southern League Champions 1975, 1976, 1977	Southern League Cup winners 1970, 1976
WOLVERHAMPTON WANDERERS (1877)					
Molineux Grounds Wolverhampton WV1 4QR 115×72 yd	53,000 61,315 v Liverpool FA Cup 5th Rd 11 February 1939	Gold/black	1888 (founder member of League) 1906–23 Div. 2 1923–24 Div. 3(N) 1924–32 Div. 2 1932–65 Div. 1 1965–67 Div. 2 1967–76 Div. 1 1976–77 Div. 2 1977– Div. 1	Div. 1 Champions 1954, 1958, 1959 Runners-up 1938, 1939, 1950, 1955, 1960 Div. 2 Champions 1932, 1977 Runners-up 1967 Div. 3(N) Champions 1924	FA Cup winners 1893, 1908, 1949, 1960 Runners-up 1889, 1896, 1921, 1939 League Cup winners 1974
WREXHAM (1873)					
Racecourse Ground Mold Road Wrexham 117×75 yd	30,000 34,445 v Manchester U FA Cup 4th Rd 26 January 1957	Red/white	1921 (founder member of Div. 3(N)) 1958–60 Div. 3 1960–62 Div. 4 1962–64 Div. 3 1964–70 Div. 4 1970–78 Div. 3 1978– Div. 2	Div. 3(N) runners-up 1933 Div. 4 runners-up 1970	FA Cup never past 6th Rd League Cup never past 5th Rd

Most League Points	Goals	Record win	Player with highest number of goals		Most League appearances	Most capped player
			Aggregate	Individual		
						WATFORD
71, Div. 4 1977–78	92, Div. 4 1959–60	10–1 v Lowestoft Town FA Cup 1st Rd 27 November 1926	Tom Barnett 144, 1928–39	Cliff Holton 42 Div. 4 1959–60	Duncan Welbourne 411, 1963–74	Frank Hoddinott 2, Wales 1921 Pat Jennings 2, N Ireland 1964
						WEST BROMWICH ALBION
60, Div. 1 1919–20	105, Div. 2 1929–30	12–0 v Darwen Div. 1 4 April 1892	Ronnie Allen 208, 1950–61	William Richardson 39 Div. 1 1935–36	Tony Brown 527, 1963–78	Stuart Williams 33, Wales 1954–62
						WEST HAM UNITED
57, Div. 2 1957–58	101, Div. 2 1957–58	8–0 v Rotherham United Div. 1 8 March 1958 Sunderland Div. 1 19 October 1968	Vic Watson 306, 1920–35	Vic Watson 41 Div. 1 1929–30	Bobby Moore 544, 1958–74	Bobby Moore 108, England 1962–73
						WIMBLEDON
44, Div. 4 1977–78	66, Div. 4 1977–78	5–0 v Southport Div. 4 17 April 1978	Roger Connell 14, 1977–78	Roger Connell 14, Div. 4 1977–78	Jeff Bryant 43, 1977–78	None
						WOLVERHAMPTON WANDERERS
64, Div. 1 1957–58	115, Div. 2 1931–32	14–0 v Crosswell's Brewery FA Cup 2nd Rd 1886–87	Bill Hartill 164, 1928–35	Dennis Westcott 37 Div. 1 1946–47	Billy Wright 491, 1946–59	Billy Wright 105, England 1946–59
						WREXHAM
61, Div. 4 1969–70 Div. 3 1977–78	106, Div. 3(N) 1932–33	10–1 v Hartlepools United Div. 4 3 March 1962	Tom Bamford 175, 1928–34	Tom Bamford 44 Div. 3(N) 1933–34	Arfon Griffiths 588, 1959–61 1962–78	Horace Blow 22, Wales 1899–1910

Ground	Capacity & Record	Shirts/shorts	League career	Honours (domestic) League	Cup
YORK CITY (1922)					
Bootham Crescent York 115×75 yd	17,000 28,123 v Huddersfield T FA Cup 5th Rd 5 March 1938	White with maroon 'Y' on front/white	1929 elected to Div. 3(N) 1958–59 Div. 4 1959–60 Div. 3 1960–65 Div. 4 1965–66 Div. 3 1966–71 Div. 4 1971–74 Div. 3 1974–76 Div. 2 1976–77 Div. 3 1977– Div. 4	Highest position 15th Div. 2 1975	FA Cup semi-finalists 1955 League Cup never past 5th Rd

LEAGUE CHAMPIONSHIPS

The most wins in the Football League championships have been the 10 by Liverpool in 1901, 1906, 1922, 1923, 1947, 1964, 1966, 1973, 1976 and 1977.

Liverpool's championship-winning effort in the 1965–66 season was remarkable in many ways, not the least of which was the fact that they called upon only 14 players to complete their Division One programme. This is an all-time record for a single season of League football.

While a club needs a considerable fortune in escaping injuries to be able to perform such a feat, Liverpool's achievement emphasised the consistency of the team. That manager Bill Shankly should find it necessary to make practically no changes at all in a team that was capable of winning the League Championship under-

lined the talent and team-work of his side. Five of the team played in every game, while another two missed only one game each. If Bobby Graham had not been called in for one game the number used would have been only 13, an impressive figure for a lengthy 42-match programme. This beat the previous record for a Championship-winning team which was created by Sunderland when they won the title in the 1891–92 season with 15 players. But Sunderland only had to play 26 matches.

When Liverpool won the League Championship in the 1946–47 season they were captained by a popular local discovery, Jack Balmer, who was at the time one of the most experienced inside-forwards in Division One. Balmer's uncles had played for Everton and he himself had been signed as an amateur by the Goodison Park club in 1935, but unfortunately for them they allowed him to go and he was snapped up by Liverpool whom he served for 17 years.

Apart from winning a League Championship medal in 1946–47, Balmer achieved record-breaking fame with a hat-trick of goals in each of three consecutive Division One games: v Portsmouth (H) 9 November, v Derby County (A) 16 November (when he actually scored four goals), and v Arsenal (H) 23 November.

Liverpool have an unmatched sequence in Football League history: for the last 13 seasons they have never finished below fifth place in Division One. They were first four times, second four times, third twice and fifth three times.

Liverpool have been Division One champions and their reserves Central League champions three times during the 1970s: in 1972–73,

Most League Points	Goals	Record win	Player with highest number of goals		Most League appearances	Most capped player
			Aggregate	Individual		
						YORK CITY
62, Div. 4 1964–65	92, Div. 3(N) 1954–55	9–1 v Southport Div. 3(N) 2 February 1957	Norman Wilkinson 125, 1954–66	Bill Fenton 31 Div. 3(N) 1951–52 Arthur Bottom 31 Div. 3(N) 1955–56	Barry Jackson 481, 1958–70	Peter Scott 5, N Ireland 1976–78

1975–76 and 1976–77. The only other clubs to have achieved a similar 'two-teams double' even once since the war have been: Arsenal, Chelsea, Manchester United, Wolverhampton Wanderers and Derby County.

Recent attempts to increase the points award for prolific scoring tend to overlook the fact that the chief honours certainly do not always go to the teams with the most goals. The proof is that in the last 17 seasons there were no more than four in which the Division One championship was won by the team with the best scoring returns.

Stoke City have spent more seasons in Division One (46) without having ever been champions than any other club. Everton have completed their 75th season in Division One in 1977–78. No other club in the Football League has had such a lengthy association with the top division. They have had seven championship titles.

Football League history was made by Ipswich Town players Roy Bailey, Lawrence Carberry, John Elsworthy, Ted Phillips and Jim Leadbetter when they won Division Three, Two and Division One championship medals with one club in the 1950s and early 1960s.

The complete Huddersfield Town defence of goalkeeper, two full-backs and three halves: John Wheeler; Ron Staniforth, Laurie Kelly; Bill McGarry, Don McEvoy and Len Quested were unchanged throughout the 42 Division Two matches during 1952–53. Outside-left Vic Metcalfe was another ever-present player in the side which won promotion after finishing as runners-up.

SUCCESS SEQUENCES
(League Championship Teams)

Sunderland after losing 4–3 on their own ground at Newcastle Road to Wolverhampton Wanderers on 15 September 1890 went 44 games in three years without losing another League game at home until 9 December 1893 when Blackburn Rovers beat them 3–2. This was followed by another run of 37 home games without defeat before losing 1–0 to Bury on 1 September 1896. This represented an aggregate of 82 League games at home with only one defeat.

They also won all their home League matches in 1891–92, the only occasion that this has been accomplished in Division One, and there was not one drawn game among their overall results. Sunderland also failed to score only once in the 1891–92 season and again in 1892–93. During this period they registered 193 goals in 56 League games.

Aston Villa did not lose a League game on their own ground at Perry Barr from 15 September 1894 when they were beaten 2–1 by Sunderland until 26 September 1896 when Everton also won by the odd goal in three. The sequence covered 29 home matches without defeat.

After Sheffield Wednesday were beaten 2–1 by Small Heath on their own ground at Owlerton, 19 April 1902, they did not concede more than a single goal at home in 30 Division One matches until Small Heath were beaten 3–2 on 27 February 1904.

Huddersfield Town's 1–0 defeat against Newcastle United on their own ground at Leeds

Road was their only defeat in 32 home matches over a period of more than eighteen months. This sequence began on 17 January 1925 after losing 2–1 to West Ham United and lasted until 4 September 1926 when they were beaten 2–0 by Birmingham.

Leeds United after losing 5–1 to Burnley at Turf Moor on 19 October 1968 had a run of 34 League games in which they were unbeaten. This is a Football League record. It included 28 matches in the 1968–69 season and six in 1969–70. The sequence ended on 30 August 1969 when Everton beat them 3–2 at Goodison Park. During this run they were unbeaten away on 17 consecutive occasions.

Burnley, after losing 2–0 away to Bradford City on 4 September 1920, had a run of 30 League games without defeat before losing 3–0 to Manchester City on 26 March 1921. This is a Football League record for the longest run in a single season. Burnley did however lose an F.A. Cup tie at Hull City 3–0 during this sequence.

The previous season Burnley had finished runners-up in the League Championship to West Bromwich Albion but there was no hint of a record performance when they began the 1920–21 season by losing their first three games and scoring just one goal. But that third defeat (2–0 away to Bradford City) was their last in the League until they were beaten 3–0 away to Manchester City six months later.

That remarkable achievement, never beaten in a single season of League football, was duly

FOOTBALL LEAGUE CHAMPIONS

Season Ending	Champions	Matches	Points	W	D	L	F	A	Pts	W	D	L	F
1889	PRESTON NORTH END	22	40	10	1	0	39	7	21	8	3	0	35
1890	PRESTON NORTH END	22	33	8	1	2	41	12	17	7	2	2	30
1891	EVERTON	22	29	9	0	2	39	12	18	5	1	5	24
1892	SUNDERLAND	26	42	13	0	0	55	11	26	8	0	5	38
1893	SUNDERLAND	30	48	13	2	0	58	17	28	9	2	4	42
1894	ASTON VILLA	30	44	12	2	1	49	13	26	7	4	4	35
1895	SUNDERLAND	30	47	13	2	0	51	14	28	8	3	4	29
1896	ASTON VILLA	30	45	14	1	0	47	17	29	6	4	5	31
1897	ASTON VILLA	30	47	10	3	2	36	16	23	11	2	2	37
1898	SHEFFIELD UNITED	30	42	9	4	2	27	14	22	8	4	3	29
1899	ASTON VILLA	34	45	15	2	0	58	13	32	4	5	8	18
1900	ASTON VILLA	34	50	12	4	1	45	18	28	10	2	5	32
1901	LIVERPOOL	34	45	12	2	3	36	13	26	7	5	5	23
1902	SUNDERLAND	34	44	12	3	2	32	14	27	7	3	7	18
1903	SHEFFIELD WEDNESDAY	34	42	12	3	2	31	7	27	7	1	9	23
1904	SHEFFIELD WEDNESDAY	34	47	14	3	0	34	10	31	6	4	7	14
1905	NEWCASTLE UNITED	34	48	14	1	2	41	12	29	9	1	7	31
1906	LIVERPOOL	38	51	14	3	2	49	15	31	9	2	8	30
1907	NEWCASTLE UNITED	38	51	18	1	0	51	12	37	4	6	9	23
1908	MANCHESTER UNITED	38	52	15	1	3	43	19	31	8	5	6	38
1909	NEWCASTLE UNITED	38	53	14	1	4	32	20	29	10	4	5	33
1910	ASTON VILLA	38	53	17	2	0	62	19	36	6	5	8	22
1911	MANCHESTER UNITED	38	52	14	4	1	47	18	32	8	4	7	25
1912	BLACKBURN ROVERS	38	49	13	6	0	35	10	32	7	3	9	25
1913	SUNDERLAND	38	54	14	2	3	47	17	30	11	2	6	39
1914	BLACKBURN ROVERS	38	51	14	4	1	51	15	32	6	7	6	27
1915	EVERTON	38	46	8	5	6	44	29	21	11	3	5	32
No National competition 1916, 1917, 1918 or 1919 regional leagues in operation													
1920	WEST BROMWICH ALBION	42	60	17	1	3	65	21	35	11	3	7	39
1921	BURNLEY	42	59	17	3	1	56	16	37	6	10	5	23
1922	LIVERPOOL	42	57	15	4	2	43	15	34	7	9	5	20
1923	LIVERPOOL	42	60	17	3	1	50	13	37	9	5	7	20
1924	HUDDERSFIELD TOWN	42	57	15	5	1	35	9	35	8	6	7	25
1925	HUDDERSFIELD TOWN	42	58	10	8	3	31	10	28	11	8	2	38
1926	HUDDERSFIELD TOWN	42	57	14	6	1	50	17	34	9	5	7	42
1927	NEWCASTLE UNITED	42	56	19	1	1	64	20	39	6	5	10	32
1928	EVERTON	42	53	11	8	2	60	28	30	9	5	7	42
1929	SHEFFIELD WEDNESDAY	42	52	18	3	0	55	16	39	3	7	11	31
1930	SHEFFIELD WEDNESDAY	42	60	15	4	2	56	20	34	11	4	6	49

appreciated in the illuminated address which the Football League presented to the club, describing Burnley as 'individually meritorious and collectively brilliant'.

This side included four of the team that had won the Cup in 1914 and there was only one newcomer to the squad that had finished Division One runners-up in 1919–20. Outstanding among their players at this time were the long-service goalkeeper Jerry Dawson; one of the finest 90 minute centre-halves of all-time, club captain Tommy Boyle, and Bob Kelly, their artistic inside-forward famed for his elusive body swerve.

Dawson, an England international, spent nearly 23 years with the club, Boyle who also played for his country played over 200 League games for them and Kelly who cost £275 was sold for £6,000 after 12 years' service.

Thirty games without defeat put a severe strain on the side, although it should be mentioned that this League run was broken by that shock Cup defeat by Hull City in the Third Round. After Manchester City had broken Burnley's run they only won two of their last eight games. That run, however, was enough to see them through to the Championship, finishing five points ahead of Manchester City after leading the table for more than five months.

Leeds United were undefeated in the first 29 matches of the 1973–74 season before losing 3–2 at Stoke City on 23 February 1974. This is a Football League record from the start of the season.

A	Pts	Goal Average	No of Players	Ever Present	Facts and Feats
8	19	3.36	18	2	Had an 11 point lead and also won FA Cup without conceding a goal
18	16	3.23	19	3	Led from 16 November but only had a two point margin over Everton
17	11	2.86	21	3	Reversed position and two point gap in leading from Preston
25	16	3.57	15	2	Achieved a record run of 13 successive wins starting on 14 November
19	20	3.33	15	3	First Football League club to score 100 goals in a single season
29	18	2.80	24	1	Finished six points ahead of runners-up Sunderland the previous champions
23	19	2.66	16	2	Only team to win at Villa in the League; third title in four years
28	16	2.60	17	2	Won with a four point margin and scored ten more goals than nearest rivals
22	24	2.43	17	4	Achieved the 'double'. Won by 11 points and unbeaten in last 11 games
17	20	1.86	23	1	Unbeaten in first 14 matches. Clinched title v Bolton on 8 April
27	13	2.23	24	1	Level with Liverpool before the last game. Villa beat them 5–0
17	22	2.26	21	2	For fifth consecutive season scored more goals than any other in Division One
22	19	1.73	18	3	Unbeaten in last 12 games but had to win their last match for the title
21	17	1.47	19	1	Goalkeeper Ned Doig (12th season) kept clean sheet 15 times
29	15	1.58	23	3	Only seven goals were conceded at home; an unequalled achievement
18	16	1.41	22	2	Only once did they concede more than a single goal in games at home
21	19	2.11	21	nil	Won their last two away matches to take the title by one point
31	20	2.07	21	1	First to win the championships of Division Two and Division One successively
34	14	1.94	27	nil	Did not drop a point at home until their last against Sheffield United
29	21	2.13	25	nil	Finished nine points ahead of their nearest rivals Aston Villa
21	24	1.71	25	1	Record points despite losing 9–1 at home to Sunderland in December
23	17	2.21	18	nil	Mid-season spell of 15 games without defeat and were five points clear
22	20	1.89	26	nil	Title clinched on last day with 5–1 home win over Sunderland
33	17	1.57	21	nil	The 10 goals conceded at home were a better ratio than previously attained
26	24	2.26	22	1	New points record after failing to win one of the first seven games
27	19	2.05	21	1	Led from the start; Danny Shea scored 27 Division One goals
18	25	2.00	24	nil	Bob Parker scored 35 goals but lowest points total for 12 years
26	25	2.47	18	1	New record points and nine ahead of Burnley. First to over a century of goals
20	22	1.88	23	1	Record of thirty matches without defeat from 6 September to 26 March
21	23	1.50	22	2	Kept their goal intact in 17 matches and led by six points
18	23	1.66	19	3	Only 31 goals conceded and on 21 occasions prevented opposition from scoring
24	22	1.42	22	1	Closest finish only .024 of a goal in front of Cardiff City
18	30	1.64	22	nil	Did not concede more than two goals in any one match in their two point lead
43	23	2.19	24	nil	Third consecutive title. George Brown scored 25 League goals
38	17	2.28	21	3	Record 19 hone wins for champions. Hughie Gallacher scored 36 goals
38	23	2.42	24	2	William Ralph 'Dixie' Dean scored a League record 60 goals in 39 games
46	13	2.04	22	4	Only three matches won away the poorest for a title winning team
37	26	2.50	22	1	Division One record 105 goals and ten points ahead of runners-up

Season Ending	Champions	Matches	Points	W	D	L	F	A	Pts	W	D	L	F
1931	ARSENAL	42	66	14	5	2	67	27	33	14	5	2	60
1932	EVERTON	42	56	18	0	3	84	30	36	8	4	9	32
1933	ARSENAL	42	58	14	3	4	70	27	31	11	5	5	48
1934	ARSENAL	42	59	15	4	2	45	19	34	10	5	6	30
1935	ARSENAL	42	58	15	4	2	74	17	34	8	8	5	41
1936	SUNDERLAND	42	56	17	2	2	71	33	36	8	4	9	38
1937	MANCHESTER CITY	42	57	15	5	1	56	22	35	7	8	6	51
1938	ARSENAL	42	52	15	4	2	52	16	34	6	6	9	25
1939	EVERTON	42	59	17	3	1	60	18	37	10	2	9	28
No National competition 1940, 1941, 1942, 1943, 1944, 1945 or 1946 regional leagues in operation													
1947	LIVERPOOL	42	57	13	3	5	42	24	29	12	4	5	42
1948	ARSENAL	42	52	15	3	3	56	15	33	8	10	3	25
1949	PORTSMOUTH	42	58	18	3	0	52	12	39	7	5	9	32
1950	PORTSMOUTH	42	56	12	7	2	44	15	31	10	2	9	30
1951	TOTTENHAM HOTSPUR	42	60	17	2	2	54	21	36	8	8	5	28
1952	MANCHESTER UNITED	42	57	15	3	3	55	21	33	8	8	5	40
1953	ARSENAL	42	54	15	3	3	60	30	33	6	9	6	37
1954	WOLVERHAMPTON WANDERERS	42	57	16	1	4	61	25	33	9	6	6	35
1955	CHELSEA	42	52	11	5	5	43	29	27	9	7	5	38
1956	MANCHESTER UNITED	42	60	18	3	0	51	20	39	7	7	7	32
1957	MANCHESTER UNITED	42	64	14	4	3	55	25	32	14	4	3	48
1958	WOLVERHAMPTON WANDERERS	42	64	17	3	1	60	21	37	11	5	5	43
1959	WOLVERHAMPTON WANDERERS	42	61	15	3	3	68	19	33	13	2	6	42
1960	BURNLEY	42	55	15	2	4	52	28	32	9	5	7	33
1961	TOTTENHAM HOTSPUR	42	66	15	3	3	65	28	33	16	1	4	50
1962	IPSWICH TOWN	42	56	17	2	2	58	28	36	7	6	8	35
1963	EVERTON	42	61	14	7	0	48	17	35	11	4	6	36
1964	LIVERPOOL	42	57	16	0	5	60	18	32	10	5	6	32
1965	MANCHESTER UNITED	42	61	16	4	1	52	13	36	10	5	6	37
1966	LIVERPOOL	42	61	17	2	2	52	15	36	9	7	5	27
1967	MANCHESTER UNITED	42	60	17	4	0	51	13	38	7	8	6	33
1968	MANCHESTER CITY	42	58	17	2	2	52	16	36	9	4	8	34
1969	LEEDS UNITED	42	67	18	3	0	41	9	39	9	10	2	25
1970	EVERTON	42	66	17	3	1	46	19	37	12	5	4	26
1971	ARSENAL	42	65	18	3	0	41	6	39	11	4	6	30
1972	DERBY COUNTY	42	58	16	4	1	43	10	36	8	6	7	26
1973	LIVERPOOL	42	60	17	3	1	45	19	37	8	7	6	27
1974	LEEDS UNITED	42	62	12	8	1	38	18	32	12	6	3	28
1975	DERBY COUNTY	42	53	14	4	3	41	18	32	7	7	7	26
1976	LIVERPOOL	42	60	14	5	2	41	21	33	9	9	3	25
1977	LIVERPOOL	42	57	18	3	0	47	11	39	5	8	8	15
1978	NOTTINGHAM FOREST	42	64	15	6	0	37	8	36	10	8	3	32

SUCCESS SEQUENCES
(Other Teams)

Liverpool were unbeaten in all 28 matches (winning 22, drawing 6) in Division Two during the 1893–94 season. They also won their 29th match, the extra 'Test Match' (used to decide promotion and relegation between the top two divisions) and the first two matches of the 1894–95 season in Division One before losing 2–1 to Aston Villa on 8 September 1894. In all there had been 31 games without defeat. They were the first club to win the Division Two championship without losing.

Plymouth Argyle did not lose on their own ground at Home Park between 25 March 1921 and 25 August 1923 during a sequence of 50 League and Cup matches (47 Division Three (Southern Section) games and three F.A. Cup ties).

Stockport did not lose on their own ground at Edgeley Park between 2 April 1927 and 5 October 1929 during a sequence of 51 League and Cup matches (48 Division Three (Northern Section) games and three F.A. Cup ties).

Reading did not lose on their own ground at Elm Park between 8 April 1933 and 15 January 1936 during a sequence of 55 Division Three (Southern Section) matches.

A	Pts	Goal Average	No of Players	Ever Present	Facts and Feats
32	33	3.02	22	1	Record 66 points but their 127 goals was one fewer than Villa's total
34	20	2.76	20	nil	Had a run of 10 undefeated matches after losing twice to runners-up Arsenal
34	27	2.80	23	1	Cliff Bastin's 33 goals set a Division One record for an outside forward
28	25	1.78	24	1	Highbury's attendance record was twice broken first at 68,828 then 69,070
29	24	2.73	25	nil	Third successive title. Crowds soared to 70,544 and 73,295
41	20	2.59	23	2	Raich Carter and Bob Gurney each scored 31 goals; the last such Division One feat
39	22	2.54	22	4	Only ninth in January they were unbeaten in their last 22 matches
28	18	1.83	29	nil	Unusually high number of team changes and only one point clear
34	22	2.09	22	1	Everton won their first six matches. Tommy Lawton scored 35 goals
28	28	2.00	26	nil	Defeat for Stoke gave the title to Liverpool who had completed their programme
17	26	1.92	19	2	Unbeaten in their first 17 matches and led from opening day's programme
30	19	2.00	18	2	Champions without internationals, seven players made 40 or more appearances
23	22	1.76	25	2	Clinched the title on the last day of the season by .393 of goal average
23	24	1.95	19	2	Took the lead in December and lost only one of their last 12 matches
31	24	2.26	24	1	Defeated Arsenal, who also had an outside chance, 6–1 in last game
34	21	2.30	21	nil	Won last game 3–2 and the title by one tenth of a goal from Preston
31	24	2.28	22	1	First club to achieve the championships of three divisions
28	25	1.92	20	2	Eighth at half-way stage they only established themselves in April
31	21	1.97	24	1	Equalled record of 11 points margin. Undefeated in last 14 games
29	32	2.45	24	nil	Points total highest for 26 years and won the title by eight points
26	27	2.45	21	nil	Had a run of 18 undefeated matches between September and December
30	28	2.61	22	nil	Were unbeaten in last 13 games in which they collected 23 points
33	23	2.02	18	3	Never led until they won their last match away to Manchester City
27	33	2.73	17	4	Equalled points record; won record first 11 matches; achieved the 'double'
39	20	2.21	16	3	Regular side cost under £30,000 and were paid approximately £25 a week
25	26	2.00	20	2	£300,000 side unbeaten at home and watched there by 1,120,888
27	25	2.19	17	3	Recovered from an indifferent start with nine points from nine matches
26	25	2.11	18	4	Achieved the title only by .686 of a goal from Leeds United
19	25	1.88	14	5	Nine players appeared in 40 or more matches. Arsenal's seven titles equalled
32	22	2.00	20	2	Unbeaten in their last 20 matches in which they registered 31 points
27	22	2.04	21	1	Did not top Division until 29 April and won last four League matches
17	28	1.57	17	4	Lowest goals total since Offside Law changed. Highest ever points
15	29	1.71	17	4	Had a nine points winning margin and beat all opposition at least once
23	26	1.69	16	3	With ten games left were six points behind leaders but achieved 'double'
23	22	1.64	16	2	Began with 12 undefeated games and won by a point after three others faltered
23	23	1.71	16	3	Equalled Arsenal's eight championship titles. Only one home match lost
13	30	1.57	20	2	Started with a record 29 games without defeat and won by five points
31	21	1.59	16	2	An ever changing leadership and the lowest points total for 20 years
10	27	1.57	19	2	Won their final game at Wolves for a record ninth title
22	18	1.47	17	3	Only unbeaten home side and point from last game, but one provided no 10
16	28	1.64	16	1	Unbeaten after 19 November and won by seven points

Millwall were undefeated in the first 19 matches of the 1959–60 season in Division Four. They also hold the Football League record for the longest home run without defeat. After losing their last match of 1963–64 season at The Den they were unbeaten in 59 consecutive League games on their own ground before losing 2–1 to Plymouth Argyle on 14 January 1967.

Gillingham did not lose on their own ground at Priestfield Stadium between 6 April 1963 and 10 April 1965 during a sequence of 52 League and Cup matches (48 Division Four games, three League Cup matches and one in the F.A. Cup).

In the 1928–29 season Cardiff City had one of the best defences in Division One, yet they were relegated. Indeed they conceded fewer goals than any other side in their division. Unfortunately they could not score goals themselves.

Whereas Aston Villa, the top scoring side in the division scored 98 goals in third place, Cardiff's total was only 43. But they conceded only 59 goals which was two less than the next best defensive record.

Cardiff's defence that season included Irish international Tom Farquharson, 13 years a first choice goalkeeper for them in the period between the two world wars, while they also had in centre-forward and captain Fred Keenor capped

32 times by Wales. Alas, this particular Cardiff side lacked goal-scoring opportunists. Yet it is rare for a side to concede fewer goals than any other but still finish at the bottom of their division.

The highest number of consecutive F.A. Cup-ties completed by a single club without defeat was recorded by Blackburn Rovers between December 1883 and December 1886 when they had a sequence of 24 such matches. In 1881–82 they played 35 matches without defeat before losing 1–0 to Old Etonians in the 1882 F.A. Cup Final.

Bristol Rovers were undefeated between 31 March 1973 and 2 February 1974 during a sequence of 32 Division Three matches. It included 27 from the start of the 1973–74 season. They had also gone 27 without defeat in 1952–53.

Bury equalled the achievement of Preston North End by winning the F.A. Cup in 1902–03 without conceding a goal in five matches for a goal record of 12–0. Preston's total for 1888–89 was 11–0 from five matches.

Bradford City achieved the highest number of consecutive F.A. Cup ties without a goal being conceded when they played 12 matches in the 1910–11 and 1911–12 seasons.

Port Vale prevented their opponents from scoring in 30 of their 42 Division Three (Northern Section) matches in 1953–54.

Millwall did not concede a goal in 11 consecutive matches during their Division Three (Southern Section) programme during 1925–26. York City also did not concede a goal in 11 consecutive Division Three matches during 1973–74 season.

Tottenham Hotspur won their first eleven Division One matches in the 1960–61 season, a Football League record for a start to a League programme. Their effort was stopped on 10 October 1960 when Manchester United held them to a 1–1 draw.

Aston Villa were responsible for the most consecutive Football League matches any team ever played without a 0–0 draw. They fulfilled 170 such fixtures in Division One between goalless games against Manchester United on 27 August 1928 and Liverpool on 10 September 1932.

Between 25 October and 13 December inclusive in 1969 Torquay United played eight Division Three drawn games in a row, an all-time record for any Football League club.

No other team experienced such a blank period before its first Football League away goal in a season as Exeter City did in the 1923–24 season. It was scored at Swindon on 16 February in the team's fourteenth Division Three (Southern Section) away match of the season.

During one period of the 1946–47 season Sunderland actually lost seven Division One home matches in succession, yet during the same time they won five, lost only three, and drew one of nine away games.

LEAGUE JOTTINGS

London has not been without Division One football since 1904 and Manchester since 1903, but neither can match Liverpool's distinction that since the Football League's 1888 formation the city has had at least one club in the premier grade every season.

Bolton Wanderers, Burnley and Everton are the only clubs which have played in the Football League in every season, including both war periods, since its 1888 inception. The only clubs which have not failed to figure in the F.A. Cup competition proper during that time have been Aston Villa, Blackburn Rovers, Derby County, Nottingham Forest, Notts County, Preston North End, Sheffield Wednesday and Wolverhampton Wanderers.

The Football League has always been indulgent to new clubs which have to seek re-election. The following clubs had to ask to be voted back at the end of their first season, and in every case a reprieve was granted: Orient, Bournemouth, Brentford, Gillingham, Halifax Town, Rochdale, Torquay United and Workington.

Burton-on-Trent is the only Provincial city or town which used to have two Football League clubs at the same time, but now has none. Burton United were in Division Two from 1892–93 to 1906–07 inclusive, and Burton Wanderers were in Division Two with them from 1894–95 to 1896–97.

The record for Football League appearances is the 824 by Terry Paine for Southampton and Hereford United, 1957 to 1977.

Everton was the first club to draw a home gate of over 40,000 for a Football League game. The occasion was the first League derby with Liverpool on 13 October 1894, Liverpool having been promoted to Division One the previous season. Nearly 44,000 paid £1,026 to see an exciting game which Everton won 3–0, a score which did not give a fair reflection of the closeness of the game. Everton had one of the most powerful sides in the country at this time, finishing runners-up to Sunderland that season.

Notts County was the first club to have a point deducted for playing an ineligible player in a Division One game. The player in question was their amateur centre-forward Tinsley Lindley who had appeared in their team against Aston Villa on 9 November 1889 when he was still not properly registered. Notts County, however, appealed against the League's decision and had it reversed although they were forced to pay a £30 fine instead.

The question of playing unregistered players was causing the Football League much consternation at this time and the Notts County case prompted them to introduce a rule whereby the offence would automatically mean the deduction of two points. Sunderland were the first to fall foul of this decision when some 10 months later they had two points deducted from their total as well as being fined £50 for playing Scottish international Ned Doig in their side against West Bromwich Albion before the player had completed the qualifying period of 14 days registration, the rule at that time.

The first club to climb from Division Three to Division One was Portsmouth who were promoted to Division Two in 1924 and to Division One three years later. The star of this rapid rise was Billy 'Farmer' Haines from Frome, one of the most popular and consistent goalscorers the club has ever had. When they were promoted to Division Two in 1923–24 Haines scored 28 League goals and would have achieved more but for an injury which kept him out of the side for several games.

In one remarkable match at Wolverhampton during the next season he scored his hat-trick in the last six minutes and Portsmouth won 5–0. When promotion was gained to Division One in the 1926–27 season it was a tight squeeze and on the last day Portsmouth just pipped Manchester City on goal average despite City winning their final game 8–0 against Bradford City. Portsmouth finished their programme with a 5–1 win over Preston North End with Haines getting four goals to bring his total for the season to 40 League goals, which remains a club record.

Among current Division One members Arsenal is the only club which did not gain its place by promotion from Division Two. They finished sixth in that division in 1914–15, but were elected to Division One when the competition was resumed in 1919 after the first World War and the two divisions extended by the addition of two clubs each.

Originally it had been thought that the League would favour the bottom two clubs of Division One in 1915, Chelsea and Spurs, and return them to the upper division along with the top two of Division Two, Derby County and Preston North End. But Sir Henry Norris, the Arsenal Chairman, so successfully canvassed every member of the Management Committee and also gained the full support of the League President, John McKenna, that when it came to the vote Arsenal were preferred to Tottenham Hotspur. This surprise did nothing to improve the strained relationship between these two North London clubs at the time.

No other player ever contributed to so many Division One championship titles as George Male. As Arsenal's right-back he played with them in six seasons when they were champions: 1930–31, 1932–33, 1933–34, 1934–35, 1937–38 and 1947–48.

On the evening of 2 April 1949 Southampton led Division Two by eight points but they failed to gain promotion at the end of the season.

THE LEAGUE'S GREATEST RIVALRY

Everton v Liverpool

Everton were founded in 1878 as St. Domingo Church Sunday School team, becoming Everton the following year. Liverpool came into being in 1892 following a split which led to the Everton club moving from Anfield to Goodison Park.

In League matches the results at Goodison have been (Everton score first):

Season	Score	Season	Score
1894–95	3–0	1931–32	2–1
1896–97	2–1	1932–33	3–1
1897–98	3–0	1933–34	0–0
1898–99	1–2	1934–35	1–0
1899–1900	3–1	1935–36	0–0
1900–01	1–1	1936–37	2–0
1901–02	4–0	1937–38	1–3
1902–03	3–1	1938–39	2–1
1903–04	5–2	1946–47	1–0
1905–06	4–2	1947–48	0–3
1906–07	0–0	1948–49	1–1
1907–08	2–4	1949–50	0–0
1908–09	5–0	1950–51	1–3
1909–10	2–3	1962–63	2–2
1910–11	0–1	1963–64	3–1
1911–12	2–1	1964–65	2–1
1912–13	0–2	1965–66	0–0
1913–14	1–2	1966–67	3–1
1914–15	1–3	1967–68	1–0
1919–20	0–0	1968–69	0–0
1920–21	0–3	1969–70	0–3
1921–22	1–1	1970–71	0–0
1922–23	0–1	1971–72	1–0
1923–24	1–0	1972–73	0–2
1924–25	0–1	1973–74	0–1
1925–26	3–3	1974–75	0–0
1926–27	1–0	1975–76	0–0
1927–28	1–1	1976–77	0–0
1928–29	1–0	1977–78	0–1
1929–30	3–3		

At Anfield the results have been (Liverpool score first):

Season	Score	Season	Score
1894–95	2–2	1931–32	1–3
1896–97	0–0	1932–33	7–4
1897–98	3–1	1933–34	3–2
1898–99	2–0	1934–35	2–1
1899–1900	1–2	1935–36	6–0
1900–01	1–2	1936–37	3–2
1901–02	2–2	1937–38	1–2
1902–03	0–0	1938–39	0–3
1903–04	2–2	1946–47	0–0
1905–06	1–1	1947–48	4–0
1906–07	1–2	1948–49	0–0
1907–08	0–0	1949–50	3–1
1908–09	0–1	1950–51	0–2
1909–10	0–1	1962–63	0–0
1910–11	0–2	1963–64	2–1
1911–12	1–3	1964–65	0–4
1912–13	0–2	1965–66	5–0
1913–14	1–2	1966–67	0–0
1914–15	0–5	1967–68	1–0
1919–20	3–1	1968–69	1–1
1920–21	1–0	1969–70	0–2
1921–22	1–1	1970–71	3–2
1922–23	5–1	1971–72	4–0
1923–24	1–2	1972–73	1–0
1924–25	3–1	1973–74	0–0
1925–26	5–1	1974–75	0–0
1926–27	1–0	1975–76	1–0
1927–28	3–3	1976–77	3–1
1928–29	1–2	1977–78	0–0
1929–30	0–3		

Overall Record

EVERTON	43	WINS
LIVERPOOL	40	WINS
DRAWN	35	
TOTAL	118	

LEAGUE POINTS

Most points in single season

Leeds United achieved 67 points in 42 Division One matches in 1968–69. They managed only 66 goals, the lowest score at the time by a championship winning side since the Offside Law was changed in 1925. But the 26 goals conceded was the best for League champions in a 42-match programme. Leeds lost only two League games, which was another record. They were also unbeaten in their last 28 matches, 14 of them played away.

Tottenham Hotspur achieved 70 points in 42 Division Two matches in 1919–20. They won their first seven matches and only suffered their initial defeat in the thirteenth at Bury on 8 November. They were also unbeaten at home where only two visitors escaped with a point. Tottenham failed to score in only two matches from a total of 102 goals.

Aston Villa achieved 70 points in 46 Division Three matches in 1971–72. Their most successful spell came from mid-January to mid-March when an unbeaten run produced 19 points out of a possible 22. Their 32 wins was also a record for the division, with 20 of these successes coming at home.

Nottingham Forest achieved 70 points in 46 Division Three (Southern Section) matches in 1950–51. Their 110 goals established a club record, while the 30 wins was also a record for the division. Wally Ardron set up a club record with 35 goals.

Bristol City also achieved 70 points in 46 Division Three (Southern Section) matches in 1954–55. They were champions, nine points ahead of Leyton Orient. And of their 101 goals, John Atyeo scored 28 and Jimmy Rogers 25 goals. City also set up a record of 30 wins for the division. Yet Orient had actually led the division in mid-season.

Doncaster Rovers achieved 72 points in 42 Division Three (Northern Section) matches in 1946–47. They completed the double of home and away wins over twelve of their rivals. Five players between them collected 109 of the club's 123 League goals, with Clarrie Jordan top scorer with 41. Two other division records were achieved with 33 wins and only three defeats.

Lincoln City achieved 74 points in 46 Division Four matches in 1975–76. They also set up a record of 32 wins and only four defeats. They had two unbeaten runs of 14 matches; the first from mid-October to the end of the season. Their 111 goals was the first three-figure total in the League since 1966–67. Only once however did the side reach as many as six goals.

Fewest points in single season

Leeds United achieved only 18 points in 42 Division One matches 1946–47. Six matches were won, all at home, and only one draw was achieved away and that to Brentford, the side who were relegated with Leeds but had achieved seven more points than United.

Queen's Park Rangers achieved only 18 points in 42 Division One matches in 1968–69. They had won promotion from Division Two for the first time the previous season. During the 1968–69 term they equalled their heaviest defeat when beaten 8–1 by Manchester United on 19 March 1969. Their four wins all came at home and only three points were derived away. And they finished 12 points beneath the second from bottom club Leicester City.

Glossop achieved only 18 points in 34 Division One matches in 1899–1900. It was their only season in the division and they won just four matches. The club resigned from the League after the war in 1919.

Notts County achieved only 18 points in 34 Division One matches in 1904–05. They won only five matches but despite finishing bottom were re-elected to Division One on its extension to 20 clubs.

Woolwich Arsenal achieved only 18 points in 38 Division One matches in 1912–13. They won only three matches. They did not win promotion to Division One but were elected to it on the extension to 22 clubs in 1919.

Doncaster Rovers achieved only eight points in 34 matches in Division Two in 1904–05. Their nearest rivals were 12 points away. They were not re-elected. Originally they gained admission in 1901 but dropped out two years later only to be re-elected in 1904. Subsequently they returned to the League as members of Division Three (Northern Section) in 1923.

Loughborough Town achieved only eight points in 34 Division Two matches in 1899–1900. They won only one match and were not re-elected. They conceded 100 goals. Yet the previous season they had beaten Darwen 10–0 for their highest scoring victory.

Rochdale achieved only 21 points in 46 Division Three matches in 1973–74. They won only twice, including once away in September. In February a home match with Cambridge United attracted only 450 spectators.

Merthyr Town achieved only 21 points in 42 Division Three (Southern Section) matches in 1924–25 and equalled this figure in 1929–30. They won eight matches in the former season suffering 29 defeats but only six in the latter when they conceded a record 135 goals and were not re-elected.

Queen's Park Rangers achieved only 21 points in 42 matches in Division Three (Southern Section) in 1925–26. Their nearest rivals were 14 points above them.

Rochdale achieved only 11 points in 40 matches in Division Three (Northern Section) in 1931–32. They suffered 33 defeats, including 17 in succession. They also suffered a record 13 consecutive home defeats after beating New Brighton 3–2 on 7 November 1931. Wigan Borough's withdrawal from the League meant only 40 matches were played that season.

Workington achieved only 19 points in 46 matches in Division Four in 1976–77. Only two points came from their last 13 games and 102 goals were conceded. They finished bottom six points behind their nearest rivals and were not re-elected.

LEAGUE GOALS

Fewest goals conceded in single season
Liverpool conceded only 24 goals in 42 Division One matches in 1968–69 and equalled this feat in 1970–71. But though they had been runners-up to Leeds United in the former season with 61 points they could only finish fifth in the latter term with ten fewer points. In both seasons they conceded only ten goals at home and 14 away, while they did not let in more than two goals in any one match.

Nottingham Forest conceded only 24 goals in 42 Division One matches in 1977–78. They were champions, seven points ahead of Liverpool. They conceded only eight goals at home and 16 away and kept a clean sheet in 25 games overall.

Manchester United conceded only 23 goals in 42 Division Two matches in 1924–25. Only a late revival in which they took as many points in their last six matches as they had achieved in the previous 11, enabled them to gain promotion in second place. Significantly they drew their last match at Barnsley 0–0.

Southampton conceded 21 goals in 42 Division Three (Southern Section) matches in 1921–22. They were champions and promoted but with two matches remaining Plymouth Argyle had led them by four points. However, while Southampton won twice, Plymouth lost their last two games and were edged out on goal average.

Port Vale conceded 21 goals in 46 Division Three (Northern Section) matches in 1953–54. The three games they lost also established a record for fewest defeats. Only five goals were conceded at home in four matches. Port Vale kept a clean sheet in 30 games overall. And in winning the championship they had an 11 point lead over Barnsley the runners-up.

Bristol Rovers conceded 33 goals in 46 Division Three matches in 1973–74. Though they were top after completing their programme, Oldham Athletic overtook them and York City were level on 61 points with an inferior goal average. Rovers had managed only 12 points from their last 12 matches after 42 from the first 27 games.

Peterborough United conceded 33 goals in 46 Division Three matches in 1977–78. Seven of these came in two matches at the end of the season and cost them promotion as they finished fourth with an inferior goal difference, to Preston North End.

Gillingham conceded 30 goals in 46 Division Four matches in 1963–64. They were champions on goal average despite the fact that they scored only 59 goals, one more than Carlisle United had actually conceded. Carlisle scored 113 themselves but Gillingham were divisional champions by ·018 of a goal.

Fewest goals scored in single season

Leicester City scored only 26 goals in 42 Division One matches in 1977–78. Three goals on one occasion was their highest total. They failed to score at all in 23 matches. They finished bottom, with an inferior goal difference to Newcastle United and ten points beneath the third relegated club West Ham United.

Watford scored only 24 goals in 42 Division Two matches in 1971–72. They also failed to score more than two goals in any one match and did not score at all in 23. In the second half of the season they achieved only six goals in 21 matches.

Crystal Palace scored only 33 goals in 42 Division Three (Southern Section) matches in 1950–51. Though they reached four goals on two occasions, they failed to score at all in 24 games.

Crewe Alexandra scored only 32 goals in 42 Division Three (Northern Section) matches in 1923–24. They did however manage to achieve 27 points, two more than the bottom two clubs.

Stockport County scored only 27 goals in 46 Division Three matches in 1969–70. Three goals on one occasion was their highest total. They failed to score at all in 25 matches. They finished bottom, seven points beneath their nearest rivals Barrow.

Bradford (Park Avenue) scored only 30 goals in 46 Division Four matches in 1967–68. They did not score more than two goals in any one match and failed to score at all in 22. They won four matches and drew 15 but finished bottom, eight points beneath their nearest rivals Workington.

Workington scored only 30 goals in 46 Division Four matches in 1975–76. Three goals on one occasion was their highest score. In fact five goals came in their last two matches, both of which were away, their only wins on travel. They failed to score at all in 23 matches and they finished bottom.

Most goals scored in single season (Team)

Aston Villa scored 128 goals in 42 Division One matches during 1930–31. They scored in every home match and failed in only three away. Eighty-six goals came at home and in 20 games overall four goals or more were recorded. At Villa Park, Middlesbrough were beaten 8–1; Manchester United 7–0; Huddersfield Town 6–1 and Arsenal 5–1. Villa also won 6–1 at Huddersfield and 4–0 at Birmingham. Top scorer was Pongo Waring with 49 goals, while Eric Houghton had 30. Yet Villa could only finish runners-up, seven points behind Arsenal the champions.

Middlesbrough scored 122 goals in 42 Division Two matches during 1926–27. On three occasions they scored seven goals: against Portsmouth and Swansea at home and also at Grimsby, while they managed six on two other occasions. Portsmouth in fact finished eight points behind them but were also promoted. Yet Middlesbrough took only one point and scored just one goal in their first four League matches. In the fourth they brought in George Camsell who ended the season as their top scorer with 59 goals. His total included eight hat-tricks.

Millwall scored 127 goals in 42 Division Three (Southern Section) matches in 1927–28. Unbeaten at home where they dropped only two points, Millwall also won 11 times away and finished ten points ahead of second placed Northampton Town. Millwall achieved 9–1 wins against Torquay United and Coventry City as well as scoring seven goals once and six on four occasions including once away. However, they themselves were also beaten 5–0 and 6–1 away.

Bradford City scored 128 goals in 42 Division Three (Northern Section) matches in 1928–29. They managed double figures in their opening League game at home to Rotherham United whom they defeated 11–1, in what proved to be the club's record victory. Promotion was not decided until the last match of the season, however, with Stockport County finishing one point behind them. Top scorer Albert Whitehurst, secured during the season, was leading scorer with 24 goals in only 15 matches, including seven in succession against Tranmere Rovers on 6 March 1929 in an 8–0 win.

City not only habitually scored more goals than the opposition but they were so often in total command that they prevented their opponents from scoring. In one run of five League games during March that season they reached a total of 29 goals without reply in this sequence: 8–0, 8–0, 5–0, 5–0 and 3–0. Indeed, around this period this astonishing team netted 43 goals in 12 games during which they conceded only two goals and not more than one in a particular game. Yet the club had faced liquidation at the end of the previous season and was almost wound up.

Queen's Park Rangers scored 111 goals in 46 Division Three matches in 1961–62. But they could only finish no higher than fourth place and Bournemouth who were third edged them out on goal average despite scoring 42 goals fewer.

Peterborough United scored 134 goals in 46 Division Four matches in 1960–61. Seven goals were reached twice, six on four occasions including once away at Stockport, who were ironically the only side to prevent Peterborough from scoring at home during the season. Terry Bly was top scorer with 52 League goals, a record for the division. The second best supported team in the division at home with an average of 14,222, Peterborough produced the highest support away with 12,182 on average in their first season in the Football League.

Most goals against in single season (Team)

Blackpool conceded 125 goals in 42 Division One matches during 1930–31. Their heaviest defeat, 10–1, a club record, was against Huddersfield Town on 13 December 1930. Seven goals were conceded on three occasions, including at home to Leeds United in a 7–3 defeat. But Blackpool escaped relegation by one point, finishing above Leeds. The previous season they had won promotion as Division Two champions with record points and goals.

Darwen conceded 141 goals in 34 Division Two matches during 1898–99. It proved the last season in the club's eventful eight season League history and they suffered three 10–0 defeats away, gathering only nine points from a possible 68 and were not re-elected.

Merthyr Town conceded 135 goals in 42 Division Three (Southern Section) matches in 1929–30. They were bottom, nine points beneath their nearest rivals. Coventry City still have the cheque they received as their share of the receipts from a midweek match at Merthyr's Penydarren Park in April 1930 which amounted to 18s 4d (92p). Merthyr were not re-elected in what was their third plea for re-admission. Between September 1922 and September 1925 they had created a Football League record with a run of 61 away games without a win. And in 1924–25 they suffered 29 defeats overall in 42 matches, a record for the division.

Nelson conceded 136 goals in 42 Division Three (Northern Section) matches in 1927–28. These included conceding nine goals in one match, eight in another and seven in a third. But they had had their own scoring successes earlier. In 1924–25 they scored seven on two occasions, while in their most prolific season 1926–27 a total of 104 goals included two more scores of seven. In 1925–26 they also scored seven goals in successive games.

Accrington Stanley conceded 123 goals in 46 Division Three matches in 1959–60. But only once did they concede as many as six goals. And they took more points (14) from away matches than at home.

Hartlepools United conceded 109 goals in 46 Division Four matches in 1959–60. Seven goals were conceded once and six on two occasions.

LEAGUE WINS

Most wins in single season

Tottenham Hotspur won 31 of their 42 Division One matches in 1960–61. They finished eight points ahead of Sheffield Wednesday to win the championship with 66 points. Of their 115 goals all but 14 from their most regularly called upon five forwards. The same season they achieved the League and Cup double, the third team to accomplish the feat. Only four other sides have scored more goals in the history of Division One.

Tottenham Hotspur also won 32 of their 42 Division Two matches in 1919–20. Nineteen of these came from home wins but it was a 3–1 win at Stoke on 10 April that ensured the club of winning the championship.

Plymouth Argyle won 30 of their 42 Division Three (Southern Section) matches in 1929–30. They had finished as runners-up six times in succession during the previous eight seasons. But not until the 19th match did they lose and their total of 68 points was a club record. Yet they started the season £6,000 in debt.

Millwall won 30 of their 42 Division Three (Southern Section) matches in 1927–28. Nineteen of these came from home wins where only two points were dropped in drawn matches.

Cardiff City won 30 of their 42 Division Three (Southern Section) matches in 1946–47. Eighteen of these came from home wins where just three points were dropped in drawn matches. Only 11 goals were conceded at home.

Nottingham Forest won 30 of their 46 Division Three (Southern Section) matches in 1950–51. Sixteen of these came from home wins. Only six matches were lost overall and ten drawn. The club also achieved a record 70 points and a record total of 110 goals. Thirty-two points were contributed from away matches.

Bristol City also won 30 of their 46 Division Three (Southern Section) matches in 1954–55. Thirteen came from away wins. The club also achieved a record 70 points.

Doncaster Rovers won 33 of their 42 Division Three (Northern Section) matches in 1946–47. They won 18 away matches, taking 37 points, lost only three times overall and established a record 72 points.

Aston Villa won 32 of their 46 Division Three matches in 1971–72. Twenty matches were won at home including 11 consecutively between October and March.

Lincoln City won 32 of their 46 Division Four matches in 1975–76. Twenty-one of these came from home wins. Only two points were dropped in drawn games on their own ground. The club also set records for most wins, most points and fewest defeats in a season in the division.

Record home wins in single season

Brentford won all 21 games in Division Three (Southern Section) in 1929–30.

Record away wins in single season

Doncaster won 18 of 21 games in Division Three (Northern Section) in 1946–47.

Most drawn games in single season

Tranmere Rovers drew 22 of their 46 Division Three matches in 1970–71. They finished 18th in the division, drawing 11 times at home and 11 away in gaining 42 points.

Aldershot drew 22 of their 46 Division Four matches in 1971–72. They drew 13 at home, nine away and finished 17th in the division with 40 points.

Chester drew 22 of their 46 Division Three matches in 1977–78. They drew eight at home, 14 away and finished fifth in the division with 54 points.

LEAGUE DEFEATS

Most defeats in single season

Leeds United suffered 30 defeats in 42 Division One matches in 1946–47. Ten came from home matches and 20 away. Only six matches were won all at home.

Blackburn Rovers suffered 30 defeats in 42 Division One matches in 1965–66. Fourteen came from home matches and 16 away. Eight matches were won and they included 6–1 and 5–0 wins at home and 4–1 and 3–0 successes away.

Tranmere Rovers suffered 31 defeats in 42 Division Two matches in 1938–39. They finished 14 points beneath their nearest rivals and picked up only one point from away games.

Newport County suffered 31 defeats in 46 Division Three matches in 1961–62. Twelve of these came from home matches. Their heaviest defeat was 8–1 at Notts County.

Merthyr Town suffered 29 defeats in 42 Division Three (Southern Section) matches in 1924–25. Their 21 points was a record low for the division.

Rochdale suffered 33 defeats in 40 Division Three (Northern Section) matches in 1931–32. Only 11 points were taken, including just one away from home. 135 goals were conceded and their nearest rivals were 13 points above them.

Workington suffered 32 defeats in 46 Division Four matches in 1975–76. Fourteen of these came from home matches and only 21 points were achieved. The record would have been worse but for the club recording their only two away wins in the last two games of the season.

Fewest defeats in single season

Preston North End went through 22 Division One matches in 1888–89 without a defeat. Only four points were dropped, including just one at home to Aston Villa on 10 November, the runners-up who finished 11 points behind them.

Leeds United suffered only two defeats in 42 Division One matches in 1968–69. These occurred on 28 September at Manchester City when they lost 3–1 and at Burnley on 19 October when they were beaten 5–1. After this defeat Leeds had a run of 28 undefeated matches until the end of the season.

Liverpool went through 28 Division Two matches without defeat in 1893–94. They won 22 and drew six of their matches. They then won their test match for promotion and drew the first two games of the following season to establish a run of 31 matches without defeat.

Burnley suffered only two defeats in 30 Division Two matches in 1897–98. They won 20 and drew eight of their games. Included among the 80 goals they scored was a 9–3 victory over Loughborough Town.

Bristol City suffered only two defeats in 38 Division Two matches in 1905–06. They won 30 and drew six of their matches. Thirty-one of their points came from away matches which produced 13 wins and five draws. They also won 14 consecutive League matches.

Leeds United suffered only three defeats in 42 Division Two matches in 1963–64. They won 24 matches which was one fewer than runners-up Sunderland who finished two points below them.

Queen's Park Rangers suffered five defeats in 46 Division Three matches in 1966–67. They won 26 and drew 15 of their matches. They finished 12 points ahead of runners-up Middlesbrough and scored 103 goals while conceding only 38. The same season they won the League Cup.

Southampton suffered only four defeats in 42 Division Three (Southern Section) matches in 1921–22. They conceded just 21 goals, a record for the division. Their 61 points was also a club record. Among their wins was an 8–0 success over Northampton Town. However they won 23 matches, two fewer than Plymouth Argyle who finished as runners-up on goal average behind them.

Plymouth Argyle suffered only four defeats in 42 Division Three (Southern Section) matches in 1929–30. Their 68 points was a club record. They conceded only 38 goals and won 30 of their matches.

Port Vale suffered only three defeats in 46 Division Three (Northern Section) matches in 1953–54. They won 26 matches and drew 17 two figures which were better than those of any of their rivals and they finished 11 points ahead of Barnsley, the runners-up.

Doncaster Rovers suffered only three defeats in 42 Division Three (Northern Section) matches in 1946–47. Of their record 33 wins, 18 came away and they established a record of 72 points as well.

Wolverhampton Wanderers suffered only three defeats in 42 Division Three (Northern Section) matches in 1923–24. Twenty-four matches were won, one fewer than achieved by the runners-up Rochdale who finished a point behind. Fifteen matches were drawn by Wolves and only 27 goals conceded one more than Rochdale.

Lincoln City suffered only four defeats in 46 Division Four matches in 1975–76. They won 32 matches, achieved a record 74 points and scored 111 goals.

Fewest wins in single season

Stoke achieved only three wins in 22 Division One matches in 1889–90. They finished bottom with 10 points, only two fewer than the previous season when they had won only four matches. They failed to gain re-election but subsequently returned to the League in 1891 when it was extended to 14 clubs.

Woolwich Arsenal achieved only three wins in 38 Division One matches in 1912–13. They also amassed just 18 points. They scored only 26 goals, finished bottom and were relegated to the Second Division.

Loughborough Town achieved only one win in 34 Division Two matches in 1899–1900. They drew six games but finished bottom, 10 points beneath their nearest rivals Luton Town. They scored only 18 goals and conceded 100. They failed to gain re-election.

Merthyr Town achieved six wins in 42 Division Three (Northern Section) matches in 1929–30. They drew nine but finished bottom nine points behind Gillingham.

Rochdale achieved four wins in 40 Division Three (Northern Section) matches in 1931–32. They suffered 33 defeats, including 17 in succession, as well as a record 13 consecutive home defeats.

Rochdale achieved only two wins in 46 Division Three matches in 1973–74. They played the last 22 matches without a win and achieved only nine points from them in drawn games.

Southport achieved only three wins in 46 matches in Division Four in 1976–77. But they managed to finish six points above the bottom club Workington.

LEADING LEAGUE GOALSCORERS 1946–1978 DIVISION ONE

Season	Leading scorer	Team	Goals	Club total	Club's final League position
1946–47	Dennis Westcott	Wolverhampton Wanderers	37	98	3rd
1947–48	Ronnie Rooke	Arsenal	33	81	1st
1948–49	Willie Moir	Bolton Wanderers	25	59	14th
1949–50	Dickie Davis	Sunderland	25	83	3rd
1950–51	Stan Mortensen	Blackpool	30	79	3rd
1951–52	George Robledo	Newcastle United	33	98	8th
1952–53	Charlie Wayman	Preston North End	24	85	2nd
1953–54	{ Jimmy Glazzard	Huddersfield Town	29	78	3rd
	{ Johnny Nicholls	West Bromwich Albion	29	86	2nd
1954–55	Ronnie Allen	West Bromwich Albion	27	76	17th
1955–56	Nat Lofthouse	Bolton Wanderers	33	71	8th
1956–57	John Charles	Leeds United	38	72	8th
1957–58	Bobby Smith	Tottenham Hotspur	36	93	3rd
1958–59	Jimmy Greaves	Chelsea	33	77	14th
1959–60	Dennis Viollet	Manchester United	32	102	7th
1960–61	Jimmy Greaves	Chelsea	41	98	12th
1961–62	{ Ray Crawford	Ipswich Town	33	93	1st
	{ Derek Kevan	West Bromwich Albion	33	83	9th
1962–63	Jimmy Greaves	Tottenham Hotspur	37	111	2nd
1963–64	Jimmy Greaves	Tottenham Hotspur	35	97	4th
1964–65	{ Jimmy Greaves	Tottenham Hotspur	29	87	6th
	{ Andy McEvoy	Blackburn Rovers	29	83	10th
1965–66	Roger Hunt	Liverpool	30	79	1st
1966–67	Ron Davies	Southampton	37	74	19th
1967–68	{ George Best	Manchester United	28	89	2nd
	{ Ron Davies	Southampton	28	66	16th
1968–69	Jimmy Greaves	Tottenham Hotspur	27	61	6th
1969–70	Jeff Astle	West Bromwich Albion	25	58	16th
1970–71	Tony Brown	West Bromwich Albion	28	58	17th
1971–72	Francis Lee	Manchester City	33	77	4th
1972–73	Bryan Robson	West Ham United	28	67	6th
1973–74	Mick Channon	Southampton	21	47	20th
1974–75	Malcolm Macdonald	Newcastle United	21	59	15th
1975–76	Ted MacDougall	Norwich City	23	58	10th
1976–77	{ Malcolm Macdonald	Arsenal	25	64	8th
	{ Andy Gray	Aston Villa	25	73	4th
1977–78	Bob Latchford	Everton	30	76	3rd

DIVISION TWO

Season	Leading scorer	Team	Goals	Club total	Club's final League position
1946–47	Charlie Wayman	Newcastle United	30	95	5th
1947–48	Eddie Quigley	Sheffield Wednesday	23	66	4th
1948–49	Charlie Wayman	Southampton	32	69	3rd
1949–50	Tommy Briggs	Grimsby Town	35	74	11th
1950–51	Cecil McCormack	Barnsley	33	74	15th
1951–52	Derek Dooley	Sheffield Wednesday	46	100	1st
1952–53	Arthur Rowley	Leicester City	39	89	5th
1953–54	John Charles	Leeds United	42	89	10th
1954–55	Tommy Briggs	Blackburn Rovers	33	114	6th
1955–56	Bill Gardiner	Leicester City	34	94	5th
1956–57	Arthur Rowley	Leicester City	44	109	1st
1957–58	Brian Clough	Middlesbrough	40	83	7th
1958–59	Brian Clough	Middlesbrough	42	87	13th
1959–60	Brian Clough	Middlesbrough	39	90	5th
1960–61	Ray Crawford	Ipswich Town	39	100	1st
1961–62	Roger Hunt	Liverpool	41	99	1st
1962–63	Bobby Tambling	Chelsea	35	81	2nd
1963–64	Ron Saunders	Portsmouth	33	79	9th
1964–65	George O'Brien	Southampton	34	83	4th
1965–66	Martin Chivers	Southampton	30	85	2nd
1966–67	Bobby Gould	Coventry City	24	74	1st
1967–68	John Hickton	Middlesbrough	24	60	6th
1968–69	John Toshack	Cardiff City	22	67	5th
1969–70	John Hickton	Middlesbrough	24	55	4th
1970–71	John Hickton	Middlesbrough	25	60	7th
1971–72	Bob Latchford	Birmingham City	23	60	2nd
1972–73	Don Givens	Queen's Park Rangers	23	81	2nd
1973–74	Duncan McKenzie	Nottingham Forest	26	57	7th
1974–75	Brian Little	Aston Villa	20	69	2nd
1975–76	Derek Hales	Charlton Athletic	28	61	9th
1976–77	Mickey Walsh	Blackpool	26	58	5th
1977–78	Bob Hatton	Blackpool	22	59	20th

DIVISION THREE

Season	Leading scorer	Team	Goals	Club total	Club's final League position
1958–59	Jim Towers	Brentford	32	76	3rd
1959–60	Derek Reeves	Southampton	39	106	1st
1960–61	Tony Richards	Walsall	36	98	2nd
1961–62	Cliff Holton	Northampton Town (36) and Walsall (1)	37	85 (NT)	8th (NT)
1962–63	George Hudson	Coventry City	30	83	4th
1963–64	Alf Biggs	Bristol Rovers	30	91	12th
1964–65	Ken Wagstaff	Mansfield Town and Hull City	8 23	95 91	3rd 4th
1965–66	Les Allen	Queen's Park Rangers	30	95	3rd
1966–67	Rodney Marsh	Queen's Park Rangers	30	103	1st
1967–68	Don Rogers	Swindon Town	25	74	10th
	Bobby Owen	Bury	25	91	2nd
1968–69	Brian Lewis	Luton Town	22	74	3rd
	Don Rogers	Swindon Town	22	71	2nd
1969–70	George Jones	Bury	26	75	19th
1970–71	Gerry Ingram	Preston North End	22	63	1st
	Dudley Roberts	Mansfield Town	22	64	7th
1971–72	Ted MacDougall	Bournemouth & B.A.	35	73	3rd
	Alf Wood	Shrewsbury Town	35	73	12th
1972–73	Bruce Bannister	Bristol Rovers	25	77	5th
	Arthur Horsfield	Charlton Athletic	25	69	11th
1973–74	Billy Jennings	Watford	26	64	7th
1974–75	Dixie McNeil	Hereford United	31	64	12th
1975–76	Dixie McNeil	Hereford United	35	86	1st
1976–77	Peter Ward	Brighton & Hove Albion	32	83	2nd
1977–78	Alex Bruce	Preston North End	27	63	3rd

Continued on page 92

Left: Peter Ward, 32 goals for Brighton & Hove 1976–77. Above: Jimmy Greaves, six times Division One top goalscorer. Below left: Terry Bly 52 goals for Peterborough United 1960–61. Below Malcolm Macdonald, twice Division One leading scorer in 1974–75 and 1976–77.

DIVISION FOUR

Season	Leading scorer	Team	Goals	Club total	Club's final League position
1958–59	Arthur Rowley	Shrewsbury Town	37	101	4th
1959–60	Cliff Holton	Watford	42	92	4th
1960–61	Terry Bly	Peterborough United	52	134	1st
1961–62	Bobby Hunt	Colchester United	41	104	2nd
1962–63	Ken Wagstaff	Mansfield Town	34	108	4th
	Colin Booth	Doncaster Rovers	34	64	16th
1963–64	Hugh McIlmoyle	Carlisle United	39	113	2nd
1964–65	Alick Jeffrey	Doncaster Rovers	36	84	9th
1965–66	Kevin Hector	Bradford (P.A.)	34	102	11th
1966–67	Ernie Phythian	Hartlepools United	23	66	8th
1967–68	Roy Chapman	Port Vale	25	61	18th
	Les Massie	Halifax Town	25	52	11th
1968–69	Gary Talbot	Chester	22	76	14th
1969–70	Albert Kinsey	Wrexham	27	84	2nd
1970–71	Ted MacDougall	Bournemouth & B.A.	42	81	2nd
1971–72	Peter Price	Peterborough United	28	82	8th
1972–73	Fred Binney	Exeter City	28	57	8th
1973–74	Brian Yeo	Gillingham	31	90	2nd
1974–75	Ray Clarke	Mansfield Town	28	90	1st
1975–76	Ronnie Moore	Tranmere Rovers	34	89	4th
1976–77	Brian Joicey	Barnsley	25	62	6th
1977–78	Steve Phillips	Brentford	32	86	4th
	Alan Curtis	Swansea City	32	87	3rd

DIVISION THREE SOUTH

Season	Leading scorer	Team	Goals	Club total	Club's final League position
1946–47	Don Clark	Bristol City	36	94	3rd
1947–48	Len Townsend	Bristol City	29	77	7th
1948–49	Don McGibbon	Bournemouth & B.A.	30	69	3rd
1949–50	Tommy Lawton	Notts County	31	95	1st
1950–51	Wally Ardron	Nottingham Forest	36	110	1st
1951–52	Ronnie Blackman	Reading	39	112	2nd
1952–53	Geoff Bradford	Bristol Rovers	33	92	1st
1953–54	Jack English	Northampton Town	28	82	5th
1954–55	Ernie Morgan	Gillingham	31	77	4th
1955–56	Sammy Collins	Torquay United	40	86	5th
1956–57	Ted Phillips	Ipswich Town	42	101	1st
1957–58	Sam McCrory	Southend United	31	90	7th
	Derek Reeves	Southampton	31	112	6th

DIVISION THREE NORTH

Season	Leading scorer	Team	Goals	Club total	Club's final League position
1946–47	Clarrie Jordan	Doncaster Rovers	41	123	1st
1947–48	Jimmy Hutchinson	Lincoln City	32	81	1st
1948–49	Wally Ardron	Rotherham United	29	90	2nd
1949–50	Peter Doherty	Doncaster Rovers	26	66	1st
1950–51	Jack Shaw	Rotherham United	37	103	1st
1951–52	Andy Graver	Lincoln City	36	121	1st
1952–53	Jimmy Whitehouse	Carlisle United	29	82	9th
1953–54	Jack Connor	Stockport County	31	77	10th
1954–55	Jack Connor	Stockport County	30	84	9th
	Arthur Bottom	York City	30	92	4th
1955–56	Bob Crosbie	Grimsby Town	36	76	1st
1956–57	Ray Straw	Derby County	37	111	1st
1957–58	Alf Ackerman	Carlisle United	35	80	16th

Week in the Life of a Club

Aldershot Football Club was founded in December 1926 and gained admittance to the Southern League in the 1927–28 season. In 1932 they were elected to the Football League, Division Three (Southern Section) and remained in it until becoming founder members of Division Four in 1958.

The club won promotion to Division Three for the first time in 1973 but were relegated at the end of the 1975–76 season.

A rebuilding programme was instituted with the restarting of the youth team and a reserve side playing in midweek. In 1977–78 this was further emphasised when the reserves entered a Saturday competition.

Aldershot was chosen as not only the first club in any normal alphabetical list of the Football League members but as one typical of an average, progressive organisation from one of the lower divisions.

Manager: Tommy McAnearney; Trainer: John Anderson.

Monday 21 March 1977
Manager: 9.00 am Checked on injuries, drew up training plan for the week, dealt with correspondence. 10–12.30 pm Trained and analysed previous Saturday's game. After lunch, telephoned contacts until 4.30 pm.
Secretary: 8.45 am Dealt with wages, correspondence and general administration. (Lunch 12.30–1.30 pm) Discussed minor policies with Chairman until 7.30 pm.
Trainer: Treated injured players, conducted training sessions under supervision of team manager, packed kit for away match at Halifax.

Discussing promotion ideas in the club's commercial section.

Tuesday 22 March
Manager: 9.00 am Checked on team squad, left for Halifax at 10.00 am. Stopped for pre-match meal at Oldham. Left afterwards with travelling director. Result of Match: lost 2–0.
Secretary: 8.45 am Prepared players' contracts, allocated dates for local cup matches, correspondence, general administration, prepared programme notes for Saturday's home match, prepared press statement.
Trainer: (as for team manager) Accompanied team back, stopping for meal after match.

Wednesday 23 March
Manager: 9.30 am Dealt with correspondence, telephoned contacts, supervised players who did not travel to Halifax, organised travel arrangements for match v Huddersfield, left 12.30 pm on scouting mission.
Secretary: 8.45 General administration, discussion with team manager on next season's League entries, interviewed prospective office staff. Discussion with Chairman until 7.00 pm.
Trainer: Arrived back with team after breakfast, prepared laundry on arrival at ground.

Thursday 24 March
Manager: 9.00 am Normal training, checked on injuries incurred at Halifax, discussed team selection for Saturday's match with trainer, short afternoon training and fitness tests.
Secretary: 8.45 am Attended to accounts of company, match preparation for Saturday, had lunch with local press representative, general administration.
Trainer: Training session, treatment of injuries, checked on boots, medical kit check, treatment.

Aldershot Football Club Secretary M. A. Cosway and his secretary Mrs V. Knight.

Friday 25 March

Manager: 9.00 am Training and pre-match talk with players.

Secretary: 8.45 am Discussed with promotions manager re-commercial managers' meeting at Leicester on previous Wednesday, general administration, correspondence.

Trainer: Liaison with team manager and training, prepared kit for Saturday.

Saturday 26 March

Manager: Called at office 10.30 am Last minute alterations. Hour for lunch, returned to ground 1.45 pm.

Secretary: 9.30 am Collected items for match day operation, supervised staff and final check on administration for the match, socialised with visiting officials and own directors. After lunch ensured smooth running of afternoon, dealt with gate receipts at match, supervised two part-time office assistants, three others in tea room.

Trainer: (as for team manager)

Result of Match: Aldershot 0 Barnsley 1.

Sunday 27 March

Manager: At ground for youth team match 11.00 am kick-off. Afternoon trials at training ground.

Secretary: 9.00 am At ground for youth game, supervised staff.

Trainer: Attended youth team match.

General

Office assistants: (1) every morning for six days a week engaged on general manual duties. Cleaner mornings five days a week. (General office assistant Monday–Friday: typing and general clerical duties.)

Promotion office: staffed six days a week, promotions manager, two full-time assistants and typist, full-time canvasser. Open 9.30 am. Administering distribution of lottery tickets and draw, deal with meeting at Leicester on Wednesday 23 March. Dealt with agents' dance arrangements and met club secretary.

Steve Bambridge, Aldershot apprentice in the boot room. He was the club's youngest debutant at 16 during 1976–77.

Playing staff: 20 professionals including two on loan from other clubs. Three of these on light training after injuries. Fourteen travelled to Halifax.

Supporters Club: Dealt with catering on match day and operation of souvenir shop, recruiting members. Committee once a month.

Groundsmen: Attention to pitch and Recreation Ground requirements as and when required.

Turnstiles: Eighteen operators on match day. Stewards head man informs Secretary of float required. Approximately 40 people in all. Prepare cash bags and float, take turnstile readings and inform stewards of posts from 10.00 am. 1.30 pm Gate staff arrived.

Programme sellers: Eight sellers report 1.30 pm on match day.

Radio shots: Operated by supporters club, manned on match days playing record requests.

Police: Policing arrangements nine on average, paid by club for duration of match and four men from security firm.

St John: Six volunteers on match day, the service for which the club makes an annual donation.

Board of Directors (five): Responsible for policy of Aldershot Football Club. One director attended match at Halifax. All present v Huddersfield. Frequently call in at Club offices during the week. Board meeting once a fortnight.

Youth team manager and trainer present Thursday night for training purposes and Sunday matches.

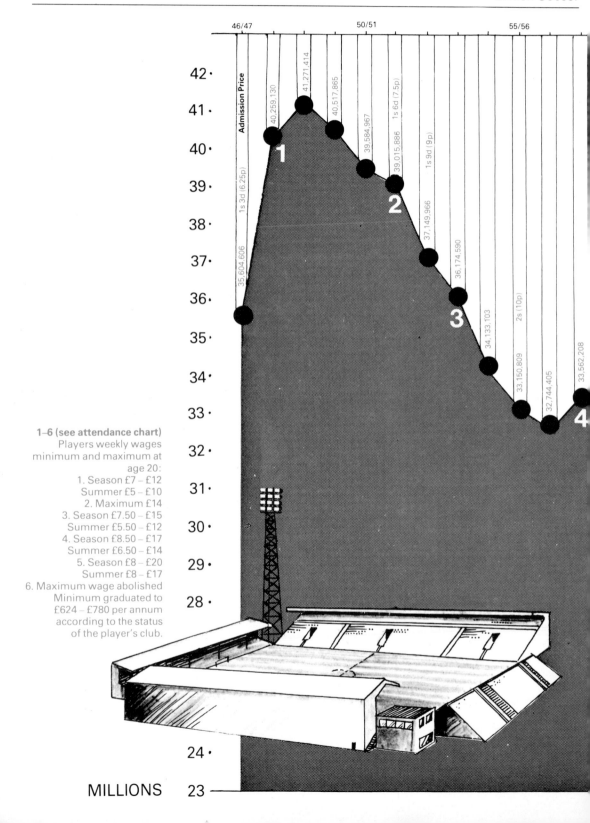

46/47 50/51 55/56

42 ·
41 ·
40 ·
39 ·
38 ·
37 ·
36 ·
35 ·
34 ·
33 ·
32 ·
31 ·
30 ·
29 ·
28 ·

24 ·

MILLIONS 23 —

Admission Price

1s 3d (6.25p)

35,604,606

40,259,130

41,271,414

40,517,865

39,584,967

39,015,886 1s 6d (7.5p)

37,149,966 1s 9d (9p)

36,174,590

34,133,103 2s (10p)

33,150,809

32,744,405

33,562,208

1

2

3

4

1–6 (see attendance chart)
Players weekly wages
minimum and maximum at
age 20:
1. Season £7 – £12
Summer £5 – £10
2. Maximum £14
3. Season £7.50 – £15
Summer £5.50 – £12
4. Season £8.50 – £17
Summer £6.50 – £14
5. Season £8 – £20
Summer £8 – £17
6. Maximum wage abolished
Minimum graduated to
£624 – £780 per annum
according to the status
of the player's club.

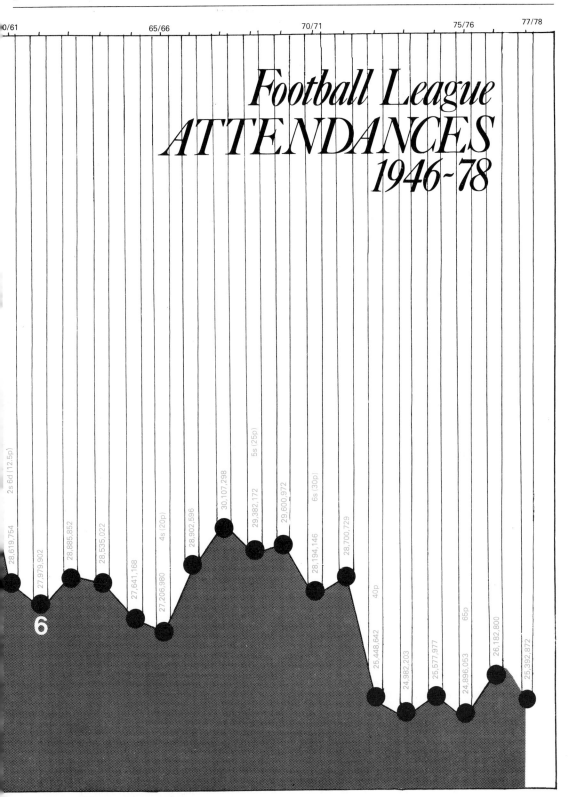

Football League
ATTENDANCES
1946~78

6

2s 6d (12.5p)

28,619,754

27,979,902

28,885,852

28,535,022

27,641,168

4s (20p)

27,206,980

28,902,596

30,107,298

5s (25p)

29,382,172

29,600,972

6s (30p)

28,194,146

28,700,729

40p

25,448,642

24,982,203

25,577,977

65p

24,896,053

26,182,800

25,392,872

FOOTBALL LEAGUE CUP ATTENDANCES

Season	Aggregate	Games	Average
1960–61	1,204,580	112	10,755
1961–62	1,030,534	104	9,909
1962–63	1,029,893	102	10,097
1963–64	945,265	104	9,089
1964–65	962,802	98	9,825
1965–66	1,205,876	106	11,376
1966–67	1,394,553	118	11,818
1967–68	1,671,326	110	15,194
1968–69	2,064,647	118	17,497
1969–70	2,299,819	122	18,851
1970–71	2,038,809	117	17,425
1971–72	2,397,154	123	19,489
1972–73	1,935,474	120	16,129
1973–74	1,722,629	132	13,050
1974–75	1,901,094	127	14,969
1975–76	1,841,735	140	13,155
1976–77	2,236,636	147	15,215
1977–78	*(Figures not available at time of going to press)*		

The League Cup was first contested in the 1960–61 season, having been inaugurated at the AGM of the Football League in May 1960. Entry was optional and it was not until 1969–70 that all 92 Football League clubs entered.

The 112 matches in the original competition attracted an attendance of 1,204,580 for an average of 10,755 and in 1968–69 crowds topped two million for the first time when 2,064,647 watched the 118 games for an average of 17,497.

Until the 1966–67 season the final was decided on a home and away aggregate over two matches. In 1967 the one match final was held at Wembley and has remained there.

Entries per season:

1960–61	87	1965–66	83
1961–62	82	1966–67	90
1962–63	80	1967–68	90
1963–64	82	1968–69	91
1964–65	82	1969–70	92
		and since	92

Season	Winners	Runners-up	Result	Venue
1960–61	**Aston Villa**	Rotherham United	Rotherham United 2 Aston Villa 0 Aston Villa 3 Rotherham United 0	
1961–62	**Norwich City**	Rochdale	Rochdale 0 Norwich City 3 Norwich City 1 Rochdale 0	
1962–63	**Birmingham City**	Aston Villa	Birmingham City 3 Aston Villa 1 Aston Villa 0 Birmingham City 0	
1963–64	**Leicester City**	Stoke City	Stoke City 1 Leicester City 1 Leicester City 3 Stoke City 2	
1964–65	**Chelsea**	Leicester City	Chelsea 3 Leicester City 2 Leicester City 0 Chelsea 0	
1965–66	**West Bromwich Albion**	West Ham United	West Ham United 2 West Bromwich Albion 1 West Bromwich Albion 4 West Ham United 1	
1966–67	**Queen's Park Rangers**	West Bromwich Albion	Queen's Park Rangers 3 West Bromwich Albion 2	Wembley
1967–68	**Leeds United**	Arsenal	Leeds United 1 Arsenal 0	Wembley
1968–69	**Swindon Town**	Arsenal	Swindon Town 3 Arsenal 1	Wembley
1969–70	**Manchester City**	West Bromwich Albion	Manchester City 2 West Bromwich Albion 1	Wembley
1970–71	**Tottenham Hotspur**	Aston Villa	Tottenham Hotspur 2 Aston Villa 0	Wembley
1971–72	**Stoke City**	Chelsea	Stoke City 2 Chelsea 1	Wembley
1972–73	**Tottenham Hotspur**	Norwich City	Tottenham Hotspur 1 Norwich 0	Wembley
1973–74	**Wolverhampton Wanderers**	Manchester City	Wolverhampton Wanderers 2 Manchester City 1	Wembley
1974–75	**Aston Villa**	Norwich City	Aston Villa 1 Norwich City 0	Wembley
1975–76	**Manchester City**	Newcastle United	Manchester City 2 Newcastle United 1	Wembley
1976–77	**Aston Villa**	Everton	Aston Villa 0 Everton 0 Aston Villa 1 Everton 1 Aston Villa 3 Everton 2	Wembley Hillsborough Old Trafford
1977–78	**Nottingham Forest**	Liverpool	Nottingham Forest 0 Liverpool 0 Nottingham Forest 1 Liverpool 0	Wembley Old Trafford

Scottish Football

SCOTTISH FOOTBALL ASSOCIATION

The Scottish Football Association was formed on 13 March 1873 at a meeting in Dewar's Hotel, Bridge Street, Glasgow, called by the Queen's Park club for the purpose of arranging a Scottish Cup competition. Eight clubs constituted the organisation: Queen's Park, Clydesdale, Dumbreck, Vale of Leven, Eastern, Third Lanark Volunteer Reserves and Granville, and word was also received from Kilmarnock of their interest in joining. Within a year these eight had been joined by Alexandra Athletic, Southern, Blythswood, Western, Renton and Dumbarton.

SCOTTISH F.A. CUP

The Scottish F.A. Cup competition was first organised in 1873–74. Sixteen clubs competed and Queen's Park became the winners, beating Clydesdale 2–0. They won again in the following two seasons.

No club has won the Scottish Cup on more than three successive occasions, though in addition to the early achievement of Queen's Park the same club repeated its feat in 1880–82 after Vale of Leven had done so between 1877–79. Vale of Leven's last success was when they were awarded the Cup after Rangers failed to appear for the replay following a 1–1 draw.

Rangers are the only other club to have accomplished three wins in succession. They have achieved this on three occasions: 1934–36; 1948–50 and 1962–64.

Of clubs no longer competing in the Scottish League apart from Vale of Leven, other winners have been Renton (twice), Third Lanark (twice) and St. Bernard's (once). Only one club from Division Two has won the Cup among the 22 different winners. East Fife achieved this feat in 1938 when they beat Kilmarnock 4–2 in a replay after a 1–1 draw.

In the early years of the competition there were other protests. Queen's Park were awarded the trophy when Vale of Leven did not appear for the final in 1884. In 1909 the Cup was withheld completely after two drawn games between Celtic and Rangers because of a riot, which occurred through a misunderstanding about the playing of extra time and a mob burned down the pay boxes at Hampden Park.

Celtic are the most successful club in the history of the Scottish F.A. Cup with 25 wins, followed by Rangers with 22 wins. The original trophy is still in use. It cost £56 and included in its costing a set of medals.

When Arbroath beat Bon Accord 36–0 in a Scottish Cup tie on 5 September 1885 the *Dundee Courier* reported that the event 'baffled description'. It was also considered that due to the lack of nets and the consequent waste of retrieval time the score would have been even higher. While Arbroath turned out in proper football attire the opposition wore a motley assortment of everyday working clothes without a single pair of football boots between them. What is not so surprising, considering the result which provided the highest score ever recorded in the history of British first-class football, is that the 'helpless set of innocents' who were led to the slaughter did not have their regular goalkeeper. He was Jimmy 'Sniper' Grant who had declared himself unfit the day before the game and his place was taken by one of their half-backs, Andy Lornie, who had never previously kept goal. It is believed that this unfortunate fellow gave up football shortly after this debacle in which Arbroath winger, John Petrie, registered a British first-class record by scoring 13 goals.

The Arbroath goalkeeper 'neither touched the ball with hand or foot' during this affair, and because of the rain spent most of the game sheltering under an umbrella. On the same day Dundee Harp beat Aberdeen Rovers 35–0.

Arbroath went on to score 55 goals in the Cup that season before being beaten 5–3 by Hibernian in the Fourth Round.

SCOTTISH LEAGUE

The Scottish League was originally constituted of 11 clubs: Celtic, Rangers, Third Lanark, St. Mirren, Hearts, Dumbarton, Abercorn, Cambuslang, Vale of Leven, Cowlairs and Renton. It was formed following a series of meetings in Glasgow in 1890 and its first season of competition was 1890–91. But Renton, one of the prime movers behind the League, were suspended by the Scottish Football Association after only five matches. They had failed to observe a ruling that affiliated clubs were banned from playing matches against St. Bernard's, a club already considered a professional organisation. And although the match Renton had played was against a team called Edinburgh Saints it was found that they were St. Bernard's masquerading under another name.

With Renton's record expunged from the League the teams played 18 matches and Dumbarton and Rangers finished level with 29 points each. After a play-off had been drawn 2–2 it was agreed that the two clubs should share the championship jointly.

Renton returned to the League the following season and Division Two was formed in 1893. In 1915 it was suspended during the war but reformed in 1921 when automatic promotion and relegation – with two clubs up and two down – was introduced between the two divisions.

An attempt was made to introduce a Division Three in 1925 but it did not survive its third season. It was revived in 1946 and divided into two sections four years later but in 1955 it was dropped completely when the Reserve League was founded.

In 1975 a major reorganisation of the Scottish League took place with the top ten clubs of Division One in 1974–75 forming the Premier Division while the bottom eight together with the top six of Division Two formed the new Division One. The remainder continued in Division Two. An additional club had been admitted the previous season to bring the total to an even figure of 38.

Rangers and Celtic have been the only two clubs to hold continuous membership of the top division in the Scottish League since its inception. And they have been the two most successful clubs. Rangers hold the record with 37 championship titles, including the original shared one in 1890–91. Celtic have won it 26 times. Rangers won all their 18 matches in 1898–99, a Scottish League record.

In the Scottish League Celtic were undefeated between 13 November 1915 and 21 April 1917 during a sequence of 63 matches. After losing the Scottish Cup Final in April 1966 they were undefeated in 33 matches until 12 December 1966. This sequence had extended from February 1966 for 27 League matches alone. Rangers were undefeated between 17 March 1928 and 27 March 1929 during a sequence of 38 Scottish League Division One matches.

THE SCOTTISH FOOTBALL LEAGUE CLUBS

Ground	Shirts/shorts	Honours League	Cup
ABERDEEN (1903)			
Pittodrie Park Aberdeen	Scarlet/scarlet	Premier Div. runners-up 1977–78 Div. 1 Champions 1954–55 Runners-up 1910–11, 1936–37, 1955–56, 1970–71, 1971–72	Winners 1947, 1970 Runners-up 1937, 1953, 1954, 1959, 1967, 1978
AIRDRIEONIANS (1878)			
Broomfield Park Airdrie	White/white	Div. 1 runners-up 1922–23, 1923–24, 1924–25, 1925–26 Div. 2 Champions 1902–03, 1954–55, 1973–74 Runners-up 1900–01, 1946–47, 1949–50, 1965–66	Winners 1924 Runners-up 1975

Of the clubs competing in the 1977–78 season only Berwick Rangers, Brechin City, Forfar Athletic, Meadowbank Thistle, Montrose, Stenhousemuir and Stranraer have failed to achieve promotion or win the championship of the Premier Division, Division One or Division Two.

Only one club no longer in membership has won the championship of Division One and that was Third Lanark who were champions in 1903–04. They resigned from the League at the end of the 1966–67 season after finishing eleventh in Division Two.

Bobby Skinner of Dunfermline Athletic was the first player to score over 50 goals in a season of Scottish League football. He performed this feat when Dunfermline won promotion to Division One in the 1925–26 season and his individual total was 53 League goals. The club's total of 109 goals that season also meant that they had become the first side to score over 100 goals in the Scottish Division Two.

Queen's Park (Glasgow) did not concede a goal to a Scottish club from the time they were formed on 9 July 1867 until 16 January 1875 when they defeated Vale of Leven 3–1 in the Scottish Cup semi-final in 1875–76. They had not lost a goal at all between 1867 and 1872. The club did not play their first match against outside opposition until May Day 1868 when they met a team called Thistle and beat them 2–0. Inter-club matches had been played at first: Captain's team v Secre- tary; Captain v President and Lightweights v Heavyweights.

They did not suffer any defeat until February 1876 when beaten by Wanderers in a friendly. And Vale of Leven became the first Scottish club to defeat Queen's Park in a Scottish Cup fifth round tie on 30 December 1876 when they won 2–1.

The first Scottish club to make a clean sweep of the major Scottish tournaments was Rangers in 1929–30. That season they had 14 players appearing in their League side who were already internationals or were destined to become so. They won the Scottish Cup, Scottish League, Glasgow Cup, Glasgow Charity Cup (by the toss of a coin after playing Celtic for two hours without reaching a definite result, the score being 2–2), Scottish Alliance and the Second XI Cup. The team was captained by David Meiklejohn and the leading scorer was centre-forward Jimmy Fleming.

SCOTTISH LEAGUE CUP

The Scottish League Cup was first contested in the 1945–46 season, succeeding the wartime Southern League Cup. Until 1977–78 season when it became a knock-out competition throughout it had been decided in the initial stages on a group basis with the qualifiers competing for the quarter-finals on the sudden death system.

League Cup	Record win	Highest number of Individual goals
		ABERDEEN
Winners 1946, 1956, 1977	13–0 v Peterhead, Scottish Cup, 1922–23	Benny Yorston, 38, 1929–30
		AIRDRIEONIANS
	11–1 v Falkirk, Div. 1, 1950–51	Bert Yarnall, 39, 1916–17

Ground	Shirts/shorts	Honours League	Cup
ALBION ROVERS (1881)			
Cliftonhill Park Coatbridge	Yellow/white	Div. 2 Champions 1933–34 Runners-up 1913–14, 1937–38, 1947–48	Runners-up 1920
ALLOA (1878)			
Recreation Ground Alloa	Gold/black	Div. 2 Champions 1921–22 Runners-up 1938–39, 1976–77	
ARBROATH (1878)			
Gayfield Park Arbroath	Maroon/white	Div. 2 runners-up 1934–35, 1958–59, 1967–68, 1971–72	
AYR UNITED (1910)			
Somerset Park Ayr	White/black	Div. 2 Champions 1911–12, 1912–13, 1927–28, 1936–37, 1958–59, 1965–66 Runners-up 1910–11, 1955–56, 1968–69	
BERWICK RANGERS (1881)			
Shielfield Park Tweedmouth Berwick-on-Tweed	Gold/black	Highest League position 6th, Div. 2, 1973–74	
BRECHIN CITY (1906)			
Glebe Park Brechin	Red/red	Highest League position 5th, Div. 2, 1958–59	
CELTIC (1888)			
Celtic Park Glasgow SE	Green, white/white	Premier Div. Champions 1976–77 Div. 1 Champions 1892–93, 1893–94, 1895–96, 1897–98, 1904–05, 1905–06, 1906–07, 1907–08, 1908–09, 1909–10, 1913–14, 1914–15, 1915–16, 1916–17, 1918–19, 1921–22, 1925–26, 1935–36, 1937–38, 1953–54, 1965–66, 1966–67, 1967–68, 1968–69, 1969–70, 1970–71, 1971–72, 1972–73, 1973–74 Runners-up 16 times Premier Div. Runners-up 1975–76	Winners 1892, 1899, 1900, 1904, 1907, 1908, 1911, 1912, 1914, 1923, 1925, 1927, 1931, 1933, 1937, 1951, 1954, 1965, 1967, 1969, 1971, 1972, 1974, 1975, 1977 Runners-up 14 times
CLYDE (1878)			
Shawfield Stadium Glasgow C5	White/black	Div. 2 Champions 1904–05, 1951–52, 1956–57, 1961–62, 1972–73, 1977–78 Runners-up 1903–04, 1905–06, 1925–26, 1963–64	Winners 1939, 1955, 1958 Runners-up 1910, 1912, 1949
CLYDEBANK (1965)			
Kilbowie Park Clydebank	White/white	Div. 1 runners-up 1976–77 Div. 2 Champions 1975–76	
COWDENBEATH (1881)			
Central Park Cowdenbeath	Blue/white	Div. 2 Champions 1913–14, 1914–15, 1938–39 Runners-up 1921–22, 1923–24, 1969–70	

League Cup	Record win	Highest number of Individual goals
		ALBION ROVERS
	10–0 v Brechin City, Div. 2, 1937–38	Jim Renwick, 41, 1932–33
		ALLOA
	9–2 v Forfar, Div. 2, 1932–33	Wee Crilley, 49, 1921–22
		ARBROATH
	36–0 v Bon Accord, Scottish Cup, 1885–86	Dave Easson, 45, 1958–59
		AYR UNITED
	11–1 v Dumbarton, League Cup, 1952–53	Jimmy Smith, 66, 1927–28
		BERWICK RANGERS
	8–2 v Dundee United, 1957–58	Ken Bowron, 38, 1963–64
		BRECHIN CITY
	12–1 v Thornhill, Scottish Cup, 1925–26	Willie McIntosh, 26, 1959–60
		CELTIC
Winners 1957, 1958, 1966, 1967, 1968, 1969, 1970, 1975 Runners-up 8 times	11–0 v Dundee, Div. 1, 1895–96	Jimmy McGrory, 50, 1935–36
		CLYDE
	11–1 v Cowdenbeath, Div. 2, 1951–52	Bill Boyd, 32, 1932–33
		CLYDEBANK
	7–1 v Hamilton, Div. 2, 1971–72 and v Queen's Park, Div. 2, 1970–71	Joe McCallan, 27, 1976–77
		COWDENBEATH
	12–0 v St Johnstone, Scottish Cup, 1927–28	Willie Devlin, 40, 1925–26

Ground	Shirts/shorts	Honours League	Cup
DUMBARTON (1872)			
Boghead Park Dumbarton	White/white	Div. 1 Champions 1890–91 (shared), 1891–92 Div. 2 Champions 1910–11, 1971–72 Runners-up 1907–08	Winners 1883 Runners-up 1881, 1882, 1887, 1891, 1897
DUNDEE (1893)			
Dens Park Dundee	Blue/white	Div. 1 Champions 1961–62 Runners-up 1902–03, 1906–07, 1908–09, 1948–49 Div. 2 Champions 1946–47	Winners 1910 Runners-up 1925, 1952, 1964
DUNDEE UNITED (1910)			
Tannadice Park Dundee	Tangerine/tangerine	Div. 2 Champions 1924–25, 1928–29 Runners-up 1930–31, 1959–60	Runners-up 1974
DUNFERMLINE ATHLETIC (1885)			
East End Park Dunfermline	White, black/black	Div. 2 Champions 1925–26 Runners-up 1912–13, 1933–34, 1954–55, 1957–58, 1972–73	Winners 1961, 1968 Runners-up 1965
EAST FIFE (1903)			
Bayview Park Methil	Gold/black	Div. 2 Champions 1947–48 Runners-up 1929–30, 1970–71	Winners 1938 Runners-up 1927, 1950
EAST STIRLING(SHIRE) (1881)			
Firs Park Falkirk	Black, white/black	Div. 2 Champions 1931–32 Runners-up 1962–63	
FALKIRK (1876)			
Brockville Park Falkirk	Blue/white	Div. 1 runners-up 1907–08, 1909–10 Div. 2 Champions 1935–36, 1969–70, 1974–75 Runners-up 1904–05, 1951–52, 1960–61	Winners 1913, 1957
FORFAR ATHLETIC (1884)			
Station Park Forfar	Blue/blue	Highest League position 5th, Div. 2, 1927–28	
HAMILTON ACADEMICAL (1875)			
Douglas Park Hamilton	Red, white/white	Div. 2 Champions 1903–04 Runners-up 1952–53, 1964–65	Runners-up 1911, 1935
HEART OF MIDLOTHIAN (1874)			
Tynecastle Park Edinburgh	Maroon/white	Div. 1 Champions 1894–95, 1896–97, 1957–58, 1959–60 Runners-up 1893–94, 1898–99, 1903–04, 1905–06, 1914–15, 1937–38, 1953–54, 1956–57, 1958–59, 1964–65 1977–78	Winners 1891, 1896, 1901, 1906, 1956 Runners-up 1903, 1907, 1968, 1976
HIBERNIAN (1875)			
Easter Road Park Edinburgh	Green/white	Div. 1 Champions 1902–03, 1947–48, 1950–51, 1951–52 Runners-up 1896–97, 1946–47, 1949–50, 1952–53, 1973–74, 1974–75 Div. 2 Champions 1893–94, 1894–95, 1932–33	Winners 1887, 1902 Runners-up 1896, 1914, 1923, 1924, 1947, 1958, 1972

League Cup	Record win	Highest number of Individual goals
		DUMBARTON
	8–0 v Cowdenbeath, Div. 2, 1963–64	Kenny Wilson, 38, 1971–72
		DUNDEE
Winners 1952, 1953, 1974 Runners-up 1968	10–0 v Alloa, Div. 2, 1946–47 and v Dunfermline, Div. 2, 1946–47	Dave Halliday, 38, 1923–24
		DUNDEE UNITED
	14–0 v Nithsdale, Scottish Cup, 1930–31	John Coyle, 41, 1955–56
		DUNFERMLINE
Runners-up 1950	11–2 v Stenhousemuir, Div. 2, 1930–31	Bobby Skinner, 55, 1925–26
		EAST FIFE
Winners 1948, 1950, 1954 (The only Second Division club ever to win these two cups)	13–2 v Edinburgh City, Div. 2, 1937–38	Henry Morris, 41, 1947–48
		EAST STIRLING(SHIRE)
	8–2 v Brechin City, Div. 2, 1961–62	Malcolm Morrison, 36, 1938–39
		FALKIRK
Runners-up 1948	10–0 v Breadalbane, Scottish Cup, 1922–23 and 1925–26	Evelyn Morrison, 43, 1928–29
		FORFAR ATHLETIC
	9–1 v Stenhousemuir, Div. 2, 1968–69	Davie Kilgour, 45, 1929–30
		HAMILTON ACADEMICAL
	10–2 v Cowdenbeath, Div. 1, 1932–33	David Wilson, 34, 1936–37
		HEART OF MIDLOTHIAN
Winners 1955, 1959, 1960, 1963 Runners-up 1962	15–0 v King's Park, Scottish Cup, 1936–37	Barney Battles, 44, 1930–31
		HIBERNIAN
Winners 1973 Runners-up 1951, 1969, 1975	15–1 v Peebles Rovers, Scottish Cup, 1960–61	Joe Baker, 42, 1959–60

Ground	Shirts/shorts	Honours League	Cup
KILMARNOCK (1869)			
Rugby Park Kilmarnock	White/white	Div. 1 Champions 1964–65 Runners-up 1959–60, 1960–61, 1962–63, 1963–64, 1975–76 Div. 2 Champions 1897–98, 1898–99 Runners-up 1953–54, 1973–74	Winners 1920, 1929 Runners-up 1898, 1932, 1938, 1957, 1960
MEADOWBANK THISTLE (1974)			
Meadowbank Stadium Edinburgh	Amber/black	Highest League position 11th, Div. 2, 1976–77	
MONTROSE (1879)			
Links Park Montrose	Blue/blue	Highest League position 3rd, Div. 1, 1975–76	
MORTON (1874)			
Cappielow Park Greenock	Blue, white/white	Div. 1 Champions 1977–78 Div. 1 runners-up 1916–17 Div. 2 Champions 1949–50, 1963–64, 1966–67 Runners-up 1899–1900, 1928–29, 1936–37	Winners 1922 Runners-up 1948
MOTHERWELL (1886)			
Fir Park Motherwell	Amber/amber	Div. 1 Champions 1931–32 Runners-up 1926–27, 1929–30, 1932–33, 1933–34 Div. 2 Champions 1953–54, 1968–69 Runners-up 1894–95, 1902–03	Winners 1952 Runners-up 1931, 1933, 1939, 1951
PARTICK THISTLE (1876)			
Firhill Park Glasgow NW	Red, yellow/black	Div. 1 Champions 1975–76 Div. 2 Champions 1896–97, 1899–1900, 1970–71 Runners-up 1901–02	Winners 1921 Runners-up 1930
QUEEN OF THE SOUTH (1919)			
Palmerston Park Dumfries	Blue/white	Div. 2 Champions 1950–51 Runners-up 1932–33, 1961–62, 1974–75	
QUEEN'S PARK (1867)			
Hampden Park Glasgow G42 9BA	Black, white/white	Div. 2 Champions 1922–23, 1955–56	Winners 1874, 1875, 1876, 1880, 1881, 1882, 1884, 1886, 1890, 1893 Runners-up 1892, 1900 English FA Cup runners-up 1884, 1885
RAITH ROVERS (1893)			
Stark's Park Kirkcaldy	Blue/white	Div. 2 Champions 1907–08, 1909–10 (shared), 1937–38, 1948–49 Runners-up 1908–09, 1926–27, 1966–67, 1975–76, 1977–78	Runners-up 1913

League Cup	Record win	Highest number of Individual goals
		KILMARNOCK
Runners-up 1953, 1961, 1963	11–1 v Paisley Academicals, Scottish Cup, 1929–30	Peerie Cunningham, 35, 1927–28
		MEADOWBANK THISTLE
	4–1 v Albion Rovers, Div. 2, 1975–76 and v Forfar, League Cup, 1975–76	Kenny Davidson and Jim Hancock, 8, 1976–77, Jim Hancock, 8, 1977–78
		MONTROSE
	12–0 v Vale of Leithen, Scottish Cup, 1974–75	Brian Third, 29, 1972–73
		MORTON
Runners-up 1964	11–0 v Carfin Shamrock, Scottish Cup, 1886–87	Allan McGraw, 41, 1963–64
		MOTHERWELL
Winners 1951 Runners-up 1955	12–1 v Dundee United, Div. 2, 1953–54	Willie MacFadyen, 52, 1931–32
		PARTICK THISTLE
Winners 1972 Runners-up 1954, 1957, 1959	16–0 v Royal Albert, Scottish Cup 1930–31	Alec Hair, 41, 1926–27
		QUEEN OF THE SOUTH
	11–1 v Stranraer, Scottish Cup, 1931–32	Jimmy Gray, 33, 1927–28
		QUEEN'S PARK
	16–0 v St Peter's, Scottish Cup, 1885–86	Willie Martin, 30, 1937–38
		RAITH ROVERS
Runners-up 1949	10–1 v Coldstream, Scottish Cup, 1953–54	Norman Haywood, 38, 1937–38

Ground	Shirts/shorts	Honours League	Cup
RANGERS (1873)			
Ibrox Stadium Glasgow SW	Blue/white	Premier Div. Champions 1975–76, 1977–78 Premier Div. Runners-up 1976–77 Div. 1 Champions 1890–91 (shared), 1898–99, 1899–1900, 1900–01, 1901–02, 1910–11, 1911–12, 1912–13, 1917–18, 1919–20, 1920–21, 1922–23, 1923–24, 1924–25, 1926–27, 1927–28, 1928–29, 1929–30, 1930–31, 1932–33, 1933–34, 1934–35, 1936–37, 1938–39, 1946–47, 1948–49, 1949–50, 1952–53, 1955–56, 1956–57, 1958–59, 1960–61,	Winners 1894, 1897, 1898, 1903, 1928, 1930, 1932, 1934, 1935, 1936, 1948, 1949, 1950, 1953, 1960, 1962, 1963, 1964, 1966, 1973, 1976, 1978 Runners-up 11 times 1962–63, 1963–64, 1974–75 Runners-up 21 times
ST JOHNSTONE (1884)			
Muirton Park Perth	Blue/white	Div. 2 Champions 1923–24, 1959–60, 1962–63 Runners-up 1931–32	
ST MIRREN (1876)			
St Mirren Park Paisley	Black, white/white	Div. 1 Champions 1976–77 Div. 2 Champions 1967–68 Runners-up 1935–36	Winners 1926, 1959 Runners-up 1908, 1934, 1962
STENHOUSEMUIR (1884)			
Ochilview Park Larbert	Maroon/white	Highest League position 3rd, Div. 2, 1958–59, 1960–61	
STIRLING ALBION (1945)			
Annfield Park Stirling	Red/red	Div. 2 Champions 1952–53, 1957–58, 1960–61, 1964–65, 1976–77 Runners-up 1948–49, 1950–51	
STRANRAER (1870)			
Stair Park Stranraer	Blue/white	Highest League position 4th, Div. 2, 1960–61, 1976–77	

Welsh and Irish Football

THE FOOTBALL ASSOCIATION OF WALES

The Football Association of Wales was formed in 1876. But it is the only one of the four home associations which does not have its own National League and as such is not eligible to forward a club for the European Champion Clubs Cup each year.

However, the winner of the Welsh Cup which was first contested in 1877–78 enters the European Cup-Winners Cup. The first Welsh Cup competition was won by Wrexham who defeated Druids 1–0 in the final. Wrexham have been the most successful club, having won it 21 times.

There is a Welsh League founded in 1902 which is divided regionally and includes the reserve teams of clubs who are members of the Football League.

League Cup	Record win	Highest number of Individual goals
		RANGERS
Winners 1947, 1949, 1961, 1962, 1964, 1965, 1971, 1976, 1978 Runners-up 5 times	14–2 v Blairgowrie, Scottish Cup, 1933–34	Sam English, 44, 1931–32
		ST JOHNSTONE
Runners-up 1970	8–1 v Partick Thistle, Scottish Cup, 1969–70	Jimmy Benson, 36, 1931–32
		ST MIRREN
Runners-up 1956	15–0 v Glasgow University, Scottish Cup, 1959–60	Dunky Walker, 45, 1921–22
		STENHOUSEMUIR
	9–2 v Dundee United, Div. 2, 1936–37	Evelyn Morrison, 29, 1927–28
		STIRLING ALBION
	7–0 v Albion Rovers, Div. 2, 1947–48; v Montrose, Div. 2, 1957–58; v St Mirren, Div. 1, 1959–60 and v Arbroath, Div. 2, 1964–65	Michael Lawson, 26, 1975–76
		STRANRAER
	7–0 v Brechin City, Div. 2, 1964–65	Derek Frye, 27, 1977–78

IRISH FOOTBALL ASSOCIATION

The Irish F.A. was founded on 18 November 1880. In 1921 clubs in the South of Ireland formed the Irish Free State F.A. Two years later a meeting of the four home associations agreed that the Irish F.A's jurisdiction should be confined to Northern Ireland.

Irish Cup
The Irish Football Association Cup was first contested in 1880–81 when seven clubs participated. Moyola Park became the first winners, beating Cliftonville 1–0 in the final. Linfield have been the most successful club with 30 victories.

Irish League
Eight clubs formed the original Irish League which was first contested in 1890–91. Linfield who were the initial winners have been the most successful club with 30 championships.

The Football Association of Ireland (Dublin)
The Football Association of Ireland was formed in June 1921. The Football League of Ireland came into existence two months afterwards. In 1923 the F.A. was accepted into FIFA membership.

FIFA decided in June 1954 that international teams representing the Football Association of Ireland should be referred to as the Republic of Ireland.

British International Football

BRITISH INTERNATIONAL CHAMPIONSHIP

The British International Championship began when all four home countries started playing each other. Previously matches between some of them had only been regarded as friendlies. The tournament itself began in 1883–84. If countries are level on points at the top they share the title, as goal average or goal difference does not count in determining the winner.

England have won the title outright on 31 occasions, Scotland 24, Wales seven and Ireland once. England have been concerned in all the 20 shared titles, Scotland 17, Wales and Ireland in five each.

In the overall record of matches between the four home countries, in addition to the friendlies played before the International Championship started, England and Wales met each other twice in qualifying matches for the 1974 World Cup, as did Scotland and Wales in the 1978 World Cup, Scotland played England as part of their Centenary in 1973 and Wales met England in their Centenary match in 1976.

England v Scotland

First match	Scotland 0 England 0, 30 November 1872, Glasgow
Overall record	96 matches: Scotland 38 wins, England 36, drawn 22. Goals: England 174, Scotland 163
Record win	England 9 Scotland 3, 15 April 1961, Wembley
Best individual performance	Dennis Wilshaw (England) 4 goals v Scotland, 2 April 1955, Wembley
Most appearances	Billy Wright (England) 13 appearances v Scotland

Wales v Scotland

First match	Scotland 4 Wales 0, 25 March 1876, Glasgow
Overall record	93 matches: Scotland 56 wins, Wales 16, drawn 21. Goals: Scotland 231, Wales 103
Record win	Scotland 9 Wales 0, 23 March 1878, Old Hampden
Best individual performance	Willie Paul (Scotland) 4 goals v Wales 22 March 1890, Paisley. John Madden (Scotland) 4 goals v Wales 18 March 1883, Wrexham
Most appearances	Billy Meredith (Wales) 12 appearances v Scotland Ivor Allchurch (Wales) 12 appearances v Scotland

England v Wales

First match	England 2 Wales 1, 18 January 1879, Kennington Oval
Overall record	91 matches: England 60 wins, Wales 12, drawn 19. Goals: England 235, Wales 84
Record win	Wales 1 England 9, 16 March 1896, Cardiff
Best individual performance	Steve Bloomer (England) 5 goals v Wales, 16 March 1896, Cardiff
Most appearances	Billy Meredith (Wales) 20 appearances v England

Ireland v Wales

First match	Wales 7 Ireland 1, 25 February 1882, Wrexham
Overall record	85 matches: Wales 40 wins, Ireland 26, drawn 19. Goals: Wales 175, Ireland 123
Record win	Wales 11 Ireland 0, 3 March 1888, Wrexham
Best individual performance	Joe Bambrick (Ireland) 6 goals v Wales, 1 February 1930, Belfast
Most appearances	Billy Meredith (Wales) 16 appearances v Ireland

Ireland v England

First match	England 7 Ireland 0, 24 February 1883, Liverpool
Overall record	85 matches: England 66 wins, Ireland 6, drawn 13. Goals: England 296, Ireland 78
Record win	Ireland 0 England 13, 18 February 1882, Belfast
Best individual performance	Willie Hall (England) 5 goals v Ireland, 16 November 1938, Old Trafford
Most appearances	Billy Wright (England), Billy Bingham (Ireland), Jimmy McIlroy (Ireland) and Pat Jennings (Ireland) 13 appearances each

Scotland v Ireland

First match	Ireland 0 Scotland 5, 26 January 1884, Belfast
Overall record	83 matches: Scotland 58 wins, Ireland 13, drawn 12. Goals: Scotland 248, Ireland 76
Record win	Scotland 11 Ireland 0, 23 February 1901, Hampden Park
Best individual performance	Charles Heggie (Scotland) 5 goals v Ireland, 20 March 1886, Belfast
Most appearances	Danny Blanchflower (Ireland) 13 appearances v Scotland

Youngest international players

England:	Duncan Edwards (Manchester United) 18 years 183 days, left-half v Scotland, 2 April 1955
Ireland:	Norman Kernoghan (Belfast Celtic) 17 years 80 days, outside-right v Wales, 11 March 1936
Scotland:	Denis Law (Huddersfield Town) 18 years 236 days, inside-forward v Wales, 18 October 1958
Wales:	John Charles (Leeds United) 18 years 71 days, centre-half v Ireland, 8 March 1950

(There are claims that other players have been younger, but the above examples are the only instances which have so far been proved satisfactorily.)

International mosaic

Although Danny Blanchflower holds the record with 33 consecutive appearances in the British International Championship for Northern Ireland between 1952 and 1962, two other players made more appearances overall in the competition. Billy Wright made 38 including an English record of 25 successive appearances from 14 April 1951 to 11 April 1959.

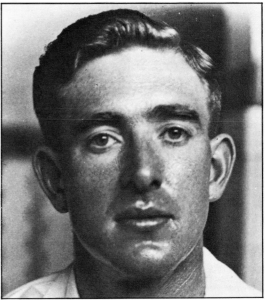

Danny Blanchflower who holds the record number of consecutive appearances in the British International Championship.

But Billy Meredith (Manchester City and Manchester United), capped on 48 occasions by Wales between 1895 and 1920, made all his appearances in the International Championship long before Wales played foreign opposition for the first time in Paris against France on 25 May 1933.

Wright set up a world record of 70 consecutive appearances which began against France on 3 October 1951 and ended against the USA on 28 May 1959.

Vivian Woodward played 61 times for England, though this figure included only 23 full internationals from 1903 to 1911. He also played in three Test matches against South Africa and six times for Great Britain in the Olympic Games in 1908 and 1912.

In the 1908–09 season, when Spurs won promotion to the First Division, it was Wood-

Vivian Woodward, footballer, international and director.

ward, an architect by profession, as well as a director of the club, who finished as their leading scorer with 19 goals in 27 Division Two games.

Acknowledged as one of football's gentlemen, Woodward was popular with his professional team-mates as well as spectators, and his scoring ability certainly helped establish Tottenham Hotspur among the country's leading clubs during the eight years he chose to remain with them. Indeed, it was a real shock when he announced his retirement in 1909 because he considered he could no longer spare the time to play football, and it was an even greater blow when, five months later, he was persuaded to turn out for Chelsea who were then sadly depleted by injuries and in danger of relegation.

He was unable to prevent them from dropping into Division Two, but the club was fortunate in being able to retain this player's services and in 1911–12, when they fought their way back into Division One, he made 14 appearances in the side. In fact he continued to play for them until the early part of the 1914–15 season when he joined the Middlesex Regiment and departed for the battlefields of France where, in 1916, he received leg wounds which finished his playing career.

This rather frail-looking footballer must be rated among the most outstanding amateurs of the 20th century because he was a player who used his brains in a more subtle style of football at a time when most centre-forwards relied on weight and strength, and because this pure approach to football brought him more than 70 goals for England in his international appearances, which were both amateur and full internationals. Obviously, any opinions he expressed in the board-room were received with appreciation and respect.

Stanley Davies made 18 appearances for Wales between 1920 and 1930 while with four different clubs: Preston North End, Everton, West Bromwich Albion and Rotherham United. During this time he turned out in six different positions: right-half (twice), left-half (once), outside-right (twice), inside-right (three times), centre-forward (six) and inside-left (four). While with West Bromwich he once scored from 30 yards in an F.A. Cup tie against Liverpool.

Before 1971 there were a few instances of players being born in one country and playing for another. But since then the international qualification rules have been altered to allow a player to represent the country of his father's birth.

An early example was Stuart Macrae, born Port Bannantyne, Bute, Scotland, who made six appearances for England at wing-half in 1883–84. Educated at Edinburgh Academy, he had captained the rugby XV there ten years earlier.

There have been many instances of players appearing in international matches for two different countries, while Ladislao Kubala and Alfredo di Stefano played for three each. Kubala was born in Hungary and first played for them at international level. Then he played for Czechoslovakia and Spain. Di Stefano played for his native Argentina, Colombia and Spain.

Tommy Pearson (Newcastle United), born in Scotland, played for England v Scotland in a wartime Red Cross international match at Newcastle on 2 December 1939 when he was pressed into service as a replacement for Eric Brook (Manchester City) who had been injured in an accident.

Stan Mortensen (Blackpool) made his international debut for Wales in wartime against his own country, at Wembley on 25 September 1943. He was reserve for England, but when Wales lost their left-half Ivor Powell with injury it was agreed that Mortensen should take his place.

Cardiff City had 17 players on their staff towards the end of the 1925–26 season all of whom had been capped. They were Fred Keenor, Billy Davies, Len Davies, Harold Beadles, Herbie Evans, Jack Evans, Jack Lewis, Jack Nicholls and Edgar Thomas, all Welsh internationals; Joe Cassidy, Jimmy Nelson, Jimmy Blair and David Lawson, Scottish internationals, and Tom Farquharson, Pat McIlvenny, Tom Watson and Tom Sloan, Irish internationals. Interestingly enough there was also Edgar Thomas, the Cardiff Corinthian, though he never actually appeared in City's League side, but was an amateur with the club during the same season having been capped the previous season for Wales against England. Towards the end of 1977–78 Manchester United had 18 full internationals on their books.

The only occasion that a Welsh international team achieved double figures was against Ireland at Wrexham, 3 March 1888 when they won 11–0. Playing a short-passing game Wales were five goals ahead at half-time, and when Jack Doughty scored the eleventh goal the Welsh team had been reduced to eight men because the others had already left 10 minutes early to catch a train. The Doughty brothers, Jack and Roger, of Newton Heath (Manchester United), scored six of their side's goals between them in this game, with Jack getting four. He was the first man to score for Wales in each of three consecutive internationals and gained a reputation as a difficult man to stop. Often in the Newton Heath side these two brothers played alongside each other in the attack and it was said that one concentrated on the defender while the other concentrated on the ball.

There has not been a full England international match held at Old Trafford, Manchester, since November 1938, or at Anfield, Liverpool, since November 1931. Yet attendances at these two venues has been higher for Manchester United and Liverpool than any other Football League clubs in recent years.

Manchester United's Denis Law twice scored four goals for Scotland in full international matches on the same ground and on the same dates in successive years. The first occasion was against Ireland on 7 November 1962, and the second against Norway on 7 November 1963.

The three goals scored by Fulham's Johnny Haynes against the USSR at Wembley on 22 October 1958 rank as the only hat-trick ever achieved for England against any of the Eastern European countries.

England's first home defeat by a side outside the United Kingdom in an international occurred on Wednesday 21 September 1949, when at Goodison Park they were beaten by the Republic of Ireland. It was also achieved by a largely experimental Republic side. England were generally in command until they came within shooting range. Even so the Republic owed much to goalkeeper Tommy Godwin, then with Shamrock Rovers but later to enjoy a lengthy Football League career with Leicester City and Bournemouth. He was one of the several heroes including defenders John Carey, Con Martin and Bud Aherne. The Republic scored once in each half, Martin from the penalty spot and Peter Farrell. Only Tom Finney of the home forwards retained his place for England's next match.

No other player in history ever figured in so many matches before he was on the losing side as Republic of Ireland international goalkeeper Pat Dunne. When he was in a Manchester United team beaten by Leeds United on 5 December 1964, it was his 20th first-class match.

The receipts for the first England v Scotland international ever held in England – at The Oval, 8 March 1873 – were £106.1.0d (£106.05). The F.A. made a profit of £73.8.6d (£73.42½) after paying expenses which included £10 for the hire of the ground from Surrey C.C.C. and £15.14.6d (£15.72½) to provide the Scottish team with lunch and dinner. The England team paid their own expenses.

When this corresponding fixture was first held at Wembley on 14 April 1934, the F.A. received £13,384.18.5d (£13,384.94) after expenses and the Wembley Stadium Company had taken their share.

Bill McCracken, famous old-time Newcastle United right-back and probably the greatest exponent of the offside trap, collected his first Irish international cap as far back as 1902 and 76 years later had just retired from scouting for Watford at 95 after a lifetime in the game. Born in Belfast, he was a full-back with Distillery and Newcastle United, played 15 times for Northern Ireland and later had lengthy managerial connections with Hull City, Millwall and Aldershot before becoming a scout with several Football League clubs.

No other goalkeeper ever made such a chastening international debut as Hugh Kelly – when Northern Ireland gave him his chance against England at Maine Road in November 1949. He had nine scored against him, yet Ireland retained him for the next match.

Sam Hardy, Elisha Scott, Tim Williamson, Jimmy Lawrence, Jerry Dawson and Ted Sagar were among international goalkeepers of earlier days who kept going in the Football League until they were turned 40. Peter Bonetti was still an active senior with Chelsea in 1977–78 at the age of 36.

Glasgow Rangers have supplied 106 players to the Scottish national team since Moses McNeil appeared against Wales on 25 March 1876. Eight others have played for Northern Ireland.

A match at Windsor Park against Ireland on 2 October 1954 set up a record for an England eleven with seven players making their international bow: Ray Wood and Bill Foulkes (Manchester United), Johnny Wheeler (Bolton Wanderers), Ray Barlow (West Bromwich Albion), Don Revie (Manchester City), Johnny Haynes (Fulham) and Brian Pilkington (Burnley).

Though the Scottish team against England in 1872 was composed entirely of Queen's Park players no attempt had been made to select a representative side and in the 1890s the England team against Wales twice included all Corinthian players who were a combined eleven most of whom also appeared with other clubs, schools, colleges and universities. The occasions were 5 March 1894 (won 5–1) at Wrexham and 8 March 1895 (drew 1–1) at Queen's Club, London.

In May 1971 Leeds United supplied eight players for two British International Championship matches. Paul Madeley, Terry Cooper and Allan Clarke appeared for England v. Ireland; Peter Lorimer, Billy Bremner and Eddie Gray for Scotland v. Wales and Gary Sprake and Terry Yorath for Wales.

Leeds also achieved a remarkable feat on 20 November 1974, by providing ten of their players for full international matches on the same day. Paul Madeley, Terry Cooper and Allan Clarke played for England v. Portugal; David Harvey, Billy Bremner, Gordon McQueen, Peter Lorimer and Joe Jordan for Scotland v. Spain; Terry Yorath for Wales v. Luxembourg; and Johnny Giles for Eire v. Turkey.

In 1973 Leeds had 14 international players on their staff. In addition to those mentioned previously they had Jack Charlton, Norman Hunter, Paul Reaney and Mick Jones (all England), Joe Jordan (Scotland) and Johnny Giles (Republic of Ireland).

The record number of players from one club playing together in an England team is seven. Frank Moss, George Male, Eddie Hapgood, Wilf Copping, Raymond Bowden, Ted Drake and Cliff Bastin of Arsenal played against Italy at Highbury on 14 November 1934. England won 3–2. Arsenal had six players in the England team v. Wales on 5 February 1936 and also v. Austria, 6 May 1936.

Linfield supplied seven of the players in the Ireland team against Scotland on 25 March 1893 in Glasgow, Scotland won 6–1.

It will not be amiss to mention here the achievements of two continental club teams in this context.

Torino supplied ten of the Italian team against Hungary on 11 May 1947: Aldo Ballarin, Virgilio Maroso, Giuseppe Grezar, Mario Rigamonti, Eusebio Castigliano, Romeo Menti II, Ezio Loik, Guglielmo Gabetto, Valentino Mazzola and Pietro Ferraris II (captain). Odd man out was goalkeeper Lucidio Sentimenti IV of the other Turin club, Juventus. Italy won 3–2.

When the Belgian goalkeeper Jean Trappeniers came on as a second-half substitute for his country against Holland on 30 September 1964 he joined Georges Heylens, Laurient Verbiest, Jean Plaskie, Jean Cornelis, Pierre Hanon, Joseph Jurion, Jacky Stockman, Johan Devrindt, Paul Van Himst and Wilfried Puis – all from Anderlecht, his own club side. Belgium won 1–0.

During the 1936–37 season Arsenal had 14 international players on their books. In addition to the seven mentioned previously, Jack Crayston, Joe Hulme, Bernard Joy, Alf Kirchen and Herbie Roberts (all England), Alex James (Scotland) and Bob John (Wales) completed the roster.

Cardiff City provided a record when they supplied the respective captains Fred Keenor and Jimmy Blair in the Wales v. Scotland, British International Championship match at Ninian Park, Cardiff, on 16 February 1924.

In the 1933–34 season Aston Villa had 15 internationals on their staff. There were ten who had played for England: Joe Beresford, George Brown, Arthur Cunliffe, Tommy Gardner, Eric Houghton, Tommy Mort, Joe Tate, Tommy Smart, Billy Walker and Pongo Waring; three for Scotland: Danny Blair, Jimmy Gibson and Joe Nibloe and a Welshman, Dai Astley.

Pongo Waring one of Aston Villa's 15 internationals in 1933–34.

Wales often experienced difficulty in raising a team for an International in the years before the first World War. Valiant efforts were made by sides which contained second or third choices in certain positions when clubs refused to release players to the Welsh F.A. One such occasion was a game against Ireland at Windsor Park, Belfast, in January 1913.

Bad weather had caused the postponement of F.A. Cup ties in England and the Welsh team had to make at least half a dozen late changes. Even then they could not muster a team without including George Lathom at right-half. He had previously played for Wales but for this game he actually travelled to Belfast as the team's trainer.

Despite their selection problems, however, Wales won with the only goal of the game which was scored in the first minute. After that Ireland did most of the attacking but the scratch Welsh team gallantly held on to their slender lead.

The last non-League amateur to appear for England in a full international was inside-forward Edgar Kail of Dulwich Hamlet. He was an amateur who could have gained a place with almost any Football League side in his day if he had chosen to turn professional. As it was he collected every honour open to him as a Dulwich Hamlet player, including 21 England amateur caps, and was a reserve for England's full international side against Ireland, Scotland and Wales, before he was finally rewarded with a full cap by playing inside-right in three of England's internationals on their continental tour of 1929. Then he scored two goals in England's 4–1 victory over France, helped them beat Belgium 5–1, and was on the losing side in Madrid when Spain won 4–3.

Between 1946 and 1948 Kevin O'Flanagan played for Ireland at Soccer and Rugby Union, and his brother Michael for Eire at Soccer and Ireland at Rugby Union. It was the only case in history of brothers both becoming internationals in two football codes.

When left-back Fred Titmus and centre-forward Bill Rawlings appeared against Wales at Anfield in March 1922 Southampton became, and still remain, the only Division Three club ever to have supplied two players to an England team for a British International Championship match.

George Best one of several Irish internationals at Manchester United capped originally as teenagers.

In November 1959 Johnny Crossan was chosen for Ireland against England at Wembley, yet at the time he was banned from playing with any Irish or English club. Then in Dutch soccer, he was under 'permanent suspension' by both the Football League and the Irish League.

Birmingham had four international goalkeepers all on their playing list simultaneously in 1929. Dan Tremelling and Harry Hibbs were full England internationals, Kenneth Tewkesbury an amateur international, and Arthur Slater a junior international.

English-born sons of Eire fathers who have won full international honours with their parent's country include David O'Leary (Arsenal), John Dempsey (Chelsea), Gerry Peyton (Fulham), Tony Grealish (Orient), Mick Kearns (Walsall) and Terry Mancini (when with Queen's Park Rangers and Arsenal).

No other club is more accustomed than Arsenal to having unusually youthful internationals on their pay-roll. Of those still at Highbury in 1977–78, Pat Rice played for Northern Ireland when only 19 and David O'Leary at 18 and Liam Brady (19) with the Republic of Ireland. Of ex-Arsenal players, Alan Ball (Southampton) and Alex Cropley (Aston Villa) were full internationals with England and Scotland respectively when in their teens, though before they joined Arsenal.

Manchester United have set up a unique sequence in the matter of assembling Northern Ireland natives who became full internationals as teenagers. Former Old Trafford stars who did so when only 17 were George Best and Jimmy Nicholson. Of contemporary United players Sammy McIlroy also did so at 17, David McCreery at 18, and Jimmy Nicholl and Chris McGrath (while with Tottenham Hotspur) when 19.

On 31 October 1974, all five countries of the British Isles won full international matches without a goal being scored against any of them. Results were: England 3, Czechoslovakia 0; Wales 2, Hungary 0; Scotland 3, East Germany 0; Sweden 0, Ireland 2; Republic of Ireland 3, Russia 0. All the losers except Sweden were East European teams.

FULL INTERNATIONAL RECORD OF THE HOME COUNTRIES

ENGLAND

Opponents	P	W	D	L	F	A
Argentina	7	3	3	1	9	6
Austria	14	8	3	3	51	21
Belgium	16	12	3	1	65	23
Bohemia	1	1	0	0	4	0
Brazil	11	1	4	6	9	8
Bulgaria	3	1	2	0	2	1
Chile	2	2	0	0	4	1
Colombia	1	1	0	0	4	0
Cyprus	2	2	0	0	6	0
Czechoslovakia	8	4	2	2	16	11
Denmark	5	4	1	0	16	4
Ecuador	1	1	0	0	2	0
Finland	5	5	0	0	22	3
France	18	13	2	3	57	24
East Germany	3	2	1	0	6	3
West Germany	14	8	2	4	30	19
Greece	2	2	0	0	5	0
Hungary	11	6	0	5	36	26
Northern Ireland	85	66	13	6	296	78
Republic of Ireland	6	3	2	1	11	6
Italy	13	6	4	3	23	17
Luxembourg	4	4	0	0	23	3
Malta	2	2	0	0	6	0
Mexico	4	2	1	1	11	2
Netherlands (Holland)	6	3	2	1	11	5
Norway	4	4	0	0	20	2
Peru	2	1	0	1	5	4
Poland	4	1	2	1	3	4
Portugal	14	8	5	1	35	16
Rumania	4	2	2	0	4	1
Scotland	96	36	22	38	174	163
Spain	11	7	1	3	26	14
Sweden	9	6	1	2	23	13
Switzerland	12	8	2	2	33	9
USA	4	3	0	1	24	5
USSR	7	3	3	1	14	7
Uruguay	6	2	2	2	7	8
Wales	91	60	19	12	235	84
Yugoslavia	11	2	5	4	15	18
Rest of Europe	1	1	0	0	3	0
FIFA	1	0	1	0	4	4
Rest of the World	1	1	0	0	2	1
Team America	1	1	0	0	3	1

SCOTLAND

Opponents	P	W	D	L	F	A
Argentina	1	0	1	0	1	1
Austria	12	3	3	6	15	24
Belgium	6	3	0	3	10	7
Brazil	5	0	2	3	1	5
Bulgaria	1	1	0	0	2	1
Cyprus	2	2	0	0	13	0
Chile	1	1	0	0	4	2
Czechoslovakia	10	5	1	4	18	16
Denmark	9	8	0	1	17	5
England	96	38	22	36	163	174
Finland	4	4	0	0	13	3
France	7	5	0	2	10	6
East Germany	2	1	0	1	3	1
West Germany	9	3	4	2	16	13
Hungary	5	1	2	2	10	12
Northern Ireland	83	58	12	13	248	76
Republic of Ireland	4	2	1	1	8	3
Italy	3	1	0	2	1	6
Iran	1	0	1	0	1	1

SCOTLAND (Cont.)

Opponents	P	W	D	L	F	A
Luxembourg	1	1	0	0	6	0
Netherlands (Holland)	7	4	1	2	11	9
Norway	6	4	1	1	20	10
Paraguay	1	0	0	1	2	3
Peru	2	1	0	1	3	3
Poland	4	1	1	2	6	7
Portugal	7	3	1	3	8	7
Rumania	2	0	2	0	2	2
Spain	6	2	2	2	13	11
Sweden	4	1	1	2	6	7
Switzerland	7	5	0	2	13	9
Turkey	1	0	0	1	2	4
Uruguay	2	0	0	2	2	10
USA	1	1	0	0	6	0
USSR	2	0	0	2	0	3
Wales	93	56	22	15	231	103
Yugoslavia	5	1	4	0	8	6
Zaire	1	1	0	0	2	0

WALES

Opponents	P	W	D	L	F	A
Austria	4	1	0	3	3	6
Belgium	2	1	0	1	6	4
Brazil	5	0	0	5	3	11
Chile	1	0	0	1	0	2
Czechoslovakia	6	2	0	4	5	7
Denmark	2	1	0	1	4	3
England	91	12	19	60	84	235
Finland	2	2	0	0	4	0
France	3	0	1	2	3	9
East Germany	4	1	0	3	7	8
West Germany	4	0	3	1	3	5
Greece	2	1	0	1	4	3
Hungary	7	3	2	2	11	10
Luxembourg	2	2	0	0	8	1
Northern Ireland	85	40	19	26	175	123
Republic of Ireland	1	1	0	0	3	2
Iran	1	1	0	0	1	0
Israel	2	2	0	0	4	0
Italy	3	0	0	3	2	9
Kuwait	2	0	2	0	0	0
Mexico	2	0	1	1	2	3
Poland	2	1	0	2	2	3
Portugal	2	1	0	1	4	4
Rumania	2	0	1	1	0	2
Scotland	92	15	22	56	103	231
Spain	2	0	1	1	2	3
Sweden	1	0	1	0	0	0
Switzerland	2	1	0	1	3	6
Rest of the UK	2	1	0	1	3	3
USSR	2	1	0	1	3	3
Yugoslavia	4	0	1	3	4	11

NORTHERN IRELAND

Opponents	P	W	D	L	F	A
Albania	2	1	1	0	5	2
Argentina	1	0	0	1	1	3
Belgium	2	1	0	1	3	2
Bulgaria	2	0	1	1	0	3
Cyprus	4	3	0	1	11	1
Czechoslovakia	2	2	0	0	3	1
England	85	6	13	66	78	296
France	3	0	1	2	3	9
Greece	2	1	0	1	3	2
Netherlands (Holland)	5	1	2	2	4	8
Israel	2	1	1	0	4	3
Iceland	2	1	0	1	2	1
Italy	4	1	1	2	6	7

NORTHERN IRELAND (Cont.)

Opponents	P	W	D	L	F	A
Mexico	1	1	0	0	4	1
Norway	2	1	0	1	4	2
Poland	2	2	0	0	4	0
Portugal	4	1	3	0	6	3
Scotland	83	13	12	58	76	248
Spain	5	0	2	3	4	12
Sweden	2	1	0	1	3	2
Switzerland	2	1	0	1	2	2
Turkey	2	2	0	0	7	1
Uruguay	1	1	0	0	3	0
USSR	4	0	2	2	1	4
Wales	85	26	19	40	123	175
West Germany	5	0	1	4	6	15
Yugoslavia	2	1	0	1	1	1

Kenny Dalglish
(see below)

		Int. Champ.	Others	Total
INTERNATIONAL APPEARANCES (ENGLAND) 50 or more				
Bobby Moore (West Ham United)	1962–1973	30	78	108
Bobby Charlton (Manchester United)	1958–1970	32	74	106
Billy Wright (Wolverhampton Wanderers)	1946–1959	38	67	105
Tom Finney (Preston North End)	1946–1956	29	47	76
Gordon Banks (Leicester City, Stoke City)	1963–1972	23	50	73
Alan Ball (Blackpool, Everton, Arsenal)	1965–1975	20	52	72
Martin Peters (West Ham, Tottenham Hotspur)	1966–1974	19	48	67
Ray Wilson (Huddersfield Town, Everton)	1960–1968	15	48	63
Jimmy Greaves (Chelsea, Tottenham Hotspur)	1959–1967	14	43	57
Johnny Haynes (Fulham)	1954–1962	16	40	56
Stanley Matthews (Stoke City, Blackpool)	1934–1956	24	30	54*
Emlyn Hughes (Liverpool)	1969–	17	37	54
INTERNATIONAL APPEARANCES (SCOTLAND) 50 or more				
Kenny Dalglish (Celtic, Liverpool)	1971–	17	40	57
Denis Law (Huddersfield Town, Manchester City, Torino, Manchester United)	1958–1974	26	29	55
Billy Bremner (Leeds United)	1965–1976	19	35	54
George Young (Rangers)	1946–1957	29	24	53
INTERNATIONAL APPEARANCES (NORTHERN IRELAND) 50 or more				
Pat Jennings (Watford, Tottenham Hotspur, Arsenal)	1964–	37	34	71
Terry Neill (Arsenal, Hull City)	1961–1973	30	30	60
Danny Blanchflower (Barnsley, Aston Villa, Tottenham Hotspur)	1949–1962	37	19	56
Billy Bingham (Sunderland, Luton Town, Everton)	1951–1963	34	22	56
Jimmy McIlroy (Burnley)	1951–1965	36	19	55
INTERNATIONAL APPEARANCES (WALES) 50 or more				
Ivor Allchurch (Swansea, Newcastle United, Cardiff City)	1950–1966	37	31	68
Cliff Jones (Swansea, Tottenham Hotspur, Fulham)	1954–1969	31	28	59

*Matthews' total would have been substantially more had the 29 war-time and Victory internationals in which he appeared been added to this total.

EUROPEAN SOCCER

UEFA

The Union of European Football Association came into being in June 1954 and is one of the six Confederations operating within FIFA. There are 34 countries in membership and its headquarters are in Berne, Switzerland.

Competitions under its control include the European Champion Clubs Cup, the European Cup-Winners Cup, the European Championship (formerly Nations Cup) and the UEFA Cup, as well as the European Under-21 Championship (formerly for Under-23s) and the European Cup for Amateurs.

EUROPEAN FOOTBALL CHAMPIONSHIP

The European Football Championship was first contested as the Nations Cup between 1958 and 1960. It is played every four years over a two-year period following the World Cup.

The winners receive the Henri Delaunay Cup, named after the former secretary of the French Football Federation and UEFA's first secretary.

Up to 1964 it was played on a knock-out basis with home and away fixtures up to the semi-finals but the third competition under its present title of the European Championship was re-styled. Teams were split into eight groups playing home and away on a League basis with the winners contesting the quarter-finals also on a home and away principle. The semi-finals, match for third and fourth place and the final have always been staged in one pre-determined country.

A further change was made for the 1978–80 competition with one country staging the final tournament comprising the eight quarter-finalists, including the host nation Italy seeded to this stage.

East European countries have dominated the competition in terms of matches won as well as providing two of the winners, the first through

---

EUROPEAN FOOTBALL CHAMPIONSHIP (FORMERLY NATIONS CUP) RECORD OF COMPETING TEAMS 1958–1976

		P	W	D	L	F	A			P	W	D	L	F	A
1	USSR	38	23	7	8	68	34	18	Scotland	18	8	5	5	22	21
2	Yugoslavia	37	19	9	9	63	40	19	Poland	22	8	5	9	34	31
3	Czechoslovakia	32	19	6	7	78	32	20	Wales	22	8	5	9	31	28
4	Spain	32	17	9	6	61	24	21	Republic of Ireland	26	8	5	13	30	46
5	Hungary	35	18	7	10	69	43	22	Northern Ireland	22	8	4	10	25	21
6	Italy	29	14	10	5	47	20	23	Turkey	22	7	5	10	16	40
7	West Germany	24	14	8	2	53	20	24	Switzerland	20	7	4	9	36	32
8	England	26	15	6	5	50	22	25	Denmark	29	6	5	18	34	62
9	France	32	13	8	11	65	49	26	Greece	19	5	6	8	24	33
10	Bulgaria	27	13	6	8	44	30	27	Norway	22	3	3	16	23	55
11	Holland	26	13	4	9	60	36	28	Luxembourg	23	1	5	17	17	87
12	Belgium	26	12	5	9	39	40	29	Albania	12	2	2	8	6	25
13	Portugal	25	11	6	8	35	32	30	Iceland	8	1	3	4	6	13
14	Rumania	27	10	8	9	51	42	31	Finland	18	0	4	14	9	41
15	East Germany	24	9	7	8	38	35	32	Malta	14	1	1	12	6	45
16	Sweden	24	9	6	9	28	33	33	Cyprus	18	1	0	17	5	77
17	Austria	23	9	4	10	43	37								

EUROPEAN CHAMPIONSHIP FINAL

Series	Final			No of entries
1958–60	(10 July 1960, Paris att. 17,966)			
	USSR (Metreveli, Ponedelnik)	(0) (1) 2	**Yugoslavia** (Netto o.g.) (1) (1) 1	17
1962–64	(21 June 1964, Madrid att. 120,000)			
	Spain (Pereda, Marcelino)	(1) 2	**USSR** (Khusainov) (1) 1	29
1966–68	(8 June 1968, Rome att. 75,000)			
	Italy (Domenghini)	(0) (0) 1	**Yugoslavia** (Dzajic) (1) (1) 1	31
Replay	(10 June 1968, Rome att. 60,000)			
	Italy (Riva, Anastasi)	(2) 2	**Yugoslavia** (0) 0	
1970–72	(18 June 1972, Brussels att. 43,437)			
	West Germany (Muller (G) 2, Wimmer)	(1) 3	**USSR** (0) 0	32
1974–76	(20 June 1976, Belgrade att. 45,000)			
	Czechoslovakia (Svehlik, Dobias)	(2) (2) 2	**West Germany** (Muller (D), Holzenbein) (1) (2) 2	32
	Czechoslovakia won 5–3 on penalties			

the USSR and the current holders Czecho-slovakia. No country has won it more than once.

EUROPEAN CHAMPION CLUBS CUP

The European Cup was first contested in 1955–56. It is open to the champion club of each of the Associations in membership of the European Union (UEFA) together with the winner of the previous competition, though the inaugural competition was by invitation.

Matches are played on a home and away basis with the aggregate score deciding the winner. In the event of a tie being drawn after extra time in the second leg then away goals count double. If still undecided, a series of penalty kicks are undertaken to determine the winner. Only one match is played in the final, which is held at a pre-determined venue.

Eighteen clubs were called together to a meeting in Paris at the invitation of Gabriel Hanot of the French sportspaper *L'Equipe* and prime mover behind the idea. They were AC Milan (Italy), Anderlecht (Belgium), Chelsea (England), Djurgaarden (Sweden), Hibernian (Scotland), Holland Sport (Holland), KB Copenhagen (Denmark), Moscow Dynamo (USSR), Partizan Belgrade (Yugoslavia), Rapid Vienna (Austria), Real Madrid (Spain), Reims (France), Rot-Weiss Essen (West Germany), Saarbrucken (The Saar), Servette (Switzerland), Sparta Prague (Czechoslovakia), Sporting Lisbon (Portugal) and Voros Lobogo (Hungary). All except Hibernian, Sparta and Moscow Dynamo actually sent representatives.

The first five competitions were won by Real Madrid (Spain), who achieved their sixth success in 1966. Latin clubs dominated the early years through Spain, Portugal and Italy before Celtic achieved a breakthrough in 1967. Then Manchester United became the first English winners the following year and Liverpool emulated their achievements ten years later. Liverpool retained the trophy in 1977–78.

Two clubs had three successive triumphs: Ajax (Holland) from 1971 to 1973 and Bayern Munich (West Germany) from 1974 to 1976.

EUROPEAN CUP

Season	Games	Goals	The Final	Attendances Overall	Average
1955–56	29	127	13–6–56, Paris, 38,000		
			Real Madrid (2) 4, Stade de Reims (2) 3	912,000	31,450
			Di Stefano, Rial 2, Marquitos; Leblond, Templin, Hidalgo		
1956–57	44	170	30–5–57, Madrid, 124,000		
			Real Madrid (0) 2, Fiorentina (0) 0	1,786,000	40,590
			Di Stefano (pen), Gento		
1957–58	48	189	28–5–58, Brussels, 67,000		
			Real Madrid (0) (2) 3, AC Milan (0) (2) 2 (a.e.t.)	1,790,000	37,290
			Di Stefano, Rial, Gento; Schiaffino, Grillo		
1958–59	55	199	2–6–59, Stuttgart, 80,000		
			Real Madrid (1) 2, Stade de Reims (0) 0	2,010,000	36,545
			Mateos, Di Stefano		
1959–60	52	218	18–5–60, Glasgow, 135,000		
			Real Madrid (3) 7, Eintracht Frankfurt (1) 3	2,780,000	50,545
			Di Stefano 3, Puskas 4; Kress, Stein 2		
1960–61	51	166	31–3–61, Berne, 28,000		
			Benfica (2) 3, Barcelona (1) 2	1,850,000	36,274
			Aguas, Ramallets (og), Coluna; Kocsis, Czibor		
1961–62	55	221	2–5–62, Amsterdam, 65,000		
			Benfica (2) 5, Real Madrid (3) 3	2,135,000	45,727
			Aguas, Cavem, Coluna, Eusebio 2; Puskas 3		
1962–63	59	214	22–5–63, London, 45,000		
			AC Milan (0) 2, Benfica (1) 1	2,158,000	36,593
			Altafini 2; Eusebio		

Season	Games	Goals	The Final	Attendances Overall	Average
1963–64	61	212	27–5–64, Vienna, 74,000 **Inter Milan (1) 3, Real Madrid (0) 1** Mazzola 2, Milani; Felo	2,180,000	35,737
1964–65	62	215	28–5–65, Milan, 80,000 **Inter Milan (1) 1, Benfica (0) 0** Jair	2,577,000	41,564
1965–66	58	234	11–5–66, Brussels, 55,000 **Real Madrid (0) 2, Partizan Belgrade (1) 1** Amancio, Serena; Vasovic	2,112,000	36,431
1966–67	65	211	25–5–67, Lisbon, 56,000 **Celtic (0) 2, Inter Milan (1) 1** Gemmell, Chalmers; Mazzola (pen)	2,248,000	34,584
1967–68	60	162	29–5–68, London, 100,000 **Manchester United (0) (1) 4, Benfica (0) (1) 1 (a.e.t.)** Charlton 2, Best, Kidd; Graca	2,544,000	42,500
1968–69	52	176	28–5–69, Madrid, 50,000 **AC Milan (2) 4, Ajax (0) 1** Prati 3, Sormani; Vasovic (pen)	2,056,000	39,540
1969–70	63	202	6–5–70, Milan, 50,000 **Feyenoord (1) (1) 2, Celtic (1) (1) 1 (a.e.t.)** Israel, Kindvall; Gemmell	2,345,000	37,222
1970–71	63	210	2–6–71, London, 90,000 **Ajax (1) 2, Panathinaikos (0) 0** Van Dijk, Kapsis (og)	2,124,000	33,714
1971–72	64	175	31–5–72, Rotterdam, 67,000 **Ajax (0) 2, Inter Milan (0) 0** Cruyff 2	2,066,976	32,280
1972–73	58	160	30–5–73, Belgrade, 93,500 **Ajax (0) 1, Juventus (0) 0** Rep	1,712,277	30,000
1973–74	60	180	15–5–74, Brussels, 65,000 **Bayern Munich (0) (0) 1, Atletico Madrid (0) (0) 1 (a.e.t.)** Schwarzenbeck; Luis		
		replay:	17–5–74, Brussels, 65,000 **Bayern Munich (1) 4, Atletico Madrid (0) 0** Muller 2, Hoeness 2	1,586,852	26,448
1974–75	55	174	28–5–75, Paris, 50,000 **Bayern Munich (0) 2, Leeds United (0) 0** Roth, Muller	1,380,254	25,096
1975–76	61	202	12–5–76, Glasgow, 54,864 **Bayern Munich (0) 1, St Etienne (0) 0** Roth	1,736,087	28,460
1976–77	61	155	25–5–77, Rome, 57,000 **Liverpool (1) 3, Borussia Moenchengladbach (0) 1** McDermott, Smith, Neal (pen); Simonsen	2,010,000	34,325
1977–78	59	172	10–5–78, London, 92,000 **Liverpool (0) 1, FC Bruges (0) 0** Dalglish	*(Figures not available at time of going to press)*	

EUROPEAN CUP-WINNERS CUP

The Cup-Winners Cup was first contested in 1960–61. It is open to the winners of national cup competitions unless the winner is eligible for the European Cup itself, when the runner-up qualifies. Similarly this applies if the cup winner is the holder of the Cup-Winners Cup.

National cup competitions were not over popular in many continental countries when the Cup-Winners Cup started, but entry into Europe has subsequently stimulated interest in domestic cups.

The first competition was organised by the Mitropa Cup Committee but since 1961–62 it has come under UEFA's Executive Committee.

The competition follows the pattern of the European Cup and English clubs have been the most successful with four successes followed by West Germany and Italy with three each.

CUP WINNERS CUP

Season	Games	Goals	The Final	Attendances Overall	Average
1960–61	18	60	1st leg, 17–5–61, Glasgow, 80,000 **Rangers (0) 0, Fiorentina (1) 2** Milan 2 2nd leg, 27–5–61, Florence, 50,000 **Fiorentina (1) 2, Rangers (1) 1** Milan, Hamrin; Scott	290,000	16,111
1961–62	44	174	10–5–62, Glasgow, 27,389 **Fiorentina (1) 1, Atletico Madrid (1) 1** Hamrin; Peiro replay: 5–9–62, Stuttgart, 45,000 **Atletico Madrid (2) 3, Fiorentina (0) 0** Jones, Mendonca, Peiro	650,000	14,733
1962–63	48	169	15–5–63, Rotterdam, 25,000 **Tottenham Hotspur (2) 5, Atletico Madrid (0) 1** Greaves 2, White, Dyson 2; Collar (pen)	1,100,000	22,916
1963–64	62	202	13–5–64, Brussels, 9,000 **MTK Budapest (1) (3) 3, Sporting Lisbon (1) (3) 3 (a.e.t.)** Sandor 2, Kuti; Figueiredo 2, Dansky (og) replay: 15–5–64, Antwerp, 18,000 **Sporting Lisbon (1) 1, MTK Budapest (0) 0** Mendes	1,300,000	20,967
1964–65	61	163	19–5–65, London, 100,000 **West Ham United (0) 2, Munich 1860 (0) 0** Sealey 2	1,100,000	18,032
1965–66	59	188	5–5–66, Glasgow, 41,657 **Borussia Dortmund (0) (1) 2, Liverpool (0) (1) 1 (a.e.t.)** Held, Yeats (og); Hunt	1,546,000	26,203
1966–67	61	170	31–5–67, Nuremberg, 69,480 **Bayern Munich (0) (0) 1, Rangers (0) (0) 0 (a.e.t.)** Roth	1,556,000	25,508
1967–68	64	200	23–5–68, Rotterdam, 60,000 **AC Milan (2) 2, SV Hamburg (0) 0** Hamrin 2	1,683,000	26,269
1968–69	51	157	21–5–69, Basle, 40,000 **Slovan Bratislava (3) 3, Barcelona (1) 2** Cvetler, Hrivnak, Jan Capkovic; Zaldua, Rexach	957,000	18,765
1969–70	64	179	29–4–70, Vienna, 10,000 **Manchester City (2) 2, Gornik Zabrze (0) 1** Young, Lee (pen); Ozlizlo	1,675,000	25,890
1970–71	67	203	19–5–71, Athens, 42,000 **Chelsea (0) (1) 1, Real Madrid (0) (1) 1** Osgood; Zoco replay: 21–5–71, Athens, 24,000 **Chelsea (2) 2, Real Madrid (0) 1** Dempsey, Osgood; Fleitas	1,570,000	23,582
1971–72	65	186	24–5–72, Barcelona, 35,000 **Rangers (2) 3, Dynamo Moscow (0) 2** Stein, Johnston 2; Estrekov, Makovikov	1,145,211	17,615
1972–73	61	174	16–5–73, Salonika, 45,000 **AC Milan (1) 1, Leeds United (0) 0** Chiarugi	908,564	15,000
1973–74	61	169	8–5–74, Rotterdam, 5,000 **FC Magdeburg (1) 2, AC Milan (0) 0** Lanzi (og), Seguin	1,105,494	18,123
1974–75	59	177	14–5–75, Basle, 13,000 **Dynamo Kiev (2) 3, Ferencvaros (0) 0** Onischenko 2, Blokhin	1,298,850	22,014

Season	Games	Goals	The Final	Attendances	
				Overall	Average
1975–76	61	189	5–5–76, Brussels, 58,000		
			Anderlecht (1) 4, West Ham United (1) 2	1,128,962	18,508
			Rensenbrink 2 (1 pen), Van der Elst 2; Holland, Robson		
1976–77	63	198	11–5–77, Amsterdam, 65,000		
			SV Hamburg (0) 2, Anderlecht (0) 0	1,537,000	24,400
			Volkert (pen), Magath		
1977–78	61	179	3–5–78, Amsterdam, 48,679	*(Figures not*	
			Anderlecht (3) 4, Austria/WAC (0) 0	*available at time*	
			Rensenbrink 2 (1 pen), Van Binst 2	*of going to press)*	

UEFA CUP

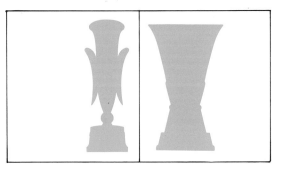

The Union of European Football Associations Cup was first contested in 1971–72. It replaced the Fairs Cup which had started in 1955 as the International Inter-City Industrial Fairs Cup and was originally designed for representative sides from cities where Industrial Fairs were annually held. The title was changed in 1969 to the European Fairs Cup.

The first competition took three years to complet and the second was played over two years. But since 1960–61 it has been organised on an annual basis. In 1971 Barcelona the first winners and Leeds United the holders met for permanent possession of the Fairs trophy, the Spanish club winning 2–1.

The same principles now apply as for the European Cup and the Cup-Winners Cup but the final is determined over two matches played home and away.

The competition is open to a certain number of clubs per country, depending on their club strength. In recent years the total entry has been 64.

Spanish clubs were the most successful in the early years but between 1968 and 1973 it was dominated by England who overall have won it seven times to Spain's six.

A London representative team entered the original Fairs Cup competition. Between June 1955 and March 1957 four matches were played home and away against Basle and Frankfurt before London qualified for the semi-finals against Lausanne and then the final against Barcelona. Results were:
Basle 0, London 5; London 3, Frankfurt 2;
London 1, Basle 0; Frankfurt 1, London 0
Lausanne 2, London 1; London 2, Lausanne 0
London 2, Barcelona 2; Barcelona 6, London 0

FAIRS/UEFA CUP

1955–58	First leg:	5–3–58, London, 45,466
		London (1) 2, Barcelona (2) 2
		Greaves, Langley (pen); Tejada, Martinez
	Second leg:	1–5–58, Barcelona, 62,000
		Barcelona (3) 6, London (0) 0
		Suarez 2, Evaristo 2, Martinez, Verges
1958–60	First leg:	29–3–60, Birmingham, 40,500
		Birmingham City (0) 0, Barcelona (0) 0
	Second leg:	4–5–60, Barcelona, 70,000
		Barcelona (2) 4, Birmingham City (0) 1
		Martinez, Czibor 2, Coll; Hooper

1960–61	First leg:	27–9–61, Birmingham, 21,005
		Birmingham City (0) 2, AS Roma (1) 2
		Hellawell, Orritt; Manfredini 2
	Second leg:	11–10–61, Rome, 60,000
		AS Roma (0) 2, Birmingham City (0) 0
		Farmer (og), Pestrin
1961–62	First leg:	8–9–62, Valencia, 65,000
		Valencia 6, Barcelona 2
		Yosu 2, Guillot 3, Nunez; Kocsis 2
	Second leg:	12–9–62, Barcelona, 60,000
		Barcelona 1, Valencia 1
		Kocsis; Guillot
1962–63	First leg:	12–6–63, Zagreb, 40,000
		Dynamo Zagreb (1) 1, Valencia (0) 2
		Zambata; Waldo, Urtiaga
	Second leg:	26–6–63, Valencia, 55,000
		Valencia (1) 2, Dynamo Zagreb (0) 0
		Mano, Nunez
1963–64	Final:	Barcelona, 24–6–64, 50,000
		Real Zaragoza (1) 2, Valencia (1) 1
		Villa, Marcelino; Urtiaga
1964–65	Final:	23–6–65, Turin, 25,000
		Ferencvaros (1) 1, Juventus (0) 0
		Fenyvesi
1965–66	First leg:	14–9–66, Barcelona, 70,000
		Barcelona (0) 0, Real Zaragoza (1) 1
		Canario
	Second leg:	21–9–66, Zaragoza, 70,000
		Real Zaragoza (1) 2, Barcelona (1) 4
		Marcelino 2; Pujol 3, Zaballa
1966–67	First leg:	30–8–67, Zagreb, 40,000
		Dynamo Zagreb (1) 2, Leeds United (0) 0
		Cercer 2
	Second leg:	6–9–67, Leeds, 35,604
		Leeds United (0) 0, Dynamo Zagreb (0) 0
1967–68	First leg:	7–8–68, Leeds, 25,368
		Leeds United (1) 1, Ferencvaros (0) 0
		Jones
	Second leg:	11–9–68, Budapest, 70,000
		Ferencvaros (0) 0, Leeds United (0) 0
1968–69	First leg:	25–5–69, Newcastle, 60,000
		Newcastle United (0) 3, Ujpest Dozsa (0) 0
		Moncur 2, Scott
	Second leg:	11–6–69, Budapest, 37,000
		Ujpest Dozsa (2) 2, Newcastle United (0) 3
		Bene, Gorocs; Moncur, Arentoft, Foggon
1969–70	First leg:	22–4–70, Brussels, 37,000
		Anderlecht (2) 3, Arsenal (0) 1
		Devrindt, Mulder 2; Kennedy
	Second leg:	28–4–70, London, 51,612
		Arsenal (1) 3, Anderlecht (0) 0
		Kelly, Radford, Sammels
1970–71	First leg:	26–5–71, Turin, 65,000
		Juventus (0) 0, Leeds United (0) 0
		(game abandoned after 51 minutes)
		28–5–71, Turin, 65,000
		Juventus (1) 2, Leeds United (0) 2
		Bettega, Capello; Madeley, Bates
	Second leg:	3–6–71, Leeds, 42,483
		Leeds United (1) 1, Juventus (1) 1
		Clarke; Anastasi
		Leeds won on away goals rule.
1971–72	First leg:	3–5–72, Wolverhampton, 45,000
		Wolverhampton Wanderers (0) 1, Tottenham Hotspur (0) 2
		McCalliog; Chivers 2
	Second leg:	17–5–72, London, 48,000
		Tottenham Hotspur (1) 1, Wolverhampton Wanderers (0) 1
		Mullery; Wagstaffe

1972–73	First leg:	10–5–73, Liverpool, 41,169
		Liverpool (3) 3, Borussia Moenchengladbach (0) 0
		Keegan 2, Lloyd
	Second leg:	25–5–73, Moenchengladbach, 35,000
		Borussia Moenchengladbach (2) 2, Liverpool (0) 0
		Heynckes 2
1973–74	First leg:	21–5–74, London, 46,281
		Tottenham Hotspur (1) 2, Feyenoord (1) 2
		England, Van Daele (og); Van Hanegem, De Jong
	Second leg:	29–5–74, Rotterdam, 68,000
		Feyenoord (1) 2, Tottenham Hotspur (0) 0
		Rijsbergen, Ressel
1974–75	First leg:	7–5–75, Dusseldorf, 45,000
		Borussia Moenchengladbach (0) 0, Twente Enschede (0) 0
	Second leg:	21–5–75, Enschede, 24,500
		Twente Enschede (0) 1, Borussia Moenchengladbach (2) 5
		Drost; Heynckes 3, Simonsen 2 (1 pen)
1975–76	First leg:	28–4–76, Liverpool, 56,000
		Liverpool (0) 3, Bruges (2) 2
		Kennedy, Case, Keegan (pen); Lambert, Cools
	Second leg:	19–5–76, Bruges, 32,000
		Bruges (1) 1, Liverpool (1) 1
		Lambert (pen); Keegan
1976–77	First leg:	4–5–77, Turin, 75,000
		Juventus (1) 1, Athletic Bilbao (0) 0
		Tardelli
	Second leg:	18–5–77, Bilbao, 43,000
		Athletic Bilbao (1) 2, Juventus (1) 1
		Irureta, Carlos; Bettega
1977–78	First leg:	26–4–78, Bastia, 15,000
		Bastia (0) 0, PSV Eindhoven (0) 0
	Second leg:	9–5–78, Eindhoven, 27,000
		PSV Eindhoven (1) 3, Bastia (0) 0
		Willy van der Kerkhof, Deijkers, van der Kuylen

EUROPEAN CUP OF THE CHAMPIONS 1955–56 to 1977–78
(listed in order of imaginary 'points' gained from matches won and drawn)

		P	W	D	L	F	A
1	Real Madrid (Sp)	115	68	17	30	293	134
2	Benfica (P)	92	46	20	26	197	110
3	Ajax (Ho)	57	34	11	12	104	52
4	Celtic (S)	58	33	11	14	118	52
5	Manchester United (E)	41	26	7	8	100	45
6	AC Milan (I)	44	26	5	13	116	59
7	Bayern Munich (WG)	40	25	7	8	93	37
8	Inter-Milan (I)	41	23	10	8	64	30
9	CSKA Sofia (Bul)	52	22	9	21	83	80
10	Juventus (I)	43	21	9	13	57	44
11	Feyenoord (Hol)	37	20	9	8	89	39
12	Atletico Madrid (Sp)	39	21	7	11	65	39
13	Dukla Prague (Cz)	39	19	10	10	68	50
14	Liverpool (E)	34	20	5	9	72	34
15	St. Etienne (F)	39	19	6	14	49	41
16	Red Star Belgrade (Y)	43	21	6	16	92	68
17	Standard Liege (Bel)	32	20	1	11	55	33
18	Borussia Moenchen-gladbach (WG)	31	15	10	6	69	31
19	Ujpest Dozsa (H)	34	16	7	11	60	50
20	Rangers (S)	37	18	3	16	66	72
21	Anderlecht (Bel)	44	16	6	22	84	89
22	Dynamo Kiev (USSR)	28	16	5	7	41	22
23	Gornik Zabrze (Pol)	31	17	3	11	52	45
24	Barcelona (Sp)	26	15	6	5	60	25
25	Rapid Vienna (A)	33	15	4	14	53	49
26	Spartak Trnava (Cz)	24	13	7	4	44	20
27	Reims (F)	24	14	3	7	63	30
28	Vasas Budapest (H)	27	12	6	9	62	34
29	Dinamo Bucharest (R)	30	13	4	13	52	55
30	PSV Eindhoven (Ho)	20	11	4	5	42	19
31	Leeds United (E)	17	12	1	4	42	11
32	Panathinaikos (Gr)	31	8	9	14	40	42
33	Legia Warsaw (Pol)	18	11	2	5	29	16
34	FC Bruges (Bel)	19	10	3	6	40	20
35	Partizan Belgrade (Y)	27	10	3	14	47	47
36	Galatasaray (T)	25	8	6	11	29	39
37	Zurich (Sw)	25	10	2	13	33	46
38	Borussia Dortmund (WG)	18	8	3	7	44	31
39	Vorwaerts (EG)	22	9	1	12	35	33
40	Hajduk Split (Y)	12	8	2	2	32	13
41	Ferencvaros (H)	16	8	2	6	36	28
42	Fiorentina (I)	13	7	4	2	14	11
43	Sparta Prague (Cz)	12	7	3	2	23	17
44	Young Boys (Sw)	15	6	5	4	27	26
45	Dynamo Dresden (EG)	16	7	3	6	28	25
46	Sporting Lisbon (P)	20	7	3	10	35	40
47	Nice (F)	14	7	2	5	29	25
48	Basle (Sw)	18	7	2	9	37	37
49	Austria/WAC (A)	19	7	2	10	24	34
50	Fenerbahce (T)	23	6	3	14	20	46
51	Derby County (E)	12	6	2	4	18	22
52	Wismut Aue (EG)	16	5	4	7	26	23
53	Slovan Bratislava (Cz)	12	6	1	5	17	19
54	Aarhus (D)	14	5	3	6	18	22
55	Malmo FF (Se)	16	6	1	9	18	34

#	Club						
56	Jeunesse Esch (L)	29	5	3	21	37	97
57	Ruch Chorzow (Pol)	10	5	2	3	17	15
58	Wiener Sportklub (A)	12	4	4	4	21	18
59	IFC Nuremberg (WG)	8	5	1	2	16	14
60	IFC Cologne (WG)	9	3	5	1	12	12
61	Ararat Erevan (USSR)	6	5	0	1	14	5
62	Eintracht Frankfurt (WG)	7	4	2	1	23	15
63	Dundee (S)	8	5	0	3	20	14
64	Carl Zeiss Jena (EG)	8	5	0	3	12	11
65	Olympiakos Piraeus (Gr)	14	3	4	7	14	21
66	Linfield (Ni)	17	3	4	10	25	48
67	DWS Amsterdam (Ho)	6	4	1	1	13	4
68	Tottenham Hotspur (E)	8	4	1	3	21	13
69	MTK Budapest (H)	8	4	1	3	24	18
70	Everton (E)	8	2	5	1	12	6
71	Atletico Bilbao (Sp)	6	4	1	1	16	14
72	Vasas Gyor (H)	8	4	1	3	16	15
73	Vojvodina (Y)	7	4	1	2	8	7
74	AEK Athens (Gr)	10	3	3	4	16	20
75	Nantes (F)	12	2	5	5	17	21
76	IFK Norkoping (Se)	12	2	5	5	14	20
77	GAIS Gothenburg (Se)	14	4	1	9	24	36
78	Arsenal (E)	6	4	0	2	13	4
79	Trabzonspor (T)	6	4	0	2	8	8
80	Schalke 04 (WG)	7	3	2	2	13	13
81	Atvidaberg (Se)	8	4	0	4	12	12
82	Servette (Sw)	9	4	0	5	16	20
83	Levski Spartak (Bul)	12	3	2	7	22	27
84	Hamburg (WG)	7	3	1	3	15	10
85	Hibernian (S)	6	3	1	2	9	5
86	IFK Malmo (Sp)	6	3	1	2	7	7
87	SW Innsbruck (A)	14	3	1	10	13	28
88	Sliema Wanderers (Ma)	14	3	1	10	10	36
89	Ipswich Town (E)	4	3	0	1	16	5
90	1860 Munich (WG)	4	3	0	1	12	4
91	Werder Bremen (WG)	4	3	0	1	11	3
92	Arges Pitesti (R)	4	3	0	1	9	4
93	Spartak Kralove (Cz)	5	2	2	1	5	5
94	Sparta Rotterdam (Ho)	6	3	0	3	12	11
95	Valencia (Sp)	6	2	2	2	6	5
96	Seville (Sp)	6	2	2	2	9	13
97	Polonia Bytom (Pol)	6	3	0	3	8	12
98	Magdeburg (EG)	8	3	0	5	15	11
99	Grasshoppers (Sw)	8	2	2	4	14	12
100	Wolverhampton Wanderers (E)	8	2	2	4	12	16
101	Lahden Reipas (Fi)	8	2	2	4	8	30
102	KB Copenhagen (D)	9	3	0	6	14	18
103	Steaua Bucharest (R)	10	2	2	6	11	21
104	Glentoran (Ni)	12	1	4	7	10	22
105	Waterford (Ei)	14	3	0	11	15	47
106	Red Star Bratislava (Cz)	4	2	1	1	8	6
107	CSKA Moscow (USSR)	4	2	1	1	5	3
108	Sarja Voroshilovgrad (USSR)	4	2	1	1	3	1
109	Hvidovre (D)	6	1	3	2	9	12
110	BK 1903 Copenhagen (D)	8	2	1	5	7	11
111	Olympique Marseille (F)	6	2	1	3	6	11
112	Petrolul Ploesti (R)	8	2	1	5	8	15
113	Djurgaarden (Se)	8	2	1	5	7	16
114	Valur (Ice)	8	1	3	4	7	25
115	Omonia Nicosia (Cy)	12	2	1	9	7	38
116	Lokomotiv Sofia (Bul)	4	2	0	2	15	13
117	Sarajevo (Y)	4	1	2	1	6	5
118	BK 1913 Odense (D)	4	2	0	2	14	14
119	Burnley (E)	4	2	0	2	8	8
120	Cagliari (I)	4	2	0	2	5	5
121	Eintracht Brunswick (WG)	5	2	0	3	5	5
122	Torino (I)	4	1	2	1	4	4
123	Gwardia Warsaw (Pol)	5	1	2	2	6	9
124	RWD Molenbeek (Bel)	4	2	0	2	6	9
125	Banik Ostrava (Cz)	4	2	0	2	5	8
126	Kilmarnock (S)	4	1	2	1	4	7
127	La Chaux-de-Fonds (Sw)	4	1	2	1	5	9
128	Vejle (D)	6	1	2	3	5	10
129	Partizan Tirana (Alb)	8	1	2	5	3	12
130	Esbjerg (D)	8	1	2	5	6	23
131	Lyn Oslo (N)	10	2	0	8	14	41
132	Monaco (F)	6	1	1	4	13	13
133	Rapid Bucharest (R)	4	1	1	2	3	3
134	Spartak Plovdiv (Bul)	4	1	1	2	3	3
135	Bologna (I)	3	1	1	1	2	2
136	Akademisk (D)	4	1	1	2	4	5
137	PAOK Salonika (Gr)	4	1	1	2	3	7
138	Nendori Tirana (Alb)	6	0	3	3	3	9
139	Akranes (Ice)	8	1	1	6	8	17
140	Besiktas (T)	8	1	1	6	3	15
141	Fredrikstad (N)	8	1	1	6	6	22
142	Dundalk (Ei)	6	1	1	4	4	20
143	Spartak Moscow (USSR)	2	1	0	1	4	4
144	Universitatea Craiova (R)	2	1	0	1	3	4
145	Trakia Plovdiv (Bul)	2	1	0	1	2	3
146	Lillestrom (N)	2	1	0	1	2	4
147	Saarbrucken (Saar)	2	1	0	1	5	7
148	LKS Lodz (Pol)	2	1	0	1	2	6
149	Torpedo Moscow (USSR)	4	0	2	2	1	5
150	Derry City (Ni)	3	1	0	2	8	15
151	Hearts (S)	4	1	0	3	4	11
152	Viking Stavanger (N)	8	1	0	7	7	16
153	HJK Helsinki (Fi)	6	1	0	5	6	15
154	Valetta (Ma)	4	1	0	3	2	12
155	UT Arad (R)	6	0	2	4	3	17
156	Hibernians (Ma)	6	0	2	4	3	17
157	Valkeakosken (Fi)	6	1	0	5	6	24
158	Spora Luxembourg (L)	5	1	0	4	7	27
159	Drumcondra (Ei)	6	1	0	5	3	25
160	Turun Palloseura (Fi)	10	1	0	9	4	28
161	Floriana (Ma)	12	0	2	10	3	49
162	Honved (H)	2	0	1	1	5	6
163	Csepel (H)	2	0	1	1	3	4
164	Dynamo Zagreb (Y)	2	0	1	1	3	4
165	Manchester City (E)	2	0	1	1	1	2
166	Skeid (N)	2	0	1	1	1	2
167	Admira (A)	2	0	1	1	0	1
168	Slask Wroclaw (Pol)	2	0	1	1	2	5
169	Valerengen (N)	2	0	1	1	2	5
170	Bohemians (Ei)	2	0	1	1	2	5
171	Glenavon (Ni)	2	0	1	1	0	5
172	Rot-Weiss Essen (WG)	2	0	1	1	1	5
173	Lausanne (Sw)	2	0	1	1	0	4
174	Distillery (Ni)	2	0	1	1	3	8
175	VOEST Linz (A)	2	0	1	1	0	5
176	Kuopion Palloseura (Fi)	6	0	1	5	4	21
177	Rosenborg (N)	6	0	1	5	6	18
178	Shamrock Rovers (Ei)	6	0	1	5	5	18
179	BK 1909 Odense (D)	6	0	1	5	6	21
180	Aris Bonnevoie (L)	6	0	1	5	6	25
181	Olympiakos Nicosia (Cy)	6	0	1	5	4	36
182	DOS Utrecht (Ho)	2	0	0	2	4	6
183	Oster Vaxjo (Se)	2	0	0	2	1	3
184	Rapid Heerlen (Ho)	2	0	0	2	3	6
185	Karl-Marx-Stadt (EG)	2	0	0	2	2	5
186	ASK Linz (A)	2	0	0	2	2	5
187	Halmstad (Se)	2	0	0	2	2	5
188	Zeljeznicar Sarajevo (Y)	2	0	0	2	1	4
189	Chemie Leipzig (EG)	2	0	0	2	2	6
190	Stal Mielec (Pol)	4	0	0	4	2	6
191	FC Porto (P)	4	0	0	4	4	9
192	Anorthosis (Cy)	2	0	0	2	1	6

193	Lierse (Bel)	2	0	0	2	0	5
194	Cork Hibs (Ei)	2	0	0	2	1	7
195	Koge (D)	2	0	0	2	1	7
196	Shelbourne (Ei)	2	0	0	2	1	7
197	Stromsgodset (N)	2	0	0	2	1	7
198	Cork Celtic (Ei)	2	0	0	2	1	7
199	HIFK Helsinki (Fi)	4	0	0	4	5	12
200	Ards (Ni)	2	0	0	2	3	10
201	Limerick (Ei)	2	0	0	2	2	9
202	Sligo Rovers (Ei)	2	0	0	2	0	6
203	Antwerp (Bel)	2	0	0	2	1	8
204	Helsinki Palloseura (Fi)	2	0	0	2	0	7
205	Avenir Beggen (L)	2	0	0	2	0	8
206	Coleraine (Ni)	2	0	0	2	1	11
207	Fram (Ice)	2	0	0	2	2	11
208	AEL (Cy)	2	0	0	2	0	12
209	Apoel (Cy)	4	0	0	4	0	13
210	Kokkolan (Fi)	2	0	0	2	0	14
211	EPA (Cy)	2	0	0	2	0	16
212	Union Luxembourg (L)	4	0	0	4	1	18
213	Crusaders (Ni)	2	0	0	2	0	19
214	KR Reykjavik (Ice)	6	0	0	6	7	35
215	IBK Keflavik (Ice)	8	0	0	8	5	35
216	Stade Dudelange (L)	4	0	0	4	1	32

(all statistics refer to completed matches and their result at the end of normal or exta time. Outcome of matches decided by the away goals rule, toss of a coin or by penalty kicks not included for the purposes of this table)

Ties in which only the first leg was played have been included but not teams who withdrew without playing. Only Dynamo Tirana (Albania) qualified on just one occasion and did not take part at all.

EUROPEAN GOALSCORERS

European Cup	Name	Club	Goals
1955–56	Milos Milutinovic	Partizan Belgrade	7
1956–57	Dennis Viollet	Manchester United	9
1957–58	Alfredo di Stefano	Real Madrid	10
1958–59	Just Fontaine	Reims	10
1959–60	Ferenc Puskas	Real Madrid	13
1960–61	Jose Aguas	Benfica	10
1961–62	Alfredo di Stefano	Real Madrid	8
1962–63	Jose Altafini	AC Milan	14
1963–64	Sandro Mazzola	Inter-Milan	8
1964–65	Jose Torres	Benfica	10
1965–66	Eusebio	Benfica	7
1966–67	Paul Van Himst	Anderlecht	6
1967–68	Eusebio	Benfica	6
1968–69	Denis Law	Manchester United	9
1969–70	Mick Jones	Leeds United	8
1970–71	Antonis Antoniadis	Panathinaikos	10
1971–72	Johan Cruyff Sylvestre Takac Lou Macari	Ajax Standard Liege Celtic	5
1972–73	Gerd Muller	Bayern Munich	11
1973–74	Gerd Muller	Bayern Munich	8
1974–75	Rene Almqvist Eduard Markarov Gerd Muller	Atvidaberg Ararat Erevan Bayern Munich	5
1975–76	Jupp Heynckes Carlos Santillana	Borussia Moenchengladbach Real Madrid	6
1976–77	Gerd Muller	Bayern Munich	5
1977–78	Allan Simonsen	Borussia Moenchengladbach	5

Johan Cruyff, top European Cup scorer in 1971–72.

Gerd Muller, four times leading European Cup goalscorer.

Goalscoring (European Cup competitions) – individual

The highest individual score in either the European Champion Cup or the Cup-Winners Cup is six goals. Lothar Emmerich scored six for Borussia Dortmund against Floriana in the first round of the Cup-Winners Cup on 10 October 1965. Kiril Milanov scored six for Levski Spartak against Reipas Lahden in a Cup-Winners Cup match in 1976–77.

Stan Bowles registered 11 goals for Queen's Park Rangers, including three goals in each of two successive UEFA Cup matches against Brann Bergen in the 1976–77 season.

Kevin Hector scored seven goals in two UEFA Cup matches against Finn Harps in 1976–77, including five in the first leg.

Ray Crawford scored five goals for Ipswich Town against Floriana in 1962–63 and Peter Osgood scored five for Chelsea in a Cup-Winners Cup match against Jeunesse Hautcharage in 1971–72.

Trevor Whymark scored four goals on two occasions for Ipswich Town in the UEFA Cup. The first occasion was on 24 October 1973 against Lazio and the second against Landskrona Bois on 28 September 1977.

Peter Lorimer scored 30 goals for Leeds United in European Cup, Cup-Winners Cup, Fairs and UEFA Cup matches between the 1965–66 season and 1976–77. This included scoring four goals against Spora Luxembourg on 3 October 1967 in the Fairs Cup.

Denis Law scored 28 goals for Manchester United in European Cup, Cup-Winners Cup and Fairs Cup matches between 1963–64 and 1968–69. He scored four goals against Waterford on 2 October 1968 and achieved three goals on four other occasions, including the first leg against Waterford on 18 September 1968 for an aggregate in the tie of seven goals.
    Law's highest scoring season was in 1968–69 when he totalled nine goals.

Three other British players have equalled this feat: Dennis Viollet for Manchester United in the 1956–57 European Cup, including four goals against Anderlecht on 26 September 1956; Derek Dougan for Wolverhampton Wanderers in the 1971–72 UEFA Cup and Alan Gilzean for Dundee in the 1962–63 European Cup.

Jose Altafini scored 14 goals for AC Milan in the 1962–63 European Cup. Lothar Emmerich also scored 14 for Borussia Dortmund in the 1965–66 Cup-Winners Cup.

Alfredo di Stefano scored 49 goals for Real Madrid in the European Cup between 1955–56 and 1963–64 and Gerd Muller 36 for Bayern Munich between 1969–70 and 1976–77.

Alfredo di Stefano, 49 goals for Real Madrid in the European Cup.

Goalscoring (European Cup competitions) – Team

Feyenoord beat Reykjavik 12–2 in a European Cup first round match on 17 September 1969. Sporting Lisbon beat Apoel Nicosia 16–1 in a Cup-Winners Cup first round match on 13 November 1963. FC Cologne beat Union Luxembourg 13–0 in a first round Fairs Cup match on 5 October 1965.

Britain in Europe

No other Football League club can claim such a long list of opponents in the three major competitions as Liverpool. They have been in conflict with teams from no fewer than 22 different countries, yet still have to meet opponents from either Denmark, Finland, Austria, Cyprus or the USSR.

Liverpool's adventures have taken them on

Jimmy Case (left) and Phil Neal: Emlyn Hughes (right) and Kevin Keegan (below, right) in European Cup Final scenes.

just about as comprehensive a tour as could be imagined. They have played in all the United Kingdom countries, Iceland, Belgium, Italy, East and West Germany, Hungary, Rumania, Poland, Holland, Sweden, Norway, Spain, Portugal, Luxembourg, Greece, Turkey, France and Switzerland.

The club is pre-eminent not only in actual achievements but also on general behaviour. They have figured in over 90 European cup matches and they have never had a player ordered off in any one of them – a striking tribute to the discipline and control of their players, often when under great provocation.

Bristol City, Middlesbrough and Norwich City were the only clubs among the 22 competing in Division One during the 1977–78 season that still have to appear in any of the three European cup competitions.

In September 1935, English international centre-half Peter O'Dowd became the first player ever bought by a French club from one in England. Valenciennes paid Chelsea £3,000 for his services.

Liverpool's 11–0 win against Stromsgodset in a European Cup-Winners Cup tie on 17 September 1974 at Anfield contained goals from nine players, a record of its kind for this century. Goalkeeper Ray Clemence and inside-right Brian Hall were the only players who failed to score.

In successive seasons in the Cup-Winners Cup non-Football League clubs qualified for the competition from Wales. In the 1962–63 season Bangor City were drawn against the Italian club Napoli. In the home leg Bangor won 2–0 and despite losing 3–1 in the second leg the Welsh side forced a play-off which was held at Highbury. Had the competition been held when away goals counted double they would have reached the next round. But the Italians finally won the play-off 2–1.

The next season of 1963–64 Borough United represented Wales. They met Sliema Wanderers (Malta) and after drawing 0–0 away beat them 2–0 at Wrexham. In the next round they were drawn against Slovan Bratislava (Czechoslovakia) and were beaten first at home 1–0 and then 3–0 away.

Moscow Dynamo

Moscow Dynamo arrived for a short tour of Britain in November 1945 and presented the following conditions to the Football Association:

They were a club side and wished to play matches against clubs, and they:

. . . could not play more than one match in seven days

. . . wished to play on the day which was normally a football day in England

. . . were unable to number their players

. . . hoped that one of their opponents would be Arsenal

. . . wished the referee who had accompanied them to officiate in one or more matches

. . . would take all their meals at the Embassy

. . . wished substitutes to be permitted (This was agreed, provided that substitutes replaced injured players)

. . . wished to practise before the match on the grounds of the clubs against which they were playing

. . . aimed to give a good exhibition of football and they did not wish much social entertainment to be arranged for them

. . . asked that ample tickets should be made available, on payment, for the Russian Colony (600) for the matches in London

. . . wished to have an assurance that the English teams would not be changed from the names submitted to them before the match unless they were first consulted

. . . wished to be given opportunities to see their opponents in action in their normal League matches

. . . were agreeable to the financial terms suggested for each of their matches, namely, that, after entertainment tax and the usual ground expenses had been deducted, the balance should be divided on a 50–50 basis (cup-tie terms) between the competing clubs. It was also agreed that the share due to the Dynamo FC should, in the first place, be sent to the Football Association, from which the administrative and other expenses incurred on their behalf should be paid.

An overcrowded Stamford Bridge in 1945 for the visit of Moscow Dynamo.

Such was the interest aroused by the visit that some 82,000 crowded into Stamford Bridge for their first match with Chelsea; spectators ringing the touchline in many places. The game ended in a 3–3 draw. Afterwards the F.A. received 34 requests for fixtures with the Russians from clubs in Britain and one or two organisations abroad.

At Ninian Park the Russian team beat Cardiff City 10–1 before a crowd of 45,000 and a third match against Arsenal at Tottenham was won 4–3 by Dynamo although it was ruined by fog and the Russians protested about the composition of the Arsenal team which had to be changed because of the unavailability of certain players who were replaced by guests. The attendance was 54,000. The Dynamo team completed their tour by drawing 2–2 with Glasgow Rangers at Ibrox Park before 90,000.

EUROPEAN CLUB DIRECTORY

(League and Cup honours to 1977 – European honours to 1978)   *Competitions started earlier in these countries

Country	Championship wins	Cup wins	European and other honours
ALBANIA	(1945) Dinamo Tirana 13; Partizan Tirana 10; 17 Nendori 5; Vlaznia 4	(1948) Dinamo Tirana 11; Partizan Tirana 8; 17 Nendori 4; Besa 1; Vlaznia 1; Labinoti 1	None
AUSTRIA	(1912) Rapid Vienna 25; Austria/WAC (previously FK Austria and WAC) 12; Admira-Energie-Wacker (previously Sportklub Admira and Admira-Energie) 8; First Vienna 6; Tirol-Svarowski-Innsbruck (previously Wacker-Innsbruck) 5; Wiener Sportklub 3; FAC 1; Hakoah 1; Linz ASK 1; Wacker Vienna 1; WAF 1; Voest Linz 1	(1919) FK Austria 19; Rapid Vienna 9; Admira-Energie-Wacker 5; First Vienna 3; Tirol-Svarowski-Innsbruck 3; Linz ASK 1; Wacker Vienna 1; WAF 1; Wiener Sportklub 1	European Cup-Winners' Cup (runners-up) Austria/WAC 1978
BELGIUM	(1896) Anderlecht 16; Union St Gilloise 11; Beerschot 7; Standard Liege 6; RC Brussels 6; FC Liege 5; Daring Brussels 5; Antwerp 4; FC Bruges 4; Lierse SK 3; Malines 3; CS Bruges 3; RWD Molenbeek 1	(1954) Anderlecht 5; Standard Liege 3; FC Bruges 3; Antwerp 1; Beerschot 1; La Gantoise 1; Lierse SK 1; Tournai 1; Waregem 1	European Cup (runners-up) FC Bruges 1978 European Cup-Winners' Cup (winners) Anderlecht 1976, 1978 (runners-up) Anderlecht 1977. European Fairs Cup (runners-up) Anderlecht 1970. UEFA Cup (runners-up) FC Bruges 1976

Country	Championship wins	Cup wins	European and other honours
BULGARIA	(1925) CSKA Sofia (previously CDNA) 19; Levski Spartak (previously Levski Sofia) 13; Slavia Sofia 6; Vladislav Varna 3; Lokomotiv Sofia 2; AS23 Sofia 1; Botev Plovdiv 1; SC Sofia 1; Sokol Varna 1; Spartak Plovdiv 1; Tichka Varna 1; Trakia Plovdiv 1; ZSK Sofia 1	(1946) Levski Spartak 12; CSKA Sofia 10; Slavia Sofia 5; Lokomotiv Sofia 2; Botev Plovdiv 1; Spartak Plovdiv 1; Spartak Sofia 1	None
CYPRUS	(1935) Apoel 11; Omonia 7; Anorthosis 6; AEL 5; EPA 3; Olympiakos 3; Chetin Kayal 1; Pezoporikos 1; Trast 1	(1935) Apoel 8; EPA 5; AEL 3; Trast 3; Chetin Kayal 2; Omonia 2; Apollon 2; Pezoporikos 2; Anorthosis 2; Paralimni 1; Olympiakos 1	None
CZECHOSLOVAKIA	(1926)* Sparta Prague 13; Slavia Prague 12; Dukla Prague (previously UDA) 9; Slovan Bratislava 6; Spartak Trnava 5; Inter-Bratislava 1; Spartak Hradec Kralove 1; Viktoria Zizkov 1; Banik Ostrava 1	(1961) Dukla Prague 4; Slovan Bratislava 4; Spartak Trnava 3; Sparta Prague 3; TJ Gottwaldov 1; Banik Ostrava 1; Lokomotiv Kosice 1	European Cup-Winners' Cup (winners) Slovan Bratislava 1969
DENMARK	(1913) KB Copenhagen 14; B93 Copenhagen 9; AB (Akademisk) 9; B 1903 Copenhagen 7; Frem 6; AGF Aarhus 4; Esbjergs FK 4; Vejle BK 3; B 1909 Odense 2; Hvidovre 2; Koge BK 2; Odense BK 1	(1955) AGF Aarhus 5; Vejle Bk 5; B 1909 Odense 3; Randers Freja 3; Aalborg BK 2; Esbjergs BK 2; Frem 1; KB Copenhagen 1; Vanlose 1	None
FINLAND	(1949)* Turun Palloseura 5; Kuopion Palloseura 5; Valkeakosken Haka 4; Lahden Reipas 3; IF Kamraterna 2; Kotkan TP 2; Helsinki JK 2; Turun Pyrkiva 1; IF Kronohagens 1; Helsinki PS 1; Ilves-Kissat 1; Kokkolan PV 1; IF Kamraterna 1; Vasa 1	(1955) Lahden Reipas 6; Valkeakosken Haka 6; Kotkan TP 3; Mikkelin 2; IFK Abo 1; Drott 1; Helsinki JK 1; Helsinki PS 1; Kuopion Palloseura 1; Pallo-Peikot 1	None
FRANCE	(1933) Saint Etienne 9; Stade de Reims 6; OGC Nice 4; Olympique Marseille 4; Nantes 4; Lille OSC 3; FC Sete 2; Sochaux 2; AS Monaco 2; Racing Club Paris 1; Roubaix-Tourcoing 1; Girondins Bordeaux 1	(1918) Olympique Marseille 9; Saint Etienne 6; Lille OSC 5; Racing Club Paris 5; Red Star 5; Olympique Lyon 3; CAS Generaux 2; AS Monaco 2; OGC Nice 2; Racing Club Strasbourg 2; Sedan 2; FC Sete 2; Stade de Reims 2; Stade Rennes 2; AS Cannes 1; Club Francais 1; Excelsior Roubaix 1; Girondins Bordeaux 1; Le Havre 1; SO Montpelier 1; Nancy-Lorraine 1; Olympique de Pantin 1; CA Paris 1; Sochaux 1; Toulouse 1	European Champions' Cup (runners-up) Stade de Reims 1956, 1959; Saint Etienne 1976 UEFA Cup (runners-up) Bastia 1978
EAST GERMANY	(1950) ASK Vorwaerts 6; Dynamo Dresden 5; Wismut Karl-Marx-Stadt 4; Carl Zeiss Jena (previously Motor Jena) 3; FC Magdeburg 3; Chemie Leipzig 2; Turbine Erfurt 2; Turbine Halle 1; Zwickau Horch 1; Empor Rostock 1	(1949) Carl Zeiss Jena 4; Chemie Leipzig 2; FC Magdeburg 2; Magdeburg Aufbau 2; Motor Zwickau 2; ASK Vorwaerts 2; Lokomotiv Leipzig 2; Dynamo Dresden 2; Dresden Einheit SC 1; Dresden PV 1; Dynamo Berlin 1; Halle Chemie SC 1; North Dessau Waggonworks 1; Thale EHW 1; Union East Berlin 1; Wismut Karl-Marx-Stadt 1; Sachsenring Zwickau 1	European Cup-Winners' Cup (winners) FC Magdeburg 1974

Country	Championship wins	Cup wins	European and other honours
WEST GERMANY	(1903) 1FC Nuremberg 9; Schalke 7; Bayern Munich 5; Borussia Moenchengladbach 5; VfB Leipzig 3; SpV Furth 3; SV Hamburg 3; Dorussia Dortmund 3; Viktoria Berlin 2; Hertha Berlin 2; Hanover 96 2; Dresden SC 2; VfB Stuttgart 2; 1FC Kaiserslautern 2; 1FC Cologne 2; Munich 1860 1; SV Werder Bremen 1; Union Berlin 1; FC Freibourg 1; Phoenix Karlsruhe 1; Karlsruher FV 1; Holstein Kiel 1; Fortuna Dusseldorf 1; Rapid Vienna 1; VfR Mannheim 1; Rot-Weiss Essen 1; Eintracht Frankfurt 1; Eintracht Brunswick 1	(1935) Bayern Munich 5; 1FC Nuremberg 3; Dresden SC 2; Karlsruher SC 2; Munich 1860 2; Schalke 4; VfB Stuttgart 2; Borussia Moenchengladbach 2; Eintracht Frankfurt 2; 1FC Cologne 2; SV Hamburg 2; Borussia Dortmund 1; First Vienna 1; VfB Leipzig 1; Kickers Offenbach 1; Rapid Vienna 1; 'Rot-Weiss Essen 1; SW Essen 1; Werder Bremen 1	World Club Championshsip (winners) Bayern Munich 1976. European Champions' Cup (winners) Bayern Munich 1974, 1975, 1976; (runners-up) Eintracht Frankfurt 1960, Borussia Moenchengladbach 1977. European Cup-Winners' Cup (winners) Borussia Dortmund 1966, Bayern Munich 1967, SV Hamburg 1977; (runners-up) Munich (1860) 1965, SV Hamburg 1968. UEFA Cup (winners) Borussia Moenchengladbach 1975; (runners-up) Borussia Moenchengladbach 1973
GREECE	(1928) Olympiakos 20; Panathinaikos 12; AEK Athens 5; Aris Salonika 3; PAOK Salonika 1	(1932) Olympiakos 16; AEK Athens 6; Panathinaikos 6; PAOK Salonika 2; Aris Salonika 1; Ethnikos 1; Iraklis 1	European Champions' Cup (runners-up) Panathinaikos 1971
HUNGARY	(1901) Ferencvaros (previously FTC) 22; MTK-VM Budapest (previously Hungaria, Bastya, and Voros Lobogo) 18; Ujpest Dozsa 16; Vasas Budapest 6; Honved 5; Czepel 4; BTC 2; Nagyvarad 1; Vasas Gyor 1	(1910) Ferencvaros 13; MTK-VM Budapest 9; Ujpest Dozsa 4; Vasas Gyor 3; Vasas Budapest 1; Bocskai 1; Honved 1; III Ker 1; Kispesti AC 1; Soroksar 1; Szolnoki MAV 1; Diosgyor 1	European Cup-Winners' Cup (runners-up) MTK Budapest 1964, Ferencvaros 1975. European Fairs Cup (winners) Ferencvaros 1965; (runners-up) Ferencvaros 1968, Ujpest Dozsa 1969
ICELAND	(1912) KR Reykjavik 20; Valur 15; IA Akranes 10; IBK Keflavik 3; Vikingur 2; IBV Vestmann 1	(1960) KR Reykjavik 7; Valur 4; IBV Vestmann 2; Fram 2; IBA Akureyri 1; Vikingur 1; IBK Keflavik 1	None
IRELAND	(1922) Shamrock Rovers 10; Shelbourne 7; Waterford 6; Bohemians 6; Cork United 5; Drumcondra 5; Dundalk 4; St Patrick's Athletic 3; St James's Gate 2; Cork Athletic 2; Sligo Rovers 2; Limerick 1; Dolphin 1; Cork Hibernians 1; Cork Celtic 1	(1922) Shamrock Rovers 20; Drumcondra 5; Dundalk 5; Bohemians 4; Shelbourne 3; Cork Athletic 2; Cork United 2; St James's Gate 2; St Patrick's Athletic 2; Cork Hibernians 2; Alton United 1; Athlone Town 1; Cork 1; Fordsons 1; Limerick 1; Transport 1; Waterford 1; Finn Harps 1; Home Farm 1	None
ITALY	(1898) Juventus 17; Inter-Milan 11; Genoa 9; AC Milan 9; Torino 8; Pro Vercelli 7; Bologna 7; Fiorentina 2; Casale 1; Novese 1; AS Roma 1; Cagliari 1; Lazio 1	(1922) Juventus 5; Torino 4; Fiorentina 4; AC Milan 4; Napoli 2; AS Roma 2; Bologna 2; Atalanta 1; Genoa 1; Inter-Milan 1; Lazio 1; Vado 1; Venezia 1	World Club Championship (winners) Inter-Milan 1964, 1965, AC Milan 1969. European Champions' Cup (winners) AC Milan 1963, 1969, Inter-Milan 1964, 1965; (runners-up) Fiorentina 1957, AC Milan 1958, Inter-Milan 1967, 1972, Juventus 1973. European Cup-Winners' Cup (winners) Fiorentina 1961, AC Milan 1968, 1973; (runners-up) Fiorentina 1962, AC Milan 1974. European Fairs Cup (winners) AS Roma 1961; (runners-up) Juventus 1965, 1971. UEFA Cup (winners) Juventus 1977

Country	Championship wins	Cup wins	European and other honours
LUXEMBOURG	(1910) Jeunesse Esch 15; Spora Luxembourg 10; Stade Dudelange 10; US Hollerich-Bonnevoie 5; Fola Esch 5; Red Boys Differdange 5; US Luxembourg 3; Sporting Luxembourg 2; Aris Bonnevoie 3; Racing Luxembourg 1; National Schifflge 1; Avenir Beggen 1; Progres Niedercorn 1	(1922) Red Boys Differdange 13; Spora Luxembourg 7; Jeunesse Esch 7; US Luxembourg 6; Stade Dudelange 4; Fola Esch 3; Alliance Dudelange 2; Progres Niedercorn 2; US Rumelange 2; Aris Bonnevoie 1; US Dudelange 1; Jeunesse Hautcharage 1; National Schifflge 1; Racing Luxembourg 1; SC Tetange 1	None
MALTA	(1910) Floriana 24; Sliema Wanderers 21; Valletta 9; Hamrun Spartans 3; Hibernians 3; St George's 1; KOMR 1	(1935) Sliema Wanderers 15; Floriana 14; Valletta 4; Hibernians 3; Gzira United 1; Melita 1	None
NETHERLANDS	(1898) Ajax Amsterdam 17; Feyenoord 12; HVV The Hague 8; Sparta Rotterdam 6; PSV Eindhoven 6; Go Ahead Deventer 4; HBS The Hague 3; Willem II Tilburg 3; RCH Haarlem 2; RAP 2; Heracles 2; ADO The Hague 2; Quick The Hague 1; BVV Scheidam 1; NAC Breda 1; Eindhoven 1; Enschede 1; Volewijckers Amsterdam 1; Limburgia 1; Rapid JC Haarlem 1; DOS Utrecht 1; DWS Amsterdam 1; Haarlem 1; Be Quick Groningen 1; SVV Scheidam 1	(1899) Ajax Amsterdam 7; Feyenoord 4; Quick The Hague 4; PSV Eindhoven 4; HEC 3; Sparta Rotterdam 3; DFC 2; Fortuna Geleen 2; Haarlem 2; HBS The Hague 2; RCH 2; VOC 2; Wageningen 2; Willem II Tilburg 2; FC Den Haag 2; Concordia Rotterdam 1; CVV 1; Eindhoven 1; HVV The Hague 1; Longa 1; Quick Njimegen 1; RAP 1; Roermond 1; Schoten 1; Velocitas Breda 1; Velocitas Groningen 1; VSV 1; VUC 1; VVV 1; ZFC 1; NAC Breda 1; Twente Enschede 1	World Club Championship (winners) Feyenoord 1970, Ajax 1972. European Champions' Cup (winners) Feyenoord 1970, Ajax 1971, 1972, 1973; (runners-up) Ajax 1969. UEFA Cup (winners) Feyenoord 1974; (runners-up) Twente Enschede 1975
NORWAY	(1938) Fredrikstad 9; Viking Stavanger 5; Lillestrom 3; Rosenborg Trondheim 3; Larvik Turn 3; Brann Bergen 2; Lyn Oslo 2; Valerengen 1; Friedig 1; Fram 1; Skeid Oslo 1; Stromgodset Dråmmen 1	(1902) Odds BK Skein 11; Fredrikstad 9; Lyn Oslo 8; Skeid Oslo 8; Sarpsborgs Fk 6; Orn Fk Horten 4; Brann Bergen 4; Miondalens IF 3; Rosenborgs BK Trondheim 3; Stromsgodset Drammen 3; Mercantile 2; Viking Stavanger 2; Grane Nordstrand 1; Kvik Halden 1; Sparta 1; Gjovik 1; Bodo-Glimt 1; Lillestrom 1	None
POLAND	(1921) Ruch Chorzow 11; Gornik Zabrze 10; Cracovia 5; Pogon Lwow 4; Wisla Krakow 5; Legia Warsaw 4; Warta Poznan 2; Polonia Bytom 2; Stal Mielec 2; Garbarnia Krakow 1; Polonia Warsaw 1; LKS Lodz 1; Slask Wroclaw 1	(1951) Gornik Zabrze 6; Legia Warsaw 5; Zaglebie Sosnowiec 3; Ruch Chorzow 2; Gwardia Warsaw 1; LKS Lodz 1; Polonia Warsaw 1; Wisla Krakow 1; Stal Rzeszow 1; Slask Wroclaw 1	European Cup-Winners' Cup (runners-up) Gornik Zabrze 1970
PORTUGAL	(1935)* Benfica 23; Sporting Lisbon 14; FC Porto 5; Belenenses 1	(1939) Benfica 15; Sporting Lisbon 8; FC Porto 4; Belenenses 2; Boavista 2; Vitoria Setubal 2; Academica Coimbra 1; Leixoes Porto 1; Sporting Braga 1	European Champions' Cup (winners) Benfica 1961, 1962; (runners-up) Benfica 1963, 1965, 1968. European Cup-Winners' Cup (winners) Sporting Lisbon 1964

Country	Championship wins	Cup wins	European and other honours
RUMANIA	(1910) Dynamo Bucharest 9; Steaua Bucharest (previously CCA) 8; Venus Bucharest 7; CSC Temesvar 6; UT Arad 6; Rapid Bucharest 4; Ripensia Temesvar 3; Petrolul Ploesti 3; Olimpia Bucharest 2; CAC Bucharest 2; Soc RA Bucharest 1; Prahova Ploesti 1; CSC Brasov 1; Juventus Bucharest 1; SSUD Resita 1; Craiova Bucharest 1; Progresul 1; Arges 1; Ploesti United 1; University of Craiova 1	(1934) Steaua Bucharest 12; Rapid Bucharest 7; Dynamo Bucharest 3; UT Arad 2; CFR Bucharest 2; Progresel 2; RIP Timisoara 2; ICO Oradeo 1; Metal Ochimia Resita 1; Petrolul Ploesti 1; Stinta Cluj 1; Stinta Timisoara 1; Turnu Severin 1; Chimia Ramnicu 1; Jiul Petroseni 1; Uni Craiova 1	None
SPAIN	(1929) Real Madrid 17; Barcelona 9; Atletico Madrid 8; Athletic Bilbao 6; Valencia 4; Betis 1; Seville 1	(1902) Athletic Bilbao 22; Barcelona 17; Real Madrid 13; Atletico Madrid 5; Valencia 4; Real Union de Irun 3; Seville 3; Español 2; Real Zaragoza 2; Arenas 1; Ciclista Sebastian 1; Racing de Irun 1; Vizcaya Bilbao 1; Real Betis 1	European Champions' Cup (winners) Real Madrid 1956, 1957, 1958, 1959, 1960, 1966; (runners-up) Real Madrid 1962, 1964, Barcelona 1961, Atletico Madrid 1974. World Club Championship (winners) Real Madrid 1960, Atletico Madrid 1975. European Cup-Winners' Cup (winners) Atletico Madrid 1962; (runners-up) Atletico Madrid 1963, Barcelona 1969, Real Madrid 1971. European Fairs Cup (winners) Barcelona 1958, 1960, 1966; Valencia 1962, 1963, Zaragoza 1964; (runners-up) Barcelona 1962, Valencia 1964, Zaragoza 1966. UEFA Cup (runners-up) Athletic Bilbao 1977
SWEDEN	(1896) Oergryte IS Gothenburg 13; Malmo FF 14; IFK Norrkoping 11; Djurgaarden 8; IFK Gothenburg 7; AIK Stockholm 8; GAIS Gothenburg 6; Boras IF Elfsborg 4; IF Halsingborg 5; Atvidaberg 2; IFK Ekilstund 1; IF Gavle Brynas 1; IF Gothenburg Fassbergs 1; Norrkoping IK Sleipner 1; Oester Vaxjo 1; Halmstad 1	(1941) Malmo FF 9; IFK Norrkoping 3; AIK Stockholm 3; Atvidaberg 2; GAIS Gothenburg 1; IFK Halsingborg 1; Raa 1; Landskrona 1; Oster Vaxjo 1	None
SWITZERLAND	(1898) Grasshoppers 16; Servette 13; Young Boys Berne 10; FC Zurich 8; Lausanne 7; FC Basle 7; La Chaux-de-Fonds 3; FC Lugano 3; Winterthur 3; FC Aarau 2; FC Anglo-Americans 1; St Gallen 1; FC Bruhl 1; Cantonal-Neuchatel 1; Biel 1; Bellinzona 1; FC Etoile la Chaux de Fonds 1	(1926) Grasshoppers 13; La Chaux-de-Fonds 6; Lausanne 6; FC Basle 5; FC Zurich 5; Young Boys Berne 5; Servette 3; FC Lugano 2; FC Sion 2; FC Granges 1; Lucerne 1; St Gallen 1; Urania Geneva 1; Young Fellows Zurich 1	None
TURKEY	(1960) Fenerbahce 7; Galatasaray 5; Besiktas 3; Trabzonspor 2	(1963) Galatasaray 6; Goztepe Izmir 2; Fenerbahce 2; Altay Izmir 1; Ankaragucu 1; Eskisehirspor 1; Besiktas 1; Trabzonspor 1	None
USSR	(1936) Dynamo Moscow 11; Spartak Moscow 9; Dynamo Kiev 8; CSKA Moscow 6; Torpedo Moscow 3; Dynamo Tbilisi 1; Saria Voroshilovgrad 1; Ararat Erevan 1	(1936) Soartak Moscow 9; Torpedo Moscow 5; Dynamo Moscow 5; CSKA Moscow 4; Dynamo Kiev 4; Donets Shaktyor 2; Lokomotiv Moscow 2; Ararat Erevan 2; Karpaty Lvov 1; Zenit Leningrad 1; Dynamo Tbilisi 1	European Cup-Winners' Cup (winners) Dynamo Kiev 1975; (runners-up) Dynamo Moscow 1972

Country	Championship wins	Cup wins	European and other honours
YUGOSLAVIA	(1923) Red Star Belgrade 12; Hajduk Split 8; Partizan Belgrade 7; Gradjanski Zagreb 5; BSK Belgrade 5; Dynamo Zagreb 3; Jugoslovija Belgrade 2; Concordia Zagreb 2; HASK Zagreb 1; Vojvodina Novi Sad 1; FC Sarajevo 1; Zeljeznicar 1	(1947) Red Star Belgrade 9; Partizan Hajduk Split 7; BSK Belgrade 2; Belgrade 5; Dynamo Zagreb 4; OFK Belgrade 2; Vardar Skoplje 1	European Champions' Cup (runners-up) Partizan Belgrade 1966. European Fairs Cup (winners) Dynamo Zagreb 1967; (runners-up) Dynamo Zagreb 1966

BRITISH CLUBS IN EUROPE

FOOTBALL LEAGUE CLUBS

Season	Competition	Round	Date	Opponents (Country)	Venue	Result		Scorers
ARSENAL								
1971–72	European Cup	1	15–9–71	Stromsgodset (Norway)	A	W	3–1	Simpson, Marinello, Kelly
			29–9–71		H	W	4–0	Kennedy, Radford 2, Armstrong
		2	20–10–71	Grasshoppers	A	W	2–0	Kennedy, Graham
			3–11–71	(Switzerland)	H	W	3–0	Kennedy, George, Radford
		QF	8–3–72	Ajax (Holland)	A	L	1–2	Kennedy
			22–3–72		H	L	0–1	
1963–64	Fairs Cup	1	25–9–63	Staevnet (Denmark)	A	W	7–1	Strong 3, Baker 3, MacLeod
			22–10–63		H	L	3–2	Skirton, Barnwell
		2	13–11–63	Liege (Belgium)	H	D	1–1	Anderson
			18–12–63		A	L	1–3	McCullough
1969–70	Fairs Cup	1	9–9–69	Glentoran (Northern	H	W	3–0	Graham 2, Gould
			29–9–69	Ireland)	A	L	0–1	
		2	29–10–69	Sporting Lisbon (Portugal)	A	D	0–0	
			26–11–69		H	W	3–0	Radford, Graham 2
		3	17–12–69	Rouen (France)	A	D	0–0	
			13–1–70		H	W	1–0	Sammels
		QF	11–3–70	Dynamo Bacau (Rumania)	A	W	2–0	Sammels, Radford
			18–3–70		H	W	7–1	George 2, Sammels 2, Radford 2, Graham
		SF	8–4–70	Ajax (Holland)	H	W	3–0	George 2 (1 pen), Sammels
			15–4–70		A	L	0–1	
		F	22–4–70	Anderlecht (Belgium)	A	L	1–3	Kennedy
			28–4–70		H	W	3–0	Kelly, Radford, Sammels
1970–71	Fairs Cup	1	16–9–70	Lazio (Italy)	A	D	2–2	Radford 2
			23–9–70		H	W	2–0	Radford, Armstrong
		2	21–10–70	Sturm Graz (Austria)	A	L	0–1	
			4–11–70		H	W	2–0	Storey (pen), Kennedy
		3	2–12–70	Beveren (Belgium)	H	W	4–0	Graham, Kennedy 2, Sammels
			16–12–70		A	D	0–0	
		QF	9–3–71	FC Cologne (West	H	W	2–1	McLintock, Storey
			23–3–71	Germany)*	A	L	0–1	
ASTON VILLA								
1975–76	UEFA Cup	1	17–9–75	Antwerp (Belgium)	A	L	1–4	Graydon
			1–10–75		H	L	0–1	
1977–78	UEFA Cup	1	14–9–77	Fenerbahce (Turkey)	H	W	4–0	Gray, Deehan 2, Little
			28–9–77		A	W	2–0	Deehan, Little
		2	19–10–77	Gornik Zabrze (Poland)	H	W	2–0	McNaught 2
			2–11–77		A	D	1–1	Gray
		3	23–11–77	Athletic Bilbao (Spain)	H	W	2–0	Iribar own goal, Deehan
			7–12–77		A	D	1–1	Mortimer
		QF	1–3–78	Barcelona (Spain)	H	D	2–2	McNaught, Deehan
			15–3–78		A	L	1–2	Little
BIRMINGHAM CITY								
1955–56	Fairs Cup	Gp.D	15–5–56	Inter-Milan (Italy)	A	D	0–0	
			17–4–57		H	W	2–1	Govan 2
			22–5–56	Zagreb (Yugoslavia)	A	W	1–0	Brown
			3–12–56		H	W	3–0	Orritt, Brown, Murphy

Season	Competition	Round	Date	Opponents (Country)	Venue	Result		Scorers
BIRMINGHAM CITY continued								
		SF	23–10–57	Barcelona (Spain)	H	W	4–3	Murphy 2, Brown, Orritt
			13–11–57		A	L	0–1	
			26–11–57		N	L	1–2	Murphy
1958–60	Fairs Cup	1	14–10–58	FC Cologne (West	A	D	2–2	Neal, Hooper
			11–11–58	Germany)	H	W	2–0	Larkin, Taylor
		QF	6–5–59	Zagreb (Yugoslavia)	H	W	1–0	Larkin
			25–5–59		A	D	3–3	Larkin 2, Hooper
		SF	7–10–59	Union St Gilloise	A	W	4–2	Hooper, Gordon, Barrett, Taylor
			11–11–59	(Belgium)	H	W	4–2	Gordon 2, Larkin, Hooper
		F	29–3–60	Barcelona (Spain)	H	D	0–0	
			4–5–60		A	L	1–4	Hooper
1960–61	Fairs Cup	1	19–10–60	Ujpest Dosza (Hungary)	H	W	3–2	Gordon 2, Astall
			26–10–60		A	W	2–1	Rudd, Singer
		QF	23–11–60	Copenhagen (Denmark)	A	D	4–4	Gordon 2, Singer 2
			7–12–60		H	W	5–0	Stubbs 2, Harris, Hellawell, own goal
		SF	19–4–61	Inter-Milan (Italy)	A	W	2–1	Harris, own goal
			3–5–61		H	W	2–1	Harris 2
		F	27–9–61	AS Roma (Italy)	H	D	2–2	Hellawell, Orritt
			11–10–61		A	L	0–2	
1961–62	Fairs Cup	1		bye				
		2	15–11–61	Espanol (Spain)	A	L	2–5	Bloomfield, Harris (pen)
			7–12–61		H	W	1–0	Auld
BURNLEY								
1960–61	European Cup	Pr		bye				
		1	16–11–60	Reims (France)	H	W	2–0	Robson, McIlroy
			30–11–60		A	L	2–3	Robson, Connelly
		QF	18–1–61	SV Hamburg (West	H	W	3–1	Pilkington 2, Robson
			15–3–61	Germany)	A	L	1–4	Harris
1966–67	Fairs Cup	1	20–9–66	Stuttgart (West Germany)	A	D	1–1	Irvine
			27–9–66		H	W	2–0	Coates, Lochhead
		2	19–10–66	Lausanne (Switzerland)	A	W	3–1	Coates, Harris, Lochhead
			25–10–66		H	W	5–0	Lochhead 3, O'Neil, Irvine
		3	18–1–67	Napoli (Italy)	H	W	3–0	Coates, Latcham, Lochhead
			8–2–67		A	D	0–0	
		QF	4–4–67	Eintracht Frankfurt	A	D	1–1	Miller
			18–4–67	(West Germany)	H	L	1–2	Miller
CARDIFF CITY								
1964–65	Cup Winners' Cup	1	9–9–64	Esbjerg (Denmark)	A	D	0–0	
			13–10–64		H	W	1–0	King
		2	16–12–64	Sporting Lisbon (Portugal)	A	W	2–1	Farrell, Tapscott
			23–12–64		H	D	0–0	
		QF	20–1–65	Real Zaragoza (Spain)	A	D	2–2	Williams, King
			3–2–65		H	L	0–1	
1965–66	Cup Winners' Cup	1	8–9–65	Standard Liege (Belgium)	H	L	1–2	Johnston
			20–10–65		A	L	0–1	
1967–68	Cup Winners' Cup	1	20–9–67	Shamrock Rovers (Eire)	A	D	1–1	King
			4–10–67		H	W	2–0	Toshack, Brown (pen)
		2	15–11–67	NAC Breda (Holland)	A	D	1–1	King
			29–11–67		H	W	4–1	Brown, Barrie Jones, Clark, Toshack
		QF	6–3–68	Moscow Torpedo (USSR)	H	W	1–0	Barrie Jones
			19–3–68		A	L	0–1	
			3–4–68		N	W	1–0	Dean
		SF	24–4–68	SV Hamburg (West	A	D	1–1	Dean
			1–5–68	Germany)	H	L	2–3	Dean, Harris
1968–69	Cup-Winners' Cup	1	18–9–68	Porto (Portugal)	H	D	2–2	Toshack, Bird (pen)
			2–10–68		A	L	1–2	Toshack
1969–70	Cup-Winners' Cup	1	17–9–69	Mjoendalen (Norway)	A	W	7–1	Clark 2, Toshack 2, Lea, Sutton, King
			1–10–69		H	W	5–1	King 2, Allan 3
		2	12–11–69	Goztepe Izmir (Turkey)	A	L	0–3	
			16–11–69		H	W	1–0	Bird
1970–71	Cup-Winners' Cup	1	16–9–70	Pezoporikos (Cyprus)	H	W	8–0	Toshack 2, Clark 2, Sutton, Gibson, King, Woodruff
			30–9–70		A	D	0–0	
		2	21–10–70	Nantes (France)	H	W	5–1	Toshack 2, Gibson, King, Phillips
			4–11–70		A	W	2–1	Toshack, Clark

Season	Competition	Round	Date	Opponents (Country)	Venue	Result		Scorers
CARDIFF CITY continued								
		QF	10–3–70	Real Madrid (Spain)	H	W	1–0	Clark
			24–3–71		A	L	0–2	
1971–72	Cup-Winners' Cup	1	15–9–71	Dynamo Berlin (East	A	D	1–1	Gibson
			15–9–71	Germany)†	H	D	1–1	Clark
1973–74	Cup-Winners' Cup	1	19–9–73	Sporting Lisbon (Portugal)	H	D	0–0	
			3–10–73		A	L	1–2	Vincent
1974–75	Cup-Winners' Cup	1	18–9–74	Ferencvaros (Hungary)	A	L	0–2	
			2–10–76		H	L	1–4	Dwyer
1976–77	Cup-Winners' Cup	Pr	4–8–76	Servette (Switzerland)	H	W	1–0	Evans
			11–8–76		A	L	1–2*	Showers
		1	15–9–76	Dynamo Tbilisi (USSR)	H	W	1–0	Alston
			29–9–76		A	L	0–3	
1977–78	Cup-Winners' Cup	1	14–9–77	Austria/WAC (Austria)	H	D	0–0	
			28–9–77		A	L	0–1	
CHELSEA								
1970–71	Cup-Winners' Cup	1	16–9–70	Aris Salonika (Greece)	A	D	1–1	Hutchinson
			30–9–70		H	W	5–1	Hutchinson 2, Hollins 2, Hinton
		2	21–10–70	CSKA Sofia (Bulgaria)	A	W	1–0	Baldwin
			4–11–70		H	W	1–0	Webb
		QF	10–3–71	FC Bruges (Belgium)	A	L	0–2	
			24–3–71		H	W	4–0	Houseman, Osgood 2, Baldwin
		SF	14–4–71	Manchester City (England)	H	W	1–0	Smethurst
			28–4–71		A	W	1–0	Weller
		F	19–5–71	Real Madrid (Spain)	N	D	1–1	Osgood
			21–5–71		N	W	2–1	Dempsey, Osgood
1971–72	Cup-Winners' Cup	1	15–9–71	Jeunesse Hautcharage (Luxembourg)	A	W	8–0	Osgood 3, Houseman 2, Hollins, Webb, Baldwin
			29–9–71		H	W	13–0	Osgood 5, Baldwin 3, Hollins (per Hudson, Webb, Houseman, Harris
		2	20–10–71	Atvidaberg (Sweden)*	A	D	0–0	
			3–11–71		H	D	1–1	Hudson
1958–59	Fairs Cup	1	30–9–58	Frem Copenhagen	A	W	3–1	Harrison, Greaves, Nicholas.
			4–11–58	(Denmark)	H	W	4–1	Greaves 2, Sillett (P), own goal
		QF	29–4–59	Belgrade (Yugoslavia)	H	W	1–0	Brabrook
			13–5–59		H	L	1–4	Brabrook
1965–66	Fairs Cup	1	22–9–65	AS Roma (Italy)	H	W	4–1	Venables 3, Graham
			6–10–65		A	D	0–0	
		2	17–11–65	Weiner SK (Austria)	A	L	0–1	
			1–12–65		H	W	2–0	Murray, Osgood
		3	9–2–66	AC Milan (Italy)	A	L	1–2	Graham
			16–2–66		H	W	2–1	Graham, Osgood
			2–3–66		A	D	1–1‡	Bridges
		QF	15–3–66	Munich 1860 (West	A	D	2–2	Tambling 2
			29–3–66	Germany)	H	W	1–0	Osgood
		SF	27–4–66	Barcelona (Spain)	A	L	0–2	
			11–5–66		H	W	2–0	own goals 2
			25–5–66		A	L	0–5	
1968–69	Fairs Cup	1	18–9–68	Morton (Scotland)	H	W	5–0	Osgood, Birchenall, Cooke, Boyle Hollins
			30–9–68		A	W	4–3	Baldwin, Birchenall, Houseman, Tambling
		2	23–10–68	DWS Amsterdam	H	D	0–0	
			30–10–68	(Holland)‡	A	D	0–0	
COVENTRY CITY								
1970–71	Fairs Cup	1	16–9–70	Trakia Plovdiv (Bulgaria)	A	W	4–1	O'Rourke 3, Martin
			30–9–70		H	W	2–0	Joicey, Blockley
		2	20–10–70	Bayern Munich (West	A	L	1–6	Hunt
			3–11–70	Germany)	H	W	2–1	Martin, O'Rourke
DERBY COUNTY								
1972–73	European Cup	1	13–9–72	Zeljeznicar (Yugoslavia)	H	W	2–0	McFarland, Gemmill
			27–9–72		A	W	2–1	Hinton, O'Hare
		2	25–10–72	Benfica (Portugal)	H	W	3–0	McFarland, Hector, McGovern
			8–11–72		A	D	0–0	

Season	Competition	Round	Date	Opponents (Country)	Venue	Result		Scorers
		QF	7-3-73	Spartak Trnava	A	D	0-0	
			21-3-73	(Czechoslovakia)	H	W	2-0	Hector 2
		SF	11-4-73	Juventus (Italy)	A	L	1-3	Hector
			25-4-73		H	D	0-0	
1975-76	European Cup	1	17-9-75	Slovan Bratislava	A	L	0-1	
			1-10-75	(Czechoslovakia)	H	W	3-0	Bourne, Lee 2
		2	22-10-75	Real Madrid (Spain)	H	W	4-1	George 3 (2 pen), Nish
			5-11-75		A	L	1-5	George
1974-75	UEFA Cup	1	18-9-74	Servette (Switzerland)	H	W	4-1	Hector 2, Daniel, Lee
			2-10-74		A	W	2-1	Lee, Hector
		2	23-10-74	Atletico Madrid (Spain)	H	D	2-2	Nish, Rioch (pen)
			6-11-74		A	D	2-2†	Rioch, Hector
		3	27-11-74	Velez (Yugoslavia)	H	W	3-1	Bourne 2, Hinton
			11-12-74		A	L	1-4	Hector
1976-77	UEFA Cup	1	15-9-76	Finn Harps (Eire)	H	W	12-0	Hector 5, James 3, George 3, Rioch
			29-9-76		A	W	4-1	Hector 2, George 2
		2	20-10-76	AEK Athens (Greece)	A	L	0-2	
			3-11-76		H	L	2-3	George, Rioch
EVERTON								
1963-64	European Cup	1	18-9-63	Inter-Milan (Italy)	H	D	0-0	
			25-9-63		A	L	0-1	
1970-71	European Cup	1	16-9-70	Keflavik (Iceland)	H	W	6-2	Ball 3, Royle 2, Kendall
			30-9-70		A	W	3-0	Royle 2, Whittle
		2	21-10-70	Borussia Moenchenglad-	A	D	1-1	Kendall
			4-11-70	bach (West Germany)	H	D	1-1†	Morrissey
		QF	9-3-71	Panathinaikos (Greece)*	H	D	1-1	Johnson
			24-3-71		A	D	0-0	
1966-67	Cup-Winners' Cup	1	28-9-66	Aalborg (Denmark)	A	D	0-0	
			11-10-66		H	W	2-1	Morrissey, Ball
		2	9-11-66	Real Zaragoza (Spain)	A	L	0-2	
			23-11-66		H	W	1-0	Brown
1962-63	Fairs Cup	1	24-10-62	Dunfermline Athletic	H	W	1-0	Stevens
			31-10-62	(Scotland)	A	L	0-2	
1964-65	Fairs Cup	1	23-9-64	Valerengen (Norway)	A	W	5-2	Pickering 2, Harvey, Temple 2
			14-10-64		H	W	4-2	Young 2, Vernon, own goal
		2	11-11-64	Kilmarnock (Scotland)	A	W	2-0	Temple, Morrissey
			23-11-64		H	W	4-1	Harvey, Pickering 2, Young
		3	20-1-65	Manchester United	A	D	1-1	Pickering
			9-2-65	(England)	H	L	1-2	Pickering
1965-66	Fairs Cup	1	28-9-65	IFC Nuremberg (West	A	D	1-1	Harris
			12-10-65	Germany)	H	W	1-0	Gabriel
		2	3-11-65	Ujpest Dosza (Hungary)	A	L	0-3	
			16-11-65		H	W	2-1	Harris, own goal
1975-76	UEFA Cup	1	17-9-75	AC Milan (Italy)	H	D	0-0	
			1-10-75		A	L	0-1	
IPSWICH TOWN								
1962-63	European Cup	Pr	18-9-62	Floriana (Malta)	A	W	4-1	Crawford 2, Phillips 2
			25-9-62		H	W	10-0	Crawford 5, Moran 2, Phillips 2, Elsworthy
		1	14-11-62	AC Milan (Italy)	A	L	0-3	
			28-11-62		H	W	2-1	Crawford, Blackwood
1973-74	UEFA Cup	1	19-9-73	Real Madrid (Spain)	H	W	1-0	own goal
			3-10-73		A	D	0-0	
		2	24-10-73	Lazio (Italy)	H	W	4-0	Whymark 4
			7-11-73		A	L	2-4	Viljoen (pen), Johnson
		3	28-11-73	Twente Enschede	H	W	1-0	Whymark
			12-12-73	(Holland)	A	W	2-1	Morris, Hamilton
		QF	6-3-74	Lokomotive Leipzig	H	W	1-0	Beattie
			20-3-74	(East Germany)†	H	L	0-1	
1974-75	UEFA Cup	1	18-9-74	Twente Enschede	H	D	2-2	Hamilton, Talbot
			2-10-74	(Holland)*	A	D	1-1	Hamilton
1975-76	UEFA Cup	1	17-9-75	Feyenoord (Holland)	A	W	2-1	Whymark, Johnson
			1-10-75		H	W	2-0	Woods, Whymark
		2	22-10-75	FC Bruges (Belgium)	H	W	3-0	Gates, Peddelty, Austin
			5-11-75		A	L	0-4	

Season	Competition	Round	Date	Opponents (Country)	Venue	Result		Scorers

IPSWICH TOWN continued

Season	Competition	Round	Date	Opponents (Country)	Venue	Result		Scorers
1977–78	UEFA Cup	1	14–9–77	Landskrona (Sweden)	A	W	1–0	Whymark
			28–9–77		H	W	5–0	Whymark 4 (1 pen), Mariner
		2	19–10–77	Las Palmas (Spain)	H	W	1–0	Gates
			2–11–77		A	D	3–3	Mariner 2, Talbot
		3	23–11–77	Barcelona (Spain)	H	W	3–0	Gates, Whymark, Talbot
			7–12–77		A	L	0–3†	

LEEDS UNITED

Season	Competition	Round	Date	Opponents (Country)	Venue	Result		Scorers
1969–70	European Cup	1	17–9–69	Lyn Oslo (Norway)	H	W	10–0	Jones 3, Clarke 2, Giles 2, Bremner, O'Grady
			1–10–69		A	W	6–0	Belfitt 2, Hibbitt 2, Jones, Lorimer
		2	12–11–69	Ferencvaros (Hungary)	H	W	3–0	Giles, Jones 2
			26–11–69		A	W	3–0	Jones 2, Lorimer
		QF	4–3–70	Standard Liege (Belgium)	A	W	1–0	Lorimer
			18–3–70		H	W	1–0	Giles (pen)
		SF	1–4–70	Celtic (Scotland)	H	L	0–1	
			15–4–70		A	L	1–2	Bremner
1974–75	European Cup	1	28–9–74	Zurich (Switzerland)	H	W	2–1	Clarke 2, Lorimer (pen), Jordan
			2–10–74		A	L	1–2	Clarke
		2	23–10–74	Ujpest Dosza (Hungary)	A	W	2–1	Lorimer, McQueen
			6–11–74		H	W	3–0	McQueen, Bremner, Yorath
		QF	5–3–75	Anderlecht (Belgium)	H	W	3–0	Jordan, McQueen, Lorimer
			19–3–75		A	W	1–0	Bremner
		SF	9–4–75	Barcelona (Spain)	H	W	2–1	Bremner, Clarke
			24–4–75		A	D	1–1	Lorimer
		F	28–5–75	Bayern Munich (West Germany)	N	L	0–2	
1972–73	Cup-Winners' Cup	1	13–9–72	Ankaragucu (Turkey)	A	D	1–1	Jordan
			28–9–72		H	W	1–0	Jones
		2	25–10–72	Carl Zeiss Jena (East Germany)	A	D	0–0	
			8–11–72		H	W	2–0	Cherry, Jones
		QF	7–3–73	Rapid Bucharest (Rumania)	H	W	5–0	Giles, Clarke, Lorimer 2, Jordan
			23–3–73		A	W	3–1	Jones, Jordan, Bates
		SF	11–4–73	Hajduk Split (Yugoslavia)	H	W	1–0	Clarke
			25–4–73		A	D	0–0	
		F	16–5–73	AC Milan (Italy)	N	L	0–1	
1965–66	Fairs Cup	1	29–9–65	Torino (Italy)	H	W	2–1	Bremner, Peacock
			6–10–65		A	D	0–0	
		2	24–11–65	Lokomotive Leipzig (East Germany)	A	W	2–1	Lorimer, Bremner
			1–12–65		H	D	0–0	
		3	2–2–66	Valencia (Spain)	H	D	1–1	Lorimer
			16–2–66		A	W	1–0	O'Grady
		QF	2–3–66	Ujpest Dosza (Hungary)	H	W	4–1	Cooper, Bell, Storrie, Bremner
			9–3–66		A	D	1–1	Lorimer
		SF	20–4–66	Real Zaragoza (Spain)	A	L	0–1	
			27–4–66		H	W	2–1	Johanneson, Charlton
			11–5–66		H	L	1–3	Charlton
1966–67	Fairs Cup	1		bye				
		2	18–18–66	DWS Amsterdam (Holland)	A	W	3–1	Bremner, Johanneson, Greenhoff
			26–10–66		H	W	5–1	Johanneson 3, Giles, Madeley
		3	18–1–67	Valencia (Spain)	H	D	1–1	Greenhoff
			8–2–67		A	W	2–0	Giles, Lorimer
		QF	22–3–67	Bologna (Italy)	A	L	0–1	
			19–4–67		H	W	1–0‡	Giles (pen)
		SF	19–5–67	Kilmarnock (Scotland)	H	W	4–2	Belfitt 3, Giles (pen)
			24–5–67		A	D	0–0	
		F	30–8–67	Dynamo Zagreb (Yugoslavia)	A	L	0–2	
			6–9–67		H	D	0–0	
1967–68	Fairs Cup	1	3–10–67	Spora Luxembourg (Luxembourg)	A	W	9–0	Lorimer 4, Greenhoff 2, Madeley, Jones, Bremner
			17–10–67		H	W	7–0	Johanneson 3, Greenhoff 2, Cooper, Lorimer
		2	29–11–67	Partizan Belgrade (Yugoslavia)	A	W	2–1	Lorimer, Belfitt
			6–12–67		H	D	1–1	Lorimer
		3	20–12–67	Hibernian (Scotland)	H	W	1–0	Gray (E)
			10–1–68		A	D	0–0	
		QF	26–3–68	Rangers (Scotland)	A	D	0–0	
			9–4–68		H	W	2–0	Lorimer, Giles (pen)

Season	Competition	Round	Date	Opponents (Country)	Venue	Result		Scorers
LEEDS UNITED continued								
		SF	1–5–68	Dundee (Scotland)	A	D	1–1	Madeley
			15–5–68		H	W	1–0	Gray (E)
		F	7–8–68	Ferencvaros (Hungary)	H	W	1–0	Charlton
			11–9–68		A	D	0–0	
1968–69	Fairs Cup	1	18–9–68	Standard Liege (Belgium)	A	D	0–0	
			23–10–68		H	W	3–2	Charlton, Lorimer, Bremner
		2	13–11–68	Napoli (Italy)	H	W	2–0	Charlton 2
			27–11–68		A	L	0–2‡	
		3	18–12–68	Hanover 96 (West	H	W	5–1	O'Grady, Hunter, Lorimer 2, Charlton
			4–2–69	Germany)	A	W	2–1	Belfitt, Jones
		QF	5–3–69	Ujpest Dosza (Hungary)	A	L	0–1	
			19–3–69		A	L	0–2	
1970–71	Fairs Cup	1	15–9–70	Sarpsborg (Norway)	H	W	1–0	Lorimer
			29–9–70		H	W	5–0	Charlton 2, Bremner 2, Lorimer
		2	21–10–70	Dynamo Dresden	A	W	1–0	Lorimer
			4–11–70	(East Germany)	A	L	1–2*	Jones
		3	2–12–70	Sparta Prague	H	W	6–0	Clarke, Bremner, Gray (E) 2, Charlton.
			9–12–70	(Czechoslovakia)				own goal
					A	W	3–2	Gray (E), Clarke, Belfitt
		QF	10–3–71	Setubal (Portugal)	H	W	2–1	Lorimer, Giles (pen)
			24–3–71		A	D	1–1	Lorimer
		SF	14–4–71	Liverpool (England)	A	W	1–0	Bremner
			28–4–71		H	D	0–0	
		F	28–5–71	Juventus (Italy)	A	D	2–2	Madeley, Bates
			3–6–71		H	D	1–1*	Clarke
1971–72	UEFA Cup	1	15–9–71	Lierse (Belgium)	A	W	2–0	Galvin, Lorimer
			29–9–71		H	L	0–4	
1973–74	UEFA Cup	1	19–9–73	Stromsgodset (Norway)	A	D	1–1	Clarke
			3–10–73		H	W	6–1	Clarke 2, Jones 2, Gray (F), Bates
		2	24–10–73	Hibernian (Scotland)	H	D	0–0	
			7–11–73		A	D	0–0†	
		3	28–11–73	Setubal (Portugal)	H	W	1–0	Cherry
			12–12–73		A	L	1–3	Liddell
LEICESTER CITY								
1961–62	Cup-Winners' Cup	1	13–9–61	Glenavon (Northern	A	W	4–1	Walsh 2, Appleton, Keyworth
			27–9–61	Ireland)	H	W	3–1	Wills, Keyworth, McIlmoyle
		2	25–10–61	Atletico Madrid (Spain)	H	D	1–1	Keyworth
			15–11–61		A	L	0–2	
LIVERPOOL								
1964–65	European Cup	Pr	17–8–64	KR Reykjavik (Iceland)	A	W	5–0	Wallace 2, Hunt 2, Chisnall
			14–9–64		H	W	6–1	Byrne, St John 2, Graham, Hunt, Stevenson
		1	25–11–64	Anderlecht (Belgium)	H	W	3–0	St John, Hunt, Yeats
			16–12–64		A	W	1–0	Hunt
		QF	10–2–65	FC Cologne (West	A	D	0–0	
			17–3–65	Germany)	H	D	0–0	
			24–3–65		N	D	2–2‡	St John, Hunt
		SF	4–5–65	Inter-Milan (Italy)	H	W	3–1	Hunt, Callaghan, St John
			12–5–65		A	L	0–3	
1966–67	European Cup	1	28–9–66	Petrolul Ploesti (Rumania)	H	W	2–0	St John, Callaghan
			12–10–66		A	L	1–3	Hunt
			19–10–66		N	W	2–0	St John, Thompson (P)
		2	7–12–66	Ajax (Holland)	A	L	1–5	Lawler
			14–12–66		H	D	2–2	Hunt 2
1973–74	European Cup	1	19–9–73	Jeunesse D'Esch	A	D	1–1	Hall
			3–10–73	(Luxembourg)	H	W	2–0	Toshack, own goal
		2	24–10–73	Red Star Belgrade	A	L	1–2	Lawler
			6–11–73	(Yugoslavia)	H	L	1–2	Lawler
1976–77	European Cup	1	14–9–76	Crusaders (Northern	H	W	2–0	Neal (pen), Toshack
			28–9–76	Ireland)	A	W	5–0	Johnson 2, Keegan, McDermott, Heighway
		2	20–10–76	Trabzonspor (Turkey)	A	L	0–1	
			3–11–76		H	W	3–0	Heighway, Johnson, Keegan
		QF	2–3–77	St Etienne (France)	A	L	0–1	
			16–3–77		H	W	3–1˙	Keegan, Kennedy, Fairclough

Season	Competition	Round	Date	Opponents (Country)	Venue	Result		Scorers

LIVERPOOL continued

Season	Competition	Round	Date	Opponents (Country)	Venue	Result		Scorers
		SF	6–4–77	Zurich (Switzerland)	A	W	3–1	Neal 2 (1 pen), Heighway
			20–4–77		H	W	3–0	Case 2, Keegan
		F	25–5–77	Borussia Moenchenglad-bach (West Germany)	N	W	3–1	McDermott, Smith, Neal (pen)
1977–78	European Cup	1		bye				
		2	19–10–77	Dynamo Dresden	H	W	5–1	Hansen, Case 2, Neal (pen), Ker
			2–11–77	(East Germany)	A	L	1–2	Heighway
		QF	1–3–78	Benfica (Portugal)	A	W	2–1	Case, Hughes
			15–3–78		H	W	4–1	Callaghan, Dalglish, McDermott,
		SF	29–3–78	Borussia Moenchenglad-bach (West Germany)	A	L	1–2	Johnson
			12–4–78		H	W	3–0	Kennedy, Dalglish, Case
		F	10–5–78	FC Bruges (Belgium)	N	W	1–0	Dalglish
1965–66	Cup-Winners' Cup	1	29–9–65	Juventus (Italy)	A	L	0–1	
			13–10–65		H	W	2–0	Lawler, Strong
		2	1–12–65	Standard Liege (Belgium)	H	W	3–1	Lawler 2, Thompson (P)
			15–12–65		A	W	2–1	Hunt, St John
		QF	1–3–66	Honved (Hungary)	A	D	0–0	
			8–3–66		H	W	2–0	Lawler, St John
		SF	14–4–66	Celtic (Scotland)	A	L	0–1	
					H	W	2–0	Lawler, St John
		F	5–5–66	Borussia Dortmund (West Germany)	N	L	1–2	Hunt
1971–72	Cup-Winners' Cup	1	15–9–71	Servette (Switzerland)	A	L	1–2	Lawler
			29–9–71		H	W	2–0	Hughes, Heighway
		2	20–10–71	Bayern Munich	H	D	0–0	
			3–11–71	(West Germany)	A	L	1–3	Evans
1974–75	Cup-Winners' Cup	1	17–9–74	Stromsgodset (Norway)	H	W	11–0	Lindsay (pen), Boersma 2, Heigh Thompson (P B) 2, Smith, Corma Hughes, Callaghan, Kennedy
			1–10–74		A	W	1–0	Kennedy
		2	23–10–74	Ferencvaros (Hungary)*	H	D	1–1	Keegan
			5–11–74		A	D	0–0	
1967–68	Fairs Cup	1	19–9–67	Malmo FF (Sweden)	A	W	2–0	Hateley 2
			4–10–67		H	W	2–1	Yeats, Hunt
		2	7–11–67	Munich 1860 (West Germany)	H	W	8–0	St John, Hateley, Thompson (P), Smith (pen), Hunt 2, Callaghan 2
			14–11–67		A	L	1–2	Callaghan
		3	28–11–67	Ferencvaros (Hungary)	A	L	0–1	
			9–1–68		H	L	0–1	
1968–69	Fairs Cup	1	18–9–68	Atletico Bilbao (Spain)‡	A	L	1–2	Hunt
			2–10–68		A	W	2–1	Lawler, Hughes
1969–70	Fairs Cup	1	16–9–69	Dundalk (Eire)	H	W	10–0	Evans 2, Smith 2, Graham 2, Law Lindsay, Thompson (P), Callagha
			30–9–69		A	W	4–0	Thompson (P) 2, Graham, Callag
		3	11–11–69	Setubal (Portugal)*	A	L	0–1	
			26–11–69		H	W	3–2	Smith (pen), Evans, Hunt
1970–71	Fairs Cup	1	15–9–70	Ferencvaros (Hungary)	H	W	1–0	Graham
			29–9–70		A	D	1–1	Hughes
		2	21–10–70	Dynamo Bucharest (Rumania)	H	W	3–0	Lindsay, Lawler, Hughes
			4–11–70		A	D	1–1	Boersma
		3	9–12–70	Hibernian (Scotland)	A	W	1–0	Toshack
			22–12–70		H	W	2–0	Heighway, Boersma
		QF	10–3–71	Bayern Munich (West Germany)	H	W	3–0	Evans 3
			24–3–71		A	D	1–1	Ross
		SF	14–4–71	Leeds United (England)	H	L	0–1	
			28–4–71		A	D	0–0	
1972–73	UEFA Cup	1	12–9–72	Eintracht Frankfurt (West Germany)	A	D	2–0	Keegan, Hughes
			26–9–72		H	D	0–0	
		2	24–10–72	AEK Athens (Greece)	H	W	3–0	Boersma, Cormack, Smith (pen)
			7–11–72		A	W	3–1	Hughes 2, Boersma
		3	29–11–72	Dynamo Berlin (East Germany)	A	D	0–0	
			13–12–72		H	W	3–1	Boersma, Heighway, Toshack
		QF	7–3–73	Dynamo Dresden (East Germany)	H	W	2–0	Hall, Boersma
			21–3–73		A	W	1–0	Keegan
		SF	10–4–73	Tottenham Hotspur (England)	H	W	1–0	Lindsay
			25–4–73		A	L	1–2*	Heighway
		F	10–5–73	Borussia Moenchenglad-bach (West Germany)	H	W	3–0	Keegan 2, Lloyd
			23–5–73		A	L	0–2	

Season	Competition	Round	Date	Opponents (Country)	Venue	Result		Scorers
LIVERPOOL continued								
1975–76	UEFA Cup	1	17–9–75	Hibernian (Scotland)	A	L	0–1	
			30–9–75		H	W	3–1	Toshack 3
		2	22–10–75	Real Sociedad (Spain)	A	W	3–1	Heighway, Callaghan, Thompson (P B)
			4–11–75		H	W	6–0	Toshack, Kennedy 2, Fairclough, Heighway, Neal
		3	26–11–75	Slask Wroclaw (Poland)	A	W	2–1	Kennedy, Toshack
			10–12–75		H	W	3–0	Case 3
		QF	3–3–76	Dynamo Dresden	A	D	0–0	
			17–3–76	(East Germany)	H	W	2–1	Case, Keegan
		SF	30–3–76	Barcelona (Spain)	A	W	1–0	Toshack
			14–4–76		H	D	1–1	Thompson (P B)
		F	28–4–76	FC Bruges (Belgium)	H	W	3–2	Kennedy, Case, Keegan (pen)
			19–5–76		A	D	1–1	Keegan
MANCHESTER CITY								
1968–69	European Cup	1	18–9–68	Fenerbahce (Turkey)	H	D	0–0	
			2–10–68		A	L	1–2	Coleman
1969–70	Cup-Winners' Cup	1	17–9–69	Atletico Bilbao (Spain)	A	D	3–3	Young, Booth, own goal
			1–10–69		H	W	3–0	Oakes, Bell, Bowyer
		2	12–11–69	Lierse (Belgium)	A	W	3–0	Lee 2, Bell
			26–11–69		H	W	5–0	Bell 2, Lee 2, Summerbee
		QF	4–3–70	Academica Coimbra	A	D	0–0	
			18–3–70	(Portugal)	H	W	1–0	Towers
		SF	1–4–70	Schalke 04 (West	A	L	0–1	
			15–4–70	Germany)	H	W	5–1	Young 2, Doyle, Lee, Bell
		F	29–4–70	Gornik Zabrze (Poland)	N	W	2–1	Young, Lee (pen)
1970–71	Cup-Winners' Cup	1	16–9–70	Linfield (Northern Ireland)	H	W	1–0	Bell
			30–9–70		A	L	1–2*	Lee
		2	21–10–70	Honved (Hungary)	A	W	1–0	Lee
			4–11–70		H	W	2–0	Bell, Lee
		QF	10–3–71	Gornik Zabrze (Poland)	A	L	0–2	
			24–3–71		H	W	2–0	Mellor, Doyle
			31–3–71		N	W	3–1	Young, Booth, Lee
		SF	14–4–71	Chelsea (England)	A	L	0–1	
			28–4–71		H	L	0–1	
1972–73	UEFA Cup	1	13–9–72	Valencia (Spain)	H	D	2–2	Mellor, Marsh
			27–9–72		A	L	1–2	Marsh
1976–77	UEFA Cup	1	15–9–76	Juventus (Italy)	H	W	1–0	Kidd
			29–9–76		A	L	0–2	
1977–78	UEFA Cup	1	14–9–77	Widzew Lodz (Poland)*	H	D	2–2	Barnes, Channon
			28–9–77		A	D	0–0	
MANCHESTER UNITED								
1956–57	European Cup	Pr	12–9–56	Anderlecht (Belgium)	A	W	2–0	Viollet, Taylor (T)
			26–9–56		H	W	10–0	Viollet 4, Taylor (T) 3, Whelan 2, Berry
		1	17–10–56	Borussia Dortmund	H	W	3–2	Viollet 2, Pegg
			21–11–56	(West Germany)	A	D	0–0	
		QF	16–1–57	Atletico Bilbao (Spain)	A	L	3–5	Taylor (T), Viollet, Whelan
			6–2–57		H	W	3–0	Viollet, Taylor (T), Berry
		SF	11–4–57	Real Madrid (Spain)	A	L	1–3	Taylor (T)
			24–4–57		H	D	2–2	Taylor (T), Charlton
1957–58	European Cup	Pr	25–9–57	Shamrock Rovers (Eire)	A	W	6–0	Whelan 2, Taylor (T) 2, Berry, Pegg
			2–10–57		H	W	3–2	Viollet 2, Pegg
		1	20–11–57	Dukla Prague	H	W	3–0	Webster, Taylor (T), Pegg
			4–12–57	(Czechoslovakia)	A	L	0–1	
		QF	14–1–58	Red Star Belgrade	H	W	2–1	Charlton, Colman
			5–2–58	(Yugoslavia)	A	D	3–3	Viollet, Charlton 2
		SF	8–5–58	AC Milan (Italy)	H	W	2–1	Viollet, Taylor (E) (pen)
			14–5–58		A	L	0–4	
1965–66	European Cup	Pr	22–9–65	HJK Helsinki (Finland)	A	W	3–2	Herd, Connelly, Law
			6–10–65		H	W	6–0	Connelly 3, Best 2, Charlton
		1	17–11–65	Vorwaerts Berlin	A	W	2–0	Law, Connelly
			1–12–65	(East Germany)	H	W	3–1	Herd 3
		QF	2–2–66	Benfica (Portugal)	H	W	3–2	Herd, Law, Foulkes
			9–3–66		A	W	5–1	Best 2, Connelly, Crerand, Charlton
		SF	13–4–66	Partizan Belgrade	A	L	0–2	
			20–4–66	(Yugoslavia)	H	W	1–0	own goal

Season	Competition	Round	Date	Opponents (Country)	Venue	Result		Scorers
MANCHESTER UNITED continued								
1967–68	European Cup	1	20–9–67	Hibernians (Malta)	H	W	4–0	Sadler 2, Law 2
			27–9–67		A	D	0–0	
		2	15–11–67	Sarajevo (Yugoslavia)	A	D	0–0	
			29–11–67		H	W	2–1	Aston, Best
		QF	28–2–68	Gornik Zabrze (Poland)	H	W	2–0	Kidd, own goal
			13–3–68		A	L	0–1	
		SF	24–4–68	Real Madrid (Spain)	H	W	1–0	Best
			15–5–68		A	D	3–3	Sadler, Kidd, Foulkes
		F	29–5–68	Benfica (Portugal)	N	W	4–1	Charlton 2, Best, Kidd
1968–69	European Cup	1	18–9–68	Waterford (Eire)	A	W	3–1	Law 3
			2–10–68		H	W	7–1	Stiles, Law 4, Burns, Charlton
		2	13–11–68	Anderlecht (Belgium)	H	W	3–0	Kidd, Law 2
			27–11–68		A	L	1–3	Sartori
		QF	26–2–69	Rapid Vienna (Austria)	H	W	3–0	Best 2, Morgan
			5–3–69		A	D	0–0	
		SF	23–4–69	AC Milan (Italy)	A	L	0–2	
			15–5–69		H	W	1–0	Charlton
1963–64	Cup-Winners' Cup	1	25–9–63	Tilburg Willen II (Holland)	A	D	1–1	Herd
			15–10–63		H	W	6–1	Setters, Law 3, Charlton, Chisnall
		2	3–12–63	Tottenham Hotspur (England)	A	L	0–2	
			10–12–63		H	W	4–1	Herd 2, Charlton 2
		QF	26–2–64	Sporting Lisbon (Portugal)	H	W	4–1	Law 3 (2 pens), Charlton
			18–3–64		A	L	0–5	
1977–78	Cup-Winners' Cup	1	14–9–77	St. Etienne (France)	A	D	1–1	Hill
			5–10–77		H	W	2–0	Pearson, Coppell
		2	19–10–77	Porto (Portugal)	A	L	0–4	
			2–11–77		H	W	5–2	Coppell 2, own goals 2, Nicholl
1964–65	Fairs Cup	1	23–9–64	Djurgaarden (Sweden)	A	D	1–1	Herd
			27–10–64		H	W	6–1	Law 3 (1 pen), Charlton 2, Best
		2	11–11–64	Borussia Dortmund (West Germany)	A	W	6–1	Herd, Charlton 3, Best, Law
			2–12–64		H	W	4–0	Charlton 2, Law, Connelly
		3	20–1–65	Everton (England)	H	D	1–1	Connelly
			9–2–65		A	W	2–1	Connelly, Herd
		QF	12–5–65	Strasbourg (France)	A	W	5–0	Connelly, Herd, Law 2, Charlton
			19–5–65		H	D	0–0	
		SF	31–5–65	Ferencvaros (Hungary)	H	W	3–2	Law (pen), Herd 2
			6–6–65		A	L	0–1	
			16–6–65		A	L	1–2	Connelly
1976–77	UEFA Cup	1	15–9–76	Ajax (Holland)	A	L	0–1	
			29–9–76		H	W	2–0	Macari, McIlroy
		2	20–10–76	Juventus (Italy)	H	W	1–0	Hill
			3–11–76		A	L	0–3	
NEWCASTLE UNITED								
1968–69	Fairs Cup	1	11–9–68	Feyenoord (Holland)	H	W	4–0	Scott, Robson (B), Gibb, Davies
			17–9–68		A	L	0–2	
		2	30–10–68	Sporting Lisbon (Portugal)	A	D	1–1	Scott
			20–11–68		H	W	1–0	Robson (B)
		3	1–1–69	Real Zaragoza (Spain)	A	L	2–3	Robson (B), Davies
			15–1–69		H	W	2–1*	Robson (B), Gibb
		QF	12–3–69	Setubal (Portugal)	H	W	5–1	Robson (B) 2, Gibb, Davies, Foggon
			26–3–69		A	L	1–3	Davies
		SF	14–5–69	Rangers (Scotland)	A	D	0–0	
			22–5–69		H	W	2–0	Scott, Sinclair
		F	29–5–69	Ujpest Dosza (Hungary)	H	W	3–0	Moncur 2, Scott
			11–6–69		A	W	3–2	Moncur, Arentoft, Foggon
1969–70	Fairs Cup	1	15–9–69	Dundee United (Scotland)	A	W	2–1	Davies 2
			1–10–69		H	W	1–0	Dyson
		2	19–11–69	Porto (Portugal)	A	D	0–0	
			26–11–69		H	W	1–0	Scott
		3	17–12–69	Southampton (England)	H	D	0–0	
			13–1–70		A	D	1–1*	Robson (B)
		QF	11–3–70	Anderlecht (Belgium)*	A	L	0–2	
			18–3–70		H	W	3–1	Robson (B) 2, Dyson
1970–71	Fairs Cup	1	23–9–70	Inter-Milan (Italy)	A	D	1–1	Davies
			30–9–70		H	W	2–0	Moncur, Davies
		2	21–10–70	Pecs Dosza (Hungary)†	H	W	2–0	Davies 2
			4–11–70		A	L	0–2	

Season	Competition	Round	Date	Opponents (Country)	Venue	Result		Scorers
NEWCASTLE UNITED continued								
1977–78	UEFA Cup	1	14–9–77	Bohemians (Eire)	A	D	0–0	
			28–9–77		H	W	4–0	Gowling 2, Craig 2
		2	19–10–77	Bastia (France)	A	L	1–2	Cannell
			2–11–77		H	L	1–3	Gowling
NOTTINGHAM FOREST								
1961–62	Fairs Cup	1	13–9–61	Valencia (Spain)	A	L	0–2	
			4–10–61		H	L	5–1	Cobb
1967–68	Fairs Cup	1	20–9–67	Eintracht Frankfurt	A	W	1–0	Baker
			17–10–67	(West Germany)	H	W	4–0	Baker 2, Chapman, Lyons
		2	31–10–67	Zurich (Switzerland)*	H	W	2–1	Newton, Moore (pen)
			14–11–67		A	L	0–1	
QUEEN'S PARK RANGERS								
1976–77	UEFA Cup	1	15–9–76	Brann Bergen (Norway)	H	W	4–0	Bowles 3, Masson
			29–9–76		A	W	7–0	Bowles 3, Givens 2, Thomas, Webb
		2	20–10–76	Slovan Bratislava	A	D	3–3	Bowles 2, Givens
			3–11–76	(Czechoslovakia)	A	W	5–2	Givens 3, Bowles, Clement
		3	24–11–76	IFC Cologne (West	H	W	3–0	Givens, Webb, Bowles
			7–12–76	Germany)	A	L	1–4*	Masson
		QF	2–3–77	AEK Athens (Greece)	H	W	3–0	Francis (2 pens), Bowles
			16–3–77		A	L	0–3†	
SHEFFIELD WEDNESDAY								
1961–62	Fairs Cup	1	12–9–61	Lyon (France)	A	L	2–4	Ellis, Young
			4–10–61		H	W	5–2	Fantham 2, Griffin, McAnearney (pen), Dobson
		2	29–11–61	AS Roma (Italy)	H	W	4–0	Fantham, Young 3
			13–12–61		A	L	0–1	
		QF	28–2–62	Barcelona (Spain)	H	W	3–2	Fantham 2, Finney
			28–3–62		A	L	0–2	
1963–64	Fairs Cup	1	25–9–63	DOS Utrecht (Holland)	A	W	4–1	Holliday, Layne, Quinn, own goal
			15–10–63		H	W	4–1	Layne 3 (1 pen), Dobson
		2	6–11–63	IFC Cologne (West	A	L	2–3	Pearson 2
			27–11–63	Germany)	H	L	1–2	Layne
SOUTHAMPTON								
1976–77	Cup-Winners' Cup	1	15–9–76	Marseille (France)	H	W	4–0	Waldron, Channon 2 (1 pen), Osgood
			29–9–76		A	L	1–2	Peach
		2	20–10–76	Carrick Rangers	A	W	5–2	Stokes, Channon 2, McCalliog, Osgood
			3–11–76	(Northern Ireland)	H	W	4–1	Williams, Hayes 2, Stokes
		QF	2–3–77	Anderlecht (Belgium)	A	L	0–2	
			16–3–77		H	W	2–1	Peach (pen), MacDougall
1969–70	Fairs Cup	1	17–9–69	Rosenborg (Norway)	A	L	0–1	
			1–10–69		H	W	2–0	Davies, Paine
		2	4–11–69	Vitoria Guimaraes	A	D	3–3	Channon, Davies, Paine
			12–11–69	(Portugal)	H	W	5–1	Gabriel, Davies 2 (1 pen), Channon, own goal
		3	17–12–69	Newcastle United	A	D	0–0	
			13–1–70	(England)*	H	D	1–1	Channon
1971–72	UEFA Cup	1	15–9–71	Atletico Bilbao (Spain)	H	W	2–1	Jenkins, Channon (pen)
			29–9–71		A	L	0–2	
STOKE CITY								
1972–73	UEFA Cup	1	13–9–72	Kaiserslautern	H	W	3–1	Conroy, Hurst, Richie
			27–9–72	(West Germany)	A	L	0–4	
1974–75	UEFA Cup	1	18–9–74	Ajax (Holland)*	H	D	1–1	Smith
			2–10–74		A	D	0–0	
SUNDERLAND								
1973–74	Cup-Winners' Cup	1	19–9–73	Vasas-Budapest	A	W	2–0	Hughes, Tueart
			3–10–73	(Hungary)	H	W	1–0	Tueart (pen)
		2	24–10–73	Sporting Lisbon (Portugal)	H	W	2–1	Kerr, Horswill
			7–11–73		A	L	0–2	

Season	Competition	Round	Date	Opponents (Country)	Venue	Result		Scorers

SWANSEA CITY

Season	Competition	Round	Date	Opponents (Country)	Venue	Result		Scorers
1961–62	Cup-Winners' Cup	1	16–19–61	Motor Jena	H	D	2–2	Reynolds, Nurse (pen)
			18–10–61	(East Germany)	A	L	1–5	Reynolds
				(in Linz, Austria)				
1966–67	Cup-Winners' Cup	1	21–9–66	Slavia Sofia (Bulgaria)	H	D	1–1	Todd
			5–10–66		A	L	0–4	

TOTTENHAM HOTSPUR

Season	Competition	Round	Date	Opponents (Country)	Venue	Result		Scorers
1961–62	European Cup	Pr	13–9–61	Gornik Zabrze (Poland)	A	L	2–4	Jones, Dyson
			20–9–61		H	W	8–1	Blanchflower (pen), Jones 3, Smith, Dyson, White
		1	1–11–61	Feyenoord (Holland)	A	W	3–1	Dyson, Saul 2
			15–11–61		H	D	1–1	Dyson
		QF	14–2–62	Dukla Prague	A	L	0–1	
			26–2–62	(Czechoslovakia)	H	W	4–1	Smith 2, Mackay 2
		SF	21–3–62	Benfica (Portugal)	A	L	1–3	Smith
			5–4–62		H	W	2–1	Smith, Blanchflower (pen)
1962–63	Cup-Winners' Cup	1		bye				
		2	31–10–62	Rangers (Scotland)	H	W	5–2	White, Greaves, Allen, Norman, own goal
			11–12–62		A	W	3–2	Greaves, Smith 2
		QF	5–3–63	Slovan Bratislava	A	L	0–2	
			14–3–63	(Czechoslovakia)	H	W	6–0	Mackay, Smith, Greaves 2, Jones, White
		SF	24–4–63	OFK Belgrade	A	W	2–1	White, Dyson
			1–5–63	(Yugoslavia)	H	W	3–1	Mackay, Jones, Smith
		F	15–5–63	Atletico Madrid (Spain)	N	W	5–1	Greaves 2, White, Dyson 2
1963–64	Cup-Winners' Cup	1		exempt				
		2	3–12–63	Manchester United	H	W	2–0	Mackay, Dyson
			10–12–63	(England)	A	L	1–4	Greaves
1967–68	Cup-Winners' Cup	1	20–9–67	Hajduk Split (Yugoslavia)	A	W	2–0	Robertson, Greaves
			27–9–67		H	W	4–3	Robertson 2, Gilzean, Venables
		2	29–11–67	Lyon (France)*	A	L	0–1	
			13–12–67		H	W	4–3	Greaves 2 (1 pen), Jones, Gilzean
1971–72	UEFA Cup	1	14–9–71	Keflavik (Iceland)	A	W	6–1	Gilzean 3, Coates, Mullery 2
			28–9–71		H	W	9–0	Chivers 3, Gilzean 2, Perryman, Coates, Knowles, Holder
		2	20–10–71	Nantes (France)	A	D	0–0	
			2–11–71		H	W	1–0	Peters
		3	8–12–71	Rapid Bucharest	H	W	3–0	Peters, Chivers 2
			15–12–71	(Rumania)	A	W	2–0	Pearce, Chivers
		QF	7–3–72	UT Arad (Rumania)	A	W	2–0	Morgan, England
			21–3–72		H	D	1–1	Gilzean
		SF	5–4–72	AC Milan (Italy)	H	W	2–1	Perryman 2
			19–4–72		A	D	1–1	Mullery
		F	3–5–72	Wolverhampton	A	W	2–1	Chivers 2
			17–5–72	Wanderers (England)	H	D	1–1	Mullery
1972–73	UEFA Cup	1	13–9–72	Lyn Oslo (Norway)	A	W	6–3	Peters, Pratt, Gilzean 2, Chivers 2
			27–9–72		H	W	6–0	Chivers 3, Coates 2, Pearce
		2	25–10–72	Olympiakos Piraeus	H	W	4–0	Pearce 2, Chivers, Coates
			8–11–72	(Greece)	A	L	0–1	
		3	29–11–72	Red Star Belgrade	H	W	2–0	Chivers, Gilzean
			13–12–72	(Yugoslavia)	A	L	0–1	
		QF	7–3–73	Setubal (Portugal)	H	W	1–0	Evans
			21–3–73		A	L	1–2*	Chivers
		SF	10–4–73	Liverpool (England)*	A	L	0–1	
			25–4–73		H	W	2–1	Peters 2
1973–74	UEFA Cup	1	19–9–73	Grasshoppers	A	W	5–1	Chivers 2, Evans, Gilzean 2
			3–10–73	(Switzerland)	H	W	4–1	Peters 2, England, own goal
		2	24–10–73	Aberdeen (Scotland)	A	D	1–1	Coates
			7–11–73		H	W	4–1	Peters, Neighbour, McGrath 2
		3	28–11–73	Dynamo Tbilisi (USSR)	A	D	1–1	Coates
			12–12–73		H	W	5–1	McGrath, Chivers 2, Peters 2
		QF	6–3–74	IFC Cologne	A	W	2–1	McGrath, Peters
			20–3–74	(West Germany)	H	W	3–0	Chievers, Coates, Peters
		SF	10–4–74	Lokomotive Leipzig	A	W	2–1	Peters, McGrath
			24–4–74	(East Germany)	H	W	2–0	McGrath, Chivers
		F	21–5–74	Feyenoord (Holland)	H	D	2–2	England, own goal
			29–5–74		A	L	0–2	

Season	Competition	Round	Date	Opponents (Country)	Venue	Result		Scorers
WEST BROMWICH ALBION								
1968–69	Cup-Winners' Cup	1	18–9–68	FC Bruges (Belgium)	A	L	1–3	Hartford
			2–10–68		H	W	2–0*	Brown (T), Hartford
		2	13–11–68	Dynamo Bucharest	A	D	1–1	Hartford
			27–11–68	(Rumania)	H	W	4–0	Lovett, Astle, Brown (T) 2 (1 pen)
		QF	15–1–69	Dunfermline Athletic	A	D	0–0	
			19–2–69	(Scotland)	H	L	0–1	
1966–67	Fairs Cup	1		bye				
		2	2–11–66	DOS Utrecht (Holland)	A	D	1–1	Hope
			9–11–66		H	W	5–2	Brown (T) 3 (1 pen), Clark, Kaye
		3	2–2–67	Bologna (Italy)	A	L	0–3	
			8–3–67		H	L	1–3	Fairfax
WEST HAM UNITED								
1964–65	Cup-Winners' Cup	1	23–9–64	La Gantoise (Belgium)	A	W	1–0	Boyce
			7–10–64		H	D	1–1	Byrne
		2	25–11–64	Sparta Prague	H	W	2–0	Bond, Sealey
			9–12–64	(Czechoslovakia)	A	L	1–2	Sissons
		QF	16–3–65	Lausanne (Switzerland)	A	W	2–1	Dear, Byrne
			23–3–65		H	W	4–3	Dear 2, Peters, own goal
		SF	7–4–65	Real Zaragoza (Spain)	H	W	2–1	Dear, Byrne
			28–4–65		A	D	1–1	Sissons
		F	19–5–65	Munich 1860	N	W	2–0	Sealey 2
				(West Germany)				
1965–66	Cup-Winners' Cup	1		bye				
		2	24–11–65	Olympiakos Piraeus	H	W	4–0	Hurst 2, Byrne, Brabrook
			1–12–65	(Greece)	A	D	2–2	Peters 2
		QF	2–3–66	Magdeburg (East	H	W	1–0	Byrne
			16–3–66	Germany)	A	D	1–1	Sissons
		SF	5–4–66	Borussia Dortmund	H	L	1–2	Peters
			13–4–66	(West Germany)	A	L	1–3	Byrne
1975–76	Cup-Winners' Cup	1	17–9–75	Lahden Reipas (Finland)	A	D	2–2	Brooking, Bonds
			1–10–75		H	W	3–0	Robson (K), Holland, Jennings
		2	22–10–75	Ararat Erevan (USSR)	A	D	1–1	Taylor (A)
			5–11–75		H	W	3–1	Paddon, Robson (K), Taylor (A)
		QF	3–3–76	Den Haag (Holland)	A	L	2–4	Jennings 2
			17–3–76		H	W	3–1*	Taylor (A), Lampard, Bonds (pen)
		SF	31–3–76	Eintracht Frankfurt	A	L	1–2	Paddon
			14–4–76	(West Germany)	H	W	3–1	Brooking 2, Robson (K)
		F	5–5–76	Anderlecht (Belgium)	N	L	2–4	Holland, Robson (K)
WOLVERHAMPTON WANDERERS								
1958–59	European Cup	Pr		bye				
		1	12–11–58	Schalke 04	H	D	2–2	Broadbent 2
			18–11–58	(West Germany)	A	L	1–2	Jackson
1959–60	European Cup	Pr	30–9–59	Vorwaerts (East Germany)	A	L	1–2	Broadbent
			7–10–59		H	W	2–0	Broadbent, Mason
		1	11–11–59	Red Star Belgrade	A	D	1–1	Deeley
			24–11–59	(Yugoslavia)	H	W	3–0	Murray, Mason 2
		QF	10–2–60	Barcelona (Spain)	A	L	0–4	
			2–3–60		H	L	2–5	Murray, Mason
1960–61	Cup-Winners' Cup	Pr		bye				
		QF	12–10–60	FK Austria (Austria)	A	L	0–2	
			30–11–60		H	W	5–0	Kirkham, Mason, Broadbent 2
		SF	29–3–61	Rangers (Scotland)	A	L	0–2	
			19–4–61		H	D	1–1	Broadbent
1971–72	UEFA Cup	1	15–9–71	Academica Coimbra	H	W	3–0	McAlle, Richards, Dougan
			29–9–71	(Portugal)	A	W	4–1	Dougan 3, McAlle
		2	20–10–71	Den Haag (Holland)	A	W	3–1	Dougan, McCalliog, Hibbitt
			3–11–71		H	W	4–0	Dougan, own goals 3
		3	24–11–71	Carl Zeiss Jena	A	W	1–0	Richards
			8–12–71	(East Germany)	H	W	3–0	Hibbitt, Dougan 2
		QF	7–3–72	Juventus (Italy)	A	D	1–1	McCalliog
			21–3–72		H	W	2–1	Hegan, Dougan
		SF	5–4–72	Ferencvaros (Hungary)	A	D	2–2	Richards, Munro
			19–4–72		H	W	2–1	Bailey, Munro
		F	3–5–72	Tottenham Hotspur	H	L	1–2	McCalliog
			17–5–72	(England)	A	D	1–1	Wagstaffe

Season	Competition	Round	Date	Opponents (Country)	Venue	Result		Scorers
WOLVERHAMPTON WANDERERS continued								
1973–74	UEFA Cup	1	26-9-73	Belenenses (Portugal)	A	W	2–0	Richards, Dougan
			3-10-73		H	W	2–1	Eastoe, McCalliog
		2	24-10-73	Lokomotive Leipzig	A	L	0–3	
			7-11-73	(East Germany)	H	W	4–1	Kindon, Munro, Dougan, Hibbitt
1974–75	UEFA Cup	1	18-9-74	Porto (Portugal)	A	L	1–4	Bailey
			2-10-74		H	W	3–1	Bailey, Daley, Dougan
WREXHAM								
1972–73	Cup Winners' Cup	1	13-9-72	Zurich (Switzerland)	A	D	1–1	Kinsey
			27-9-72		H	W	2–1	Ashcroft, Sutton
		2	25-10-72	Hajduk Split (Yugoslavia)*	H	W	3–1	Tinnion, Smallman, own goal
			8-11-72		A	L	0–2	
1975–76	Cup-Winners' Cup	1	17-9-75	Djurgaarden (Sweden)	H	W	2–1	Griffiths, Davis
			1-10-75		A	D	1–1	Whittle
		2	22-10-75	Stal Rzeszow (Poland)	H	W	2–0	Ashcroft 2
			5-11-75		A	D	1–1	Sutton
		QF	3-3-76	Anderlecht (Belgium)	A	L	0–1	
			17-3-76		H	D	1–1	Lee

*won on away goals counting double
†won on penalties
‡won on the toss of a coin

SCOTTISH LEAGUE CLUBS

Season	Competition	Round	Date	Opponents (Country)	Venue	Result		Scorers
ABERDEEN								
1967–68	Cup-Winners' Cup	1	6-9-67	KR Reykjavik (Iceland)	H	W	10–1	Munro 3, Storrie 2, Smith 2, McM
								Petersen, Taylor
			13-9-67		A	W	4–1	Storrie 2, Buchan, Munro
		2	29-11-67	Standard Liege (Belgium)	A	L	0–3	
			6-12-67		H	W	2–0	Munro, Melrose
1970–71	Cup-Winners' Cup	1	16-9-70	Honved (Hungary)†	H	W	3–1	Graham, Harper, Murray (S)
			30-9-70		A	L	1–3	Murray (S)
1968–69	Fairs Cup	1	17-9-68	Slavia Sofia (Bulgaria)	A	D	0–0	
			2-10-68		H	W	2–0	Robb, Taylor
		2	23-10-68	Real Zaragoza (Spain)	H	W	2–1	Forrest, Smith
			30-10-68		A	L	0–3	
1971–72	UEFA Cup	1	15-9-71	Celta Vigo (Spain)	A	W	2–0	Harper, own goal
			29-9-71		H	W	1–0	Harper
		2	27-10-71	Juventus (Italy)	A	L	0–2	
			17-11-71		H	D	1–1	Harper
1972–73	UEFA Cup	1	13-9-72	Borussia Moenchenglad-	H	L	2–3	Harper, Jarvie
			27-9-72	bach (West Germany)	A	L	3–6	Harper 2, Jarvie
1973–74	UEFA Cup	1	19-9-73	Finn Harps (Eire)	H	W	4–1	Miller (R), Jarvie 2, Graham
			3-10-73		A	W	3–1	Robb, Graham, Miller (R)
		2	24-10-73	Tottenham Hotspur	H	D	1–1	Hermiston (pen)
			7-11-73	(England)	A	L	1–4	Jarvie
1977–78	UEFA Cup	1	14-9-77	RWD Molenbeek	A	D	0–0	
			28-9-77	(Belgium)	H	L	1–2	Jarvie
CELTIC								
1966–67	European Cup	1	28-9-66	Zurich (Switzerland)	H	W	2–0	Gemmell, McBride
			5-10-66		A	W	3–0	Gemmell 2 (1 pen), Chalmers
		2	30-11-66	Nantes (France)	A	W	3–1	McBride, Lennox, Chalmers
			7-12-66		H	W	3–1	Johnstone, Lennox, Chalmers
		Qf	1-3-66	Vojvodina (Yugoslavia)	A	L	0–1	
			8-3-66		H	W	2–0	Chalmers, McNeill
		Sf	12-4-67	Dukla Prague	H	W	3–1	Johnstone, Wallace 2
			25-4-67	(Czechoslovakia)	A	D	0–0	
		F	25-5-67	Inter-Milan (Italy)	N	W	2–1	Gemmell, Chalmers
1967–68	European Cup	1	20-9-67	Dynamo Kiev (USSR)	H	L	1–2	Lennox
			4-10-67		A	D	1–1	Lennox

Season	Competition	Round	Date	Opponents (Country)	Venue	Result		Scorers
CELTIC continued								
1968–69	European Cup	1	18–8–68	St Etienne (France)	A	L	0–2	
			2–10–68		H	W	4–0	Gemmell (pen), Craig, Chalmers, McBride
		2	13–11–68	Red Star Belgrade (Yugoslavia)	H	W	5–1	Murdoch, Johnstone 2, Lennox, Wallace
			27–11–68		A	D	1–1	Wallace
		QF	19–2–69	AC Milan (Italy)	A	D	0–0	
			12–3–69		H	L	0–1	
1969–70	European Cup	1	17–9–69	Basle (Switzerland)	A	D	0–0	
			1–10–69		H	W	2–0	Hood, Gemmell
		2	12–11–69	Benfica (Portugal)	H	W	3–0	Gemmell, Wallace, Hood
			26–11–69		A	L	0–3‡	
		QF	4–3–70	Fiorentina (Italy)	H	W	3–0	Auld, Wallace, own goal
			18–3–70		A	L	0–1	
		SF	1–4–70	Leeds United (England)	A	W	1–0	Connolly
			15–4–70		H	W	2–1	Hughes, Murdoch
		F	6–5–70	Feyenoord (Holland)	N	L	1–2	Gemmell
1971–72	European Cup	1	16–9–70	KPV Kokkola (Finland)	H	W	9–0	Hood 3, Wilson 2, Hughes, McNeill, Johnstone, Davidson
			30–9–70		A	W	5–0	Wallace 2, Callaghan, Davidson, Lennox
		2	21–10–70	Waterford (Eire)	A	W	7–0	Wallace 3, Murdoch 2, Macari 2
			4–11–70		H	W	3–2	Hughes, Johnstone 2
		QF	10–3–70	Ajax (Holland)	A	L	0–3	
			24–3–71		H	W	1–0	Johnstone
1971–72	European Cup	1	15–9–71	BK 1903 Copenhagen (Denmark)	A	L	1–2	Macari
			29–9–71		H	W	3–0	Wallace 2, Callaghan
		2	20–10–71	Sliema Wanderers (Malta)	H	W	5–0	Gemmell, Bacari 2, Hood, Brogan
			3–11–71		A	W	2–1	Hood, Lennox
		QF	8–3–72	Ujpest Dozsa (Hungary)	A	W	2–1	Macari, own goal
			22–3–72		H	D	1–1	Macari
		SF	5–4–72	Inter-Milan (Italy)†	A	D	0–0	
			19–4–72		H	D	0–0	
1972–73	European Cup	1	13–9–72	Rosenborg (Norway)	H	W	2–1	Macari, Deans
			27–9–72		A	W	3–1	Macari, Hood, Dalglish
		2	25–10–72	Ujpest Dozsa (Hungary)	H	W	2–1	Dalglish 2
			8–11–72		A	L	0–3	
1973–74	European Cup	1	19–9–73	Turun (Finland)	A	W	6–1	Callaghan 2, Hood, Johnstone, Connelly (pen), Deans
			3–10–73		H	W	3–0	Deans, Johnstone 2
		2	24–10–73	Vejle (Denmark)	H	D	0–0	
			6–11–73		A	W	1–0	Lennox
		QF	27–2–74	Basle (Switzerland)	A	L	2–3	Wilson, Dalglish
			20–3–74		H	W	4–2	Dalglish, Deans, Callaghan, Murray
		SF	10–4–74	Atletico Madrid (Spain)	H	D	0–0	
			24–4–74		A	L	0–2	
1974–75	European Cup	1	18–9–74	Olymiakos Piraeus (Greece)	H	D	1–1	Wilson
			2–10–74		A	L	0–2	
1977–78	European Cup	1	14–9–77	Jeunesse Esch (Luxembourg)	H	W	5–0	McDonald, Wilson, Craig 2, McLaughlin
			28–9–77		A	W	6–1	Lennox 2, Edvaldsson 2, Glavin, Craig
		2	19–10–77	SW Innsbruck (Austria)	H	W	2–1	Craig, Burns
			2–11–77		A	L	0–3	
1963–64	Cup-Winners' Cup	1	17–9–63	Basle (Switzerland)	A	W	5–1	Divers, Hughes 3, Lennox
			9–10–63		H	W	5–0	Johnstone, Divers 2, Murdoch, Chalmers
		1	4–12–63	Dynamo Zagreb (Yugoslavia)	H	W	3–0	Chalmers 2, Hughes
			11–12–63		A	L	1–2	Murdoch
		QF	26–2–64	Slovan Bratislava (Czechoslovakia)	H	W	1–0	Murdoch (pen)
			4–3–64		A	W	1–0	Hughes
		SF	15–4–64	MTK Budapest (Hungary)	H	W	3–0	Johnstone, Chalmers 2
			29–4–64		A	L	0–4	
1965–66	Cup-Winners' Cup	1	29–9–65	Go Ahead Deverter (Holland)	A	W	6–0	Gallagher 2, Hughes, Johnstone 2, Lennox
			7–10–65		H	W	1–0	McBride
		2	3–11–65	Aarhus (Denmark)	A	W	1–0	McBride
			17–11–65		H	W	2–0	McNeill, Johnstone

Season	Competition	Round	Date	Opponents (Country)	Venue	Result		Scorers
CELTIC continued								
		QF	12–1–66	Dynamo Kiev (USSR)	H	W	3–0	Gemmell, Murdoch 2
			26–1–66		A	D	1–1	Gemmell
		SF	14–4–66	Liverpool (England)	H	W	1–0	Lennox
			19–4–66		A	L	0–2	
1975–76	Cup-Winners' Cup	1	16–9–75	Valur Reykjavik (Iceland)	A	W	2–0	Wilson, McDonald
			1–10–75		H	W	7–0	Edvaldsson, Dalglish, McCluskey (pen), Hood 2, Deans, Callaghan
		2	22–10–75	Boavista (Portugal)	A	D	0–0	
			5–11–75		H	W	3–1	Dalglish, Edvaldsson, Deans
		QF	3–3–76	Sachsenring Zwickau	H	D	1–1	Dalglish
			17–3–76		A	L	0–1	
1962–63	Fairs Cup	1	26–9–62	Valencia (Spain)	A	L	2–4	Carrol 2
			24–10–62		H	D	2–2	Crerand, own goal
1964–65	Fairs Cup	1	23–9–64	Leixoes (Portugal)	A	D	1–1	Murdoch
			7–10–64		H	W	3–0	Murdoch (pen), Chalmers 2
		2	18–11–64	Barcelona (Spain)	A	L	1–3	Hughes
			2–12–64		H	D	0–0	
1976–77	UEFA Cup	1	15–9–76	Wisla Krakow (Poland)	H	D	2–2	McDonald, Dalglish
			29–9–76		A	L	0–2	
DUNDEE								
1962–63	European Cup	Pr	5–9–62	IFC Cologne (West Germany)	H	W	8–1	Gilzean 3, own goal, Wishart, Robertson, Smith, Penman
			26–9–62		A	L	0–4	
		1	24–10–62	Sporting Lisbon (Portugal)	A	L	0–1	
			31–10–62		H	W	4–1	Gilzean 3, Cousin
		QF	6–3–63	Anderlecht (Belgium)	A	W	4–1	Gilzean 2, Cousin, Smith
			13–3–63		H	W	2–1	Cousin, Smith
		SF	24–4–63	AC Milan (Italy)	A	L	1–5	Cousin
			1–5–63		H	W	1–0	Gilzean
1964–65	Cup-Winners' Cup	1		bye				
		2	18–11–64	Real Zaragoza (Spain)	H	D	2–2	Murray, Houston
			8–12–64		A	L	1–2	Robertson
1967–68	Fairs Cup	1	27–9–67	DWS Amsterdam (Holland)	A	L	1–2	McLean (G)
			4–10–67		H	W	3–0	Wilson (S), McLean 2 (1 pen)
		2	1–11–67	Liege (Belgium)	H	W	3–1	Stuart 2, Wilson (S)
			14–11–67		A	W	4–1	McLean (G) 4
		3		bye				
		QF	27–3–68	Zurich (Switzerland)	H	W	1–0	Easton
			3–4–68		A	W	1–0	Wilson (S)
		SF	1–5–68	Leeds United (England)	H	D	1–1	Wilson (R)
			15–5–68		A	L	0–2	
1971–72	UEFA Cup	1	15–9–71	Akademisk Copenhagen (Denmark)	H	W	4–2	Bryce 2, Wallace, Lambie
			29–9–71		A	W	1–0	Duncan
		2	19–19–71	IFC Cologne (West Germany)	A	L	1–2	Kinninmouth
			3–11–71		H	W	4–2	Duncan 3, Wilson (R)
		3	24–11–71	AC Milan (Italy)	A	L	0–3	
			8–12–71		H	W	2–0	Wallace, Duncan
1973–74	UEFA Cup	1	19–9–73	Twente Enschede (Holland)	H	L	1–3	Stewart
			3–10–73		A	L	2–4	Johnston, Scott (J)
1974–75	UEFA Cup	1	18–9–74	RWD Molenbeek (Belgium)	A	L	0–1	
			2–10–74		H	L	2–4	Duncan, Scott (J)
DUNDEE UNITED								
1974–75	Cup-Winners' Cup	1	18–9–74	Jiul Petrosani (Rumania)	H	W	3–0	Narey, Copland, Gardner
			2–10–74		A	L	0–2	
		2	23–10–74	Bursaspor (Turkey)	H	D	0–0	
			6–10–74		A	L	0–1	
1966–67	Fairs Cup	1		bye				
		2		Barcelona (Spain)	A	W	2–1	Hainey, Seeman
			16–11–66		H	W	2–0	Mitchell, Hainey
		3	8–2–67	Juventus (Italy)	A	L	0–3	
			8–3–67		H	W	1–0	Dossing
1969–70	Fairs Cup	1	15–9–69	Newcastle United (England)	H	L	1–2	Scott
			1–10–69		A	L	0–1	
1970–71	Fairs Cup	1	15–9–70	Grasshoppers (Switzerland)	H	W	3–2	Reid (I), Markland, Reid (A)
			30–9–70		A	D	0–0	

Season	Competition	Round	Date	Opponents (Country)	Venue	Result		Scorers

DUNDEE UNITED continued

Season	Competition	Round	Date	Opponents (Country)	Venue	Result		Scorers
		2	21–10–70	Sparta Prague	A	L	1–3	Traynor
			4–11–70	(Czechoslovakia)	H	W	1–0	Gordon
1975–76	UEFA Cup	1	23–9–75	Keflavik (Iceland)	A	W	2–0	Narey 2
			30–9–75		H	W	4–0	Hall 2, Hegarty (pen), Sturrock
		2	22–10–75	Porto (Portugal)	H	L	1–2	Rennie
			5–11–75		A	D	1–1	Hegarty
1977–78	UEFA Cup	1	14–9–77	KB Copenhagen	H	W	1–0	Sturrock
			27–9–77	(Denmark)	A	L	0–3	

DUNFERMLINE ATHLETIC

Season	Competition	Round	Date	Opponents (Country)	Venue	Result		Scorers
1961–62	Cup-Winners' Cup	1	12–9–61	St Patrick's Athletic (Eire)	H	W	4–1	Melrose, Peebles, Dickson, Macdonald
			27–9–61		A	W	4–0	Peebles 2, Dickson 2
		2	25–10–61	Vardar Skoplje (Yugoslavia)	H	W	5–0	Smith, Dickson 2, Melrose, Peebles
			8–11–61		A	L	0–2	
		QF	13–2–62	Ujpest Dozsa (Hungary)	A	L	3–4	Smith, Macdonald 2
			20–2–62		H	L	0–1	
1967–68	Cup-Winners' Cup	1	18–9–68	Apoel (Cyprus)	H	W	10–1	Robertson 2, Renton 2, Barry, Callaghan (W) 2, Gardner, Edwards, Callaghan (T)
			2–10–68		A	W	2–0	Gardner, Callaghan (W)
		2	13–11–68	Olympiakos Pireaeus	H	W	4–0	Edwards 2, Fraser, Mitchell
			27–11–68	(Greece)	A	L	0–3	
		QF	15–1–69	West Bromwich Albion	H	D	0–0	
			19–2–69	(England)	A	W	1–0	Gardner
		SF	9–4–69	Slovan Bratislava	H	D	1–1	Fraser
			23–4–69	(Czechoslovakia)	A	L	0–1	
1962–63		1	24–10–62	Everton (England)	A	L	0–1	
			31–10–62		H	W	2–0	Miller, Melrose
		2	12–12–62	Valencia (Spain)	A	L	0–4	
			19–12–62		H	W	6–2	Melrose, Sinclair 2, McLean, Peebles, Smith
			6–2–63		N	L	0–1	
1964–65	Fairs Cup	1	13–10–64	Oergryte (Sweden)	H	W	4–2	McLaughlin 2, Sinclair 2
			20–10–64		A	D	0–0	
		2	17–11–64	Stuttgart (West Germany)	H	W	1–0	Callaghan (T)
			1–12–64		A	D	0–0	
		3	27–1–65	Atletico Bilbao (Spain)	A	L	0–1	
			3–3–65		H	W	1–0	Smith
			16–3–65		A	L	1–2	Smith
1965–66	Fairs Cup	1		bye				
		2	3–11–65	KB Copenhagen (Denmark)	H	W	5–0	Fleming, Paton 2, Robertson, Callaghan (T)
			17–11–65		A	W	4–2	Edwards, Paton, Fleming, Ferguson
		3	26–1–66	Spartak Brno	H	W	2–0	Paton, Ferguson (pen)
			16–2–66	(Czechoslovakia)	A	D	0–0	
		QF	16–3–66	Real Zaragoza (Spain)	H	W	1–0	Paton
			30–3–66		A	L	2–4	Ferguson 2
1966–67	Fairs Cup	1	24–8–66	Frigg Oslo (Norway)	A	W	3–1	Fleming 2, Callaghan (T)
			28–9–66		H	W	3–1	Delaney 2, Callaghan (T)
		2	26–10–66	Dynamo Zagreb*	H	W	4–2	Delaney, Edwards, Ferguson 2
			11–11–66		A	L	0–2	
1969–70	Fairs Cup	1	16–9–69	Bordeaux (France)	H	W	4–0	Paton 2, Mitchell, Gardner
			30–9–69		A	L	0–2	
		2	5–11–69	Gwardia Warsaw (Poland)	A	W	2–1	McLean, Gardner
			18–11–69		A	W	1–0	Renton
		3	17–12–69	Anderlecht (Belgium)*	A	L	0–1	
			14–1–70		H	W	3–2	McLean 2, Mitchell

HEARTS

Season	Competition	Round	Date	Opponents (Country)	Venue	Result		Scorers
1958–59	European Cup	Pr	3–9–58	Standard Liege (Belgium)	A	L	1–5	Crawford
			9–9–58		H	W	2–1	Bauld 2
1960–61	European Cup	Pr	29–9–60	Benfica (Portugal)	H	L	1–2	Young
			5–10–60		A	L	0–3	
1976–77	Cup-Winners' Cup	1	15–9–76	Lokomotive Leipzig	A	L	0–2	
			29–9–76	(East Germany)	H	W	5–1	Kay, Gibson 2, Brown, Busby
		2	20–10–76	SV Hamburg (West	A	L	2–4	Park, Busby
			3–11–76	Germany)	H	L	1–4	Gibson

Season	Competition	Round	Date	Opponents (Country)	Venue	Result		Scorers

HEARTS continued

Season	Competition	Round	Date	Opponents (Country)	Venue	Result		Scorers
1961–62	Fairs Cup	1	27–9–61	Union St Gilloise	A	W	3–1	Blackwood, Davidson 2
			4–10–61	(Belgium)	H	W	2–0	Wallace, Stenhouse
		2	6–11–61	Inter-Milan (Italy)	H	L	0–1	
			22–11–61		A	L	0–4	
1963–64	Fairs Cup	1	25–9–63	Lausanne (Switzerland)	A	D	2–2	Traynor, Ferguson
			9–10–63		H	D	2–2	Cumming, Hamilton (J)
			15–10–63		A	L	2–3	Wallace, Ferguson
1965–66	Fairs Cup	1		bye				
		2	18–10–65	Valerengen (Norway)	H	W	1–0	Wallace
			27–10–65		A	W	3–1	Kerrigan 2, Traynor
		3	12–1–66	Real Zaragoza (Spain)	H	D	3–3	Anderson, Wallace, Kerrigan
			26–1–66		A	D	2–2	Anderson, Wallace
			2–3–66		A	L	0–1	

HIBERNIAN

Season	Competition	Round	Date	Opponents (Country)	Venue	Result		Scorers
1955–56	European Cup	1	14–9–55	Rot-Weiss Essen	A	W	4–0	Turnbull 2, Reilly, Ormond
			12–10–55	(West Germany)	H	D	1–1	Buchanan (J)
		QF	23–11–55	Djurgaarden (Sweden)	H	W	3–1	Combe, Mulkerrin, own goal
			28–11–55		A	W	1–0	Turnbull (pen)
		SF	4–4–56	Reims (France)*	A	L	0–2	
			18–4–56		H	L	0–1	
1972–73	Cup-Winners' Cup	1	13–9–72	Sporting Lisbon (Portugal)	A	L	1–2	Duncan
			27–9–72		H	W	6–1	Gordon 2, O'Rourke 3, own goal
		2	25–10–72	Besa (Albania)	H	W	7–1	Cropley, O'Rourke 3, Duncan 2, Brownlie
			8–11–72		A	D	1–1	Gordon
		QF	7–3–73	Hajduk Split (Yugoslavia)	H	W	4–2	Gordon 3, Duncan
			21–3–73		A	L	0–3	
1960–61	Fairs Cup	1		Lausanne (Switzerland) Lausanne withdrew before second leg				
		QF	27–12–60	Barcelona (Spain)	A	D	4–4	McLeod, Preston, Baker 2
			22–2–61		H	W	3–2	Kinloch 2 (1 pen), Baker
		SF	19–4–61	AS Roma (Italy)	H	D	2–2	Baker, McLeod
			26–4–61		A	D	3–3	Baker 2, Kinloch
			27–5–61		A	L	0–6	
1961–62	Fairs Cup	1	4–9–61	Belenenses (Portugal)	H	D	3–3	Fraser 2, Baird (pen)
			27–9–61		A	W	3–1	Baxter 2, Stevenson
		2	1–11–61	Red Star Belgrade	A	L	0–4	
			15–11–61	(Yugoslavia)	H	L	0–1	
1962–63	Fairs Cup	1	3–10–62	Stavenet (Denmark)	H	W	4–0	Byrne 2, Baker, own goal
			23–10–62		A	W	3–2	Stevenson 2, Bryne
		2	27–11–62	DOS Utrecht (Holland)	A	W	1–0	Falconer
			12–12–62		H	W	2–1	Baker, Stevenson
		QF	13–3–63	Valencia (Spain)	A	L	0–5	
			3–4–63		H	W	2–1	Preston, Baker
1965–66	Fairs Cup	1	8–9–65	Valencia (Spain)	H	W	2–0	Scott, McNamee
			12–10–65		A	L	0–2	
			3–11–65		A	L	0–3	
1967–68	Fairs Cup	1	20–9–67	Porto (Portugal)	H	W	3–0	Cormack 2, Stevenson
			4–10–67		A	L	1–3	Stanton (pen)
		2	22–11–67	Napoli (Italy)	A	L	1–4	Stein
			29–11–67		H	W	5–0	Duncan, Quinn, Cormack, Stanton, Stein
		3	20–12–67	Leeds United (England)	A	L	0–1	
			10–1–68		H	D	1–1	Stein
1968–69	Fairs Cup	1	18–9–68	Ljubljana (Yugoslavia)	A	W	3–0	Stevenson, Stein, Marinello
			2–10–68		H	W	2–1	Davis (2 pen)
		2	13–11–68	Lokomotive Leipzig	H	W	3–1	McBride 3
			20–11–68	(East Germany)	A	W	1–0	Grant
		3	18–12–68	SV Hamburg (West	A	L	0–1	
			15–1–69	Germany)*	H	W	2–1	McBride 2
1970–71	Fairs Cup	1	16–9–70	Malmo (Sweden)	H	W	6–0	McBride 3, Duncan 2, Blair
			30–9–70		A	W	3–2	Duncan, McEwan, Stanton
		2	14–10–70	Vitoria Guimaraes	H	W	2–0	Duncan, Stanton
			28–10–70	(Portugal)	A	L	1–2	Graham
		3	9–12–70	Liverpool (England)	H	L	0–1	
			22–12–70		A	L	0–2	

Season	Competition	Round	Date	Opponents (Country)	Venue	Result		Scorers
HIBERNIAN continued								
1973–74	UEFA Cup	1	19–9–73	Keflavik (Iceland)	H	W	2–0	Black, Higgins
			3–10–73		A	D	1–1	Stanton
		2	24–10–73	Leeds United (England)†	A	D	0–0	
			2–10–74		H	D	0–0	
1974–75	UEFA Cup	1	18–9–74	Rosenborg (Norway)	A	W	3–2	Stanton, Gordon, Cropley
			2–10–74		H	W	9–1	Harper 2, Munro 2, Stanton 2, Cropley 2 (pens), Gordon
		2	23–10–74	Juventus (Italy)	H	L	2–4	Stanton, Cropley
			6–11–74		A	L	0–4	
1975–76	UEFA Cup	1	17–9–75	Liverpool (England)	H	W	1–0	Harper
			30–9–75		A	L	1–3	Edwards
1976–77	UEFA Cup	1	15–9–76	Sochaux (France)	H	W	1–0	Brownie
			29–9–76		A	D	0–0	
		2	20–10–76	Oesters Vaxjo (Sweden)	H	W	2–0	Blackley, Brownlie (pen)
			3–11–76		A	L	1–4	Smith
KILMARNOCK								
1965–66	European Cup	Pr	8–9–65	Nendori Tirana (Albania)	A	D	0–0	
			29–6–65		H	W	1–0	Black
		1	17–11–65	Real Madrid (Spain)	H	D	2–2	McLean (pen), McInally
			1–12–65		A	L	1–5	McIlroy
1964–65	Fairs Cup	1	2–9–64	Eintracht Frankfurt (West Germany)	A	L	0–3	
			22–9–64		H	W	5–1	Hamilton, McIlroy, McFadzean, McInally, Sneddon
		2	11–11–64	Everton (England)	H	L	0–2	
			23–11–64		A	L	1–4	McIlroy
1966–67	Fairs Cup	1	bye					
		2	25–10–66	Antwerp (Belgium)	A	W	1–0	McInally
			2–11–66		H	W	7–2	McInally 2, Queen 2, McLean 2 Watson
		3	14–12–66	La Gantoise (Belgium)	H	W	1–0	Murray
			21–12–66		A	W	2–1	McInally, McLean
		QF	19–4–67	Lokomotive Leipzig (East Germany)	A	L	0–1	
			26–4–67		H	W	2–0	McFadzean, McIlroy
		SF	19–5–67	Leeds United (England)	A	L	2–4	McIlroy 2
			24–5–67		H	D	0–0	
1969–70	Fairs Cup	1	16–9–69	Zurich (Switzerland)	A	L	2–3	McLean (J), Mathie
			30–9–69		H	W	3–1	McGrory, Morrison, McLean (T)
		2	19–11–69	Slavia Sofia (Bulgaria)	H	W	4–1	Mathie 2, Cook, Gilmour
			26–11–69		A	L	0–2	
		3	17–12–69	Dynamo Bacau (Yugoslavia)	H	D	1–1	Mathie
			13–1–70		A	L	0–2	
1970–71	Fairs Cup	1	15–9–70	Coleraine (Northern Ireland)	A	D	1–1	Mathie
			29–9–70		H	L	2–3	McLean (T), Morrison
MORTON								
1968–69	Fairs Cup	1	18–9–68	Chelsea (England)	A	L	0–5	
			30–9–68		H	L	3–4	Thorop, Mason, Taylor
PARTICK THISTLE								
1963–64	Fairs Cup	1	16–9–63	Glentoran (Northern Ireland)	A	W	4–1	Hainey, Yard 2, Wright
			30–9–63		H	W	3–0	Smith 2, Harvey (pen)
		2	18–11–63	Spartak Brno (Czechoslovakia)	H	W	3–2	Yard, Harvey (pen), Ferguson
			27–11–63		A	L	0–4	
1972–73	UEFA Cup	1	13–9–72	Honved (Hungary)	A	L	0–1	
			27–9–72		H	L	0–3	

Season	Competition	Round	Date	Opponents (Country)	Venue	Result		Scorers
RANGERS								
1956–57	European Cup	Pr		bye				
		1	24–10–56	Nice (France)	H	W	2–1	Murray, Simpson
			14–11–56		A	L	1–2	Hubbard (pen)
			28–11–56		N	L	1–3	own goal
1957–58	European Cup	Pr	4–9–57	St Etienne (France)	H	W	3–1	Kichenbrand, Scott, Simpson
			25–9–57		A	L	1–2	Wilson
		1	27–11–57	AC Milan (Italy)	H	L	1–4	Murray
			11–12–57		A	L	0–2	
1959–60	European Cup	Pr	16–9–59	Anderlecht (Belgium)	H	W	5–2	Millar, Scott, Matthew, Baird 2
			24–9–59		A	W	2–0	Matthew, McMillan
		1	11–11–59	Red Star Belgrade	H	W	4–3	McMillan, Scott, Wilson, Millar
			18–11–59	(Czechoslovakia)	A	D	1–1	Scott
		QF	9–3–60	Sparta Rotterdam	A	W	3–2	Wilson, Baird, Murray
			16–3–60	(Holland)	H	L	0–1	
			30–3–60		N	W	3–2	Baird 2, Millar
		SF	13–4–60	Eintracht Frankfurt	A	L	1–6	Caldow (pen)
			5–5–60	(West Germany)	H	L	3–6	McMillan 2, Wilson
1961–62	European Cup	Pr	5–9–61	Monaco (France)	A	W	3–2	Baxter, Scott 2
			12–9–61		H	W	3–2	Christie 2, Scott
		1	15–11–61	Vorwaerts (East Germany)	A	W	2–1	Caldow (pen), Brand
			23–11–61		H	W	4–1	McMillan 2, Henderson, own goal
		QF	7–2–62	Standard Liege (Belgium)	A	L	1–4	Wilson
			14–2–62		H	W	2–0	Brand, Caldow (pen)
1963–64	European Cup	Pr	25–9–63	Real Madrid (Spain)	H	L	0–1	
			9–10–63		A	L	0–6	
1964–65	European Cup	Pr	2–9–64	Red Star Belgrade	H	W	3–2	Brand 2, Forrest
			9–9–64	(Yugoslavia)	A	L	2–4	Greig, McKinnon
			4–11–64		N	W	3–1	Forrest 2, Brand
		1	18–11–64	Rapid Vienna (Austria)	H	W	1–0	Wilson
			8–12–64		A	W	2–0	Forrest, Wilson
		QF	17–2–65	Inter-Milan (Italy)	A	L	1–3	Forrest
			3–3–65		H	W	1–0	Forrest
1975–76	European Cup	1	17–9–75	Bohemians (Eire)	H	W	4–1	Fyfe 2, Johnstone, own goal
			1–10–75		A	D	1–1	Johnstone
		2	22–10–75	St Etienne (France)	H	L	0–2	
			5–11–75		A	L	1–2	MacDonald
1976–77	European Cup	1	15–9–76	Zurich (Switzerland)	H	D	1–1	Parlane
			29–9–76		A	L	0–1	
1960–61	Cup-Winners' Cup	Pr	28–9–60	Ferencvaros (Hungary)	H	W	4–2	Davis, Millar 2, Brand
			12–10–60		A	L	1–2	Wilson
		QF	15–11–60	Borussia Moenchenglad-	A	W	3–0	Millar, Scott, McMillan
			30–11–60	bach (West Germany)	H	W	8–0	Baxter, Brand 3, Millar 2, Davis, own goal
		SF	29–3–61	Wolverhampton	H	W	2–0	Scott, Brand
			19–4–61	Wanderers (England)	A	D	1–1	Scott
		F	17–5–61	Fiorentina (Italy)	H	L	0–2	
			27–5–61		A	L	1–2	Scott
1962–63	Cup-Winners' Cup	1	5–9–62	Seville (Spain)	H	W	4–0	Millar 3, Brand
			26–9–62		A	L	0–2	
		2	31–10–62	Tottenham Hotspur	A	L	2–5	Henderson, Millar
			11–12–62	(England)	H	L	2–3	Brand, Wilson
1966–67	Cup-Winners' Cup	1	27–9–66	Glentoran (Northern	A	D	1–1	McLean
			5–10–66	Ireland)	H	W	4–0	Johnston, Smith (D), Setterington, McLean
		2	23–11–66	Borussia Dortmund	H	W	2–1	Johansen, Smith (A)
			6–12–66	(West Germany)	A	D	0–0	
		QF	1–3–67	Real Zaragoza (Spain)‡	H	W	2–0	Smith, Willoughby
			22–3–67		A	L	0–2	
		SF	19–4–67	Slavia Sofia (Bulgaria)	A	W	1–0	Wilson
			3–5–67		H	W	1–0	Henderson
		F	31–5–67	Bayern Munich	N	L	0–1	
				(West Germany)				
1969–70	Cup-Winners' Cup	1	17–9–69	Steaua Bucharest	H	W	2–0	Johnston 2
			1–10–69	(Rumania)	A	D	0–0	
		2	12–11–69	Gornik Zabrze (Poland)	A	L	1–3	Persson
			26–11–69		H	L	1–3	Baxter

Season	Competition	Round	Date	Opponents (Country)	Venue	Result		Scorers

RANGERS continued

Season	Competition	Round	Date	Opponents (Country)	Venue	Result		Scorers
1971–72	Cup-Winners' Cup	1	15–9–71	Rennes (France)	A	D	1–1	Johnston
			28–9–71		H	W	1–0	MacDonald
		2	20–10–71	Sporting Lisbon (Portugal)	H	W	3–2	Stein 2, Henderson
			3–11–71		A	L	3–4*	Stein 2, Henderson
		QF	8–3–72	Torino (Italy)	A	D	1–1	Johnston
			22–3–72		H	W	1–0	Macdonald
		SF	5–4–72	Bayern Munich	A	D	1–1	own goal
			19–4–72	(West Germany)	H	W	2–0	Jardine, Parlane
		F	24–5–72	Dynamo Moscow (USSR)	N	W	3–2	Johnstone 2, Stein
1973–74	Cup-Winners' Cup	1	19–9–73	Ankaragucu (Turkey)	A	W	2–0	Conn, McLean
			3–10–73		H	W	4–0	Greig 2, O'Hara, Johnston
		2	24–10–73	Borussia Moenchenglad-	A	L	0–3	
			7–11–73	bach (West Germany)	H	W	3–2	Conn, Jackson, MacDonald
1977–78	Cup-Winners' Cup	Pr	17–8–77	Young Boys (Switzerland)	H	W	1–0	Greig
			31–8–77		A	D	2–2	Johnstone, Smith
		1	14–9–77	Twente Enschede	H	D	0–0	
			28–9–77	(Holland)	A	L	0–3	
1967–68	Fairs Cup	1	21–9–67	Dynamo Dresden	A	D	1–1	Ferguson
			4–10–67	(East Germany)	H	W	2–1	Penman, Greig
		2	8–11–67	IFC Cologne (West	H	W	3–0	Ferguson 2, Henderson
			28–11–67	Germany)	A	L	1–3	Henderson
		3		bye				
		QF	26–3–68	Leeds United (England)	H	D	0–0	
			9–4–68		A	L	0–2	
1968–69	Fairs Cup	1	18–9–68	Vojvodina (Yugoslavia)	H	W	2–0	Greig (pen), Jardine
			2–10–68		A	L	0–1	
		2	30–10–68	Dundalk (Eire)	H	W	6–1	Henderson 2, Ferguson 2, Greig, own goal
			13–11–68		A	W	3–0	Mathieson, Stein 2
		3	11–1–69	DWS Amsterdam	A	W	2–0	Johnston, Henderson
			22–1–69	(Holland)	H	W	2–1	Smith, Stein
		QF	19–3–69	Atletico Bilbao (Spain)	H	W	4–1	Ferguson, Penman, Persson, Stein
			2–4–69		A	L	0–2	
		SF	14–5–69	Newcastle United	H	D	0–0	
			22–5–69	(England)	A	L	0–2	
1970–71	Fairs Cup	1	16–9–70	Bayern Munich	A	L	0–1	
			30–9–70	(West Germany)	H	D	1–1	Stein

ST JOHNSTONE

Season	Competition	Round	Date	Opponents (Country)	Venue	Result		Scorers
1971–72	UEFA Cup	1	15–9–71	SV Hamburg	A	L	1–2	Pearson
			29–9–71	(West Germany)	H	W	3–0	Hall, Pearson, Whitelaw
		2	20–10–71	Vasas Budapest (Hungary)	H	W	2–0	Connolly (pen), Pearson
			2–11–71		A	L	0–1	
		3	24–11–71	Zeljeznicar (Yugoslavia)	H	W	1–0	Connolly
			8–12–71		A	L	1–5	Rooney

*won on away goals counting double
†won on penalties
‡won on the toss of a coin

IRISH LEAGUE CLUBS

ARDS

Season	Competition	Round	Date	Opponents (Country)	Venue	Result		Scorers
1958–59	European Cup	Pr	17–9–58	Reims (France)	H	L	1–4	Lowry
			8–10–58		A	L	2–6	Lawther, Quee
1969–70	Cup-Winners' Cup	1	17–9–69	AS Roma (Italy)	H	D	0–0	
			1–10–69		A	L	1–3	Crothers
1974–75	Cup-Winners' Cup	1	18–9–74	PSV Eindhoven (Holland)	A	L	0–10	
			2–10–74		H	L	1–4	Guy
1973–74	UEFA Cup	1	12–9–73	Standard Liege (Belgium)	H	W	3–2	Cathcart, McAvoy (pen), McAteer (pen)
			19–9–73		A	L	1–6	Guy

Season	Competition	Round	Date	Opponents (Country)	Venue	Result		Scorers

CARRICK RANGERS

1976–77	Cup-Winners' Cup	1	15–9–76	Aris Bonnevoie	H	W	3–1	Prenter 2, Connor
			6–10–76	(Luxembourg)	A	L	1–2	Irwin
		2	20–10–76	Southampton (England)	H	L	2–5	Irwin, Prenter
			3–11–76		A	L	1–4	Reid

COLERAINE

1974–75	European Cup	1	18–11–74	Feyenoord (Holland)	A	L	0–7	
			2–10–74		H	L	1–4	Simpson
1965–66	Cup-Winners' Cup	1	2–9–65	Dynamo Kiev (USSR)	H	L	1–6	Curley
			8–9–65		A	L	0–4	
1975–76	Cup-Winners' Cup	1	16–9–75	Eintracht Frankfurt	A	L	1–5	Cochrane
			30–9–75	(West Germany)	H	L	2–6	McCurdy, Cochrane
1969–70	Fairs Cup	1	17–9–69	Jeunesse D'Esch	A	L	2–3	Hunter, Murray
			1–10–69	(Luxembourg)	H	W	4–0	Dickson 2, Wilson, Jennings
		2	11–11–69	Anderlecht (Belgium)	A	L	1–6	Murray
			20–11–69		H	L	3–7	Dickson 2, Irwin
1970–71	Fairs Cup	1	15–9–70	Kilmarnock (Scotland)	H	D	1–1	Mullan
			29–9–70		A	W	3–2	Dickson 3
		3	20–10–70	Sparta Rotterdam	A	L	0–2	
			4–11–70	(Holland)	H	L	1–2	Jennings
1977–78	Cup-Winners' Cup	1	14–9–77	Lokomotive Leipzig	H	L	1–4	Tweed
				(East Germany)	A	D	2–2	Guy 2

CRUSADERS

1973–74	European Cup	1	19–9–73	Dynamo Bucharest	H	L	0–1	
			3–10–73	(Rumania)	A	L	0–11	
1976–77	European Cup	1	14–9–76	Liverpool (England)	A	L	0–2	
			28–9–76		H	L	0–5	
1967–68	Cup-Winners' Cup	1	20–9–67	Valencia (Spain)	A	L	0–4	
			11–10–67		H	L	2–4	Trainor, Magill
1968–69	Cup-Winners' Cup	1	18–9–68	Norkopping (Sweden)	H	D	2–2	Jameson, Parke
			2–10–68		A	L	1–4	McPolin

DERRY CITY

1965–66	European Cup	Pr	31–8–65	Lyn Oslo (Norway)	A	L	3–5	Wood (R), Gilbert 2
			9–9–65		H	W	5–1	Wilson 2, Crossan, Wood (R), McGeough
		1	23–11–65	Anderlecht (Belgium)	A	L	0–9	
			00–00–65		withdrew			
1964–65	Cup-Winners' Cup	1	9–9–64	Steaua Bucharest	A	L	0–3	
			16–9–64	(Rumania)	H	L	0–2	

DISTILLERY

1963–64	European Cup	Pr	25–9–63	Benfica (Portugal)	H	D	3–3	John Kennedy, Hamilton, Ellison
			2–10–63		A	L	0–5	
1971–72	Cup-Winners' Cup	1	15–9–71	Barcelona (Spain)	H	L	1–3	O'Neill
			29–9–71		A	L	0–4	

GLENAVON

1957–58	European Cup	Pr	11–9–57	Aarhus (Denmark)	A	D	0–0	
			25–9–57		H	L	0–3	
1960–61	European Cup	Pr		withdrew				
1961–62	Cup-Winners' Cup	1	13–9–61	Leicester City (England)	H	L	1–4	Jones
			27–9–61		A	L	1–3	Wilson
1977–78	UEFA Cup	1	14–9–77	PSV Eindhoven (Holland)	H	L	2–6	Malone (pen), McDonald
			28–9–77		A	L	0–5	

GLENTORAN

1964–65	European Cup	Pr	16–9–64	Panathinaikos (Greece)	H	D	2–2	Turner, Thompson
			30–9–64		A	L	2–3	Turner, Pavis
1967–68	European Cup	1	13–9–67	Benfica (Portugal)*	H	D	1–1	Colrain (pen)
			4–10–67		A	D	0–0	

Season	Competition	Round	Date	Opponents (Country)	Venue	Result		Scorers
GLENTORAN continued								
1968–69	European Cup	1	18–9–68	Anderlecht (Belgium)	A	L	0–3	
			2–10–68		H	D	2–2	Morrow, Johnston
1970–71	European Cup	1	16–9–70	Waterford (Eire)	H	L	1–3	Hall
			30–9–70		A	L	0–1	
1977–78	European Cup	1	15–9–77	Valur (Iceland)	A	L	0–1	
			29–9–77		H	W	2–0	Robson, Jamison
		2	19–10–77	Juventus (Italy)	H	L	0–1	
			2–11–77		A	L	0–5	
1966–67	Cup-Winners' Cup	1	27–9–66	Rangers (Scotland)	H	D	1–1	Sinclair
			5–10–66		A	L	0–4	
1973–74	Cup-Winners' Cup	1	19–9–73	Chimia Ramnicu	A	D	2–2	Jamison, McCreary
			3–10–73	(Rumania)	H	W	2–0	Jamison, Craig
		2	24–10–73	Brann Bergen (Norway)	A	D	1–1	Feeney
			7–11–73		H	W	3–1	Feeney, Jamison 2
		QF	5–3–74	Borussia Moenchenglad-	H	L	0–2	
			20–3–74	bach (West Germany)	A	L	0–5	
1962–63	Fairs Cup	1	26–9–62	Real Zaragoza (Spain)	H	L	0–2	
			10–10–62		A	L	2–6	Doherty 2
1963–64	Fairs Cup	1	16–9–63	Partick Thistle (Scotland)	H	L	1–4	Thompson
			30–9–63		A	L	0–3	
1965–66	Fairs Cup	1	28–9–65	Antwerp (Belgium)	A	L	0–1	
			6–10–65		H	D	3–3	Hamilton, Thompson 2
1969–70	Fairs Cup	1	9–9–69	Arsenal (England)	A	L	0–3	
			29–9–69		H	W	1–0	Henderson
1971–72	UEFA Cup	1	14–9–71	Eintracht Brunswick	H	L	0–1	
			28–9–71	(West Germany)	A	L	1–6	McCaffrey
1975–76	UEFA Cup	1	16–9–75	Ajax (Holland)	H	L	1–6	Jamison
			1–10–75		A	L	0–8	
1976–77	UEFA Cup	1	14–9–76	Basle (Switzerland)	H	W	3–2	Feeney 2, Dickenson
			29–9–76		A	L	0–3	
LINFIELD								
1959–69	European Cup	Pr	9–9–59	Gothenburg (Sweden)	H	W	2–1	Milburn 2
			23–9–59		A	L	1–6	Dickson
1961–62	European Cup	Pr	30–8–61	Vorwaerts (East Germany)	A	L	0–3	
				withdrew				
1962–63	European Cup	Pr	5–9–62	Esbjerg (Denmark)	H	L	1–2	Dickson
			19–9–62		A	D	0–0	
1966–67	European Cup	1	7–9–66	Aris Bonnevoie	A	D	3–3	Hamilton, Pavis, Scott
			16–9–66	(Luxembourg)	H	W	6–1	Thomas 3, Scott 2, Pavis
		2	26–10–66	Valerengen (Norway)	A	W	4–1	Scott, Pavis, Thomas, Shields
			8–11–66		H	D	1–1	Thomas
		QF	1–3–67	CSKA Sofia (Bulgaria)	H	D	2–2	Hamilton, Shields
			15–3–67		A	L	0–1	
1969–70	European Cup	1	17–9–69	Red Star Belgrade	A	L	0–8	
			1–10–69	(Yugoslavia)	H	L	2–4	McGraw 2
1971–72	European Cup	1	15–9–71	Standard Liege (Belgium)	A	L	0–2	
			29–9–71		H	L	2–3	Magee, Larmour
1975–76	European Cup	1	17–9–75	PSV Eindhoven (Holland)	H	L	1–2	Malone (P)
			1–10–75		A	L	0–8	
1963–64	Cup-Winners' Cup	1		bye				
		2	13–11–63	Fenerbahce (Turkey)	A	L	1–4	Dickson
			11–12–63		H	W	2–0	Craig, Ferguson
1970–71	Cup-Winners' Cup	1	16–9–70	Manchester City (England)	A	L	0–1	
			30–9–70	(England)*	H	W	2–1	Millen 2
1967–68	Fairs Cup	1	19–9–67	Lokomotive Leipzig	A	L	1–5	Pavis
			4–10–67	(East Germany)	H	W	1–0	Hamilton
1968–69	Fairs Cup	1	18–9–68	Setubal (Portugal)	A	L	0–3	
			9–10–68		H	L	1–3	Scott
PORTADOWN								
1962–63	Cup-Winners' Cup	1		bye				
		2	7–11–62	OFK Belgrade	A	L	1–5	Clements
			22–11–62	(Yugoslavia)	H	W	3–2	Burke, Jones, Cush
1974–75	UEFA Cup	1	18–9–74	Valur (Iceland)	A	D	0–0	
			1–10–74		H	W	2–1	McFaul, Morrison (pen)
		2	23–10–74	Partizan Belgrade	A	L	0–5	
			6–11–74	(Yugoslavia)	H	D	1–1	Malcolmson

INTERNATIONAL CENTURIONS

Franz Beckenbauer (Bayern Munich and West Germany)
103 International appearances 1965–1977

Date	Venue	Opponents	Result	Scored
1965				
26 September	Stockholm	v Sweden	Won 2–1	
9 October	Stuttgart	v Austria	Won 4–1	
14 November	Nicosia	v Cyprus	Won 6–0	
1966				
23 February	Wembley	v England	Lost 0–1	
23 March	Rotterdam	v Holland	Won 4–2	2 goals
4 May	Dublin	v Republic of Ireland	Won 4–0	1 goal
7 May	Belfast	v Northern Ireland	Won 2–0	
23 June	Hanover	v Yugoslavia	Won 2–0	
12 July	Sheffield	v Switzerland (WC)	Won 5–0	2 goals
16 July	Birmingham	v Argentina (WC)	Drew 0–0	
20 July	Birmingham	v Spain (WC)	Won 2–1	
23 July	Sheffield	v Uruguay (WC)	Won 4–0	1 goal
25 July	Liverpool	v USSR (WC)	Won 2–1	1 goal
30 July	Wembley	v England (WC)	Lost 2–4*	
19 November	Cologne	v Norway	Won 3–0	
1967				
22 February	Karlsruhe	v Morocco	Won 5–1	
8 April	Dortmund	v Albania	Won 6–0	
3 May	Belgrade	v Yugoslavia	Lost 0–1	
27 September	Berlin	v France	Won 5–1	
22 November	Bucharest	v Rumania	Lost 0–1	
1968				
6 March	Brussels	v Belgium	Won 3–1	
17 April	Basle	v Switzerland	Drew 0–0	
1 June	Hanover	v England	Won 1–0	1 goal
16 June	Stuttgart	v Brazil	Won 2–1	
25 September	Marseille	v France	Drew 1–1	
13 October	Vienna	v Austria	Won 2–0	
14 December	Rio de Janeiro	v Brazil	Drew 2–2	
18 December	Santiago	v Chile	Lost 1–2	
22 December	Mexico City	v Mexico	Drew 0–0	
1969				
16 April	Hampden Park	v Scotland	Drew 1–1	
10 May	Nuremberg	v Austria	Won 1–0	
21 May	Essen	v Cyprus	Won 12–0	
21 September	Vienna	v Austria	Drew 1–1	
24 September	Sofia	v Bulgaria	Won 1–0	
22 October	Hamburg	v Scotland	Won 3–2	
1970				
8 April	Stuttgart	v Rumania	Drew 1–1	
9 May	Berlin	v Republic of Ireland	Won 2–1	
13 May	Hanover	v Yugoslavia	Won 1–0	
3 June	Leon	v Morocco (WC)	Won 2–1	

Date	Venue	Opponents	Result	Scored
7 June	Leon	v Bulgaria (WC)	Won 5–2	
10 June	Leon	v Peru (WC)	Won 3–1	
14 June	Leon	v England (WC)	Won 3–2*	1 goal
17 June	Mexico City	v Italy (WC)	Lost 3–4*	
9 September	Nuremberg	v Hungary	Won 3–1	
17 October	Cologne	v Turkey	Drew 1–1	
18 November	Zagreb	v Yugoslavia	Lost 0–2	
22 November	Athens	v Greece	Won 3–1	1 goal
1971				
17 February	Tirana	v Albania	Won 1–0	
25 April	Istanbul	v Turkey	Won 3–0	
12 June	Karlsruhe	v Albania	Won 2–0	
22 June	Oslo	v Norway	Won 7–1	1 goal
27 June	Gothenburg	v Sweden	Lost 0–1	
30 June	Copenhagen	v Denmark	Won 3–1	1 goal
8 September	Hanover	v Mexico	Won 5–0	
10 October	Warsaw	v Poland	Won 3–1	
17 November	Hamburg	v Poland	Drew 0–0	
1972				
29 March	Budapest	v Hungary	Won 2–0	
29 April	Wembley	v England	Won 3–1	
13 May	Berlin	v England	Drew 0–0	
26 May	Munich	v USSR	Won 4–1	
14 June	Antwerp	v Belgium (EC)	Won 2–1	
18 June	Brussels	v USSR (EC)	Won 3–0	
15 November	Dusseldorf	v Switzerland	Won 5–1	
1973				
14 February	Munich	v Argentina	Lost 2–3	
28 March	Dusseldorf	v Czechoslovakia	Won 3–0	
9 May	Munich	v Yugoslavia	Lost 0–1	
12 May	Hamburg	v Bulgaria	Won 3–0	1 goal
16 June	Berlin	v Brazil	Lost 0–1	
5 September	Moscow	v USSR	Won 1–0	
10 October	Hanover	v Austria	Won 4–0	
13 October	Gelsenkirchen	v France	Won 2–1	
14 November	Hampden Park	v Scotland	Drew 1–1	
24 November	Stuttgart	v Spain	Won 2–1	
1974				
23 February	Barcelona	v Spain	Lost 0–1	
26 February	Rome	v Italy	Drew 0–0	
27 March	Frankfurt	v Scotland	Won 2–1	
17 April	Dortmund	v Hungary	Won 5–0	
1 May	Hamburg	v Sweden	Won 2–0	
14 June	Berlin	v Chile (WC)	Won 1–0	
18 June	Hamburg	v Australia (WC)	Won 3–0	
22 June	Hamburg	v East Germany (WC)	Lost 0–1	
26 June	Dusseldorf	v Yugoslavia (WC)	Won 2–0	
30 June	Dusseldorf	v Sweden (WC)	Won 4–2	
3 July	Frankfurt	v Poland (WC)	Won 1–0	
7 June	Munich	v Holland (WC)	Won 2–1	
4 September	Basle	v Switzerland	Won 2–1	
20 November	Piraeus	v Greece	Drew 2–2	
22 December	Valetta	v Malta	Won 1–0	
1975				
12 March	Wembley	v England	Lost 0–2	
27 April	Sofia	v Bulgaria	Drew 1–1	
17 May	Frankfurt	v Holland	Drew 1–1	
3 September	Vienna	v Austria	Won 2–0	
11 October	Dusseldorf	v Greece	Drew 1–1	
19 November	Stuttgart	v Bulgaria	Won 1–0	
20 December	Istanbul	v Turkey	Won 5–0	
1976				
28 February	Dortmund	v Malta	Won 8–0	
24 April	Madrid	v Spain	Drew 1–1	
22 May	Munich	v Spain	Won 2–0	
17 June	Belgrade	v Yugoslavia (EC)	Won 4–2*	
20 June	Belgrade	v Czechoslovakia (EC)	Drew 2–2* (lost 3–5 on penalty kicks)	
6 October	Cardiff	v Wales	Won 2–0	1 goal
17 November	Hanover	v Czechoslovakia	Won 2–0	
23 February	Paris	v France	Lost 0–1	

*after extra time
WC = World Cup (final stages)
EC = European Championship (final stages)

Beckenbauer captained West Germany for the first time against Turkey in April 1971. He was captain against Mexico and Poland (in Warsaw) the same year. From 1972 to 1977 he became the permanent captain. He also appeared in his 60th consecutive international against France in Paris in February 1977. He missed only ten matches during these twelve years.

Jozsef Bozsik (Honved and Hungary)
100 International appearances 1947–1962

Date	Venue	Opponents	Result	Scored
1947				
17 August	Budapest	v Bulgaria	Won 9–0	
14 September	Vienna	v Austria	Lost 3–4	
12 October	Bucharest	v Rumania	Won 3–0	
1948				
22 April	Budapest	v Switzerland	Won 7–4	
2 May	Vienna	v Austria	Lost 2–3	
6 June	Budapest	v Rumania	Won 9–0	
19 September	Warsaw	v Poland	Won 6–2	
3 October	Budapest	v Austria	Won 2–1	
24 October	Bucharest	v Rumania	Won 5–1	
7 November	Sofia	v Bulgaria	Lost 0–1	
1949				
10 April	Prague	v Czechoslovakia	Lost 2–5	
8 May	Budapest	v Austria	Won 6–1	
12 June	Budapest	v Italy	Drew 1–1	
19 June	Stockholm	v Sweden	Drew 2–2	
10 July	Debrecen	v Poland	Won 8–2	
16 October	Vienna	v Austria	Won 4–3	
30 October	Budapest	v Bulgaria	Won 5–0	
20 November	Budapest	v Sweden	Won 5–0	
1950				
30 April	Budapest	v Czechoslovakia	Won 5–0	
14 May	Vienna	v Austria	Lost 3–5	
4 June	Warsaw	v Poland	Won 5–2	
24 September	Budapest	v Albania	Won 12–0	
29 October	Budapest	v Austria	Won 4–3	
12 November	Sofia	v Bulgaria	Drew 1–1	
1951				
27 May	Budapest	v Poland	Won 6–0	
14 October	Witkowice	v Czechoslovakia	Won 2–1	
18 November	Budapest	v Finland	Won 8–0	
1952				
18 May	Budapest	v East Germany	Won 5–0	

On 25 and 28 May, Hungary play two matches against a Moscow Selection. Bozsik appeared in the first of these which counted as a full international.

Date	Venue	Opponents	Result	Scored
15 June	Warsaw	v Poland	Won 5–1	
22 June	Helsinki	v Finland	Won 6–1	1 goal
15 July	Turku	v Rumania (O)	Won 2–1	
21 July	Helsinki	v Italy (O)	Won 3–0	
24 July	Kotka	v Turkey (O)	Won 7–1	1 goal
28 July	Helsinki	v Sweden (O)	Won 6–0	
2 August	Helsinki	v Yugoslavia (O)	Won 2–0	
20 September	Berne	v Switzerland	Won 4–2	
19 October	Budapest	v Czechoslovakia	Won 5–0	
1953				
26 April	Budapest	v Austria	Drew 1–1	
17 May	Rome	v Italy	Won 3–0	
5 July	Stockholm	v Sweden	Won 4–2	
4 October	Prague	v Czechoslovakia	Won 5–1	
11 October	Vienna	v Austria	Won 3–2	
15 November	Budapest	v Sweden	Drew 2–2	
25 November	Wembley	v England	Won 6–3	1 goal
1954				
12 February	Cairo	v Egypt	Won 3–0	
11 April	Vienna	v Austria	Won 1–0	
23 May	Budapest	v England	Won 7–1	
17 June	Zurich	v South Korea (WC)	Won 9–0	
20 June	Basle	v West Germany (WC)	Won 8–3	
27 June	Berne	v Brazil (WC)	Won 4–2	
30 June	Lausanne	v Uruguay (WC)	Won 4–2	
4 July	Berne	v West Germany (WC)	Lost 2–3	
19 September	Bucharest	v Rumania	Won 5–1	
26 September	Moscow	v USSR	Drew 1–1	
10 October	Budapest	v Switzerland	Won 3–0	1 goal
24 October	Budapest	v Czechoslovakia	Won 4–1	
8 December	Glasgow	v Scotland	Won 4–2	1 goal
1955				
24 April	Vienna	v Austria	Drew 2–2	
11 May	Stockholm	v Sweden	Won 7–3	
15 May	Copenhagen	v Denmark	Won 6–0	

Date	Venue	Opponents	Result	Scored
20 May	Helsinki	v Finland	Won 9–1	
29 May	Budapest	v Scotland	Won 3–1	
17 September	Lausanne	v Switzerland	Won 5–4	
25 September	Budapest	v USSR	Drew 1–1	
2 October	Prague	v Czechoslovakia	Won 3–1	
16 October	Budapest	v Austria	Won 6–1	
13 November	Budapest	v Sweden	Won 4–2	
27 November	Budapest	v Italy	Won 2–0	
1956				
19 February	Istanbul	v Turkey	Lost 1–3	
29 April	Budapest	v Yugoslavia	Drew 2–2	1 goal
20 May	Budapest	v Czechoslovakia	Lost 2–4	1 goal
3 June	Brussels	v Belgium	Lost 4–5	
9 June	Lisbon	v Portugal	Drew 2–2	
16 September	Belgrade	v Yugoslavia	Won 3–1	
23 September	Moscow	v USSR	Won 1–0	
7 October	Paris	v France	Won 2–1	
14 October	Vienna	v Austria	Won 2–0	
1957				
16 June	Stockholm	v Sweden	Drew 0–0	
23 June	Budapest	v Bulgaria	Won 4–1	1 goal
15 September	Sofia	v Bulgaria	Won 2–1	
22 September	Budapest	v USSR	Lost 1–2	
6 October	Budapest	v France	Won 2–0	
10 November	Budapest	v Norway	Won 5–0	
22 December	Hanover	v West Germany	Lost 0–1	
1958				
20 April	Budapest	v Yugoslavia	Won 2–0	
7 May	Glasgow	v Scotland	Drew 1–1	
8 June	Sandviken	v Wales (WC)	Drew 1–1	
12 June	Stockholm	v Sweden (WC)	Lost 1–2	
17 June	Stockholm	v Wales (WC)	Lost 1–2	
26 October	Bucharest	v Rumania	Won 2–1	
1959				
27 September	Budapest	v USSR	Lost 0–1	
11 October	Belgrade	v Yugoslavia	Won 4–2	
25 October	Budapest	v Switzerland (sub)	Won 8–0	
8 November	Budapest	v West Germany (sub)	Won 4–3	
1961				
8 October	Vienna	v Austria	Lost 1–2	
9 December	Santiago	v Chile	Lost 1–5	
13 December	Santiago	v Chile (sub)	Drew 0–0	
23 December	Montevideo	v Uruguay (sub)	Drew 1–1	
1962				
18 April	Budapest	v Uruguay	Drew 1–1	1 goal

O = Olympic Games (final stages)
WC = World Cup (final stages)

Bozsik played in 48 consecutive internationals from 6 June 1948 to 24 October 1954. From his first appearance on 17 August 1947 until 12 June 1958 he missed only nine matches out of a total of 98 played. On two occasions during the period mentioned Hungary fielded two separate international teams on the same day, so Bozsik actually missed fewer possible appearances. He died on the eve of the 1978 World Cup finals.

Bobby Moore (West Ham United, Fulham and England)
108 International appearances 1962–1973

Date	Venue	Opponents	Result
1962			
20 May	Lima	v Peru	Won 4–0
31 May	Rancagua	v Hungary (WC)	Lost 1–2
2 June	Rancagua	v Argentina (WC)	Won 3–1
7 June	Rancagua	v Bulgaria (WC)	Drew 0–0
10 June	Vina del Mar	v Brazil (WC)	Lost 1–3
3 October	Hillsborough	v France	Drew 1–1
20 October	Belfast	v Northern Ireland	Won 3–1
21 November	Wembley	v Wales	Won 4–0
1963			
27 February	Paris	v France	Lost 2–5
6 April	Wembley	v Scotland	Lost 1–2
8 May	Wembley	v Brazil	Drew 1–1
20 May	Bratislava	v Czechoslovakia	Won 4–2
2 June	Leipzig	v East Germany	Won 2–1
5 June	Basle	v Switzerland	Won 8–1
12 October	Cardiff	v Wales	Won 4–0
23 October	Wembley	v Rest of the World	Won 2–1
20 November	Wembley	v Northern Ireland	Won 8–3

BOBBY MOORE continued

Date	Venue	Opponents	Result	Scored
1964				
11 April	Glasgow	v Scotland	Lost 0–1	
6 May	Wembley	v Uruguay	Won 2–1	
17 May	Lisbon	v Portugal	Won 4–3	
24 May	Dublin	v Republic of Ireland	Won 3–1	
30 May	Rio de Janeiro	v Brazil	Lost 1–5	
4 June	Sao Paulo	v Portugal	Drew 1–1	
6 June	Rio de Janeiro	v Argentina	Lost 0–1	
3 October	Belfast	v Northern Ireland	Won 4–3	
21 October	Wembley	v Belgium	Drew 2–2	
1965				
10 April	Wembley	v Scotland	Drew 2–2	
5 May	Wembley	v Hungary	Won 1–0	
9 May	Belgrade	v Yugoslavia	Drew 1–1	
12 May	Nuremberg	v West Germany	Won 1–0	
16 May	Gothenburg	v Sweden	Won 2–1	
2 October	Cardiff	v Wales	Drew 0–0	
20 October	Wembley	v Austria	Lost 2–3	
10 November	Wembley	v Northern Ireland	Won 2–1	
8 December	Madrid	v Spain	Won 2–0	
1966				
5 January	Liverpool	v Poland	Drew 1–1	1 goal
23 February	Wembley	v West Germany	Won 1–0	
2 April	Glasgow	v Scotland	Won 4–3	
29 June	Oslo	v Norway	Won 6–1	1 goal
3 July	Copenhagen	v Denmark	Won 2–0	
5 July	Chorzow	v Poland	Won 1–0	
11 July	Wembley	v Uruguay (WC)	Drew 0–0	
16 July	Wembley	v Mexico (WC)	Won 2–0	
20 July	Wembley	v France (WC)	Won 2–0	
23 July	Wembley	v Argentina (WC)	Won 1–0	
26 July	Wembley	v Portugal (WC)	Won 2–1	
30 July	Wembley	v West Germany (WC)	Won 4–2	
22 October	Belfast	v Northern Ireland	Won 2–0	
2 November	Wembley	v Czechoslovakia	Drew 0–0	
16 November	Wembley	v Wales	Won 5–1	
1967				
15 April	Wembley	v Scotland	Lost 2–3	
24 May	Wembley	v Spain	Won 2–0	
27 May	Vienna	v Austria	Won 1–0	
21 October	Cardiff	v Wales	Won 3–0	
22 November	Wembley	v Northern Ireland	Won 2–2	
6 December	Wembley	v USSR	Drew 2–2	
1968				
24 February	Glasgow	v Scotland	Drew 1–1	
3 April	Wembley	v Spain	Won 1–0	
8 May	Madrid	v Spain	Won 2–1	
22 May	Wembley	v Sweden	Won 3–1	
1 June	Hanover	v West Germany	Lost 0–1	
5 June	Florence	v Yugoslavia (EC)	Lost 0–1	
8 June	Rome	v USSR (EC)	Won 2–0	
6 November	Bucharest	v Rumania	Drew 0–0	
11 December	Wembley	v Bulgaria	Drew 1–1	
1969				
12 March	Wembley	v France	Won 5–0	
3 May	Belfast	v Northern Ireland	Won 3–1	
7 May	Wembley	v Wales	Won 2–1	
10 May	Wembley	v Scotland	Won 4–1	
1 June	Mexico City	v Mexico	Drew 0–0	
8 June	Montevideo	v Uruguay	Won 2–1	
12 June	Rio de Janeiro	v Brazil	Lost 1–2	
5 November	Amsterdam	v Netherlands	Won 1–0	
10 December	Wembley	v Portugal	Won 1–0	
1970				
25 February	Brussels	v Belgium	Won 3–1	
18 April	Cardiff	v Wales	Drew 1–1	
21 April	Wembley	v Northern Ireland	Won 3–1	
25 April	Glasgow	v Scotland	Drew 0–0	
20 May	Bogota	v Colombia	Won 4–0	
24 May	Quito	v Ecuador	Won 2–0	
2 June	Guadalajara	v Rumania (WC)	Won 1–0	

Date	Venue	Opponents	Result	Scored
7 June	Guadalajara	v Brazil (WC)	Lost 0–1	
11 June	Guadalajara	v Czechoslovakia (WC)	Won 1–0	
14 June	Leon	v West Germany (WC)	Lost 2–3	
25 November	Wembley	v East Germany	Won 3–1	
1971				
21 April	Wembley	v Greece	Won 3–0	
12 May	Wembley	v Malta	Won 5–0	
15 May	Belfast	v Northern Ireland	Won 1–0	
22 May	Wembley	v Scotland	Won 3–1	
13 October	Basle	v Switzerland	Won 3–2	
10 November	Wembley	v Switzerland	Drew 1–1	
1 December	Athens	v Greece	Won 2–0	
1972				
29 April	Wembley	v West Germany	Lost 1–3	
13 May	Berlin	v West Germany	Drew 0–0	
20 May	Cardiff	v Wales	Won 3–0	
27 May	Glasgow	v Scotland	Won 1–0	
11 October	Wembley	v Yugoslavia	Drew 1–1	
15 November	Cardiff	v Wales	Won 1–0	
1973				
24 January	Wembley	v Wales	Drew 1–1	
14 February	Glasgow	v Scotland	Won 5–0	
12 May	Liverpool	v Northern Ireland	Won 2–1	
15 May	Wembley	v Wales	Won 3–0	
19 May	Wembley	v Scotland	Won 1–0	
27 May	Prague	v Czechoslovakia	Drew 1–1	
6 June	Chorzow	v Poland	Lost 0–2	
10 June	Moscow	v USSR	Won 2–1	
14 June	Turin	v Italy	Lost 0–2	
14 November	Wembley	v Italy	Lost 0–1	

(WC) = World Cup (final stages)
(EC) = European Championships (final stages)

Moore was absent on only 12 occasions during his entire international career from 20 May 1962 to 14 November 1973. And he never missed more than two matches in succession.

Two other England players have reached 100 or more appearances before Moore. Billy Wright appeared in 105 matches from 28 September 1946 to 28 May 1959 and Bobby Charlton in 106 from 19 April 1958 to 14 June 1970. Wright played in the first 33 consecutive matches after the resumption of normal internationals after the war, was absent for three out of the next five and then completed an un-interrupted run of 70 matches. He captained England on a record 90 occasions. Charlton scored a record 49 goals.

Edson Arantes do Nascimento (Pele) (Santos and Brazil)
111 International appearances 1957–1971

Date	Venue	Opponents	Result	Scored
1957				
7 July	Rio de Janeiro	v Argentina (sub)	Lost 1–2	1 goal
10 July	Sao Paulo	v Argentina	Won 2–0	1 goal
1958				
14 March	Rio de Janeiro	v Bulgaria (sub)	Won 4–0	
4 May	Rio de Janeiro	v Paraguay	Won 5–1	1 goal
18 May	Sao Paulo	v Bulgaria	Won 3–1	2 goals
15 June	Gothenburg	v USSR (WC)	Won 2–0	
19 June	Gothenburg	v Wales (WC)	Won 1–0	1 goal
24 June	Stockholm	v France (WC)	Won 5–2	3 goals
29 June	Stockholm	v Sweden (WC)	Won 5–2	2 goals
1959				
10 March	Buenos Aires	v Peru	Drew 2–2	1 goal
15 March	Buenos Aires	v Chile	Won 3–0	2 goals
21 March	Buenos Aires	v Bolivia	Won 4–2	1 goal
26 March	Buenos Aires	v Uruguay	Won 3–1	
29 March	Buenos Aires	v Paraguay	Won 4–1	3 goals
4 April	Buenos Aires	v Argentina	Drew 1–1	1 goal
13 May	Rio de Janeiro	v England	Won 2–0	
17 September	Rio de Janeiro	v Chile	Won 7–0	3 goals
20 September	Sao Paulo	v Chile	Won 1–0	
1960				
29 April	Cairo	v UAR	Won 5–0	
1 May	Alexandria	v UAR	Won 3–1	3 goals
6 May	Cairo	v UAR	Won 3–0	
8 May	Malmo	v Malmo FF	Won 7–1	2 goals
10 May	Copenhagen	v Denmark	Won 4–3	
12 May	Milan	v Inter-Milan	Drew 2–2	2 goals
16 May	Lisbon	v Sporting Lisbon	Won 4–0	
9 July	Montevideo	v Uruguay	Lost 0–1	
12 July	Rio de Janeiro	v Argentina	Won 5–1	1 goal
1962				
21 April	Rio de Janeiro	v Paraguay	Won 6–0	1 goal
24 April	Sao Paulo	v Paraguay	Won 4–0	2 goals
6 May	Sao Paulo	v Portugal	Won 2–1	
9 May	Rio de Janeiro	v Portugal	Won 1–0	1 goal

PELE continued

Date	Venue	Opponents	Result	Scored
12 May	Rio de Janeiro	v Wales	Won 3–1	1 goal
16 May	Sao Paulo	v Wales	Won 3–1	2 goals
30 May	Vina del Mar	v Mexico (WC)	Won 2–0	1 goal
2 June	Vina del Mar	v Czechoslovakia (WC)	Drew 0–0	
1963				
13 April	Sao Paulo	v Argentina	Lost 2–3	
16 April	Rio de Janeiro	v Argentina	Won 4–1	3 goals
21 April	Lisbon	v Portugal	Lost 0–1	
28 April	Paris	v France	Won 3–2	3 goals
2 May	Amsterdam	v Holland	Lost 0–1	
3 May	Eindhoven	v PSV Eindhoven	Won 1–0	
5 May	Hamburg	v West Germany	Won 2–1	1 goal
12 May	Milan	v Italy	Lost 0–3	
1964				
30 May	Rio de Janeiro	v England	Won 5–1	1 goal
3 June	Sao Paulo	v Argentina	Lost 0–3	
7 June	Rio de Janeiro	v Portugal	Won 4–1	1 goal
1965				
2 June	Rio de Janeiro	v Belgium	Won 5–0	3 goals
6 June	Rio de Janeiro	v West Germany	Won 2–0	1 goal
9 June	Rio de Janeiro	v Argentina	Drew 0–0	
17 June	Oran	v Algeria	Won 3–0	1 goal
24 June	Oporto	v Portugal	Drew 0–0	
30 June	Solna	v Sweden	Won 2–1	1 goal
4 July	Moscow	v USSR	Won 3–0	2 goals
21 November	Rio de Janeiro	v USSR	Drew 2–2	1 goal
1966				
1 May	Rio de Janeiro	v Gaucho Selection	Won 2–0	
19 May	Rio de Janeiro	v Chile	Won 1–0	
4 June	Sao Paulo	v Peru	Won 4–0	1 goal
8 June	Rio de Janeiro	v Poland	Won 2–1	
12 June	Rio de Janeiro	v Czechoslovakia	Won 2–1	2 goals
15 June	Rio de Janeiro	v Czechoslovakia	Drew 2–2	1 goal
21 June	Madrid	v Atletico Madrid	Won 5–3	3 goals
25 June	Hampden Park	v Scotland	Drew 1–1	
30 June	Gothenburg	v Sweden	Won 3–2	
4 July	Stockholm	v AIK Stockholm	Won 4–2	2 goals
6 July	Malmo	v Malmo FF	Won 3–1	2 goals
12 July	Goodison Park	v Bulgaria (WC)	Won 2–0	1 goal
19 July	Goodison Park	v Portugal (WC)	Lost 1–3	
1968				
25 July	Asuncion	v Paraguay	Won 4–0	2 goals
28 July	Asuncion	v Paraguay	Lost 0–1	
31 October	Rio de Janeiro	v Mexico	Lost 1–2	
3 November	Belo Horizonte	v Mexico	Won 2–1	1 goal
6 November	Rio de Janeiro	v FIFA	Won 2–1	
13 November	Parana	v Parana Selection	Won 2–1	
14 December	Rio de Janeiro	v West Germany	Drew 2–2	
17 December	Rio de Janeiro	v Yugoslavia	Drew 3–3	1 goal
1969				
7 April	Porto Alegre	v Peru	Won 2–1	
9 April	Rio de Janeiro	v Peru	Won 3–2	1 goal
12 June	Rio de Janeiro	v England	Won 2–1	
9 July	Aracaju	v Sergipe Selection	Won 8–2	
13 July	Recife	v Pernambuco Selection	Won 6–1	1 goal
6 July	Salvador	v Bahia	Won 4–0	1 goal
1 August	Bogota	v Millionarios	Won 2–0	
6 August	Bogota	v Colombia	Won 2–0	
10 August	Caracas	v Venezuela	Won 5–0	2 goals
21 August	Rio de Janeiro	v Colombia	Won 6–2	1 goal
17 August	Asuncion	v Paraguay	Won 3–0	
24 August	Rio de Janeiro	v Venezuela	Won 6–0	2 goals
31 August	Rio de Janeiro	v Paraguay	Won 1–0	1 goal
3 September	Belo Horizonte	v Atletico Mineiro	Lost 1–2	1 goal
1970				
4 March	Porto Alegre	v Argentina	Lost 0–2	
8 March	Rio de Janeiro	v Argentina	Won 2–1	1 goal
22 March	Sao Paulo	v Chile	Won 5–0	2 goals
26 March	Rio de Janeiro	v Chile	Won 2–1	
5 April	Manaus	v Amazon Selection	Won 4–1	1 goal
12 April	Rio de Janeiro	v Paraguay	Drew 0–0	

Date	Venue	Opponents	Result	Scored
19 April	Mineirao	v Mineira Selection	Won 3–1	
26 April	Morumbi	v Bulgaria (sub)	Drew 0–0	
29 April	Rio de Janeiro	v Austria	Won 1–0	
6 May	Guadalajara	v Guadalajara	Won 3–0	1 goal
17 May	Leon	v Leon	Won 5–2	3 goals
24 May	Irapuato	v Irapuato	Won 3–0	1 goal
3 June	Guadalajara	v Czechoslovakia (WC)	Won 4–1	1 goal
7 June	Guadalajara	v England (WC)	Won 1–0	
10 June	Guadalajara	v Rumania (WC)	Won 3–2	2 goals
14 June	Guadalajara	v Peru (WC)	Won 4–2	
17 June	Mexico City	v Uruguay (WC)	Won 3–1	
21 June	Mexico City	v Italy (WC)	Won 4–1	1 goal
30 September	Rio de Janeiro	v Mexico	Won 2–1	
4 October	Santiago	v Chile	Won 5–1	1 goal
1971				
11 July	Sao Paulo	v Austria	Drew 1–1	1 goal
18 July	Rio de Janeiro	v Yugoslavia	Drew 2–2	

OUTSTANDING INTERNATIONAL PLAYERS
A century of international appearances
The following players have appeared in 100 or more matches for their countries:

Name	Country	From	To	Total	
Franz Beckenbauer	West Germany	1965	1977	103	(see p.158)
Jozsef Bozsik	Hungary	1947	1962	100	(see p.160)
Bobby Charlton	England	1958	1970	106	
Hector Chumpitaz	Peru	1963		102*	
Gylmar	Brazil	1953	1969	100	
Bobby Moore	England	1962	1973	108	(see p.161)
Bjorn Nordqvist	Sweden	1963		108*	
Pele	Brazil	1957	1971	111	(see p.163)
Leonel Sanchez	Chile	1955	1967	104	
Thorbjorn Svenssen	Norway	1947	1961	105	
Djalma Santos	Brazil	1952	1968	100	
Rivelino	Brazil	1968		108*	
Billy Wright	England	1946	1959	105	
Attouga	Tunisia	1963		109*	

*Still adding to total in 1978

INDIVIDUAL EUROPEAN RECORDS

Gerd Muller (Bayern Munich and West Germany) reached his 600th goal in competition matches alone in a West German Cup match against Eintracht Trier early in the 1977–78 season. His total was made up thus:

West German Bundesliga	339
Regional League South	35
Bundesliga Promotion Play-offs	4
West German Cup	75
West German League Cup	12
West German national team	68
European Cup	36
Cup-Winners Cup	20
Fairs Cup	7
Super Cup	3
World Club Championship	1
Total	600

His 339 Bundesliga goals, a record for the competition, were achieved from the 1965–66 season until the opening games of 1977–78. At

the end of the 1976–77 season Muller had scored 332 goals in 375 Bundesliga matches.

Muller started his career with TSV Nordlingen, his home town side in southern Germany, and joined Bayern in 1964 at the insistence of Bayern's President, Wilhelm Neudecker. In his first season Bayern were promoted to the Bundesliga and in 1965–66 he scored 15 goals in 33 matches as well as taking over in goal from Sepp Maier in one match against Hamburg.

Muller reached his 350th Bundesliga goal against Werder Bremen on 21 January 1978.

Hungary's successful run

Hungary completed an unbeaten run of 34 international matches after losing 5–3 to Austria on 14 May 1950 until they were beaten 3–2 in the World Cup Final by West Germany on 4 July 1954.

The sequence included winning the 1952 Olympic Games title in Helsinki in the final of which they defeated Yugoslavia 2–0. However, during this period there were two matches which have been a source of controversy concerning their actual international status.

Both were played against a Moscow Selection on 25 and 28 May 1952 at a time when the USSR had just started to take an interest in international football again and remained reticent to reveal themselves. But the overriding consideration about the games is that as official Hungarian records for both the country's leading international Jozsef Boszik and their top scorer Ferenc Puskas take in these games there can be no question that they were treated as full internationals.

Prior to this run, as well, the Hungarians had gone 13 years playing at home without losing. After being beaten 7–2 on 7 November 1943 in Budapest they began in their next full international on 19 August 1945 by beating Austria 2–0 and continued successfully until 20 May 1956 when they lost 4–2 to Czechoslovakia.

There were two outstanding performances during this time. They won 6–3 at Wembley against England on 25 November 1953 and completed a double over the English on 23 May 1954 with a 7–1 success in Budapest. Their November win against England was the first time England had lost at home to a continental team.

On one occasion during this period Hungary fielded two full international sides on the same day. On 4 October 1953 one team won 5–1 in Prague against Czechoslovakia while the other eleven drew 1–1 in Sofia against Bulgaria.

Sandor Kocsis scored 75 goals in 68 international appearances for Hungary from 1948 to 1956. He would almost certainly have added to his total had he not left his native country at the time of the political uprising to continue his career in Spain.

INTERNATIONAL GOALSCORING

Ferenc Puskas (Hungary) 84 international appearances. Scored 83 goals in following matches:

Year	Opponents	Venue	No. of goals
1945	Austria	H	1
	Rumania	H	2
1946	Luxembourg	A	3
1947	Austria	H	1
	Italy	A	1
	Yugoslavia	A	1
	Rumania	A	2
1948	Switzerland	H	2
	Rumania	H	2
	Rumania	A	3
1949	Czechoslovakia	A	1
	Austria	H	3
	Poland	H	2
	Austria	A	2
	Bulgaria	H	2
	Sweden	H	1
1950	Czechoslovakia	H	2
	Austria	A	1
	Poland	A	2
	Albania	H	4
	Austria	H	3
1951	Poland	H	2
	Finland	H	2
1952	Moscow Selection	A	1
	Poland	A	2
	Finland	A	1
	Rumania	A	1
	Turkey	A	2
	Sweden	A	1
	Yugoslavia	A	1
	Switzerland	A	2
1953	Italy	A	2
	Sweden	A	1
	Czechoslovakia	A	1
	England	A	2
1954	Egypt	A	2
	England	H	2
	South Korea	A	2
	West Germany	A	1
	West Germany	A	1
1955	Norway	A	1
	Sweden	A	2
	Finland	A	1
	Switzerland	A	2
	USSR	H	1
	Sweden	H	1
	Italy	H	1
1956	Turkey	A	1
	Belgium	A	1
	Yugoslavia	A	1
	Austria	A	1

Puskas left Hungary at the time of the uprising in 1956 and then played in Spain. He made four international appearances for Spain.

SOCCER IN THE AMERICAS

SOUTH AMERICA

The South American Championship for the 'Copa America' was first contested in 1916. It is open to the national teams of countries affiliated to the South American Confederation (CONMEBOL). It has been organised at irregular intervals but was in decline after the start of the Libertadores Cup in 1960 until revived in 1975.

The tournament was originally played in one country with each team playing the other once on

Year	Country/Venue	Teams	Matches	Goals	Champions	Pts
1916	Argentina, Buenos Aires	4	6	18	Uruguay	5
1917	Uruguay, Montevideo	4	6	21	Uruguay	6
1919	Brazil, Rio de Janeiro (1)	4	7	26	Brazil	7
1920	Chile, Valparaiso	4	6	16	Uruguay	5
1921	Argentina, Buenos Aires	4	6	14	Argentina	6
1922	Brazil, Rio de Janeiro (2)	5	11	23	Brazil	7
1923	Uruguay, Montevideo	4	6	18	Uruguay	6
1924	Uruguay, Montevideo	4	6	15	Uruguay	5
1925	Argentina, Buenos Aires (3)	3	6	26	Argentina	7
1926	Chile, Santiago de Chile	5	10	55	Uruguay	8
1927	Peru, Lima	4	6	37	Argentina	6
1929	Argentina, Buenos Aires	4	6	23	Argentina	6
1935	Peru, Lima*	4	6	18	Uruguay	6
1937	Argentina, Buenos Aires (4)	6	16	68	Argentina	10
1939	Peru, Lima	5	10	47	Peru	8
1941	Chile, Santiago de Chile*	5	10	32	Argentina	8
1942	Uruguay, Montevideo (5)	7	21	81	Uruguay	12
1945	Chile, Santiago de Chile*	7	21	89	Argentina	11
1946	Argentina, Buenos Aires*	6	15	61	Argentina	10
1947	Ecuador, Guayaquil	8	28	102	Argentina	13
1949	Brazil, Rio de Janeiro (6)	8	29	130	Brazil	14
1953	Peru, Lima (7)	7	21	67	Paraguay	10
1955	Chile, Santiago de Chile	6	15	73	Argentina	9
1956	Uruguay, Montevideo*	6	15	38	Uruguay	9
1957	Peru, Lima	7	21	101	Argentina	10
1959	Argentina, Buenos Aires	7	21	86	Argentina	11
1959	Ecuador, Guayaquil*	5	20	39	Uruguay	7
1963	Bolivia, La Paz & Cochabamba	7	21	91	Bolivia	11
1967	Uruguay, Montevideo	6	15	49	Uruguay	9
1975	(Reorganised on home and away basis)	10	25	79	Peru	N/A

*extraordinary tournaments

1: play-off: Brazil 1   Uruguay 0
2: play-off: Brazil 3   Paraguay 1; Uruguay withdrew
3: two legs were played (home and away)
4: play-off: Argentina 2   Brazil 0
5: Chile withdrew
6: play-off: Brazil 7   Paraguay 0
7: play-off: Paraguay 3   Brazil 2 (organised by the Paraguayan Football League)

a League basis. Teams level on points had to play-off to determine the winner. But the 1975 competition was reorganised to provide for three groups of three countries in each playing home and away with the winners qualifying for home and away semi-finals together with the previous winners (Uruguay) seeded to this stage.

Between the start of the competition and 1920 only Argentina, Brazil, Chile and Uruguay entered. Paraguay made their first appearance in 1921, Bolivia in 1925, Peru the following year, Ecuador in 1939 and Colombia in 1945. Venezuela, where professional football was not introduced until the 1960s, did not make their first appearance until 1967 but the 1975 series was the first in which all ten possible nations participated.

The initial tournament was held in 1916 as a pilot for later ones and was considered as an Extraordinary Competition as indeed were many subsequent tournaments arranged without pre-determination though officially recognised by the governing body.

Argentina has been the most successful country, winning on 12 occasions followed by Uruguay with 11 titles and Brazil with only three. However, Brazil have not always either entered or sent their strongest available selection to compete. In 1975 they entered a state selection side only, not the full national team.

SOUTH AMERICAN CUP

(Libertadores Cup)

The Libertadores Cup was first contested in 1960 as the South American Champion's Club Cup, an international club competition following closely on the principles of its European equivalent and open to champion teams of the South American Confederation (CONMEBOL).

The first two competitions were played on a knock-out basis with home and away matches similar to the European Cup but in 1962 it was altered with teams placed in groups on a league basis. In 1965 it was decided that the runners-up in national championships could enter along with the winners. The name was also changed then to the Libertadores Cup.

Brazil was opposed to this idea because they considered it was not financially a proposition for their clubs and withdrew for several years. By 1969 the Cup had become so unwieldy that clubs

were refusing to release players for international matches in order to fulfil the fixtures and this was one of the causes of the demise of the South American Championship.

In 1970 the tournament was streamlined to reduce the number of matches played and the 1977 edition had five groups of four teams in each playing each other home and away and similarly two semi-final groups composed of three teams in each. The winners of these two groups met in the final. The competition is so organised that clubs from the same country cannot meet in the final.

The Uruguayan club Penarol have made the most appearances in the competition, playing in 17 of the 18 tournaments. Argentinian clubs have been the most successful winning on 11 occasions, with Independiente individually having won it alone on six occasions in 1964, 1965, 1972, 1973, 1974 and 1975.

COPA LIBERTADORES RECORD 1960-77

		P	W	D	L	F	A
1	Penarol (U)	146	71	33	42	243	154
2	Nacional (U)	113	54	30	29	194	112
3	Universitario (Pe)	91	35	24	32	123	119
4	River Plate (Arg)	74	37	17	20	138	84
5	Independiente (Arg)	72	37	16	19	104	64
6	Boca Juniors (Arg)	60	34	13	13	86	44
7	Olimpia (Par)	76	26	23	27	102	99
8	Vruzeiro (Br)	42	29	5	8	96	46
9	Cerro Portena (Par)	64	22	18	24	93	97
10	Palmeiras (Br)	44	28	4	12	73	43
11	Guarani (Par)	59	21	17	21	78	74
12	Estudiantes (Arg)	37	26	4	7	55	23
13	Universidad (Ch)	52	23	10	19	91	79
14	Deportivo Cali (Co)	51	20	12	19	77	75
15	Colo Colo (Ch)	51	19	9	23	87	95
16	Universidad de Chile (Ch)	50	18	8	24	67	76
17	Emelec (E)	51	17	10	24	62	81
18	Union Espanola (Ch)	41	15	11	15	51	54
19	Barcelona (Ec)	45	15	11	19	53	60
20	Milonarios (Co)	44	15	10	19	54	55
21	Rosario Central (Arg)	30	16	7	7	44	29
22	Sporting Cristal (Pe)	42	12	15	15	49	60
23	Racing Club (Arg)	27	16	6	5	54	26
24	Deportivo Italia (V)	44	14	9	21	44	81
25	Liga Deportivo U. (Ec)	31	13	8	10	47	41
26	Bolivar (Bo)	35	11	10	14	48	55
27	Santos (Br)	22	14	3	5	60	32
28	Sao Paulo (Br)	23	12	7	4	39	18
29	Jorge Wilsterman (Bo)	38	11	9	18	39	70
30	Nacional (Ec)	30	11	7	12	33	36
31	Alianza (Pe)	34	10	7	17	36	54
32	Portuguesa (V)	22	8	8	6	24	23
33	Botafogo (Br)	17	10	3	4	30	23
34	Indep. Santa Fe (Co)	28	6	8	14	37	64
35	Internacional Porto Alegre (Br)	16	8	3	5	21	17
36	San Lorenzo (Arg)	15	7	4	4	26	10

		P	W	D	L	F	A			P	W	D	L	F	A
37	Nacional Medellin (Co)	18	5	5	8	18	24	63 Union Magdalena (Co)		6	2	1	3	7	8
38	Dep. Municipal (Bo)	20	6	3	11	39	49	64 Defensor Arica (Pe)		6	1	3	2	5	6
39	Galacia (V)	42	5	5	32	33	79	65 Palestino (Ch)		6	2	1	3	5	6
40	Huracan (Arg)	11	6	2	3	19	12	66 Defensor (U)		6	1	3	2	5	7
41	Libertad (Par)	16	5	4	7	14	21	67 America (Co)		10	1	3	6	12	22
42	Oriente Petroleo (Bo)	18	5	3	10	20	33	68 31st October (Bo)		10	2	1	7	11	28
43	Deportivo Por. (V)	18	5	3	10	16	34	69 Chaca Petroleo (Bo)		12	2	1	9	8	22
44	The Strongest (Bo)	16	4	4	8	18	39	70 Nautico (Br)		6	1	2	3	7	8
45	Wanderers (Ch)	12	4	3	5	20	22	71 Atletico Mineiro (Br)		6	0	4	2	5	6
46	Deportivo Cuenca (Ec)	13	4	3	6	13	20	72 Union San Felipe (Ch)		6	1	2	3	5	8
47	America (Ec)	12	4	2	6	13	22	73 Univer. Catolica (Ec)		6	1	2	3	2	5
48	Defensor Lima (Pe)	10	4	1	5	8	12	74 Atletico Junior (Co)		6	1	2	3	5	9
49	Dep. Ind. Medellin (Co)	10	4	1	5	15	21	75 U.D. Canarias (V)		6	1	2	3	3	7
50	Union Huaral (Pe)	12	2	5	5	12	22	76 Nacional (Co)		6	2	1	3	5	6
51	Fluminese (Br)	6	4	0	2	16	6	77 Deportivo Lara (V)		10	1	2	7	5	16
52	Newell's Old Boys (Arg)	7	3	2	2	9	9	78 Bahia (Br)		4	1	1	2	4	7
53	Valencia (V)	16	2	4	10	16	35	79 Wanderers (U)		6	1	1	4	8	10
54	Sport Boys (Pe)	14	2	3	9	12	18	80 Ninth October (Ec)		10	1	1	8	14	28
55	Huachipato (Ch)	6	2	2	2	10	10	81 Rangers (Ch)		10	1	1	8	11	26
56	Wanderers (V)	6	3	0	3	6	8	82 Sporting Luqueno (Par)		6	1	0	5	5	14
57	Alf. Ugarte Puno (Par)	6	1	0	5	5	14	83 Guabira (Bo)		6	1	0	5	2	15
58	Juan Aurich (Pe)	8	2	2	4	14	20	84 Club Always Ready (Bo)		6	0	2	4	2	17
59	Deportivo Quito (Ec)	10	1	4	5	7	19	85 Universitario (Bo)		6	0	2	4	2	19
60	Corinthians (Br)	6	2	1	3	10	6	86 Aurora (Bo)		4	0	1	3	2	14
61	Vasco da Gama (Br)	6	1	3	2	7	7	87 Litoral (Bo)		6	0	1	5	1	14
62	Everton (Ch)	6	2	1	3	7	8	88 Everest (Ec)		2	0	0	2	1	14

Key to countries:
Arg: Argentina; Bo: Bolivia; Br: Brazil; Ch: Chile; Co: Colombia; Ec: Ecuador; Par: Paraguay; Pe: Peru; U: Uruguay; V: Venezuela.

COPA LIBERTADORES

Year	Winner	Entries	Matches	Goals	Attendances	Average
1960	Penarol (Uruguay)	8	13	39	335,000	25,000
1961	Penarol	9	16	52	428,000	26,875
1962	Santos (Brazil)	10	25	101	742,000	29,680
1963	Santos	9	19	63	763,000	40,195
1964	Independiente (Argentina)	10	25	89	665,000	26,620
1965	Independiente	10	27	72	883,700	32,720
1966	Penarol	17	94	218	2,331,500	24,803
1967	Racing (Argentina)	19	114	355	1,796,300	17,335
1968	Estudiantes (Argentina)	21	93	232	2,150,800	27,424
1969	Estudiantes	17	74	211	1,739,400	23,500
1970	Estudiantes	19	88	253	1,805,100	20,153
1971	Nacional (Uruguay)	21	73	196	2,232,700	30,584
1972	Independiente	20	69	176	1,825,300	26,452
1973	Independiente	19	66	190	2,185,363	33,111
1974	Independiente	21	76	178	1,912,114	25,160
1975	Independiente	21	76	208	2,244,369	29,531
1976	Cruzeiro (Brazil)	21	77	211	1,769,616	22,982
1977	Boca Juniors (Argentina)	(No figures available at time of going to press)				

BRAZILIAN CHAMPIONSHIPS

The first Brazilian championship for the Copa Brasil was organised in 1971 after several previous attempts to formulate a more comprehensive national competition.

In addition each state organises its own championship and because of the size of the country, 2,340 miles from north to south and only slightly less from east to west, the difficulties of an overall tournament were obvious.

In 1933 a competition was held between teams from the two traditionally strongest states of Guanabara (the city of Rio de Janeiro) and Sao Paulo and was revived in 1950 as a more regular event with the winner considered as the unofficial national champion.

This Rio–Sao Paulo tournament was expanded into the first national championship in 1967 under the name of the Silver Cup in which teams from five states participated. The Brazilian Sports Federation took over the organisation of the cup in 1968 and brought the number of competing states to seven. In 1971 it was increased to eight and subsequently expanded to include all 22 Brazilian states.

The 1977 tournament had 62 clubs originally split into six groups, being reduced to 40 clubs, then 22, with a total of 485 matches being played altogether.

Brazilian Champions
(Rio-Sao Paulo tournament)
1950   Corintians
1951   Palmeiras
1952   Portuguesa
1953   Corintians
1954   Corintians
1955   Portuguesa
1956   Not played
1957   Fluminense
1958   Vasco da Gama
1959   Santos
1960   Fluminense
1961   Flamengo

1962   Botafogo
1963   Santos
1964   Santos and Botafogo (shared)
1965   Palmeiras
1966   Corintians, Santos, Vasco da Gama and
         Botafogo
         (shared)

Silver Cup
1967   Palmeiras
1968   Santos
1969   Palmeiras
1970   Fluminense

Copa Brasil
1971   Atletico Mineiro
1972   Palmeiras
1973   Palmeiras
1974   Vasco da Gama
1975   Internacional Porto Alegre
1976   Internacional Porto Alegre

SOUTH AMERICAN DIRECTORY

Country	Championship wins
Argentina (1893–)	Boca Juniors 17; Racing Club 15; River Plate 14; Alumni 9; Independiente 9; San Lorenzo 8; Huracan 5; Lomas 5; Belgrano 3; Estudiantes de la Plata 2; Porteno 2; Estudiantil Porteno 2; Dock Sud 1; Chacarita Juniors 1; Lomas Academicals 1; Quilmes 1; English High School 1; Gimnasia y Esgrima La Plata 1; Sportivo Barracas 1; Newell's Old Boys 1. (National League 1967–): Boca Juniors 3; Rosario Central 2; San Lorenzo 2; Independiente 1; Velez Sarsfield 1; River Plate 1.
Bolivia (1914–)	The Strongest 17; Bolivar 10; Jorge Wilsterman 6; Deportivo Municipal 4; Litoral 3; Universitario 3; Always Ready 2; Chaco Petrolero 2; Colegio Militar 1; Oriente Petrolero 1; Nimbles Sport 1; Deportivo Militar 1; Nimbles Rail 1; Ayacucho 1; Ferroviario 1; Guabira 1.
Brazil	(Rio League 1906–): Fluminense 22; Flamengo 18; Botafogo 12; Vasco da Gama 13; America 7; Bangu 2; San Christavao 1; Paysandu 1. (Sao Paulo League 1902–): *SE Palmeiras 18; Corinthians 16; Santos 13; Sao Paulo 11; Paulistano 8; SP Athletic 4; AA des Palmeiras 3; Portuguesa 3; Sao Bento; Germania 2; Americano 2; Internacional 1. *formerly Palestra Italia
Chile (1933–)	Colo Colo 11; Universidad de Chile 7; Magallanes 4; Audax Italiano 4; Union Espanola 4; Universidad Catolica 4; Everton 3; Wanderers (Valpariso) 2; Santiago Morning 1; Green Cross 1; Hauchipato 1; Palestino 1; Union San Felipe 1.
Colombia (1948–)	Millionarios 10; Independiente Santa Fe 6; Deportivo Cali 5; Independiente Medellin 2; Nacional Medellin 2; Deportes Caldas 1; Atletico Nacional 1; Atletico Quindio 1; Union Magdalena 1.
Ecuador (1957–)	Barcelona 4; Emelec 4; Liga Deportiva Universitaria 3; Nacional 3; Everest 2; Deportivo Quito 2.
Paraguay (1906–)	Olimpia 24; Cerro Porteno 18; Libertad 8; Guarani 7; Nacional 6; Sporting Luqueno 2; Presidente Hayes 1. (National Championship 1976–): Olimpia 1.
Peru (1928–)	Alianza 14; Universitario 14; Sport Boys 5; Sporting Cristal 5; Deportivo Municipal 4; Atletico Chalaco 2; Mariscal Sucre 2; Union Huaral 1; Defensor Lima 1.
Uruguay (1900–)	Penarol 33; Nacional 31; River Plate 4; Montevideo Wanderers 3; Defensor 1; Rampla Juniors 1. (Major League 1975–): Nacional 3.
Venezuela (1956–)	Deportivo Italia 5; Deportivo Portugues 3; Deportivo Galicia 3; Portuguesa 3; Valencia 2; Lasalle 1; Tiquire Aragua 1; Celta Deportivo 1; Lara 1; Union Deportiva Canarias 1.

Colour Supplement

Maracana Stadium, Rio de Janeiro the world's largest football ground (Colorsport)

Ray Clemence holding the European Cup trophy in 1977
(All-Sport Photographic)

Celtic (hooped shirts) appeal for a penalty against Inter
Milan in the 1967 European Cup Final in Lisbon (Syndication
International)

Manchester United's 1968 European Cup winning squad. Back row left to right Bill Foulkes, John Aston, Jimmy Rimmer, Alex
Stepney, Alan Gowling, David Herd. Middle: David Sadler, Tony Dunne, Shay Brennan, Pat Crerand, George Best, Francis
Burns, Jack Crompton (trainer). Front: Jimmy Ryan, Nobby Stiles, Denis Law, Matt Busby (Manager), Bobby Charlton, Brian

WILL'S CIGARETTES

PLAYER'S CIGARETTES.

A. WOOD.

WILL'S CIGARETTES

A. McSPADYEN (PARTICK THISTLE)

WILL'S CIGARETTES

B. JONES (ARSENAL)

J. ROBINSON (SHEFFIELD WEDNESDAY)

WILL'S CIGARETTES

G. ALSOP (WALSALL)

PLAYER'S CIGARETTES.

JOE BRADFORD

WILL'S CIGARETTES

P. DOHERTY (MANCHESTER CITY)

PLAYER'S CIGARETTES.

F. BARSON

CARRERAS CIGARETTES

DAVID JACK
ARSENAL (1ST DIVISION)

WILL'S CIGARETTES

H. CARTER (SUNDERLAND)

PLAYER'S CIGARETTES

W. H. WALKER

WILL'S CIGARETTES

J. HAMPSON BLACKPOOL

Olympic Stadium, Munich (Syndication International)

River Plate Stadium, Buenos Aires (Syndication International)

The teams line up for the 1966 World Cup Final with England in red and West Germany in white (Gerry Cranham)

George Cohen (red shirt) tackles West Germany's Sigi Held in the 1966 World Cup Final at Wembley (Syndication International)

Action from the 1970 World Cup Final in Mexico between Brazil (yellow shirts) and Italy.

West Germany's Gerd Muller (green shirt) scores with a near post header against Australia despite the presence of defenders Jack Reilly (1) and Doug Utjesenovic (2) (All-Sport Photographic)

An incident in the Brazilian goalmouth in the match against Yugoslavia (All-Sport Photographic)

Johan Neeskens (orange shirt) takes a shot for Holland in the 1974 World Cup Final against West Germany (Syndication International)

Above: Tottenham Hotspur F.C. and the cockerel (Gerry Cranham)

Above: Brazilian supporter (Syndication International)

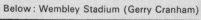

Below: Wembley Stadium (Gerry Cranham)

Leeds United supporters
(Syndication International)

Right: Dressing room; left to right Cliff Jones, Jimmy Greaves and Terry Dyson of Tottenham Hotspur (Gerry Cranham)

Below: Rosettes (Gerry Cranham)

Denis Law in action (Syndication International)

The Football League playing career of Sir Stanley Matthews C.B.E., spanned 33 years from his debut for Stoke City in 1932 at 17 until his last appearance with the same club in 1965 at the age of 50. He also played for Blackpool from 1947 to 1961. All told he made 701 League appearances and scored 71 goals, played in 54 full internationals plus another 29 wartime and Victory games. With his wartime club appearances he made well over 1,000 senior outings. He also won an F.A. Cup winners medal in 1953 and two runners-up awards in 1948 and 1951. Matthews played in 13 Inter-League matches and for Great Britain against the Rest of Europe in 1947 and 1955. Another unique double came when he was elected the first Footballer of the Year in 1948 and the first European Footballer of the Year in 1956. He was Footballer of the Year again in 1963. (Syndication International)

Arsenal F.C. August 1971 after the League and Cup 'double'. B
row left to right: Bob McNab, Ray Kennedy, Bob Wilson, J
Roberts, Geoff Barnett, Peter Simpson, Peter Marinello. Front: Sar
Nelson, Peter Storey, John Radford, Pat Rice, Frank McLintock, E
Kelly, George Graham, George Armstrong. Missing from pict
Charlie George. (Syndication International)

Arsenal Stadium, Highbury (Gerry Cranh

WORLD CUP Qualifying Countries 1978

ARGENTINA

AUSTRIA

BRAZIL

FRANCE

W. GERMANY

HOLLAND

HUNGARY

IRAN

ITALY

MEXICO

PERU

POLAND

SCOTLAND

SPAIN

SWEDEN

TUNISIA

(Syndication International)

(Colorsport)

Adios Pele

COSMOS NO. 10
IS NOW RETIRED!
IT WILL NEVER
BE WORN AGAIN.

Adios, Pele. On 1 October 1977 in New York he played one half for Cosmos, the other for Santos (green) his only two clubs, then retired. (Syndication International)

(Colorsport)

WORLD CLUB CHAMPIONSHIP

The World Club Championship, sometimes known as the Intercontinental Cup, was first contested in 1960 between the winners of the European Champions Club Cup and the South American Champions Club Cup, the latter competition having been started primarily to provide a world finalist.

Originally organised by UEFA, the European governing body, and CONMEBOL for South America, this unofficial club championship of the world did not have the blessing of FIFA until it had been in existence for several years.

Up to 1968 it was played with home and away legs on a points basis, which meant that a win for each side or two drawn matches would necessitate a play-off. Until 1964 this had to take place on the ground of the country at home in the second leg. Even as late as 1968 it had to be played in the same continent but in 1969 it was decided on an aggregate of goals.

The competition has been marred by violent incidents and resulted in several European clubs refusing to participate. Thus clubs other than those qualified to represent Europe have been featured and in 1975 no competition was played at all because no agreement could be reached over suitable dates.

World Club Championship

year
1960   Real Madrid (Spain) beat Penarol (Uruquay) 0–0, 5–1
1961   Penarol (Uruguay) beat Benfica (Portugal) 0–1, 5–0, 2–1
1962   Santos (Brazil) beat Benfica (Portugal) 3–2, 5–2
1963   Santos (Brazil) beat AC Milan (Italy) 2–4, 4–2, 1–0
1964   Inter-Milan (Italy) beat Independiente (Argentina) 0–1, 2–0, 1–0
1965   Inter-Milan (Italy) beat Independiente (Argentina) 3–0, 0–0
1966   Penarol (Uruguay) beat Real Madrid (Spain) 2–0, 2–0
1967   Racing Club (Argentina) beat Celtic (Scotland) 0–1, 2–1, 1–0

1968   Estudiantes (Argentina) beat Manchester United (England) 1–0, 1–1
1969   AC Milan (Italy) beat Estudiantes (Argentina) 3–0, 1–2
1970   Feyenoord (Holland) beat Estudiantes (Argentina) 2–2, 1–0
1971   Nacional (Uruguay) beat Panathinaikos (Greece) 1–1, 2–1
1972   Ajax (Holland) beat Independiente (Argentina) 1–1, 3–0
1973   Independiente (Argentina) beat Juventus (Italy) 1–0
1974   Atletico Madrid (Spain) beat Independiente (Argentina) 0–1, 2–0
1975   Independiente (Argentina) and Bayern Munich (West Germany) could not agree on dates
1976   Bayern Munich (West Germany) beat Cruzeiro (Brazil) 2–0, 0–0

PELE

Pele (Edson Arantes do Nascimento) scored his 1,000th goal in all matches on 19 November 1969. The occasion was a Silver Cup tournament match between his club Santos and Vasco da Gama played at the Maracana Stadium in Rio de Janeiro.

The game itself held little other importance, since neither club had much chance of progressing in the competition, but a crowd of 75,157 was present in expectation of the milestone.

Pele did manage to hit the post with one shot but generally found the Vasco goalkeeper in fine form until 12 minutes before the end of the match with the score 1–1 when Pele was tripped in the penalty area. Referee Manoel Amaro de Lima awarded a penalty to Santos and Rildo came up to take the kick but as the crowd were chanting 'Pele, Pele' the Santos captain gave the ball to him.

Pele scored with a low shot into the corner of the net. Immediately his jersey was torn off to reveal a silver shirt with the figure 1,000 on it. He was carried shoulder high around the ground by spectators who had invaded the pitch.

The game finally restarted and when it came to its conclusion with Santos 2–1 winners, the stadium president Dr. Abelard Franca unveiled a bronze plaque to commemorate the historical event.

Pele (born in Tres Coracoes, 1940) first played football in Bauru in the state of Sao Paulo. He came to the attention of Waldemar de Brito, a former Brazilian World Cup player and manager of the local Division Two team.

He never once attempted to curb Pele's obvious natural ability but corrected his faults and encouraged him. When Pele was 15 he suggested that he join Santos where he made quick progress.

Of many feats of individual brilliance it is unlikely that any were surpassed by the occasion at the Maracana Stadium against Fluminense when he dribbled from his own penalty area beating seven players before scoring. It earned him the 'Goal de Placa' (commemorative plate goal).

Pele retired originally on 2 October 1974 after playing for Santos against Ponte Preta having won many honours, including appearing in three World Cup winning tournaments for Brazil in 1958, 1962 and 1970 as well as playing for the team in 1966.

In 1975 he was persuaded to come out of retirement and signed a three-year contract with New York Cosmos on 11 June.

Pele played his last match on 1 October 1977 in New Jersey before a crowd of 75,646. The occasion was a friendly between Cosmos and the only other team that Pele had played with, Santos.

It was Pele's 1,363rd match and he managed to celebrate with a goal, the 1,281st of his career.

NORTH AMERICAN SOCCER

The game in the United States of America has become increasingly popular and the impression is that it is a comparatively recent innovation in the country. However, that is far from the truth, for as long ago as 1894 Football League players were being tempted to cross the Atlantic to try their luck with clubs in America.

That year Baltimore club sent an agent to England to try and secure players for a new professional League formed in the States to keep baseball players occupied out of season. They merely wanted a sprinkling of real footballers to launch the scheme properly by coaching the baseball players and assist generally. It was hoped that visiting teams like Sunderland would go out there to play in exhibition matches. On Wednesday, 3 October 1894 the American agent set sail in the *Teutonic* accompanied by Wallace, Little, Calvey and Ferguson of Manchester City and Davies of Sheffield United who was also a former Manchester City player. It was reported that they went for £10 down and £4 to £5 per week. Two other City players – Nash and Mann – had also arranged to go but changed their minds at the last minute.

Jealous of the Baltimore club's enterprise, others in the U.S.A. immediately pressurised the authorities to examine the situation and inquire as to the terms under which these players were induced to visit the U.S.A. The moot point was whether the contract law reached sport and government lawyers were asked to prove whether or not the men went 'under contract to play on salary'. There was also talk of violation of alien contract labour law.

The agent in question denied that he had made contracts to bring footballers from England, stating that they had come over either to visit relatives or to get work at their trades without any idea of playing football for a living.

In any event, the men did not have much chance of playing, for the League was so poorly supported that it folded up almost as soon as it began. The English players were only too glad to return home steerage instead of saloon passengers as they had been on the outward journey. They all received a period of suspension by the F.A. As for the visit of Sunderland, the club never made the trip at this time because there was no adequate guarantee forthcoming.

The North American Soccer League was started in 1968 after two competitions had been in opposition the previous year. One was the officially sanctioned United Soccer Association and the other the National Professional Soccer League.

Where two teams had existed in one city the problem was solved by moving one team to another venue. The USA League imported nine whole teams on a temporary basis mostly from England and they played under other names,

The New York Cosmos duo of Giorgio Chinaglia and Pele which was part of the reason for the game's take-off in the USA.

while the NPSL began their competition with ten new clubs.

Between 1968 and 1975 the NASL enjoyed a mushroom existence, the number of competitors switching from 17, 5, 6, 8, 8, 9, 15 and then 20 in 1975; 44 different teams were involved in the period, although several switched franchise to other cities.

Only St. Louis Stars remained in constant membership, while though Dallas Tornado were in the USA in 1967 they remained in the NASL.

Progress was slow and in an effort to make the game more appealing as a spectator sport in a country unused to it, six points were awarded for a win, one bonus point for each goal scored to a maximum of three per team and drawn matches were ruled out; a 'shoot-out' sudden death penalty shot, rather like that used in ice hockey when one player takes on the goalminder, was used to determine the winner.

If one player was responsible for popularising the game it was Pele, signed by New York Cosmos in 1975. Crowds flocked to the matches

in which Pele was appearing and in 1976 an exhibition match between Seattle Sounders and New York Cosmos attracted a record crowd of 58,128.

Aided by the signing of Franz Beckenbauer (West Germany), Giorgio Chinaglia (Italy) and Carlos Alberto (Brazil), Cosmos who became just that when moving to the Giants Stadium in East Rutherford, New Jersey, broke further attendance records in 1977 when they won the League.

In the regular schedule of matches visits from Tampa Bay Rowdies and Rochester Lancers produced respective crowds of 57,828 and 73,669. Cosmos average 34,142 for home games and 25,369 away.

In the play-offs Tampa Bay were watched by 62,394 and Los Angeles by 57,191. But on 14 August these figures were eclipsed when 77,691 attended the match with Fort Lauderdale Strikers. They were rewarded by seeing Cosmos win 8–3, though Pele was not among the scorers.

GOALS AND GOALSCORERS

MAJOR RECORDS

Highest scores – Teams
First-class match
Arbroath 36 Bon Accord 0, Scottish Cup first round, 5 September 1885
International
England 13 Northern Ireland 0, 18 February 1882
F.A. Cup
Preston North End 26 Hyde United 0, first round, 15 October 1887
Football League
Newcastle United 13 Newport County 0, Division Two, 5 October 1946
Stockport County 13 Halifax Town 0, Division Three (Northern Section), 6 January 1934
Scottish League
Celtic 11 Dundee 0, Division One, 26 October 1895
East Fife 13 Edinburgh City 2, Division Two, 11 December 1937

Aggregate
Tranmere Rovers 13 Oldham Athletic 4, Division Three (Northern Section), 26 December 1935

Most goals in a season
Football League
134 goals by Peterborough United, Division Four, 1960–61 in 46 matches
Scottish League
142 goals by Raith Rovers, Division Two, 1937–38 in 34 matches

Most goals – Individual
Match
13 goals by John Petrie for Arbroath v. Bon Accord, Scottish Cup first round, 5 September 1885
Career
1,329 goals by Artur Friedenreich in Brazilian football between 1910–1930

Individuals				
Seven players have scored more than 350 goals in Football League and Scottish League games:				
Name	Clubs	Years	Goals	Games
Arthur Rowley	West Bromwich Albion, Leicester City, Shrewsbury Town	1946–65	434	619
Jimmy McGrory	Celtic, Clydebank	1922–38	410	408
Hughie Gallacher	Airdrieonians, Newcastle United, Chelsea, Derby County, Notts County, Grimsby Town, Gateshead	1921–39	387	541
Dixie Dean	Tranmere Rovers, Everton, Notts County	1923–39	379	437

Name	Clubs	Years	Goals	Games
Hugh Ferguson	Motherwell, Cardiff City, Dundee	1916–30	361	422
Jimmy Greaves	Chelsea, Tottenham Hotspur, West Ham United	1957–71	357	516
Steve Bloomer	Derby County (two spells), Middlesbrough	1892–1914	352	600

McGrory, who was the only one of these seven players to actually score more goals than the number of matches in which he participated, reached a total of 550 goals in all first-class matches: Scottish League 410, Scottish Cup 77, Glasgow Cup 33, Glasgow Charity Cup 18, Representative matches 12.

At the start of the 1971–72 season, when McGrory was Celtic's public relations officer, he was honoured on the 50th anniversary of joining the club when he opened the new cantilever stand at Celtic Park.

Right: Dixie Dean (right) scores for Everton against Arsenal. Below: Jimmy McGrory of Celtic. Below right: Arthur Rowley scorer of 434 League goals.

Jimmy Greaves scored more Division One goals than any other player in Football League history and six times finished as the leading scorer in the division: 1958–59 Chelsea 33 goals; 1960–61 Chelsea 41; 1962–63 Tottenham Hotspur 37; 1963–64 Tottenham Hotspur 35; 1964–65 Tottenham Hotspur 29; 1968–69 Tottenham Hotspur 27. He was the youngest player to complete a century of Football League goals at the age of 20 years and 261 days when he achieved this feat on 19 November 1960 for Chelsea against Manchester City. His 200th League goal was achieved while he was with Tottenham Hotspur in December 1963 when he was 23 years 290 days old.

Dixie Dean scored 37 hat-tricks during his Football League career of 16 seasons. He also headed more goals than any other player in Division One. Yet while with Tranmere Rovers in March 1925 he had suffered a fracture of the skull in a motor cycle accident. William Ralph Dean was given the nickname of Dixie at Tranmere by supporters because of his curly black hair. But he never really liked it and prefers close friends to call him Bill.

Dixie Dean registered the highest total in England, having scored 82 goals in 1927–28: Division One 60, F.A. Cup 3, Inter-League 6, International trials 8, Internationals 5. In all matches that season his total was 100.

Dean achieved his 200th League goal after 199 matches; his 300th in 310 games and had scored 362 goals after 400 League games. In 502 matches including League, Cup, International, representative and charity games he scored 473 goals. His total for England was 18 goals in 16 matches.

Hugh Ferguson, a Scotsman, scored the goal for Cardiff City which took the F.A. Cup out of England into Wales for the first and only time in 1927.

Steve Bloomer, who scored a pre-war record for England of 28 goals in 24 international matches, included in his record one unofficial international against Germany in 1901. Upon retiring in 1914 he went to coach in Germany and was interned there for the period of World War One.

The highest number of goals scored in one season of first-class football in the British Isles is 96. This total was achieved by Fred Roberts, the Glentoran centre-forward, during the 1930–31 season: Irish League 55, Irish Cup 4, City Cup 28, Antrim Shield 7, Belfast Charity Cup 2.

Joe Bambrick had previously scored 94 goals for Linfield at centre-forward in 1929–30: Irish League 50, Irish Cup 7, City Cup 10, Antrim Shield 5, Belfast Charity Cup 9, Inter-League 5, Gold Cup 1, Conder Cup 1, Internationals 6.

In Scotland the record for goalscoring in one season is held by Jimmy Smith who scored 84 goals in 1927–28 for Ayr United: Scottish League Division Two 66, Scottish Cup 2, Ayr Charity Cup 1, other matches 15.

Jimmy McGrory scored 410 League goals in 408 appearances between 20 January 1923 and 16 October 1937 chiefly for Celtic but also for Clydebank with whom he spent the 1923–24 season on loan which accounted for 30 games and 13 of these goals. Including goals in international matches and cup-ties, his total was 550.

Though he scored half this figure with his head, in a match against Dunfermline Athletic on 14 January 1928 all eight of his goals came from his feet. Yet he made only seven appearances for Scotland.

Evelyn Morrison holds the individual scoring record of two different Scottish League clubs. He had established himself as the highest scorer for Stenhousemuir during the 1927–28 season. He had scored 29 League goals before he was transferred to Falkirk in January 1928. In the second half of the season he managed another 19 goals for Falkirk and in 1928–29 he reached 43 League goals to set up a record for his new club. In 1928 Stenhousemuir had lost their club's records in a fire which destroyed the stand.

The highest individual achievement by one player in Great Britain was made by outside right John Petrie when he scored 13 of the 36 goals scored by Arbroath v. Bon Accord in the Scottish Cup, 5 September 1885.

Ten goals have been scored by a single player on two occasions. Gerry Baker scored 10 goals for St. Mirren v. Glasgow University in a Scottish Cup first round match on 30 January 1960. St Mirren won 15–0. Baker was born in New York and played for Chelsea, Motherwell, St. Mirren, Manchester City, Hibernian and Ipswich Town.

Arthur Rowley was handicapped because when he entered first-class football wartime regional matches were still being played, and after making senior appearances for Manchester United while still an amateur he turned professional with West Bromwich Albion in 1944.

He overtook McGrory's record by scoring his 411th League goal for Shrewsbury Town against Millwall on 26 September 1962.

Steve Bloomer was one of the most prolific goalscorers of all time. An inside-right, he played in the Football League for Derby County and Middlesbrough from 1892 to 1914 scoring 352 goals in 600 League appearances. Those figures should be considered in the light of the fact that this slightly built player from Cradley Heath did his goalscoring under the old offside law when an attacker needed three opponents between himself and the goal to keep onside. It was because of this that Bloomer scored nearly all of his goals either by direct shots or by dribbling through the opposition, for he was seldom able to move in close enough to head any goals.

Bloomer devoted himself to scoring goals, and indeed, his critics said that he concentrated so much on this aspect of his play that he did very little else; to use a modern term, his 'work-rate' was not all that it might have been. But goalscoring remains the most important facet of the game and Bloomer concentrated on developing his shooting power through constant practice. He had what was often described as the knack of instant shooting. He could, of course, hit the ball equally well with either foot and the majority of his shots were barely above ground level. Closest resemblance to Bloomer in more recent times has probably been Jimmy Greaves.

Unlike many outstanding Football League players who seldom produce their best form in internationals, Bloomer was nearly always prominent when playing for England. As clear proof he scored 28 goals in 28 internationals, figures which provide him with one of the best averages among all-time England goalscorers.

Unfortunately, in the 19th century, newspaper reporters did not always consider it necessary to name the actual goalscorers in their account of matches, and when they did there were often contradictions between one reporter and another. This makes it difficult to be really certain just how many goals Steve Bloomer actually scored in some of his games. There is, for instance, confusion about England's scorers when they beat Wales 9–1 at Cardiff on 16 March 1896. Some reports credit Steve Bloomer with 5, G. O. Smith 2, and one each by John Goodall and Billy Bassett, while others give the scorers as Bloomer 4, Smith 3, and Bassett 2. But if one accepts the statement of J. A. H. Catton of the *Athletic News,* who probably reported on more England internationals than anyone else at this period and was one of the most respected football reporters of his day, then Steve Bloomer really did score five goals on that occasion, a figure which has been equalled but never beaten by an England international.

While on the subject of goalscoring and the contradictions one finds in various 19th-century reports, even the result of at least one international game has been in dispute. On 20 March 1899 England beat Wales 4–0 at Bedminster, Bristol, or was it 4–1? 'Association Football' by N. L. Jackson, published later the same year, gives the result as 4–0 and so did the *Sporting Chronicle* and *Athletic News* annuals. But when *Gamages* first published their annual in 1909 the result was given as 4–1, and amazingly enough the *Athletic News* annuals changed from 4–0 to 4–1 in their editions published during World War I. If Wales did score a goal in that game then nobody has yet discovered the identity of the scorer.

Joe Payne scored 10 goals for Luton Town v. Bristol Rovers in a Division Three (Southern Section) match on 13 April 1936. Luton won 12–0.

This unique individual goalscoring feat in Football League history was performed at Kenilworth Road, Luton, on a cold rainy Easter Monday which later produced sleet and the man who made his name that day was a red-haired collier from the Chesterfield area.

Until that day Payne had been nothing more than an average wing-half or full-back with Luton Town, but because of the absence through injury of both the club's regular centre-forwards it was decided to give him a run in that position against Bristol Rovers.

Having previously made only three League appearances, Payne was obviously intent on making the most of this unexpected opportunity

Ted Drake (right) who once scored seven goals for
Arsenal against Aston Villa.

to show his prowess in attack but even he could
not have anticipated the afternoon's events.

He completed a hat-trick in the first half, and
after the interval Jack Ellis in the Bristol Rovers
goal must have wished that he had been elsewhere that day, for with George Stephenson
creating most of the openings Payne more than
doubled his score with seven other goals,
including three in eight minutes.

Oddly enough it was first thought that his
second-half tally was only six but after the game
the referee confirmed that when Martin rushed
in to bundle both goalkeeper and ball into the
back of the net, following up a Joe Payne header
for Luton's seventh goal, the ball had already
crossed the line and the goal belonged to Payne.
Goal timings: 23 mins., 40, 43, 49, 55, 57, 65, 76,
84 and 86.

Payne started his career with Bolsover
Colliery, then graduated to Biggleswade Town,
Luton, Chelsea, West Ham United and Millwall
where he retired in 1947 through injury. In 1942
he twice broke his ankle. He made a brief come-
back with Worcester City in 1952. He made one
appearance for England.

Nine goals have been registered on five occasions. The first was by Jimmy Simpson for
Partick Thistle v. Royal Albert in a Scottish Cup
first round match on 17 January 1931. Partick
won 16–0.

Jimmy Smith scored nine goals for Rangers v.
Blairgowrie in a Scottish Cup first round match
on 20 January 1934. Rangers won 14–2. In the
1933–34 season he was leading scorer in the
Scottish Division One with 41 goals.

'Bunny' Bell scored nine goals for Tranmere Rovers v. Oldham Athletic on 26 December 1935. Tranmere won 13–4. Victory was no surprise for Tranmere who were top of Division Three (Northern Section) at the time, having lost only one game so far that season, but obviously the manner of the Boxing Day victory even exceeded their expectations.

Bell was only a part-time professional at this stage of his career, being a shipping clerk in Liverpool and training in the evenings. He regarded football as a hobby.

On this memorable occasion he scored five goals in the first half and four after the interval. In that second half he also missed a penalty, and but for this he would still be in the record books today as top scorer in a Football League game, but this record was taken by Joe Payne only four months after Bell's nine-goal effort.

Joe Baker scored nine goals for Hibernian v. Peebles Rovers in a Scottish Cup second round match on 11 February 1961. Hibernian won 15–1. Baker, the younger brother of Gerry Baker, was born in Liverpool and was originally employed by a Wishaw firm making railway wagons. He played for Coltness United, Armadale Thistle, Hibernian, Torino (Italy), Arsenal, Nottingham Forest, Sunderland, Hibernian (again) and Raith Rovers. He played eight times for England. He became the first professional to appear for England while with a club outside the Football League. In 1959–60 he scored a club record 42 Scottish League goals for Hibernian. That season at Airdrie on 24 October 1959, Hibs won 11–1, gaining a 3–0 lead at half-time and then completely over-running the home side in the second half. Baker scored three times.

Ted MacDougall scored nine goals for Bournemouth v. Margate in an F.A. Cup first round match on 20 November 1971, a record score in the competition proper. Bournemouth won 11–0. MacDougall was the leading scorer in Division Four during 1970–71 season with 42 goals and the following season finished top in Division Three with 35 goals. In 1975–76 he was the leading scorer in Division One for Norwich City with 23 goals. In 1976–77 season he reached his 200 League goal in a career spent with Liverpool, York City (with whom he made his League debut), Bournemouth, Manchester United,

West Ham United, Norwich City and Southampton. He played seven times for Scotland.

In Division One the highest individual score is seven goals, achieved by two players, Jimmy Ross and Ted Drake. Ross scored all seven goals for Preston North End v. Stoke on 6 October 1888. Preston, playing at home, won 7–0. Ross, inside-right, played for St. Bernards, Preston, Liverpool, Burnley and Manchester City.

Drake scored all seven goals for Arsenal on Aston Villa's ground at Villa Park on 14 December 1935. Arsenal won 7–1. He was a tough, bustling centre-forward and it is doubtful whether any player took more hard knocks during a first-class career. Drake would risk almost anything to score goals and he often paid the penalty for his boldness with leg injuries, but he was resilient and was seldom kept out of the side. Indeed, his outstanding performance took place on a day when his left knee was already bandaged.

Arsenal were at Villa Park where the struggling home club had been in the news after spending freely in the transfer market in an effort to avoid relegation to Division Two. Most of the home crowd had come to see one of their latest signings, Scottish international wing-half Alex Massie, but it soon became clear that it was Drake who was to command everyone's attention.

He began the game by taking a nasty tumble onto the track which surrounded the pitch as he chased the ball out of play in one of his typically determined runs. But in 15 minutes he had put Arsenal ahead and had completed his hat-trick by the interval. His efforts did not end there. In the second half he went on to score another hat-trick in the space of 12 minutes, and the remarkable feature about this goalscoring spree was that he had scored six times with six consecutive shots. His seventh attempt then rebounded from the bar before he was able to round off an astonishing afternoon's performance by hitting a seventh goal with his eighth shot in the last minute of the game.

Jack Palethorpe scored Villa's consolation goal and after the game Drake was presented with the ball which was autographed by both teams.

Drake scored well over 200 goals before a spinal injury finally put paid to his illustrious career in a war-time game at Reading during 1944.

He had started with Southampton Schools and then played for Winchester City, Southampton and Arsenal. Later he had managerial connections with Hendon, Reading, Chelsea and briefly with Barcelona (as assistant manager). He played five matches for England.

One of the most outstanding individual goal-scoring performances of the post-war era occurred in a Scottish League Division One game at Falkirk on 17 March 1962. Top-of-the-League club Rangers were the visitors that day and surprisingly enough they did some experimenting with their team, switching Jimmy Millar from centre-forward to wing-half in place of Harold Davis who moved to centre-half.

Outside-right Willie Henderson moved over to the opposite wing from where Davie Wilson switched to centre-forward. Falkirk were thoroughly beaten 7–1 and Wilson hit six of the goals, five of them in the second half. Rangers retained the same experimental line-up the following Saturday at home to Dundee but were beaten 1–0. After that Wilson returned to his normal place on the left-wing.

Since the Football League's 1888 formation, only two players have achieved hat-tricks for England in full international matches on their own club's ground. Ted Drake (Arsenal) did so against Hungary at Highbury on 3 December 1936, and Jack Rowley (Manchester United) against Ireland on 16 November 1949 at Maine Road, where United, like City, played all their home matches at that time because their own Old Trafford ground was unfit because of wartime bomb damage.

Jim Cookson (West Bromwich Albion) in September 1927 completed the quickest-ever century of Football League goals – in his 89th match. David Halliday (Sunderland) in March 1928 completed the fastest in Division One – in his 101st game. Brian Clough (Sunderland) in September 1961 completed the quickest Football League 200 – in his 219th match.

Brian Clough who completed the quickest 200 League goals.

Leading International Goalscorers (all time)		
England	Bobby Charlton	49
Northern Ireland	Billy Gillespie	13
Scotland	Denis Law	30
Wales	Trevor Ford	23
Republic of Ireland	Don Givens	17
Olympic Games	Sophus Nielsen (Denmark)	13 in 1908 and 1912
	Antal Dunai (Hungary)	13 in 1968 and 1972
	Ferenc Bene (Hungary)	12 in 1964
Copa Libertadores	Daniel Onega (River Plate)	18 in 1966

Before Pele scored his century of goals in 1969 two other players were credited with similar milestones. The first was Artur Friedenreich, a Brazilian who was said to have scored 1,329 goals between 1910 and 1930. He was in the first Brazilian international team against Exeter City in 1914 during which he lost two teeth in a tackle.

Franz 'Bimbo' Binder, an Austrian, scored 1,006 goals in 756 matches between 1930 and 1950. He was capped by his native country and also Germany when Austria was annexed by the Nazi regime.

The record individual score for a single season in the F.A. Cup competition proper is 15 goals achieved by Alex Brown of Tottenham Hotspur when they won the trophy in 1900–01.

A Scot from Glenbuck, Brown was obviously a fine opportunist and his scoring ability in the Cup ties of 1900–01 earned him the name of 'Alexander the Great'. He scored in every round and including replays only failed to register once in Tottenham's run of eight Cup ties – first round: Preston North End 1–1 (Brown), replay 4–2 (Cameron, Brown 3); second round: beat Bury 2–1 (Brown 2); third round: Reading 1–1 (Kirwan), replay 3–0 (Brown 2, Copeland); semi-final: West Bromwich Albion 4–0 (Brown 4); final: Sheffield United 2–2 (Brown 2), replay 3–1 (Cameron, Smith, Brown).

Brown's most remarkable display was in scoring all four goals against West Bromwich at Villa Park, which was almost like beating the Midland club on their home ground. All four of the goals were scored in the second half. He achieved the first with a neat header from a perfectly placed centre by outside-left John Kirwan; the second from a corner-kick; the third with a mighty 30-yard drive, and the fourth from an accurate centre by John Cameron following a neat passing movement.

Brown played twice for Scotland, against England. The first time in 1902 was on the occasion of the Ibrox disaster when he scored his side's goal in a 1–1 draw, and the second was two years later after he had moved to Middlesbrough. But on this occasion he failed to score and Scotland were beaten 1–0.

Goals in Division Two seem more difficult to achieve than in any of the other three grades. No player in Division Two has led the Football League scoring list since Liverpool's Roger Hunt did so with 41 goals in the 1961–62 season and no player in Division Two has reached the 30 mark in a season since Martin Chivers did so for Southampton in 1965–66.

TEAMS

In the 1925–26 season Manchester City scored a total of 31 goals in the F.A. Cup: in the third round they defeated Corinthians 4–0 (after a 3–3 draw); fourth round Huddersfield Town 4–0; fifth round Crystal Palace 11–4; sixth round Clapton Orient 6–1; semi-finals Manchester United 3–0; final lost 1–0 to Bolton Wanderers.

City then had goalscorers of the calibre of 'Boy' Browell, Frank Roberts and Tommy Johnson, but in contrast to their Cup record that season City were relegated from Division One, for although they had scored 89 League goals they conceded 100. This was the first season under the new offside law and goals were plentiful. Thus 120 goals in League and Cup games failed to bring success.

At the end of the 1936–37 season Manchester City were Division One champions and Manchester United were relegated.

In 1937–38 Manchester City were concerned in the only case in Football League history of a relegated team having scored more goals than any other in the division and also returned a credit goal average. They descended to Division Two with a goal record of 80–77, three more than champions Arsenal scored. That same season Manchester United were promoted.

Blackpool created the unique record of scoring more away than home goals in two successive seasons when they hit 18 (home) and 23 (away) in Division One in 1966–67 and 33 (home) and 38 (away) in Division Two in 1967–68.

Saturday 7 October 1967 was the end of a week in which Chelsea manager Tommy Docherty resigned after being given a month's suspension by the F.A. It was the day in which the club figured in the record books after being on the receiving end of a 7–0 defeat by Leeds United. The goals were scored by Albert Johanneson, Jimmy Greenhoff, Jackie Charlton, Peter Lorimer, Eddie Gray, Billy Bremner and an 'own goal' by Marvin Hinton. It was the first time in League history that as many as seven different players had scored for one team in a single game.

QUICK SCORING

It is often claimed that the fastest goal on record in British first-class football was that scored by Bradford Park Avenue centre-forward, Jim Fryatt, in a Division Four game against Tranmere Rovers on 25 April 1964. According to the referee, Mr R. J. Simons of Carlisle, who always timed goals, this remarkable effort was scored only four seconds after the kick-off.

There is no doubt that the goal was scored quickly but the facts seem to indicate that the referee must have been mistaken in his precise timing. At the kick-off Fryatt tapped the ball to his nearest colleague and immediately made straight for the edge of the Tranmere Rovers penalty area 37 yards away, arriving there in time to receive a pass from another team-mate and shoot past John Heath in the Rovers goal.

Bradford manager Jimmy Scoular said that they had been trying this move for some time but

this was the first occasion it had succeeded. However, even he found it hard to believe that the goal had taken only four seconds. While Fryatt was making his 37-yard dash the ball went in turn to four of his colleagues before he received that final pass.

It is generally accepted that the fastest goals have been scored in six seconds. Albert Mundy achieved it for Aldershot against Hartlepool United in Division Four on 25 October 1958 and Keith Smith of Crystal Palace equalled the feat against Derby County on 12 December 1964.

In between Barrie Jones also made it in six seconds on his debut for Notts County against Torquay United on 31 March 1962.

Jimmy Fryatt (right) points to his wristwatch clearly certain that his four seconds goal was a legitimate record in the Football League. Others differ . . .

GOAL EVENTS

It has not happened on many occasions that a player has scored a hat-trick when making his professional debut, but remarkably enough Burnley have had two players with somewhat similar names perform this feat.

On 10 October 1936 Burnley beat Tottenham Hotspur 3–1 and all three of their goals were scored by Tommy Lawton, destined to become one of England's most outstanding centre-forwards. Lawton had previously been playing in the Burnley senior side as an amateur but he signed professional forms on his 17th birthday and it was four days later that he achieved his first hat-trick in the Football League.

Burnley's other 17-year-old with a hat-trick to celebrate his first senior appearance was Ian Lawson. His initial senior game was in the F.A. Cup on 5 January 1957 when Burnley beat Chesterfield 7–0 in a third round match. Lawson actually did better than Lawton because he scored four times.

In April 1926 Burnley had conceded more goals than any team in the Football League and were in a perilous position only two points ahead of Manchester City at the foot of Division One. They

had won only three of their last dozen games and were understandably perplexed to know which eleven to select for their visit to Birmingham on 10 April.

They had already tried six different centre-forwards that season but among six late changes to the team printed in the Birmingham programme was outside-left Louis Page, switched to centre-forward for his first appearance in that position with the Lancashire club.

This experiment paid off, for Burnley made headline news with an astonishing 7–1 victory and Page the experimental centre-forward scored six of his side's goals, including three in succession in each half. Indeed, in the second half he achieved three in four minutes. John Bruton scored one for Burnley in between Page's two hat-tricks while Joe Bradford did not register Birmingham's consolation goal until four minutes from time.

Considering that Page excelled as an opportunist and had previously scored 16 goals for Burnley that season as a winger, it is perhaps rather surprising that he had not already been tried at centre-forward, but those were the days when the centre-forward berth was considered to be one of the most highly specialised positions on the field.

Page's six-goal centre-forward debut was all the more remarkable because it made him the first player in that particular season to score as many as six in a League game, despite the fact that it was late in the season and it was the highest scoring campaign in Football League history up to that time.

Remember it was the first season under the new offside rule whereby an attacker needed only two instead of three opponents between himself and the goal-line to keep him onside.

Page made over 400 League appearances with Stoke, Northampton Town, Burnley, Manchester United and Port Vale during his career from 1919 to 1933 and twice played for England in the 1926–27 season, though both times at outside-left; England being especially well served at centre-forward in those days by the inimitable Dixie Dean.

Incidentally, Burnley took seven points from their last five games in 1925–26 and escaped relegation.

James McClelland scored all five goals by which Middlesbrough defeated Leeds United 5–1 in an F.A. Cup third round tie on 9 January 1926. On the same day his son Charles, who was to become a Blackburn Rovers centre-forward, was born.

On 27 October 1962, winger John McClelland hit an away hat-trick in his home city. He scored all the goals in a 3–0 win by Queen's Park Rangers in a Division Three match at Bradford, where he had been born.

Stanley Mortensen, an outstanding England centre- or inside-forward of the early post-war era, scored for Blackpool in every F.A. Cup round in which the club appeared over a period of more than four seasons. During this time from 1945–46 to 1949–50 Blackpool played in 12 rounds and Mortensen failed to score only in a couple of replays. The actual run of consecutive Cup games in which he scored was nine.

The best post-war scoring feat by any player when appearing in a Football League match against his former club was achieved when Jimmy McIntosh hit five goals for Blackpool on 5 May 1948, in Division One match away against Preston North End.

Only one player since the war has achieved two Football League hat-tricks on successive days. Cliff Holton managed this feat for Watford against Chester and Gateshead respectively on 15 and 16 April 1960, in Division Four matches.

In less than three months from the start of the 1950–51 season Eddie Brown had played in three Division Two games against Bury and scored in all of them – two for Preston North End and one for Southampton.

After Jack Howarth had scored for Aldershot at York on 29 September 1973, the City, with Scottish goalkeeper Graeme Crawford in action, did not concede a solitary goal in any of their next 11 Division Three matches. The goal that ended the spell was scored on 22 December by Howarth, for Aldershot in the return fixture between the teams.

In a Division Three match on 2 September 1972, Charlton Athletic's Vincent O'Kane was penalised for a handling offence and York City right-back John Mackin's penalty-kick was saved. A minute later Mackin was penalised for handling and O'Kane converted the penalty.

Playing for Newcastle United against Doncaster Rovers in a Football League Cup-tie on 8 October 1973, Malcolm Macdonald scored three times. Against Queen's Park Rangers in a Division One Match on the same date a year later, he scored three times.

Playing for Rotherham United against Bournemouth on 10 October 1972, Carl Gilbert scored both his team's goals in a 7–2 home defeat and then had three scored against him after he had become the emergency substitute goalkeeper.

Brian Flynn who joined Leeds United in the 1977–78 season scored in a full international (for Wales v. Scotland at Cardiff on 17 May 1975) and in a Football League Cup-tie (two for Burnley at Hereford on 9 September 1975) before he achieved his first goal in the Football League v. Everton on 31 January 1976.

Playing for Rotherham United in the Division Three (Northern Section) match, Walter Ardron scored four goals against Carlisle United on 13 September 1947 and four against Hartlepool United on 13 September 1948.

The first four goals scored by Alf Wood out of five for Shrewsbury Town in their 7–1 win over Blackburn Rovers in Division Three on 2 October 1971 came from first-half headers. The fifth was a second-half penalty.

The first full-back to score a hat-trick in a Division One game was Stan Lynn whose three included two penalties for Aston Villa against Sunderland on 11 January 1958. He was the most prolific scoring full-back in League history, for in a first-class career extending from 1946 to 1966, during which he served Accrington Stanley, Aston Villa and Birmingham City, Lynn scored 64 goals.

However, he was not the first full-back in League history to reach the 50-goal mark. Jack Brownsword (Hull City and Scunthorpe United) just beat him by 10 days when he scored his 50th League goal for Scunthorpe United v. Derby County on 20 March 1964. That was Brownsword's last League goal before retiring to become Scunthorpe's trainer. Lynn was the only player who appeared in League matches in 20 consecutive peacetime seasons following the last war.

Brentford's four principal goalscorers in Division Three matches in the 1963–64 season were Johnny Dick, a Scot, Dai Ward (Welshman), Billy McAdams (from Northern Ireland) and Mike Block (English).

Queen's Park Rangers' forward line in a Division Three match against Port Vale in April 1965 was a five countries affair – George Wood (a Scot), Billy McAdams (Irish), Stewart Leary (South African), Brian Bedford (Welsh) and John Collins (English).

In the 1937–38 season Arsenal became the only club which ever had in its simultaneous service five Englishmen all credited with career centuries of Football League goals. They were Joe Hulme, Ray Bowden, Ted Drake, George Hunt and Cliff Bastin, all of whom were England internationals.

David Herd was one of the most prolific goalscorers in post-war football (228 goals for Stockport County, Arsenal, Manchester United and Stoke City) but one of his scoring feats is probably unique in the annals of the game. On 26 November 1966 he scored a goal against three different goalkeepers in a single match. This was at Old Trafford when Manchester United beat Sunderland 5–0. Herd scored four of those goals, the first three being against three different goal-keepers – Jim Montgomery, Charlie Hurley and John Parke, in that order.

All six goals in a Division One match between Chelsea (Ron Tindall three and Peter Brabrook) and Newcastle United (Len White two) on 5 November 1960 were headed in for a Football League record.

Peter Osgood and Stan Bowles, though not considered the most prolific domestic goal-scorers, were nonetheless the only two operating in the 1977–78 season who had ever hit a hat-trick in each of two legs in a European Cup-tie. Osgood, later at Southampton, did it for Chelsea in the Cup-Winners Cup against Jeunesse Haut-charage (Luxembourg) in the 1971–72 season, and Bowles for Queen's Park Rangers in the UEFA Cup against Brann Bergen (Norway) in 1976–77.

Cyril Done was the only player in history who scored more than twice as many Football League goals as anyone else for each of two clubs in the same season. In that of 1954–55 he scored 15 for Tranmere Rovers and 13 for Port Vale (to whom he was transferred on 14 December); six being the season's second best individual contribution for each club.

Birmingham-born Jimmy Brown was responsible for an outsize scoring oddity in the sense that when he had hit all his first three goals of a season he had spread the feat over three competitions! He did that with Preston North End during 1976–77 in the Football League Cup, the F.A. Cup, and then in Division Four in that order.

In the 1965–66 season John Byrom's goals in the 26 Division Two matches in which he appeared with Blackburn Rovers totalled three, but in six F.A. Cup games he managed to score seven times.

Peter Kitchen (Orient) was the only player operating in the 1977–78 season who scored within two minutes of the kick-off in each of the first two Football League matches of his career – with Doncaster Rovers against Shrewsbury Town on 27 November 1970 and Swansea on 5 December.

Peter Kitchen of Orient – a quick scorer for Doncaster Rovers on two notable occasions.

Ronnie Allen, who has managed all three 'w' clubs in his native Midlands – Walsall, Wolverhampton Wanderers and West Bromwich Albion, was the only player to have scored Football League goals in all the first 18 post-war seasons.

Ronnie Allen.

One of the least-mentioned but most remarkable scoring records belongs to Tommy Wright, a full-back of the post-war era who was capped at all levels for England and who made over 300 Football League appearances for Everton between 1964 and 1974 before injury forced his retirement. Not only did this player score two of the quickest 'own goals' in League history, but he had the misfortune to do so on consecutive Saturdays – one in 33 seconds v. Liverpool, 4 March 1972, and the other in 32 seconds v. Manchester City on 11 March.

Only two players still on active service in 1977–78 claim hat-tricks in the Football League, F.A. Cup, Football League Cup, and one or other of the European cups: Leeds United's Peter Lorimer and Tony Brown of West Bromwich Albion.

Within a period of 18 months in 1964 and 1966 Ted Phillips scored goals in all four Football League divisions: with Ipswich Town (First), Orient (Second), Luton Town (Third) and Colchester United (Fourth). No other player ever did that so quickly.

Outside-left George Bowater scored one of the goals by which York City beat Burton Town away in the F.A. Cup first round in November 1934. Later, transferred from one club to the other, he scored one of the goals by which Burton beat York away in the Cup's first round in November 1935.

John Galley ranks as the only player in the game's history who achieved hat-tricks when making his Football League debut with two clubs – and in an away match in each instance. He did it with Rotherham United at Coventry in December 1964 and for Bristol City at Hudders-field in December 1967. He also scored at Fulham on his December debuts for Wolver-hampton Wanderers in 1962 and for Nottingham Forest in 1972.

No contemporary player ever matched a feat once achieved by Millwall and former Manchester City, Shrewsbury Town, Hull City and Middlesbrough striker Alf Wood. On 2 October 1961 he scored five goals in Shrewsbury's 7–1 win against Blackburn Rovers. All the first four came

from first-half headers and the last from the penalty spot.

It has happened only twice in Football League history that a player has achieved a hat-trick on his wedding day. Bill Poyntz did it for Leeds United against Leicester City on 20 February 1922, and Bill Holmes for Southport against Carlisle United on 30 October 1954. Brian Clough scored four times for Middlesbrough on his 24th birthday against Swansea Town on 21 March 1959.

In the 1969–70 season Steve Earle, later with Leicester City, scored all his first 11 goals for Fulham in away matches; in 1973–74 Halifax Town striker Mick Bullock hit 10 of his first 11 for Orient away; in 1976–77 all Mick Vinter's first 10 for Notts County were achieved away, as were 14 of Trevor Phillips' for Rotherham United.

Newcastle United's captain in the 1977–78 season, Geoff Nulty, is credited with the latest goal ever known to have been scored in a Football League match. On 27 March 1971 he hit a dramatic equaliser for Burnley in a 2–2 Division One home draw against Ipswich Town. It was timed officially as having been scored one second from the finish.

In a Highbury match on 17 December 1955, Arsenal left-back Dennis Evans, hearing a whistle, thought it sounded the end of the game, and flicked the ball casually into his own net. Hull Referee Frank Coultas awarded a goal and later said: 'The game was not over. The whistle came from the crowd.'

Playing for Tottenham Hotspur against Burnley in a home match on 5 October 1974, Mike England and John Pratt both put through their own goal during the first half. After the interval both scored for their own side.

A goal from left-back Peter Aldis for Aston Villa against Sunderland in a Division One match on 1 September 1952 was thought to have been the longest-distance headed goal ever seen in the Football League. It was scored from 35 yards.

John Goodchild made only one Division Two appearance for Sunderland in the 1960–61 season, yet it brought him an away hat-trick against Leeds United. Clinton Boulton figured in 32 League games for Torquay United in season 1976–77, and the only goals he scored were three at Doncaster in the second of them.

So-called 'open goals' are regularly missed, but one of the most freakish incidents on record occurred in the Scotland v. England international at Hampden Park on 13 April 1929. England were awarded a free-kick, apparently against the Scottish goalkeeper for 'carrying'.

There appeared to be some confusion among the players as to whether this was a direct or an indirect, the whole of the Scottish team with the exception of their goalkeeper retired to behind

the ball which was placed only six yards out from the centre of the goal.

The Scottish goalkeeper stood to one side against an upright, fearing the shot might hit him and go into the net, and, therefore, all that England had to do to score was for Bill Wainscoat (Leeds United), the kicker, to tap the ball to a colleague to drive home. But as Wainscoat side-footed the ball, a Scottish player dashed through and cleared. Obviously this player had not been 10 yards from the ball, and this incident caused a great deal of comment about the general inability or reluctance of referees to enforce this rule. Scotland won this game 1–0 with a goal scored from a corner-kick by Alex Cheyne in the last minute.

INTERNATIONAL GOALSCORING

Gerd Muller (West Germany) 62 international appearances. Scored 68 goals in following matches:

Year	Opponents	Venue	No. of goals
1967	Albania	H	4
	France	H	1 (sub)
	Yugoslavia	H	1
1968	Austria	A	1
	Cyprus	A	1
1969	Wales	H	1
	Scotland	A	1
	Austria	H	1
	Cyprus	H	4
	Austria	A	1
	Scotland	H	1
1970	Morocco	A	1
	Bulgaria	A	3
	Peru	A	3
	England	A	1
	Italy	A	2
	Hungary	H	2
	Turkey	H	1
1971	Albania	A	1
	Turkey	A	2
	Norway	A	3
	Denmark	A	1
	Mexico	H	3
	Poland	A	2
1972	England	A	1
	USSR	H	4
	Belgium	A	2
	USSR	A	2
	Switzerland	H	4
1973	Czechoslovakia	H	2
	USSR	A	1
	Austria	H	2
	France	H	2
1974	Hungary	H	2
	Australia	H	1
	Yugoslavia	H	1
	Poland	H	1
	Holland	H	1

Muller announced his retirement from international matches only after the World Cup Final against Holland.

INTERNATIONAL GOALSCORING

Bobby Charlton (England) 106 international appearances. Scored 49 goals in following matches:

Year	Opponents	Venue	No. of goals
1958	Scotland	A	1
	Portugal	H	2
	Northern Ireland	A	2
	USSR	H	1
1959	Scotland	H	1
	Italy	H	1
	USA	A	3
	Sweden	H	1
1960	Scotland	A	1
	Northern Ireland	A	1
	Luxembourg	A	3
	Wales	H	1
1961	Mexico	H	3
	Luxembourg	H	2
	Northern Ireland	H	1
1962	Argentina	A	1
1963	Czechoslovakia	A	1
	East Germany	A	1
	Switzerland	A	3
	Wales	A	1
1964	Portugal	A	1
	USA	A	1 (sub)
1965	Scotland	H	1
	Austria	H	1
1966	Scotland	A	1
	Yugoslavia	H	1
	Mexico	H	1
	Portugal	H	2
	Wales	H	1
1967	Wales	A	1
	Northern Ireland	H	1
1968	Spain	H	1
	Sweden	H	1
	USSR	A	1
1969	Wales	H	1
1970	Northern Ireland	H	1
	Colombia	A	1

MISCELLANY

Abandoned games

The 12 December 1891 was a particularly cold day and the sleet and snow which was falling during the game between Burnley and Blackburn Rovers did not help to keep either team in a congenial mood. Play was extremely rough and as they were already 3–1 in arrears many of the Rovers players seemed reluctant to resume after the interval. Indeed, the second half was several minutes old before they were again at full strength, but then after another 10 minutes something happened which led to one of the most peculiar scenes ever witnessed in a Division One match.

A player from either side came to blows and were immediately ordered off, but on leaving the field they were followed by the whole of the Blackburn team with the single exception of goalkeeper Herbie Arthur who manfully stuck to his position.

The referee re-started the game and, not surprisingly, Burnley easily beat their solitary opponent, whereupon he quite rightly appealed for offside. When, however, the goalkeeper delayed in taking the free-kick the referee abandoned the game.

Events were not much less farcical that same freezing Saturday over at Deepdale where Preston North End were playing Notts County. This game was played to a finish in wretched conditions, but during the second half the County's trainer came on the field and took off six of his men. With their captain Jimmy Oswald already ordered off early in the game, this reduced the Notts side to only four men. However, one player soon returned and County played out the remaining time with only two forwards and three defenders. Preston won 6–0.

The Division One game between Sheffield Wednesday and Stoke on 6 April 1895 was abandoned 15 minutes from time with the score at 0–0 when someone threw mud at the referee, Mr J. Lewis of Blackburn. When the game was replayed 11 days later, Stoke won 4–2.

On 28 December 1895 at Everton the referee enraged a section of the crowd by abandoning the game against Small Heath (now Birmingham City) after 37 minutes when Everton were leading 1–0. It was raining heavily at the time and the pitch was under water. Most of the crowd dispersed without incident but a large number refused to move and were joined by 'street loafers', who had entered when the gates were thrown open. They advanced on the offices, smashing windows and the face of the clock while throwing stones at those club officials and policemen who tried to reason with them. A cry of 'fire the stands' was heard, but fortunately the police called for reinforcements and two contingents soon arrived, drew their batons and quickly cleared the ground.

One of the most remarkable Football League games ever played was a Division One clash between Sheffield Wednesday and Aston Villa in 1898–99. Part of it at least took place at Wednesday's former ground at Olive Grove on 26 November 1898. Because of bad light the game was abandoned with 10½ minutes remaining and Wednesday leading 3–1.

Instead of taking the more usual course of ordering the game to be replayed in full or even accept the score as the final result, the League insisted that the last 10½ minutes had to be played. This brief skirmish eventually took place at Olive Grove nearly four months later on 13 March 1899 when the Wednesday added a further goal and so clinched victory 4–1.

The F.A. Cup semi-final second replay between Sheffield United and Liverpool at Fallowfield, Manchester, on 27 March 1899 was abandoned at half-time because of crowd encroachment. The ground was not large enough for the 30,000 spectators who eventually pushed down wire barriers and spilled onto the pitch. Police urged them back beyond the touchlines and the match started at four o'clock.

But after half an hour's play, during which time Liverpool had opened the scoring, the crowd came on again and the players were taken off. Some form of order was restored and the game was re-started. But half-time was not reached until ten minutes to six and the referee then abandoned the match. Sheffield eventually won 1–0 at the fourth attempt three days later at Derby.

On 20 February 1904 an F.A. Cup match was abandoned and the replay ordered to take place on another ground. This was the second round tie between Tottenham Hotspur and Aston Villa at White Hart Lane. In order to accommodate as many fans as possible the Tottenham club had placed seats inside the fence around the edge of the touch-line and during the interval the occupants of these seats led an invasion of the pitch. It was found impossible to resume the game despite pleas from the referee and players. Consequently the referee had to declare the game abandoned, which so angered a section of the crowd that there were ugly scenes before the stadium was eventually cleared.

A meeting of the F.A. Council two days later blamed the Tottenham Hotspur club for the debacle, fined them £350 and ordered the tie to be replayed on 25 February at Villa Park.

So Spurs played what should have been a home tie away but it did not prevent them from winning by a solitary goal from Bristol Jack Jones.

One of the most astonishing incidents ever to take place in the Football League was seen at Middlesbrough on 3 April 1915 in a Division One game with Oldham Athletic.

To appreciate the shock of the afternoon's events it should be noted that the Latics were at this time enjoying the most successful season in the club's history and were in sight of winning the Football League Championship. This was the Easter weekend and Oldham were in third position behind Blackburn Rovers and Manchester City. Having already won 1–0 at Newcastle on Good Friday , they were confident of getting at least a point against Middlesbrough who had just been beaten 4–1 by Sunderland.

From Oldham's point of view, however, the game at Middlesbrough was a complete fiasco. The home team were in such aggressive form that they scored three goals in the first 20 minutes, and when the score was 4–1 early in the second half a number of the Oldham players began to lose their self-control, as it was reported by the *Athletic News*.

One of the Oldham full-backs that day was Billy Cook, who was also a well-known Lancashire cricketer. A penalty was awarded against him for a tackle on Jackie Carr, and when another similar incident occurred involving the same two players the referee ordered Cook to leave the field. Cook had other ideas, however, and an argument ensued between the player and the referee. Cook simply refused to leave the field and the referee gave him a minute to get off. But Cook still stood his ground. The referee declared the game abandoned and walked off accompanied by the players.

Cook was suspended for 12 months and ordered to pay the cost of a Commission of Enquiry. Although there was still 33 minutes left for play at the time of the abandonment, the League ordered the result to stand.

Oldham finished that season as runners-up in the League Championship, only one point behind Everton.

The Football League ordered a score to stand when a game between Barrow and Gillingham had to be abandoned because of bad light with 15 minutes remaining for play. It was a Division Four game on 9 October 1961 at Holker Street, Barrow, and it had started late because Gillingham missed their train and were forced to charter an aeroplane to fly up.

The score after 75 minutes was 7–0 in Barrow's favour.

The Division One match between Manchester United and Manchester City at Old Trafford on 27 April 1974 was abandoned five minutes before time when spectators invaded the pitch after City had scored the first goal. The result was allowed to stand. United lost 1–0 and were relegated after 36 years in the division. City's scorer was Denis Law, a former United player.

Accidental coincidence
In August 1966, Colchester United half-back Bobby Blackwood broke his jaw in a collision with Queen's Park Rangers striker Les Allen in a Division Three match. In the return game in December, Blackwood broke his jaw again in a collision with . . . Les Allen.

Amateur Football
The highest number of Football League appearances made by an amateur in the Football League in the period since World War Two is 89 by Mike Pinner, who played four times in goal for

Cambridge in the University match (captaining them in 1954) and established himself as England's Amateur International 'keeper, playing in nearly 50 games. He also played for the famous 'Oxbridge' amateur club Pegasus.

Pinner made his Football League debut with Aston Villa in 1954–55, and before Leyton Orient persuaded him to turn professional at the age of 28 in October 1963 he had played in the Football League for Sheffield Wednesday, Queen's Park Rangers, Manchester United, Chelsea and Swansea Town, in addition to Orient. In the 1957–58 season Sheffield Wednesday had five professional goalkeepers on their staff, but for a period they preferred Pinner to any of them in their senior side.

Arsenal's team which defeated Stoke City by an only goal at Highbury on 19 October 1946 included three amateurs – Bernard Joy, Dr Kevin O'Flanagan and an Icelander, Albert Gudmundsson.

The late Maurice Edelston was responsible for the only case in history of an amateur achieving two Football League hat-tricks in three days – for Reading against Crystal Palace and Southend in the first week of September 1946.

The record number of England amateur international appearances was established by Rod Haider, the Hendon captain and half-back, who played on 65 occasions for his country up to 1974.

The F.A. Amateur Cup was competed from 1892–93 to 1973–74. Its most successful club was Bishop Auckland who won it ten times in 1896, 1900, 1914, 1921, 1922, 1935, 1939, 1955, 1956 and 1957.

The competition ended when the F.A. withdrew official recognition of amateur footballers, but a new cup, the F.A. Challenge Vase, was immediately introduced and was open to non-Football League clubs, excluding those in the F.A. Challenge Trophy.

The Challenge Trophy was instituted in 1969–70 for non-Football League clubs and both this competition and the Vase have held their finals at the Empire Stadium, Wembley.

One of the most astonishing results in the annals of football history was the 5–0 defeat of Preston North End by the renowned amateur team the Corinthians, at Richmond Athletic Ground on Monday 18 November 1889. In order to appreciate the enormity of the Corinthians' success on that occasion it should be remembered that Preston were then the most powerful combination in the country, having recently completed the League and Cup double. Indeed, two days before their visit to Richmond they had beaten Everton 5–1 on the Liverpool club's ground and Everton were then considered to be second only to Preston.

Of course, Preston tried to make excuses for their severe beating at the hands of the university and public school men, but apart from the score they could not disguise the fact that they were throroughly outplayed on this occasion. Maybe the professionals had not treated the game too seriously, but they certainly received a good deal of adverse publicity from those who believed that they should have been able to do much better as a team of fully-trained professionals against amateurs who played only for the fun of it. Obviously Preston took the criticism to heart, for in another meeting between these two sides later the same season at Richmond the professionals won 1–0 to restore their prestige.

Corinthians were formed in the 1880s and with few exceptions only public school and university men were admitted as members. And until the 1922–23 season they did not enter competitions except for charity matches. They had been the first English soccer club to play outside Europe when they made a tour of South Africa in 1897. In 1939 they amalgamated with the Casuals.

Awards
The Football Writers Association, founded in 1947, has elected a Footballer of the Year at the end of each season since 1947–48. Stanley Matthews (1948 and 1963), Tom Finney (1954 and 1957) and Danny Blanchflower (1958 and 1961) have each won it more than once.

Matthews was also the first winner of the European Footballer of the Year award in 1956 organised annually by France Football and chosen each December by a panel of journalists from various European countries who award marks to five players of their choice in order of preference. Three players have won it more than once: Johan Cruyff (Holland) in 1971, 1973 and 1974; Franz Beckenbauer (West Germany) 1972 and 1976, and Alfredo di Stefano (Argentina, Colombia and Spain) 1957 and 1959.

Attendance records

Any match
205,000 (199,854 paid) for the Brazil v. Uruguay match in the 1950 World Cup final series on 16 July 1950 at the Maracana Stadium, Rio de Janeiro.

European Cup
136,505 for the Celtic v. Leeds United semi-final at Hampden Park, Glasgow, on 15 April 1970.

International
149,547 for the Scotland v. England international at Hampden Park, Glasgow, on 17 April 1937.

F.A. Cup final
160,000 (estimated) for the Bolton Wanderers v. West Ham United match at Wembley on 28 April 1923 (counted admissions were 126,047).

Scottish Cup final
146,433 for the Celtic v. Aberdeen final at Hampden Park, Glasgow, on 24 April 1937.

Football League
Division One: Manchester United v. Arsenal at Maine Road, 17 January 1948, 83,260.

Division Two: Aston Villa v. Coventry City at Villa Park, 30 October 1937, 68,029.

Division Three (Southern Section): Cardiff City v. Bristol City at Ninian Park, 7 April 1947, 51,621.

Division Three (Northern Section): Hull City v. Rotherham United at Boothferry Park, 25 December 1948, 49,655.

Division Three: Aston Villa v. Bournemouth at Villa Park, 12 February 1972, 48,110.

Division Four: Crystal Palace v. Millwall at Selhurst Park, 31 March 1961, 37,774.

Scottish League: Rangers v. Celtic, Ibrox Park, 2 January 1939, 118,567.

In 1949 the Football League record for aggregate attendances at one day's matches was beaten twice in successive days. The figures on 27 December of 1,226,098 exceeded the previous highest ever, and on the following day they were 1,253,572.

In the 1965–66 season Hull City's Division Three average home League attendance of 22,828 was over 9,000 more than that of Blackburn Rovers, Division One, whose average was 13,513.

Stockport County have been concerned in a novel kind of 'hat-trick'. In the 1974–75 season they had two attendances of 2,047 at Division Four home games, two of 2,780 in 1975–76, and two of 3,004 during 1976–77.

South America and Africa have similar awards organised respectively since 1971 and 1970. Elias Figueroa (Chile) won the South American title for the third year in succession in 1976.

Since 1967–68 the Golden Boots Award has gone to the top goalscorer in Europe. Dudu Georgescu (Dynamo Bucharest) established a new record in 1976–77 with 47 goals.

Bachelors

One outstanding example of a large playing staff of bachelors with a Football League club was that of Wolves in the 1937–38 season. Not one of their 40 players was a married man.

Benefits

Football League clubs may permit a Testimonial match to be arranged on behalf of any player who has completed 10 years or more in the service of a club, providing the consent of the Management Committee of the League is obtained.

Best man

When Arsenal forward George Graham was married in London on the morning of Saturday 16 September 1967, his best man was the Tottenham Hotspur inside-left Terry Venables. In the afternoon they were on opposing sides in a Division One 'derby' match at Highbury.

Birthplaces

The scenes of famous Scottish battles of long ago are recalled by the birthplaces of three contemporary Football League players. Bristol City's Don Gillies is a native of Glencoe, Sheffield United's Eddie Colquhoun of Prestonpans, and Grimsby Town's Garry Liddell of Bannockburn . . . Former Bradford City winger Arthur Thorpe was born at Lucknow.

Black players

In 1909 Walter Daniel Tull, son of a West Indian father and English mother, became the first-ever Football League coloured player with Tottenham Hotspur. The first-ever coloured director of a Football League club was Ismail Gibrail, a native of British Somalia, who was elected to Blackpool's board in December 1967. He was the managing director of a Blackpool tea and coffee firm.

More coloured players are figuring in the cosmopolitan Football League nowadays than at any previous period, but the only one who ever scored a century of goals in the competition did so between the wars. London-born Jack Leslie registered 134 goals for Plymouth Argyle between the 1921–22 abd 1934–35 seasons inclusive.

Bookends

The 1913–14 season was the only one in Football League history in which clubs in the same provincial city or town finished in the first and last positions in the same division. Notts County were Division Two champions and Forest were at the bottom.

Bookings

The all-time record for a block booking in a Football League match was set up at Old Trafford on 27 December 1971. In a match against Manchester United Cannock referee Dennis Turner booked five Coventry City players in one swoop – Chris Cattlin, Ernie Machin, Bobby Parker, Chris Chilton and Ian St John.

Broadcasting and Television

The first match broadcast on the radio was the Division One game between Arsenal and Sheffield United at Highbury on 22 January 1927. The first Football League match to be covered by television was the Division One match between Blackpool and Bolton Wanderers on 10 September 1960. The first cup-tie televised other than the final was the fifth round match between Charlton Athletic and Blackburn Rovers on 8 February 1947.

Christmas present

Harry Jackson, a centre-forward, was the only player ever transferred on successive Christmas Eves – from Manchester City to Preston North End in 1947 and to Blackburn Rovers in 1948.

Clergymen

In Division Two in the 1912–13 season Wolverhampton Wanderers provided the only case in Football League history of two clergymen playing together in the same side. The Rev. K. R. G. Hunt was one of the half-backs and the Rev. W. C. Jordan a forward.

Costly kick

When Peter Knowles (who quit Soccer in September 1969 when he left Wolverhampton Wanderers to become a full-time Jehovah's Witness) headed a goal in a match at Portsmouth in February 1967, he was so delighted that he kicked the ball over the stand and out of the ground. It was not retrieved and Knowles later received a bill, which he paid, for £7 10s from Portsmouth asking for the cost of a new one.

Close calls

One of the most remarkable recoveries ever made to escape relegation was that achieved by Lincoln City in the 1957–58 season when they were struggling at the foot of Division Two. At the beginning of January the City were firmly embedded on the bottom and remained there for most of February and March, but then with the signing of players like left-back Geoff Smith from Sheffield United and centre-forward Ron Harbertson from Darlington, there were signs of a revival, but nobody expected the astonishing transformation that took place after losing their first two home games in April, 3–1 to Stoke City and 3–1 to Barnsley.

Most of the crtitics had already written Lincoln City off as having no chance of avoiding relegation while preferring fellow strugglers Notts County to escape the drop. But Lincoln then revived to such effect that they won five games in a row, including three away from home. Even so they still had to draw their last game of the season to be able to overtake Notts County on goal average and send them down along with Doncaster Rovers. City did better than that, for they made it six in a row by defeating Cardiff City 3–1 at Sincil Bank.

Sunderland had a shaky start to the 1912–13 season in Division One. They failed to win any of their first seven games in which they collected only two points but then achieved such a transformation that they went on to win the Championship by a margin of four points ahead of Aston Villa, collecting a new record total of 54 points.

More than that, they almost completed the League and Cup 'double', for they reached the Cup Final only to lose by a single goal to the Aston Villa side that had pushed them all the way in the League. Sunderland's poor opening was the worst ever made by a Championship-winning team and it was not until nearly two-thirds of the season's fixtures had been completed that they succeeded in climbing into one of the top three League places.

Sunderland's transformation had started in October when they signed Glossop's goal-keeper, Joe Butler, for £3,000 and secured a new right-back, Charlie Gladwin from Blackpool.

Cricketing footballers
Since the 1960s Chris Balderstone (Huddersfield Town and Carlisle United), Graham Cross (Leicester City, Brighton and Hove and Preston North End) and Ted Hemsley (Sheffield United and Doncaster Rovers) have all completed at least 15 years of all-the-year-round sport activity in the Football League and first-class cricket. But none has yet matched the late Andy Ducat, who maintained a career at both games with Villa and Arsenal and Surrey, for 18 years from 1906 to 1924.

Both Willie Watson and Ken Taylor were born in Yorkshire's West Riding, both entered Huddersfield Town's senior side and Yorkshire's cricket team when in their teens, both opened the England innings to Test cricket, both were with Bradford's rival Soccer clubs at the same time, and both have since settled permanently in South Africa after taking on coaching appointments there.

No other county cricket teams ever contained, in the same season, so many players who were or had been Football League professionals as that of Gloucestershire in 1966. There were seven such in their side: Arthur Milton, Barrie Meyer, Ronnie Nicholls, Dave Smith, Syd Russell, Harold Jarman and Bob Etheridge.

Current Aston Villa director and ex-England winger Eric Houghton made his debut in first-class cricket with Warwickshire against India at Edgbaston – in August 1946 – in the same month in which he began his 20th season as a Villa professional footballer.

England teams in Test cricket have included players born all over the globe but in Soccer only Bill Perry (ex-Blackpool) and current Ipswich Town midfield performer Colin Viljoen, both born in South Africa, have been the only post-war full English internationals from abroad, while Scotland, Wales and Eire often use non-nationals.

Chris Balderstone became the only man to play in first class cricket and soccer on the same day. He batted for Leicester against Derbyshire at Chesterfield on 15 September 1975 and an hour later, after a hectic car journey, he turned out for Doncaster Rovers in a Division Four match at home to Brentford.

Debuts
One of the unhappiest debuts ever made in the Football League was that of Stan Milton when he began his career with Halifax Town in the 1933–34 season. The club's first-team goal-keeper, Walter Shirlaw, was unable to take his place in the side which went to Stockport on 6 January (the only game he missed that season) and so Milton the reserve team goalkeeper was called upon to deputise. Unfortunately for Milton his side met a Stockport combination in their most devastating form.

The County had already established themselves as one of the most prolific goalscoring sides in the League that season but against Halifax they really excelled themselves by scoring 13 goals without reply.

Though such an experience was enough to disillusion any young goalkeeper, Milton remained with Halifax for three years and then joined York City and was still with them as reserve team goalkeeper at the outbreak of World War Two.

Many players have scored within a minute of their Football League debut: Bernard Evans (Wrexham) 25 seconds, 15 September 1954; Barrie Jones (Notts County) six seconds, 31 March 1962; Peter Ward (Brighton and Hove) 50 seconds, 27 March 1976; Keith Bertschin (Ipswich Town) one minute, 17 April 1976; Jeremy Charles (Swansea City) one minute, 14 August 1976 (in a League Cup tie), and Graham Baker (Southampton) 58 seconds, 12 November 1977.

Appearing at left-back for Middlesbrough against Bolton Wanderers on 18 December 1937, George Hardwick became the only player in Football League history to put through his own goal in the first minute of his debut match. Yet he went on to play for England in 13 full international matches.

No other player now in the game ever made a start in top-level soccer quite like that of Liverpool's Steve Heighway. In September 1970 Liverpool gave him his debut in a Football League Cup replay against Mansfield Town. On the following day he also made his international bow with the Republic of Ireland against Poland in Dublin.

Malcolm Clarke had the unique experience of never making contact with the ball at all on his Football League debut. On 25 September 1965, playing for Leicester City against Leeds United, he went on as a substitute 90 seconds from the end and had not had a kick when the whistle was blown for full time.

Graham Moore ranks as the only player who ever scored a last-minute equalising goal when he both made his Football League and also his international championship debut. He did it with Cardiff City at Brighton on 13 September 1958 and with Wales against England at Cardiff on 17 October 1959.

The only case between 1919 and 1965 of a player having the misfortune to be sent off when making his Football League debut was John Burns, a Rochdale half-back against Stockport County on 29 October 1921. Since then there have been four other instances: Gerald Casey (Tranmere Rovers) v. Torquay United in August 1967; Bryan Myton (Middlesbrough) v. Cardiff City in September 1968; Kevin Tully (Blackpool) v. Burnley in December 1972; and David Esser (Rochdale) v. Halifax in August 1977.

Delayed action
Mansfield Town's first Division Three home goal of the 1971–72 season, scored by John Fairbrother against Plymouth Argyle on 18 December, was not registered until they had played for seven minutes short of 14 hours on the ground in the Football League during the season. It was their tenth home League game. Yet they had previously scored six times in two F.A. Cup ties at home, 4–3 v. Chester and 2–2 v. Tranmere Rovers.

Directors
There have been more instances than usual in the last few years of uncommonly youthful directors being recruited by the Football League clubs, some being even younger than many players in the game. But Charlton Athletic chairman Michael Gliksten still claims two all-time records in this field. He was the youngest-ever League club director at 18 and the youngest-ever member of the League Management Committee at 23.

In the 1946–47 season Scottish international forward Tommy Walker had the unique experience of playing in 48 League games. After he had played in nine matches with Hearts in the Scottish League he moved to Chelsea and appeared in 39 in Division One with them before the season's end. He later became the manager and a director in turn with Hearts.

George Gillen, who in July 1967 was a Torquay hotelier of 75, was then credited with being the only man to have been a director of three Football League clubs – Torquay United from 1945 to 1954, Exeter City 1954 to 1957 and 1959 to 1966, and Plymouth Argyle 1957 to 1958.

Arsenal director and former general manager Bob Wall, now 65, has been at Highbury for 49 years. In that time the club have been Division One champions eight times and F.A. Cup winners on four occasions.

Former League professionals who were directors of clubs in 1977–78 made the equivalent of a complete team: Joe Mercer and Jimmy Hill (Coventry City), Sir Matt Busby (Manchester United), Eric Houghton (Aston Villa), Sir Alf Ramsey (Birmingham City), Stanley Seymour (Newcastle United), George Reader (Southampton), Freddie Pye (Stockport County), Gordon Pallister (Barnsley), Frank Walton (Southend United) and Ernie Tagg (Crewe Alexandra).

Disasters
A total of 301 people were killed and over 500 injured at the National Stadium, Lima, Peru on 24 May 1964. Six minutes before the end of a match between Peru and Argentina, the referee disallowed a goal for Peru and a riot started. Police used tear gas but the casualties occurred in the panic to get out of the ground.

Two air crashes decimated the teams of Torino and Manchester United respectively in 1949 and

1958. On 14 May 1949 the entire team of Italian League champions Torino which contained eight international players were killed when the plane on which they were returning from a match in Lisbon crashed at Superga outside Turin. All the reserves, manager, trainer and coach were among the 28 who died.

On 6 February 1958 the aircraft carrying the Manchester United team home from a European Cup match in Belgrade crashed on take-off at Munich airport killing seven players, the club secretary, coach, trainer, eight journalists, the co-pilot, a steward and two other passengers. An eighth player subsequently died from his injuries.

Double-sided

Sam Wynne created a record by scoring two goals for each side in a single Football League game. He scored with a free kick and a penalty kick for Oldham as well as twice putting through his own goal against Manchester United in a Division Two game on 6 October 1923.

(Chris Nicholl emulated this achievement on 20 March 1976, scoring twice in open play for Aston Villa and conceding two at the other end for Leicester City.)

Jimmy Oakes, a full-back for Hanley, Staffordshire, who played for Port Vale and Charlton Athletic in pre-war days, had the distinction of playing for both of those clubs in the same Football League game.

On Boxing Day 1932 he was left-back for Port Vale in a Division Two game against Charlton Athletic at The Valley when the match was abandoned because of bad light. Three weeks later Oakes was transferred from Port Vale to Charlton Athletic, and when the abandoned fixture was played on 26 April 1933 he was Charlton's left-back and helped them beat Port Vale 2–1.

Centre-forward Andy Graver, playing for Stoke City, had the unique experience of appearing against one or other of his former clubs in four successive Saturdays in 1956: v. Leicester City away (F.A. Cup) on 28 January; Lincoln City away (League) on 4 February; Leicester City home (League) on 11 February and Newcastle United away (F.A. Cup) on 18 February.

A unique record was set up in season 1959–60 when 16st. Sam Evans turned out for Hull in the Rugby League, in which he had previously also played for Hull Kingston Rovers – and also for Hull City in the Football League.

Embarrassment

A Notts County team defeated by Nottingham Forest 5–0 in a Division Two match on 10 October 1953 included five players who had all been with Forest. They were: Aubrey Southwell, Tom Johnston, Bill Baxter, Tot Leverton and Jack Edwards.

Endeavour

If Hull City ever rise to Division One they will have to plead guilty to having taken longer over it than any other club that ever reached it. They have already had 62 seasons in Division Two and Three. Similarly, no other club had been striving longer than Wrexham to climb into Division Two. They had been actively engaged in this for 49 seasons before winning promotion in 1977–78.

Fair play

In view of the number of players who have been at odds with referees from time to time it is worth recording that the vast majority of players, including several with really long careers, never once found themselves sent off or even cautioned.

An outstanding example considering the number of matches in which he played was John Atyeo, who appeared in over 600 League and Cup games as centre-forward with Bristol City between 1951 and 1966. When one remembers that he scored 350 goals in those games, as well as five in six appearances for England, it is obvious that he must have received considerable physical attention from opposing defenders, but despite this his conduct was above reproach.

Billy Wright, the first player ever to appear in 100 internationals (his total was 105), also went through a lengthy career without ever being cautioned or sent off. Since a large slice of Wright's career was spent as a centre-half then it is obvious that he used only the cleanest form of tackling to halt the opposition. He served his entire first-class career with Wolverhampton Wanderers and played in over 500 League and cup games during one of the most successful period's in the club's history when the pressures were considerable.

Another player with over 500 League and Cup appearances to his credit with never a single caution to mar his record was Billy Liddell, who joined Liverpool straight from school in 1937 and made his last appearance for the club 23 years later. Noted for the power of his shooting, this Scot, who also made 28 appearances for his country, was idolised by the crowd and was Liverpool's top scorer in eight post-war seasons, either as a winger or at centre-forward.

After being admitted to the Football League in 1921 Southport never had a player sent off in a peace-time match in the competition until Walter Taylor, a back, was dismissed at Halifax on 18 October 1952. It was Southport's 1,027th Division Three (Northern Section) match.

Frank Saul's dismissal in a match at Burnley on 4 December 1965, ended the longest spell any club ever had without having a player sent off in a Football League peace-time match. Spurs' previous such case had been when Cecil Poynton was ordered off in a game at Stoke on 27th October 1928.

During the entire 20 seasons between the two World Wars such was their exemplary record that the only Arsenal player ever ordered off in a Division One match was Welsh goalkeeper Dai Lewis in a game at Sunderland in April 1926.

Fatalities
Among a number of players who have accidentally lost their lives during the course of a match one of the most dramatic concerned Sam Wynne, the Bury full-back, who collapsed when taking a free-kick against Sheffield United at Bramall Lane on 30 April 1927. He was carried to the dressing room where he died, primarily because of pneumonia.

Fines
The record fine imposed on a Football League club was £10,000 on Derby County in April 1970 following allegations of administration irregularities. They were also banned from playing in Europe for a year.

Football Association Charity Shield
The Charity Shield match was first played in 1908 between Manchester United, champions of the

Football League, and Queen's Park Rangers, champions of the Southern League. United won 4–0 after a 1–1 draw. It has been held at irregular intervals until more recent times when the F.A. Cup holders have met the League champions annually.

Fixtures
No club in modern times has fulfilled such a strenuous and congested programme in a similar period as the one experienced by West Bromwich Albion when they played seven matches in 10 days between 20 and 29 April inclusive in 1912, these comprising an F.A. Cup final and replay plus five Division One matches.

Barnsley and West Bromwich Albion drew the F.A. Cup final of 1912 and had to replay on the following Wednesday. On the Monday, two days after the original match and two days before the replay, Barnsley played a Division Two game against Derby County and Albion one in the Division One against Everton.

Bradford Park Avenue created a post-war record in November and December 1952 when they fulfilled seven consecutive home fixtures, five in Division Three and two in the F.A. Cup.

The shortest close season in history in the Football League extended for only 70 days. The 1946–47 season went on until 14 June because of an accumulation of weather postponements, and the 1947–48 campaign began on 23 August.

Stoke City created an all-time record in the 1954–55 season in meeting Bury seven times without being beaten. They defeated them in the fifth meeting of an F.A. Cup third round tie, won a Division Two home match and drew one away.

In December and January of season 1957–58 Queen's Park Rangers created the post-war record for the most consecutive Football League matches played by a team which returned the same result in every case. Six Division Three (Southern Section) games in succession played by them all ended 1–1.

The Central League nowadays is restricted to the reserve teams of Football League clubs, but it was not always so. Crewe Alexandra, Port Vale,

Rochdale, Southport and Tranmere Rovers all played in the Central League immediately before they entered the Football League just after World War One.

Coventry City's first and reserve teams have been responsible for travel records. In the 1925–26 season the City and Ashington supplied the widest-ever geographical club extremes in the Division Three (Northern Section). It is an identical set-up in the Central League today with the reserve teams of Coventry and Newcastle United as far apart.

On 25 March 1961, Gillingham, whose ground was under suspension, played a Division Four 'home' match against Wrexham at Gravesend. It was the only time a Football League fixture in peace-time has ever been fulfilled on a non-League club's ground.

The longest distance any team travelled between fulfilling Football League fixtures on successive days was undertaken by Swansea Town when they played a Division Two match at Plymouth on Good Friday, 10 April 1936, and another at Newcastle a day later.

Floodlights

The 1950s saw the arrival of floodlit football. The first match played under floodlights took place at Bramall Lane, Sheffield, on 14 October 1878, when the electric power was generated on the ground by two portable engines driving Siemen's dynamos. There were four lamps, one in each corner of the ground erected on 30ft. high wooden towers and the illuminating powers of each was said to equal 8,000 standard candles. Such was the novelty of the occasion that it attracted a crowd said to have numbered nearly 20,000, and this factor was aided by the fact that it was a crisp, clear moonlit night.

The team chosen for this auspicious occasion were both from various clubs in the Sheffield area and victory by 2–0 went to the one captained by W. E. Clegg, an England international, later Sir William Clegg and Lord Mayor of Sheffield, over a team captained by his brother, J. C. Clegg, also an England international, and who later became Sir Charles Clegg, President of the Football Association.

Two weeks later another football match by floodlight was played at the Lower Aston Grounds, Aston, Birmingham, when a Birmingham representative team beat Nottingham Forest 2–1, while the first floodlight match ever seen in London followed at The Oval on 4 November 1878, when Clapham Rovers drew 2–2 with the Wanderers. This London affair was not so successful as the original game at Sheffield, for the lights were affected by a high wind and were insufficient to provide an even illumination over the whole ground. One report suggested that if more lights had been provided it would have been possible to dispense with the use of reflectors for following the play.

The first Football League match played under lights was the Division One game between Portsmouth and Newcastle United at Fratton Park on 22 February 1956. On 14 September 1955 floodlights were first used in an F. A. Cup tie for the replay between Kidderminster Harriers and Brierley Hill Alliance.

Floodlights were first switched on during an international tie in England at Wembley on 30 November 1955. England beat Spain 4–1. The first played entirely under lights was at the same venue on 20 November 1963. England beat Northern Ireland 8–3.

Foreign players in the U.K.

No German-born player ever figured in Football League matches during the 20 seasons between the two wars, but five who have done so since the last war have been: Bert Trautmann (introduced to League matches by Manchester City), Alous Eisentrager (Bristol City), Dietmar Bruck (Coventry City), Wilf Smith (Sheffield Wednesday) and Roy Tunks (Rotherham United).

In the 1946–47 season Port Vale's manager was Gordon Hodgson and their trainer Ken Fish. Both were South Africans, both stood six feet tall and both were former Aston Villa centre-forwards. Hodgson had played three times for England in 1930–31.

No Football League club has recruited players from more overseas countries than Charlton Athletic. They have included natives of Mexico, Singapore, India, Jamaica, Holland, New Zealand and South Africa.

Gregarious

Only six clubs have met all the other 90 (apart from Wigan Athletic and Wimbledon) in Football League matches, but six more are within an ace of completing the circuit. Huddersfield Town have played all but Mansfield Town; Barnsley all but Oxford United; Luton Town all but Cambridge United; Port Vale all but Sunderland; and Bradford City and Oldham Athletic all but Ipswich Town. Cambridge United's promotion to Division Two at the end of the 1977–78 season reduced the number to five.

Grimsby Town claim to have met more different teams in Football League matches than any other club in the country. They have been in conflict with over 100 in having met all the other current 91 clubs and also 12 no longer in the League.

The promotions and relegations of recent seasons mean that clubs which have operated in all four Football League divisions now total 13 – two in Bradford, Brentford, Bury, Carlisle United, Coventry City, Crystal Palace, Grimsby Town, Luton Town, Huddersfield Town, Northampton Town, Notts County and Oldham Athletic.

Coventry City rank as the only club to have operated in all four Football League divisions and also both Southern and Northern Sections of the former Division Three as well as the old Southern League.

Handicap

Bobby Thomson had a long Football League career as a centre-forward with Chelsea and Charlton Athletic before and after the 1914–18 war, yet he had only one eye. At the age of seven he had been blinded in the left eye through a youthful companion accidentally thrusting a lighted firework into it. He not only made good with Chelsea but even led them in the F.A. Cup Final of 1915. A local lad from Croydon, Thomson when asked how he managed to overcome his handicap used to say 'when the ball is coming my way I shut my good eye and play from memory'.

One of this remarkable player's most exciting games was in a war-time London Combination match in 1916 when he scored seven of the 11 goals his side registered against Luton Town. That season Thomson scored 39 goals in 31 first-team games.

Honours

Terry Venables was the first player to win international honours for England at five different levels: schoolboy, youth, amateur, Under-23 and full. His first full international award came on 21 October 1964 against Belgium.

Injuries

Hull City goalkeeper Billy Bly used to be viewed as just about Soccer's most-injured player of all time, but Stoke City's contemporary centre-half Denis Smith must be regarded as something of a rival. He has had five broken legs, four broken noses, a cracked ankle, broken collar-bone, chipped spine, many broken fingers and toes, and over 100 stitches.

During his 23 years with Hull before he signed for Weymouth in December 1961, Bly sustained 13 fractures to hands, feet, legs and ribs.

Innovations

Sam Widdowson of Nottingham Forest is credited with the introduction and registering of shinguards in 1874. Forest also claim to have been the first club to adopt the referee's whistle (1878), the crossbar instead of tape (1875) as well as oval-section goal-posts.

Goal nets have been an accepted feature of football equipment for many years and it is surprising to recall that it was more than 10 years after crossbars came into general use in the first-class game before anyone thought of the idea of using nets. During this period there were innumerable arguments about whether or not the ball had actually passed between the posts and under the bar.

Credit for inventing and introducing nets to the game goes to Mr J. A. Brodie, a former Rugby player who was City Engineer of Liverpool when he discussed his idea with Bob Lythgoe, a former goalkeeper with the Druids and secretary of the Liverpool and District F.A. Lythgoe assured Brodie of the soundness of the idea which was then patented. John Bentley of Bolton, later to become President of the Football League, invited Brodie to demonstrate his net at Bolton and only one was used in a friendly between Bolton and Nottingham Forest on New Year's Day 1891.

It was an obvious success and the first important game at which Brodie's patented nets were used was the North v. South game at Nottingham on 12 January 1891. During the following month the F.A. Council approved their use, although at that time they could not make them compulsory 'Until some satisfactory arrangement can be made with the patentee as to price to be charged to the clubs.'

Three months later the F.A. recommended the use of nets in all F.A. Cup ties and at a meeting in September that same year the Football League decided that all clubs must provide nets by 1 November. The price quoted for their purchase at that time was £3 12s 6d (£3.625).

It is generally considered that Chelsea were the main cause of the rule being introduced which prevents the unrestricted signing of new players after a certain stage in the season. Originally the last date for new signings in the Football League was 16 March and more recently this was changed to the second Thursday in March.

The idea is to prevent clubs buying players late in the season to clinch promotion or avoid relegation, and during the last few weeks of the 1909–10 season Chelsea entered the transfer market in a desperate bid to avoid dropping into Division Two. Unfortunately for them the venture made little difference to their performance and they won only two of their last 11 games.

Even so, a win at Tottenham in the last game of the season would have saved them from relegation and this local derby created a great deal more interest than usual. But Spurs sealed Chelsea's fate with a 2–1 victory, and the irony of it was that the winning goal was scored by Percy Humphreys whom Spurs had signed from Chelsea earlier in that campaign. That summer the League introduced their new rule restricting transfers.

Inter-League matches
The first Inter-League match was between the Football League and the Football Alliance on 20 April 1891. At various times there have been similar games involving the Football League v. Scottish League; Irish League; League of Ireland; Southern League; also the Scottish League v. Irish League; Southern League; League of Ireland. Irish League v. Southern League. Football League v. International Football Combination of Denmark; Italian League; Belgian League. Scottish League v. Italian League. Irish League v. Italian League and Irish League v. League of Ireland.

Internationals
The most international appearances recorded by a player from the British Isles are the 108 by Bobby Moore for England between 1962–73.

Outside these islands the record is less easy to trace because of the difficulty in determining the actual number of matches played of a representative nature by some foreign countries.

Irish connection
Eire international midfield player Gerry Daly will always be able to claim a place of his own in the game's records. When he left Manchester United for Derby County in March 1977 for around £160,000 he became the first Irishman, from either North or South, ever sold for a six-figure fee – and his was the 147th such deal effected by a Football League club.

Limited Companies
The first football club to become a Limited Liability Company was Small Heath in 1888. They changed their name to Birmingham in 1905 and added City to their title in 1945. Of the present 92 League clubs only Nottingham Forest are not a limited company. They are run by a committee.

Local Derby
A 0–0 draw at White Hart Lane on 27 September 1975 was the first Football League peace-time match ever to have been played between Arsenal and Tottenham Hotspur, the 79th in the series, starting in season 1909–10, without a goal being registered in it.

Longest game
War-time conditions necessitated cup-ties being completed at the first attempt and as a result two of them took over three hours each. On 14 April 1945 in the second round of the Football League North, War Cup Cardiff City and Bristol City played for three hours 22 minutes before the deciding goal was scored for Cardiff by B. Rees. After normal time the teams had been level at 2–2 and in accordance with war-time rules an extra ten minutes each way had been completed without further score.

On 30th March 1946 the second leg of a Division Three (North) Cup tie between

Stockport County and Doncaster Rovers lasted 203 minutes before bad light stopped play at 6.43 pm with the score at 4–4. Doncaster won the replay.

Longevity

The Football League record for long-service belongs to Ted Sagar who joined Everton on 26 March 1929 and retired in May 1953 after 24 years and one month. He kept goal for them in 465 League matches, a relatively low figure as his career spanned the war years and did not include such regional games in which he played between 1939 and 1946. Born in Moorend, Yorkshire, he had been originally turned down by Hull City.

On 26 March 1929 this young miner who had been playing in goal for the Thorne Colliery team signed on at Goodison Park. He became not only the longest serving club member Everton ever had but one of the most accomplished goal-keepers in the League.

Players have been known to demand transfer as soon as they have lost their place in the side but Sagar twice fought his way back into the Everton team after being dropped. After making eight appearances in the 1929–30 season he did not make a League appearance the following season when Bill Coggins was first choice, but he came back the next year.

When Sagar returned from war service with the Fifth Divisional Signals in Italy he found George Burnett filling his position in the League side, but Sagar again proved his worth in the reserves and was able to regain his place in the League side. When he finally decided to retire in May 1953 he had also established a club record for peace-time Football League appearances. He also made four appearances for England.

Bob Crompton signed for his local club Blackburn Rovers in October 1896 and remained with them as a full-back until May 1920, a period of 23 years seven months. After retiring he extended his service, becoming honorary manager in 1931, director and honorary adviser with the club. He also had a brief spell as manager of Bournemouth in 1935–36.

He was the first player who made 500 Football League appearances with one club. Right-back Crompton performed this feat by making his 500th appearance away to Notts County on 10 October 1914, when this Division One game ended in a 1–1 draw. He was then aged 35 and had

been with the club for 19 years. He made his final appearance for Blackburn in a Division One game at Bradford Park Avenue on 23 February 1920 when Rovers were beaten 5–2.

An outstanding personality both on and off the field, Crompton was noted for his fair but fearless tackling and accurate kicking with either foot. He finished his career as team-manager of his original club from March 1938 until his death in March 1941.

Crompton only gained the honour of being the first man to make 500 Football League appearances for a single club by six months, for in April 1915 Sheffield Wednesday's Scottish centre-forward Andy Wilson reached this mark in a Division One game at Bradford City. Unfortunately he did not celebrate with a goal, for the Wednesday were beaten 1–0. Indeed, there was no celebration at all, for in those days little heed was paid to such statistics and probably did not even appreciate that such a landmark had been reached by the centre-forward who had joined them from Clyde in 1900.

Born at Irvine, Ayrshire, Wilson was a gifted ball-playing type of centre-forward in the true Scottish tradition and he scored 200 peace-time Football League goals in 502 appearances for the Wednesday before making his final appearance for them in 1919–20. He made 41 appearances for England. In later years he became manager of Bristol Rovers, Oldham Athletic and Stockport County.

The Scottish League record was set up by Alec Smith who made his first appearance for Rangers in April 1894 and was a senior choice over the next 21 years at outside-left. Right-back Alec McNair equalled this period of service, completing 21 years with Celtic in 1925.

The two Potteries clubs are unique in having both included in their senior side at one time or another three players who had all turned 40. Stoke City did so with Stanley Matthews, Tom Brittleton and Bob McGrory and Port Vale with Tom Holford, Howard Matthews and Arthur Bridgett. Brittleton and McGrory played for Stoke between the wars, and Matthews did so in February 1965 when 50. The other three all played for Port Vale between the wars.

After an absence from the Football League of over 11 years, Port Vale brought back former

England and Sunderland winger Arthur Bridgett at the age of 39 in November 1923. After leaving Sunderland he had been manager of both South Shields and North Shields and had then been out of the game for several years. He made his League come-back for Port Vale against Clapton Orient in a Division Two game on 10 November 1923 and scored the winning goal. In all Bridgett made 14 appearances in Division Two games that season and scored seven goals.

The Football League careers of two players who appeared in the same side in the same season spanned an unbroken period of 44 years. They were Billy Meredith and Joe Spence, who were in the Manchester United forward line in season 1919–20. Meredith began his League career in October 1894, and Spence did not finish his until season 1937–38.

Bobby Collins, one-time Scottish international forward who became caretaker manager of Hull City in 1977, is not generally known to have been responsible for the longest post-war career any player has had in League life. It began with Celtic in the 1949–50 season and ended with Oldham Athletic in April 1973, 23 years later.

Terry Paine holds the record of Football League appearances, having made 824 between 1957 and 1977. Winchester-born, he played for Winchester Schools and Winchester Corinthians before joining Winchester City. Here he attracted the attention of Southampton and signed for them in February 1957.

An outside-right, he made 713 League appearances for the club as well as scoring 160 League goals, both club records, before joining Hereford United in 1974.

He became player-coach with his new club and reached his 800th League appearance overall on 4 September 1976 in a home match against Burnley. On 16 October he played to retire after the match against his former team Southampton on his 806th League outing.

But Hereford were having a particularly unhappy time in Division Two and after a run of nine matches during which they managed only one point, Paine was persuaded to return just three weeks after his last appearance against Chelsea on 6 November.

He continued until 11 May 1977 when he retired for a second time, the occasion once more being graced by the presence in opposition of Southampton in his 824th League appearance.

Paine played 19 times for England during his career. He was given a free transfer by Hereford.

Jimmy Dickinson made 764 League appearances for Portsmouth as a wing-half from 1946 to 1965, the last of them on his 40th birthday. He would have added to this total but for the war period, having originally joined the club as an amateur in 1943 after completing service in the Royal Navy.

A Hampshire man born in Alton, he played on 48 occasions for England and was awarded the M.B.E. in 1964. After retiring he became Public Relations Officer and scout for the club until 1968 when he was appointed Secretary. In 1977 he was persuaded to become the club's manager.

Roy Sproson made 761 League appearances for Port Vale as either a wing-half or full-back from 1950 to 1972. The following year he was appointed the club's manager but was dismissed in 1977.

John Trollope made 738 League appearances for Swindon Town as a full-back from 1960 to 1978. This included 368 consecutive appearances between 3 April 1961 and 24 August 1968, the sequence being ended by a broken arm.

Harold Bell holds the record for the highest number of consecutive League appearances. From the opening match of the 1946–47 season he was ever present for Tranmere Rovers until he was left out of the side against Gateshead on 30 August 1955 after 401 Division Three (North Section) matches.

Including all senior matches during this period he registered 459 appearances, including 26 F.A. Cup games, 22 Liverpool Senior Cup matches and 10 Cheshire Bowl appearances.

The nearest he came to breaking this sequence occurred one week when he felt unwell with a sore throat. Consultation with the club's doctor diagnosed tonsilitis but he recovered by the weekend and played as normal.

A centre-half during this sequence, he later regained his place as a full-back and remained with the club until given a free transfer in 1961. His aggregate total of 595 League matches for the club would certainly have been higher, as he had joined Tranmere originally as a teenager in 1939 and seven seasons were lost to his possible record when he made regional league appearances during the war period.

Stanley Matthews made a total of 701 League appearances between 1932 and 1965 during a career with Stoke City (twice) and Blackpool. But this total included three appearances at the start of the 1939–40 season which was abandoned and replaced by regional football when World War Two started. He would also have added to his total but for this fact.

MANAGERS

Because of the pre-war status of the secretary-manager and the post-war trend towards managers and general managers it is difficult to make an accurate assessment of the length of service, but Sir Matt Busby, C.B.E., who was manager or general manager of Manchester United from October 1945 until June 1971 when he became a club director, had spent 25 years eight months in the position during the club's most successful period. During this time United won five Division One Championships, finished runners-up on another seven occasions, won three F.A. Cup competitions and finished runners-up another three times. They also won the European Cup in 1968.

In 1977–78 Brian Clough equalled the achievement of Herbert Chapman in managing two different League Championship winning teams. Clough, the Nottingham Forest manager, had previously won the Division One title in 1972 with Derby County, while Chapman's successes had come with Huddersfield Town in 1924 and 1925 and Arsenal in 1931 and 1933.

Six men have both played for and then become managers of League championship winning teams: Ted Drake, Bill Nicholson, Alf Ramsey, Joe Mercer, Dave Mackay and Bob Paisley.

Bill Nicholson and the Tottenham Hotspur background he knew so well.

Bob Paisley, Liverpool manager, treasures his OBE.

Name	Position	Player	Manager
Drake	Centre-forward	Arsenal 1933–34 1934–35 1937–38	Chelsea 1954–55
Nicholson	Right-half	Tottenham Hotspur 1950–51	Tottenham Hotspur 1960–61
Ramsey	Right-back	Tottenham Hotspur 1950–51	Ipswich Town 1961–62
Mercer	Left-half	Everton 1938–39 Arsenal 1947–48 1952–53	Manchester City 1967–68
Mackay	Left-half	Tottenham Hotspur 1960–61	Derby County 1974–75
Paisley	Wing-half	Liverpool 1946–47	Liverpool 1975–76 1976–77

Nine different men have played in and managed F.A. Cup-winning teams: Matt Busby, Peter McWilliam, Joe Mercer, Don Revie, Jimmy Seed, Bill Shankly, Joe Smith, Bob Stokoe and Billy Walker.

Name	Position	Player	Manager
Busby	Right-half	Manchester City 1934	Manchester United 1948, 1963
McWilliam	Left-half	Newcastle United 1910	Tottenham Hotspur 1921
Mercer	Left-half	Arsenal 1950	Manchester City 1969
Revie	Centre-forward	Manchester City 1956	Leeds United 1972
Seed	Inside-right	Tottenham Hotspur 1921	Charlton Athletic 1947
Shankly	Right-half	Preston North End 1938	Liverpool 1965, 1974
Smith	Inside-left	Bolton Wanderers 1923, 1926	Blackpool 1953
Stokoe	Centre-half	Newcastle United 1955	Sunderland 1973
Walker	Centre-forward	Aston Villa 1920	Sheffield Wednesday 1935 Nottingham Forest 1959

Marching orders

The total number of players sent off in Football League matches during the post-war period have been as follows:

1946–47	12	1957–58	27	1968–69	51
1947–48	5	1958–59	20	1969–70	37
1948–49	10	1959–60	19	1970–71	28
1949–50	14	1960–61	18	1971–72	36
1950–51	7	1961–62	25	1972–73	83
1951–52	14	1962–63	35	1973–74	76
1952–53	15	1963–64	45	1974–75	97
1953–54	14	1964–65	46	1975–76	89
1954–55	13	1965–66	46	1976–77	100
1955–56	20	1966–67	50	1977–78	*(Figures not available at time of going to press)*
1956–57	15	1967–68	48		

In a Division Three match at Hull on Christmas Day in 1936 Ambrose Brown, a Scottish inside-right, playing for Wrexham, became, as he still remains, the only player ever sent off in the first minute of a Football League game.

On 20 November 1976 nine players were sent off – three in Division One and six in the first round of the F.A. Cup – a record for dismissals in one day.

The highest number of players sent off in the Football League in one day is eight on 5 October 1974. In the F.A. Cup there were also eight dismissed in the first round on 9 January 1915.

The record number of players ordered off in a Football League match is three. It happened on two occasions, firstly to Plymouth Argyle who had three of their players dismissed on 10 March 1974 in a Division Three match at Port Vale and to Oxford United on 21 February 1976 at Blackpool.

Jimmy Turnbull, as Manchester United's centre-forward, was dismissed in matches against Aston Villa on 16 October 1909 and Sheffield United on 23 October, the only occasion that a player was ever sent off twice in successive Football League matches.

The first England player to be sent off in a full international was Alan Mullery against Yugoslavia in a European Championship match in Florence, Italy, on 5 June 1968. And the British International Championship had been in existence for nearly a century before any player was ordered off in a match in the tournament. The first-ever such instance arose in October 1966 when Linfield outside-right Billy Ferguson was dismissed when turning out for Ireland at Windsor Park, Belfast, in a match won by England.

Rodger Wylde of Sheffield Wednesday and John Middleton of Bradford City both scored once and then found themselves sent off the field in the same games. But Reading striker John Murray achieved a hat-trick while playing for Bury against Doncaster Rovers in March 1973 before being dismissed himself.

Memorial

The Duncan Edwards Football Club, a memorial to the Manchester United and England half-back who was a victim of the Munich air crash in February 1958, was formed in his native Dudley in September 1959. It was the only time a club has been named after a player.

Name games

In April 1966 Peter O'Sullivan, then a 35-year-old bricklayer and a Liverpool supporter, went to a local registrry office and had his newly-born daughter officially named: Paula St John Lawrence Lawler Byrne Strong Yeats Stevenson Callaghan Hunt Milne Smith Thompson Shankly Bennett Paisley O'Sullivan.

Professional Soccer, though not the Sport Of Kings, is arguably the King of Sports and a study of the names of some of those who had figured in it in modern times suggests that it has an aristocratic tone all of its own. At all events Football League players in recent years have included King, Queen, Prince, Duke, Earl, Lord, Baron and Knight.

Few people connected in any capacity with the Football League have such a succession of christian names as the man whom Northampton promoted from trainer to manager in 1977. He is London-born erstwhile Arsenal and Bristol Rovers half-back John Frederick James Petts, who was given the same names as his father and three uncles.

A pre-war West Bromwich Albion centre-half owned the longest string of names of any Football League player in history. He was christened Arthur Griffith Stanley Sackville Redvers Boscawen Trevis. But everybody called him 'Bos'! Conversely, the shortest-named was ex-Arsenal, Manchester United and Scotland half-back Ian Ure.

Mansfield Town's Glasgow-born full-back Sandy Pate carries the name of renowned wartime military leaders. His christian names are Alexander Montgomery.

Bob Hope, the Scot who has appeared with West Bromwich Albion, Birmingham City and Sheffield Wednesday during the 1970s, is by no means the first Football League player to bear the same name as someone famous in other spheres than soccer. Winston Churchill used to play for Chelsea, Baden Powell for Darlington, Charlie Chaplin for Wolverhampton Wanderers and Antony Eden for Aston Villa.

In the 1949–50 season, Leslie, Herbert, Antony and Jeff Smith were Aston Villa players, Bill Smith secretary and Norman and Edward Smith directors . . . In 1966–67 Chester's playing staff included seven of the Jones clan: Bryn, Les, Ray, Howard, Bobby, David and Keither.

Two players both named Francis Lee studied together at Horwich Technical College in Lancashire and formed the right wing in the same side. Both later became professionals with Lancashire clubs, Preston North End and Bolton Wanderers, and both had trials with Lancashire County Cricket Club.

In the 1950–51 season Rotherham United ran four teams, and each was captained by a Williams; the first by Horace, the second by Danny, the third by Ken and the fourth by Bobby. There was no relationship between any of them.

Early in the second half of an F.A. Cup second round tie against Nuneaton Borough on 20 November 1971, Torquay United withdrew ex-Coventry City defender Brian Hill. His substitute was the unrelated former Bristol City winger Brian Hill.

Dennis Thrower used to be an Ipswich Town wing half-back, Tony Goodgame a Fulham half-back, Fred Forward Portsmouth's outside-right, Peter Tough a Norwich City inside-left, Alf Steward Manchester United's goalkeeper, Frank Shooter a Norwich City centre-forward, and Ivor Scorer a Bristol Rovers half-back.

The most appropriately-named pair of club-mates ever known in the Football League were together with Lincoln City in season 1958–59. Centre-half Ray Long stood 6ft 3in and outside-left Joe Short 5ft 2in.

Jack, James and John were international players with Arsenal's successful team of the 1930s. Then Derby County assembled the most extensive company ever known of players with surnames that are found in more common use as christian names. Their team in the 1970s included James, George, Hector, Thomas and Daniel.

The same surname occurs nine times among the lists of players who have represented all four home countries in International Championship matches. Players named Brown, Cook, Harris, Hunter, Kelly, Martin, Russell, Thompson and Turner have appeared for England, Scotland, Ireland and Wales.

Friday signs on Tuesday, but began on Sunday. Interpreted, it means that Cardiff City striker Robin Friday first became a Football League professional with Reading on Tuesday 22 January 1974, but made his debut in the competition on the following 10 February in a Sunday match against Exeter City during the season when League matches were permitted on the Sabbath because of the three-day working week then operating.

Liverpool players in Division One matches between the wars included Elisha Scott (an Irishman), Robert Ireland (Scot), Sam English (Irish) and George Poland (Welsh). And Don Welsh (English) managed the club after the Second World War.

Nemesis
Hull City are probably not sorry that they will not have to visit Chelsea in the foreseeable future. When they first played at Stamford Bridge in September 1905 they did manage to score a goal in a 5–1 defeat, but since then they have fulfilled 11 more Division Two fixtures at Chelsea and have not been able to score in any of them.

Never too late
There have been few other Football League matches in the post-war era quite like one on 18 September 1965, in the matter of a team becoming overwhelming victors after losing a first-minute goal. In a home Division One match against Wolverhampton Wanderers, Southampton were one down after 35 seconds, yet won 9–3.

Nicknames
Most football clubs have nicknames and many of them have more than one. Some nicknames have gone out of fashion while new names have taken their place. For instance, one seldom hears Charlton Athletic being referred to nowadays by their old nickname of the Haddicks, or Swindon Town mentioned as the Moonrakers, but those names were commonly in use at one period with the respective clubs. Now their supporters more often prefer to refer to both of them as the Robins.

Nicknames generally fall into five categories. (1) One of the principal occupations of the town – Crewe (the Railwaymen), Grimsby (the Mariners), Luton and Stockport (the Hatters), Barnsley (the Colliers); (2) from the name of the club's ground – Fulham are known as the Cottagers because their ground is Craven Cottage, Bradford City as the Paraders because their ground is Valley Parade; (3) the club colours – Liverpool (the Reds), Birmingham City (the Blues); (4) animals, birds and insects (some of these also arise out of the club colours) – Norwich City play in yellow and are known as the Canaries, Newcastle United play in black and white and are known as the Magpies; (5) derived from the name of the club – Hamilton Academical (the Accies), Middlesbrough (the Borough), Orient (the Os), Hartlepool (the Pool).

However, other club nicknames are not so obvious and tracing their derivation is often interesting.

Arsenal are known as the Gunners because the club was originally formed at the Woolwich Arsenal; Plymouth Argyle are known as the Pilgrims because the Pilgrim Fathers sailed from Plymouth to America; Southampton are the Saints because the club was originally Southampton St Mary's; Sheffield Wednesday, the Owls because they used to play at Owlerton; Bury as the Shakers ever since they were giving such outstanding performances in the Lancashire Senior Cup in 1891–92 that their Chairman was heard to exclaim 'We'll give them a shaking up, in fact we are the "Shakers"!'

Millwall's nickname of Lions is supposed to have been derived from their days on the Isle of Dogs when during a cup-tie a supporter urged them on with a cry of 'Come on Millwall, eat 'em up!' A fellow spectator replied: 'What do you think they are, Lions?' It was soon adopted and when the club moved headquarters for the last time to date they called their new ground The Den.

Numbering of Players
Players were first numbered in the F.A. Cup Final in 1933. But they ran from 1 to 22 thus:

EVERTON

Sagar 1

Cook 2   Cresswell 3

Britton 4   White 5   Thomson 6

Geldard 7   Dunn 8   Dean 9   Johnson 10   Stein 11

Brook 12   McMullan 13   Herd 14   Marshall 15   Toseland 16

Bray 17   Cowan 18   Busby 19

Dale 20   Cann 21

Langford 22

MANCHESTER CITY

There were several isolated instances of Football League clubs numbering players in League matches in the late 1920s and 1930s but it did not become compulsory until the 1939–40 season.

Odd Soccer World

An all-amateur club known as the Argonauts once applied to join the Football League. Dick Sloley, who had played for the Corinthians around the time of the first World War and had been a member of the Great Britain team in the Olympic Games, was the prime mover in the formation of the Argonauts in 1927.

Sloley was concerned about the number of public schools changing to rugby and wanted to give the amateurs a boost. As it was, the new club was properly constituted with the Earl of Lonsdale as president, while the vice-presidents included the then headmasters of Westminster and Harrow.

Wembley Stadium was lined up for home matches and then application was made for membership of Division Three (Southern Section) at the League's AGM in 1928. The fact that this amateur club gathered 16 votes shows how much of an impression their efforts had made. Many a professional club has since been less well received. But not for the first or last time the League members that year preferred to re-elect the bottom clubs. Thus, on this occasion, Torquay United and Merthyr Town received 42 votes and 27 votes respectively, while the Argonauts did at least have the satisfaction of receiving more support than Kettering or Peterborough.

The following year they made a second application, but while the two bottom clubs (Exeter City and Gillingham) were again re-elected the Argonauts collected only five votes, although even this comparatively low figure was still more than Aldershot, Kettering, Thames and Llanelly. After that disappointment the idea was dropped.

Oldest

The oldest player to have appeared in a Football League match was Neil McBain who kept goal for New Brighton against Hartlepool United on 15 March 1947 at the age of 52 years 4 months.

McBain was manager of the club at the time and as a result of a mishap his side found itself short of two players at Hartlepool. He managed to utilise the services of an amateur player for outfield duty while he himself filled the other position in goal.

His playing career had been spent as a half-back with Ayr United, Manchester United, Everton and St. Johnstone. A Scot born in Campbeltown, he made three appearances for Scotland in the 1920s.

Sir Stanley Matthews was the oldest ever to appear in a Division One game. When he made his 701st and final league appearance for Stoke City against Fulham on 6 February 1965 he was 50 years 5 days.

Billy Meredith was the oldest to appear in an F.A. Cup match in the competition proper. He was 49 years 8 months when he played for Manchester City against Newcastle United in the semi-final on 29 March 1924. Meredith had actually made his debut against Newcastle thirty years before.

Newcastle themselves provided the oldest in an F.A. Cup Final when Billy Hampson played at right-back against Aston Villa at the age of 41 years 8 months.

Meredith was also the oldest to turn out in a British International Championship match when he played for Wales against England on 15 March 1920 at Highbury. He was then in his 46th year.

In the 1928–29 season Halifax Town fielded two goalkeepers who were both over 40 years of age. Their regular goalkeeper was 44-year-old Howard Matthews, a Welshman who made his Football League debut with Oldham Athletic as far back as 1908, but when both he and reserve goalkeeper Cliff Binns were unavailable through injury, trainer Bob Suter volunteered to fill his position.

Suter, who had first appeared in the League with Notts County some 28 years earlier, had not played in the competition for seven years and was aged 47 years 9 months when he once again pulled on the goalkeeper's jersey for his club's Division Three (Northern Section) game at home to South Shields on 20 April 1929. Halifax lost 2–0. Four days later he played again at Darlington when they were beaten again by a similar score.

One further interesting point about Suter's

career is that the loyally served Notts County for 12 seasons during which time, largely owing to the consistency of Albert Iremonger, he made only eight League appearances.

The oldest player ever to make his Division One debut in the Football League was Scottish international inside-forward Andy Cunningham. It was in the 1929–30 season when Newcastle United were going through a difficult period that they signed this player from Glasgow Rangers in an attempt to pull their forward line together. Cunningham was aged 38 and 2 days when he played for Newcastle at Leicester on 2 February 1929 and helped his new side gain a 1–1 draw which was their first point in six away games. He was subsequently appointed player-manager. In all he made 122 League appearances for the club before retiring.

He was also the oldest Scottish player ever transferred to a club in England and he had started his career with Kilmarnock in 1911, before moving on to Rangers in 1920.

In Accrington Stanley's last season in the Football League in 1961–62 they sent a letter to Sylvester Bickerton, of Padiham, inviting him to have a trial. There was only one snag – Sylvester was . . . 71.

Olympic Games

Football has been officially included in the Olympic Games tournaments from 1908 to 1976 with the exception of the 1932 series held in Los Angeles. Since World War Two the competition has been dominated by Eastern European countries who have invariably used their full national teams. Hungary were the winners in 1952, 1964 and 1968 and no other country has won it more than twice.

An exhibition match had been staged in the 1900 Olympics in Paris between the Upton Park club and a French side which London's representatives won 4–0. In 1904 the tournament in St. Louis included three teams and a Canadian side Galt F.C. won it, while in the 1906 Intercalated Olympics in Athens the competition was won by Denmark.

FIFA took over the organisation in 1908 but now all National Associations who are members of the world governing body are eligible providing they can satisfy their own Olympic Committee that they are non-professionals.

In 1920 Belgium were awarded the final against Czechoslovakia when their opponents left the field just before half-time in protest against some of the referee's decisions, including one of their players sent off for kicking an opponent. Belgium were leading 2–0 at the time, and Czechoslovakia was disqualified from the competition.

Year	Winners	Runners-up	Third
1908	Great Britain	Denmark	Holland
1912	Great Britain	Denmark	Holland
1920	Belgium	Spain	Holland
1924	Uruguay	Switzerland	Sweden
1928	Uruguay	Argentina	Italy
1932	No competition		
1936	Italy	Austria	Norway
1948	Sweden	Yugoslavia	Denmark
1952	Hungary	Yugoslavia	Sweden
1956	USSR	Yugoslavia	Bulgaria
1960	Yugoslavia	Denmark	Italy
1964	Hungary	Czechoslovakia	East Germany
1968	Hungary	Bulgaria	Japan
1972	Poland	Hungary	USSR and East Germany
1976	East Germany	Poland	USSR

Venues: 1908 London; 1912 Stockholm; 1920 Antwerp; 1924 Paris; 1928 Amsterdam; 1936 Berlin; 1948 London; 1952 Helsinki; 1956 Melbourne; 1960 Rome; 1964 Tokyo; 1968 Mexico City; 1972 Munich; 1976 Montreal.

Overcoming adversity

When Coventry City defeated Aldershot by 7–1 in a Division Four match on 22 November 1958, they achieved the biggest-ever Football League win by any team left with depleted forces. They had already lost goalkeeper Jim Sanders with a broken leg, and substitutes had not then become permissible.

Overtime

A Football League Cup-tie between Southampton and Leeds United on 5 December 1960 did not finish until 10.10 pm, the latest time at which first-class Soccer has ever been played in England. Power failures caused hold-ups lasting for 62 minutes.

Penalties

The penalty kick was introduced in 1890–91 by the Irish Football Association. The Football Association accepted it in the following close season. The first man to score with a penalty kick in the Football League was James Heath for Wolverhampton Wanderers v. Accrington, 14 September 1891. However, considering that name it is a coincidence that probably the first penalty kick to be scored in senior English football was scored for Newton Heath (Lancashire and Yorkshire Railway) v. Blackpool in a Lancashire League game, Saturday 5 September 1891. Newton Heath later became Manchester United.

It is worth recalling that for many years after the penalty kick was introduced in 1891 the true blue amateurs always refused to take advantage by fouling a player or deliberately handling the ball was something they believed only professionals would entertain, and they considered that it was only the professionals that the F.A. had in mind when they agreed to the introduction of the penalty kick. It therefore became the practice whenever an amateur team was awarded a penalty to either refuse to take it or gently tap the ball into the goalkeeper's hands.

One of the most famous amateur sides of all times, the Corinthians, were among the strongest objectors to the penalty kick, and for several years most of the old boys' teams that competed in the Arthur Dunn Cup (which was not introduced until 11 years after the penalty kick) still refused to take advantage of it.

The highest number of penalty kicks awarded to one team in a League game is four to Burnley against Grimsby Town, Division Two, 13 February 1909. Burnley missed three of them, or rather they were saved by the Grimsby goalkeeper Walter Scott, who established a record in the process.

His goalkeeping performance on that occasion can rarely have been excelled in the Football League, for apart from saving three out of four penalties he made many other fine saves.

Grimsby defended robustly that afternoon at Turf Moor and it was from a free-kick for a foul that Walter Abbot put Burnley ahead after 16 minutes. In a ten-minute spell before the interval Burnley were awarded three penalties in quick succession. Dick Smith took the first two and

Scott saved them both. Then Abbot was given the job of taking the third and this time Scott was beaten. But when, soon after the interval, Abbott took a fourth penalty after he had been fouled, Scott saved again.

Grimsby were down to 10 men for most of this game, so it was understandable that goalkeeper Scott was accorded a deserved ovation when the game ended with his side losing only 2–0.

The scoring champion among goalkeepers in a single season of Football League matches is Arnold Birch. Between 1919 and 1927 he made 168 League appearances with Sheffield Wednesday and Chesterfield and it was with the latter club in season 1923–24 that he created a record by scoring five goals in Division Three (Northern Section) matches, all of them from penalties.

However, that was the only season in which Birch scored any goals and his career total of five was exceeded by Ernald Scattergood who registered eight goals during his career with Derby County and Bradford which extended from 1907 to 1925. Ernald's son Ken also played for Derby County just before World War Two.

A missed penalty cost Cardiff City the League Championship in 1923–24, a title which has eluded them ever since. City needed to win their final game – at Birmingham – to have captured the coveted trophy. When in the second half with neither side having scored, Cardiff were awarded a penalty after a defender had blatantly handled a shot from Len Davies which would have probably found the net, victory and the League Championship seemed within their grasp.

But no-one wanted the responsibility of taking a penalty with so much at stake and it seemed that no-one had been previously instructed to fulfil this task. So the youthful Davies stepped forward to take his first penalty and hit the ball so close to Dan Tremelling that the Birmingham goalkeeper was able to hold the ball.

After this draw it needed some fine calculations to show that Cardiff City had missed the Championship by only .024 of a goal, as Huddersfield Town's goal average was that fraction higher.

In a F.A. Cup tie in December 1921, Benny Smith, a Norwich City full-back, struck such a hard shot from the penalty spot that Leach, the Metrogas goalkeeper, was knocked out and Smith hit the rebound into the unguarded net. The luckless goalkeeper was carried off. Norwich won this fifth qualifying round tie 2–1 on the Old Kent Road ground and Smith's penalty might well have been the hardest shot ever seen.

Aldershot goalkeeper Glen Johnson saved three shots from the same penalty kick against Newport County on 26 February 1977. The kick in the last minute of the game was ordered to be re-taken twice by the referee. After the third successful save Johnson made a gesture to the official, was shown the yellow card for ungentlemanly conduct and subsequently fined by the F.A. Disciplinary Committee. Aldershot won 4–0.

Manchester City missed three penalties in a Division One match against Newcastle United on 27 January 1912. They drew 1–1. City also missed a penalty against Newcastle in the last match of the 1925–26 season and were relegated from Division One. A draw would have saved them but they were beaten 3–2. Yet the highest number of penalty kicks converted by one player in a single season is 13 by Francis Lee for Manchester City in Division One during the 1971–72 season.

Billy Cook, the Everton right-back, scored from the penalty spot in three consecutive Division One matches for Everton over Christmas 1938: v. Blackpool (home) 24 December; v. Derby County (home) 26 December and v. Derby County (away) 27 December.

All four penalty kicks awarded in the F.A. Cup Final since it was switched to Wembley in 1923 have been converted, by Preston North End (1938), Blackpool (1948), West Bromwich Albion (1954) and Tottenham Hotspur (1962).

Three players failed with the same penalty kick in a Division Two match at Portsmouth on 22 September 1973. Notts County were awarded the penalty and Kevin Randall missed. A re-take was ordered and Don Masson hit the crossbar. From another attempt Brian Stubbs had his shot saved.

Players Union
The professional Footballers Association was formed as the Football Players and Trainers Union on 2 December 1907 after two previous attempts to form a union had been made in 1893 and 1898.

Pools
The first football pools were started in 1923.

Prison soccer
Among a number of thoroughly well-organised and extremely useful Soccer teams of prisoners which play in local leagues is the longest-standing at Wakefield Jail in Yorkshire. Of course, they play all their matches at home behind 'closed gates'.

Profit and loss
When Stoke City made a profit of £476,766, then the biggest on record by any club, on the 1976–77 season, they had been responsible for both the Football League's highest-ever profit and also the peak figure for the most massive deficit. That was when they lost £448,342 during 1974–75.

Nearby situated Crewe Alexandra reported a record loss of £45,773 in 1977 their centenary year. Donations of £4,935 from fund-raising efforts and a profit of £3,462 on their social club helped to reduce the season's debit to £37,715 but the club finished with liabilities of £95,596 made up by a bank overdraft of £41,380 and £54,216 owed to creditors.

Progress
Ronnie Williams played in Newcastle United's third team in a League match on Wednesday 26 September 1934. Three days later he led the Wales attack at Cardiff in a full international match against England.

Promotional flair
Hugh Jacobson, a left-back, was the only player who ever made maximum Football League appearances three times with the same club which won promotion in all three. He did it in helping Grimsby Town to ascend from Division Three in the 1925–26 season and from Division Two in 1928–29 and 1933–34.

Centre-half Chris Nicholl has achieved a unique hat-trick of quick promotion. He signed for Halifax Town in October 1968, and at the season's end they rose from Division Four. He moved to Luton Town in September 1969, and at that season's close they climbed out of Division Three. He signed for Aston Villa in March 1972 and two months later they, too, were promoted from Division Three. Transferred to Southampton he was in their Division Two promotion side in 1977–78.

Goalkeeper Bob Anderson ranks as the only player who, since the war, has been with two clubs in the same city when both won promotion from the same division. He was with Bristol Rovers when they won Division Three (Southern Section) promotion in 1953 and Bristol City when they achieved a similar success in 1955.

Receipts

The record receipts for a soccer game is the £500,000 (excluding radio and television fees) for the Arsenal v. Ipswich Town, F.A. Cup Final at Wembley on 6 May 1978.

Referees

The first official reference to a referee in Association Football appeared in the F.A. Challenge Cup rules in 1871. But his role was still not as one in complete control until 20 years later.

The weekday activities of one and another of the 100-plus on the Football League list of referees throw up a remarkable variety of occupations. Just about the most unusual of any referee in modern times must surely be that of Bristol's David Biddle – the city's police fingerprint expert.

On 21 December 1935 the train taking Mr B. Ames from the Midlands to referee a Division Three (Southern Section) match between Exeter City and Bristol Rovers was held up through fog and one of the linesmen had to take over the whistle until the referee's belated arrival at St. James' Park 20 minutes after the kick-off. The man who acted as linesman during that period was Exeter City's reserve centre-forward Jimmy McCambridge, who was a former Bristol Rovers player.

The Coventry City v. Southend United match in January 1962 had been in progress for three minutes before it was noticed that both teams were playing in blue and white. Referee Arthur Holland stopped play and Coventry changed into red shirts on the field.

Probably the only occasion in first-class football when a player asked the referee to leave the field took place at Hampden Park in the annual Sheffield v. Glasgow inter-city match on 22 September 1930. Sheffield were playing in white shirts and black shorts, and the referee, Mr J. Thomson of Burnbank, wore a white shirt and black shorts without a jacket. Captaining Sheffield was inside-right Jimmy Seed, and as soon as he found that he was passing the ball to the referee in error, he asked Mr Thomson to stop the game and put on a jacket. The referee duly obliged.

A freak goal that enabled Barrow to go to the top of Division Three in November 1968 was scored against Plymouth Argyle by Scottish striker George McLean. A harmless-looking shot by him was travelling wide of the goal when it struck Manchester referee Ivan Robinson and was diverted off course and into the net.

In April 1952 Huddersfield Town were beaten 1–0 at Tottenham by a freak goal. Eddie Baily played the ball twice when taking a corner-kick and yet when he centred with that second kick and Len Duquemin headed it into the net the referee allowed the goal to stand despite protests from a desperate Huddersfield side that was struggling to avoid relegation and needed every point.

The referee had positioned himself about five yards in from the corner flag and had been struck in the back by Baily's first kick before the Spurs player ran forward to centre the rebound.

Huddersfield were relegated but won promotion at the end of the 1952–53 season.

In the matter of supplying F.A. Cup final referees, Bolton is an easy first among all provincial towns and cities. Since the 1914–18 war J. T. Howcroft, A. E. Fogg, J. H. Clough, K. Dagnall and R. Matthewson, all of Bolton, have refereed the final. Sheffield is the only other town or city to have provided even three.

The entire London area persistently remains almost completely barren in producing top-class referees. Among the 100 referees on the Football League list in 1977–78 only two based at Isleworth and Uxbridge are from anywhere in the London area. And Ken Aston, of Ilford, ranks as the sole referee from the region of the capital who has controlled any of the post-war F.A. Cup finals. He refereed the 1963 match between Manchester United and Leicester City.

Nineteen players were sent off in the second leg of a Pinto Duran Cup match between Chile and Uruguay on 25 June 1975 in Santiago. Ten minutes before the end the match ended in a brawl and the referee sent off ten Chileans and nine Uruguayans.

The trouble began after 78 minutes when a Chilean defender put through his own goal to give Uruguay a 3–1 lead. Uruguay had also won the first leg 1–0 in Montevideo.

A player from each side began fighting and in the fracas which followed it was 15 minutes before the sent-off Uruguayans could leave the field with the rest of their team because the crowd was pelting them with missiles.

But a week later referee Sergio Vasquez of Chile was suspended and fined by the Chilean Referees Association for 'letting things get out of hand'.

On 4 January 1977 Uruguayan referee Hector Pedro Rodriguez, in charge of his first international, sent six Ecuador players off in Montevideo in a match against Uruguay. The match was abandoned in the 75th minute with the score 1–1.

Relegation blues

Bobby Owen was with three clubs in the 1976–77 season, and all suffered relegation. It was a tie-up unique in Football League history. From Carlisle United (relegated from Division Two) he went on loan to Northampton Town (who descended from Division Three) in October and to Workington (voted out of Division Four) in December. Once with Manchester City and Bury, he joined Doncaster Rovers in 1977–78.

By the time left-back Paul Garner was 21 he had been involved in four instances of relegation. With Huddersfield Town he went down from Division One in 1971–72; Division Two in 1972–73, and Division Three in 1974–75, and from Division One with Sheffield United in 1975–76.

Centre-half Colin Waldron has had the misfortune of have been concerned in four relegation instances. He was with Bury when they dropped out of Division Two in the 1966–67

season, and has gone down from Division One with Burnley in 1970–71 and again in 1975–76 and with Sunderland in 1976–77.

Centre-forward George Jones has been with clubs which finished in the depths in all four divisions. He went down from Division One with Blackburn Rovers in season 1965–66; Division Two with Bury in 1966–67 and again in 1968–69; Division Three with Bury in 1970–72 and Halifax Town in 1975–76, and was with Southport, re-elected to Division Four in 1976–77 and then were voted out in 1978.

One-time Middlesbrough forward Jimmy Lawson was with Huddersfield Town when they descended from Division One in 1972; Division Two in 1973 and Division Three in 1975 and with Halifax Town when they were compelled to seek re-election to Division Four at the end of 1976–77.

In 50 years of Football League activity before the war there was only one case – now-defunct Bradford Park Avenue – of a club being relegated twice in successive seasons. But in just over 30 years since then such a double descent has befallen all these: Doncaster Rovers, Lincoln City, Notts County, Brighton and Hove, Northampton Town, Fulham, Huddersfield Town, Crystal Palace and York City.

In the last 50 years 12 clubs have gone out of the Football League and never returned to it: Aberdare, Accrington Stanley, Ashington, Barrow, Bradford Park Avenue, Durham, Gateshead, Merthyr, Nelson, New Brighton, Thames and Wigan Borough. Workington and Southport, the last to go, may come under the same category. If these two have an idea they will ever get back, one particularly chilling fact might give them second thoughts. It is that since the 1914–18 war only three clubs ever achieved such a return after they had once lost their place: Gillingham, Lincoln City and Newport County.

Requiem

Leeds City won a Division Two match away against Wolverhampton Wanderers by 4–2 on 4 October 1919. It was the last match they ever played. During the following week they were expelled from the Football League and disbanded after having been found guilty of making illegal payments to players during the war.

Reversal of fortunes
In Swindon Town's first-ever Football League season of 1920–21 they defeated Luton Town by 9–1 in their opening match, but in their second they lost to Southampton by 4–0. They were the most widely-contrasting results on record in a team's first two League games in a season.

On 28 October 1905, Hull City's full-strength team lost a Division Two home game against Manchester United by 1–0, but their reserves won an F.A. Cup away tie against Denaby United by 2–0. On 17 October 1908, a full-strength team lost a Division Two home game to Grimsby Town by 2–0, but their reserves won an F.A. Cup tie away against Denby Dale by 11–0.

Royalty
The Duke of Edinburgh has said that all his sons are keenly interested in sport, and that they prefer football to polo. When Prince Charles was at Cheam School in Surrey in his early years he was given special soccer coaching by former Manchester City, Charlton Athletic and Southampton full-back Syd Cann.

Of those on Leicester City's board of directors in 1977–78, chairman Syd Needham has been awarded the O.B.E. and former chairman Len Shipman the C.B.E., while former manager and player Frank McLintock also owns the C.B.E.

Thirty-three past and present Football League players have now received awards in Royal Honours Lists, and they comprise 26 English, three Scottish, three Welsh and just one Irish. The one man from across the Irish Sea is Arsenal goalkeeper Pat Jennings, who was awarded the M.B.E. in 1976.

King George V was the first reigning monarch to attend a Football League match outside London when he saw the Manchester City v. Liverpool Division One match at Hyde Road on 27 March 1920. He was also the first to watch an F.A. Cup Final when he attended the Burnley v. Liverpool final at the Crystal Palace on 25 April 1914.

Saved
Four current Division One or Two clubs have never played in the Third, yet have finished last in the Second. Burnley (1902–03), Leicester City (1903–04), Blackpool (1908–09 and 1912–13) and Birmingham (1909–10) all did so at a time when there was no Division Three and all were re-elected. But Blackpool were relegated to the Third at the end of 1977–78.

Savings
When Hartlepools United were in the throes of a financial crisis in November 1966, manager Brian Clough decided to work for nothing until the situation eased and live on his savings in the meantime.

Scots in English football
The rare fact about this Accrington Stanley eleven, which played against York City in a Division Three (Northern Section) match in April 1955: McQueen; Ashe, Harrower; Hunter, Ryden, Sneddon; Devlin, Currie, Stewart, Wright, Scott was that it was the first all-Scottish team to turn out for an English club for well over 70 years.

One Football League club after another has lost heavily in recent years in selling to Scottish clubs players who had cost them far more than they collected. The biggest fee any English club has received in any such deal was the £120,000 paid by Hibernian to Everton for Joe Harper in January 1974.

It has happened only twice in around 40 years that the then exciting record transfer fee paid by a Football League club was made out to one in Scotland. The first instance was when Derby County paid Morton £15,000 for inside-forward Billy Steel in June 1947. The second occurred when Kenny Dalglish signed from Celtic in August 1977 costing Liverpool £440,000.

Size
Several goalkeepers of 5ft. 7in. have figured in the Football League in recent years, but the smallest ever known was Jerry Best, who kept for Coventry City and Halifax Town between the wars. The tallest of all time was Bill Carr, a Bournemouth goalkeeper of the mid-twenties who possessed a height of 6ft. 8¾in.

Substitutes
England's first substitute in a full international match was Jimmy Mullen (Wolverhampton Wanderers), who took over from the injured Jackie Milburn after ten minutes of the game against Belgium in Brussels on 18 May 1950.

Bobby Knox, a Barrow forward, scored the first Football League goal by a substitute against Wrexham on 21 August 1965. He was the first number twelve to save a penalty-kick when, as an emergency goalkeeper, he did so against Doncaster Rovers on the following 27 December.

Sunday matches
The first Football League game to be played on a Sunday was between Millwall and Fulham on the morning of 20 January 1974 during the industrial crisis of the three-day working week.

Supporters Clubs
The National Federation of Football Supporters Clubs was formed in 1927.

Survivor
Few managers survive to put in well over a decade with the same non-League club, but that is what has been achieved by Terry Bly, whose feat of collecting 52 Division Four goals for Peterborough United in the 1960–61 season still stands as a Football League post-war record. In October 1964 he became manager of the Southern League club Grantham and was still in charge of them in 1977–78.

Suspensions
A number of players have been suspended from the game sine die following serious offences, although many of those suspensions were subsequently lifted, but the player who claimed to have suffered more suspensions than any other was Frank Barson, one of the country's most accomplished centre-halves in the 1920s. Indeed, he was such an outstanding prospect that he was chosen to play for England in one game soon after World War One and there is no doubt that, but for his reputation with referees, he would have won many more appearances for his country.

A powerfully built Yorkshireman from Barnsley, Barson made his League debut with his local club in the 1911–12 season and soon earned a reputation for his hard-tackling and generally robust play. His first serious trouble came in 1914–15 when Barnsley were making a bid for promotion to Division One, although the actual game in which the particular incident occurred to this wholehearted player was a Cuptie at Everton when Barnsley lost 3–0. Both Barson and Everton's George Harrison were sent off and subsequently suspended for a month.

During World War One, Barson received a two months suspension for a foul on a Birmingham winger and then in October 1919 he was transferred to Aston Villa at a time when they looked like slipping into Division Two. Barson proved such an asset that Villa rose to ninth position that term and also won the F.A. Cup. But in the final Barson was actually warned about his conduct by referee Jack Howcroft before the kick-off.

At the beginning of the following season Barson received a 14 days suspension because he missed the opening game after refusing to live in Birmingham, and before that season was over the club had suspended him for another seven days.

Despite these problems Manchester United thought so highly of him as a player that they paid Villa the large sum at the time of £5,000 for his transfer in 1922 and he remained with this club for six seasons.

Incidentally, Barson was reported to have left the Villa after a row when the directors had ordered his friend, Stan Fazackerley of Everton, out of the Villa dressing-room after a game and Barson refused to apologise. He also refused to re-sign for the Villa and the League would not allow the club to pay him a share of the transfer fee as his accrued share of benefit.

In 1928 he moved to Watford and this is where he ran into his longest suspension. On 29 September Watford were beaten 6–2 at home by Fulham, Barson was sent off following an incident involving a Fulham player. The referee needed police protection and the Watford supporters raised a petition signed by 5,000 people claiming that the only reason their centre-half had been sent off was because his name was Barson. They claimed that if he had been called Smith, Jones or Brown the referee would have ignored the incident in question. The plea failed at F.A. headquarters where they considered the player's past record and suspended him for the remainder of that season – seven months.

In the summer of 1930 Barson moved to Wigan Borough, then a Division Three (Northern Section) club, and in a game against Accrington Stanley that December he was sent off for an alleged foul on Jack Ferguson and this time he received a three months suspension and a £5 fine. And the 1930–31 season was this outstanding personality's last as a player in the Football League although he was subsequently sent off a number of times while player-manager of Rhyl Athletic.

Between the wars there were instances of players being suspended for a whole season for mis-behaviour. But in over 30 post-war years the longest term imposed on any Football League player for match offences was five months in December 1971 on Manchester United's Kevin Lewis, who survived the ordeal and later joined Stoke City.

The longest-ever suspension on Football League players for match misbehaviour, as distinct from bribery offences, affected Willie Cook (Oldham Athletic left-back) from 16 April 1915 to 30 April 1916 and Cyril Hunter (Gateshead centre-half) from 22 April 1931 to the end of the 1931–32 season.

Manchester United finished a point ahead of Chelsea in the bottom three places of Division One in the 1914–15 season with Tottenham Hotspur last of all, but when normal peace-time football resumed in 1919 Tottenham dropped into Division Two while Arsenal were elected to take their place in the newly enlarged Division One. But Chelsea escaped relegation because in 1914–15 Manchester United and Liverpool had taken part in a 'fixed' match. Manchester United had won it but an enquiry had shown that a number of players taking part had agreed to 'fix' the result so that they could profit from fixed-odd betting. The outcome of that game had affected Chelsea's position near the foot of the table.

The Football Association permanently sus-pended seven of the players, four on one side and three on the other, who had taken part in this Division One match on 2 April 1915. In 1919 a number of these suspensions were lifted in appreciation of war service. Enoch West, the Manchester United centre-forward, was one of them, but the ban on him was lifted in November 1945 – 30 years later. It was the longest suspen-sion that was subsequently lifted, ever to have been imposed on a Football League professional.

Tie
In Division One 1907–08 Blackburn Rovers and Woolwich Arsenal finished with identical records, not only in the number of games won, lost and drawn, but also in the number of goals scored and conceded – W12 L14 D12 F51 A63. Nothing like this ever happened before or since.

Togetherness
Trevor Ford, Ray Daniel, Ivor Allchurch, John Charles, Mel Charles and Barrie Jones all spent their early careers with Swansea Town, all moved to English clubs, all became Welsh inter-nationals, and were all later recruited by Cardiff City on returning to South Wales.

In the 1937–38 season Charlton Athletic's pro-fessional staff included four centre-backs, John Oakes, Frank Rist, Bert Tann and George Hunt, all of whom had had previous service with Clapton Orient.

Tours
Oxford University were the first English team to make an overseas tour when they visited Germany in 1875.

Two in one
Queen's Park Rangers defender Dave Clement played in two matches for the club against Watford on the same Saturday in 1966 – in the South-East Counties League in the morning and in the Football Combination in the afternoon. He finished on the winning side both times.

Goalkeeper Fred Swift played for Oldham Athletic against Preston North End in a Division Two match at Deepdale on the morning of Easter Monday 2 April 1934, and for their reserves against Preston Reserves in a Central League game at Boundary Park in the afternoon.

Transfers
Transfer fees have been considered as private and confidential by the Football League since 1922 and are not officially disclosed.

The first four-figure transfer fee was £1,000 for the transfer of Alf Common from Sunderland to Middlesbrough in February 1905.

David Jack was transferred from Bolton Wan-derers to Arsenal in October 1928 for £10,890 in the first five-figure move and Tony Hateley was concerned in the most probable six-figure transfer when he joined Chelsea from Aston Villa in October 1966 for £100,000.

The record transfer fee received for an English player was thought to be £500,000 when Liverpool transferred Kevin Keegan to Hamburg of the West German Bundesliga.

The highest transfer deal between British clubs was transacted in February 1978 when Manchester United signed Gordon McQueen from Leeds United for £495,000.

The first £1 million transfer involving one player was probably the £922,000 paid by the Spanish club Barcelona for the services of Johan Cruyff of Ajax Amsterdam of Holland in August 1973. Cruyff's share of the transfer was reported to be approximately £400,000.

Sunderland was probably the first football club in the world to pay a transfer fee of as much as £5,000 for a player. That was in 1922 when they signed Hull City's Scottish international centre-half, Mick Gilhooley. Unfortunately, because of injury he only made 20 League appearances during his stay at Roker Park although he made something of a come-back with Bradford City in 1925.

Blackpool are the only club which has sold two goalkeepers for six-figure fees: John Burridge to Aston Villa for £100,000 in September 1975 and George Wood to Everton for £140,000 in August 1977.

Two of the oddest series of transfers of recent times concern a pair of three-times clubmates. Mike Culleton and Terry Bailey both signed as teenagers from Port Vale, who later discarded them. Both moved to the Northern Premier League with Stafford Rangers, from whom both were brought back by Vale, with whom they were during 1977–78.

Travelling man
Few, if any, other British-born players have had to travel so far from his club when going home as John Buchanan. He was born at Dingwall in the north of Scotland, so during his service with Northampton town and Cardiff City in turn a round trip home and back has meant a trek of around 1,500 miles.

Versatile Varsity
The rival seats of learning at Oxford and Cambridge have produced outstanding figures in many ages and many spheres, but Ron Atkinson claims to be the only Soccer personality who has won honours with the clubs of both cities. As a player he helped Oxford United to rise from Division Four to Two; then he managed Cambridge United, whom he led to the Division Four title in the 1976–77 season.

Versatility
Gordon Nisbet of West Bromwich Albion made his first League appearance as a goalkeeper and his next as a full-back, a position he kept subsequently with the club and later when transferred to Hull City.

Tony Read was the recognised Luton Town goalkeeper when he was experimented as a striker in the 1965–66 season when he scored 16 goals in Division Four, including a hat-trick against Notts County on 20 November.

Wanderers
Inside-forward Leslie Roberts, born at Redditch, played with more Football League clubs (16) than any other player in history. Between 1921 and 1936 he was with Aston Villa, Chesterfield, Sheffield Wednesday, Bristol Rovers, Merthyr Town, Bournemouth, Bolton Wanderers, Swindon Town, Brentford, Manchester City, Crystal Palace, Chester, Rochdale, Rotherham United and New Brighton in that order, and also had a spell with Scunthorpe United who were then members of the Midland League.

Between 1946 and 1958 outside-left Alan Daley played for Mansfield Town, Hull City, Bangor City, Worksop Town, Doncaster Rovers, Boston United, Scunthorpe United, Corby Town, Mansfield (again), Stockport County, Crewe Alexandra and Coventry City in that order.

Barnsley-born Joe Hooley has played for Barnsley, Sheffield United, Workington, Bradford Park Avenue, Bedford Town, Accrington Stanley, Dover, Ramsgate, Burton Albion, Holbeach United and Poole Town. Since then he has coached Sudan's national team, Alfreton, Colchester United, in Iceland twice, Norway twice, Worksop Town and in Germany. And he was only 38 in 1977.

Brian Birch was a forward with Manchester United, Wolverhampton Wanderers, Oldham Athletic, Exeter City, Lincoln City, Barrow and Boston United before he began something like a world tour as a coach. Countries in which he has taught the Soccer gospel include Australia, Turkey, Egypt and Sweden in 1977 at the age of 43.

Harold Mather was a Burnley full-back for 18 years before and after the war, but in the next seven years he had eight jobs elsewhere as manager, coach or trainer. In that time he was with Nelson, Hull City, Kettering Town, Colwyn Bay, Grimsby Town, in South Africa and Iraq and with Accrington Stanley.

Ian Macfarlane is a Scot in English Soccer who has also moved around. He left Aberdeen as a back for Chelsea in August 1956, passed on to Leicester City and since he turned to coaching has been with Bath City, Sheffield Wednesday, Sunderland, Newcastle United, Carlisle United, Middlesbrough, Manchester City, back to Sunderland and in 1977 linked up with Leicester again.

Few goalkeepers develop such a rolling-stone flair as former England international Tony Waiters. In the last 10 years he has been a Blackpool player, a coach with Liverpool, Burnley, Coventry City, Tranmere Rovers, and the England Youth team, a Chelsea scout, Plymouth Argyle's manager and a coach in Vancouver in Canada's Far West – and all when under the age of 40.

Former Bradford City, Nottingham Forest, Newcastle United, Birmingham City, Sheffield United, Norwich City and Aston Villa, English-born but Welsh international Trevor Hockey is credited with having been the youngest-ever player to turn out on all 92 Football League grounds. He had completed the circuit by the time he was 25.

Irish international half-back Tommy Casey who played in the 1958 World Cup has had an affinity with sea breezes. He played for Bangor in Northern Ireland, later with Bournemouth, Newcastle United and Portsmouth, then coached or managed Everton and Grimsby Town, and in 1977 was seen on the coast still, again coaching, in Iceland.

Scottish inside-forward Frank Sharp was with three Football League clubs in two days in

February 1969. Carlisle United loaned him to Southport, recalled him on 18 February and transferred him to Cardiff City on 19 February.

Yorkshire-born goalkeeper Steve Sherwood was with three League clubs in four days. In season 1976–77 he left Chelsea for Fulham on a month's loan on a Tuesday, but on the following Friday he was sold to Watford.

Len Richley, a native of the North East, fulfilled post-war assignments with four of the area's Football League clubs. He followed spells as a half-back with Sunderland and Hartlepool and one as Darlington's manager by becoming Newcastle United's chief scout.

The wives of many football folk must often tire of constant domestic upheavals. Take the case of Peter Taylor, who has been associated with Brian Clough at Middlesbrough, Derby, Brighton, and now Forest, and who earlier put in service with Coventry City and Burton Albion. During his career he has moved house fourteen times.

War-time oddities
Rules had to be relaxed during World War Two. In one match Norwich City defeated Brighton & Hove Albion 18–0; the visitors being composed of five players, a couple of Norwich reserves and soldiers recruited on the ground.

Weather
The weather was so inclement at Blundells Park on 6 February 1912 that 10 minutes from the end of the Grimsby Town v. Leicester Fosse match with Grimsby leading 4–0 some of the visitors, then facing a biting wind, left the field, either singly or in pairs until there were only five of the team remaining.

The Fosse trainer walked to the line and together with goalkeeper Frank Mearns made further protests about the conditions – it was raining and sleeting heavily. But after consulting his linesmen referee A. Adams of Nottingham ordered play to continue. Grimsby Town made little effort to add to their score in the few minutes that remained and won 4–0.

The men who had left the field claimed that it was not a protest against conditions but because they were genuinely ill.

The hottest weather in which Football League matches were ever played was that on the opening day of the 1906–07 season. It reached 90°F in the shade in some parts of the country, and many players collapsed through sheer exhaustion. Five of Manchester City did so in a game against Woolwich Arsenal. Arsenal did not seem to mind for they went on to win 4–1 while City finished this Division One game with only six men, on 1 September 1906.

Every season brings long and abortive journeys for this team and that because of weather postponements, and whenever such a situation arises Carlisle United have rueful and painful memories. In December 1965 they travelled all the way to Plymouth for a match that had to be called off. No other team ever travelled that far for a game that could not be played. Distance involved: 778 miles round trip.

Only two Football League matches in the whole of this century have had to be postponed because fog prevented the visiting team reaching its destination. It happened to Rotherham United at Hartlepool on 22 December 1934 and to Millwall at Swansea on 21 December 1946.

A match between Bolton Wanderers and Sheffield Wednesday in 1894 was postponed because it was 'very windy'. Another 80 years elapsed before another Football League fixture was called off because of high winds. It was one between Newcastle United and Liverpool on 28 December 1974.

Women's football
Women's clubs have been in existence since the 1890s. One of the most famous was Dick Kerr's XI formed in 1894 at Preston. The Football Association recognised women's football in 1969.

Women in football
More Football League clubs have given the secretary's job to a woman in recent years than ever before. In the 1977–78 season Chelsea had Christine Mathews acting in that capacity, and Colchester United (Mrs E. Scott) and Scunthorpe United (Mrs S. Louth) provided the other examples. Crystal Palace, Halifax Town and Exeter City also have had women secretaries.

World Championships
In 1888, after West Bromwich Albion's surprise 2–1 victory in the F.A. Cup Final over Preston North End and Renton's 6–1 thrashing of Cambuslang in the Scottish Cup Final, the two winning sides met for what was billed as 'The Championship of the World'.

The game was played at Hampden Park on 19 May 1888 in heavy rain coupled with spasmodic thunder and lightning. The pitch was inches deep in water and there were interruptions in each half when the players had to leave the field to allow the worst downpours to pass over. But while these conditions obviously upset the visitors, Renton revelled in them and ran out 4–0 winners.

West Bromwich Albion claimed that because of the state of the pitch and the interruptions the game could not be considered a test, but many Scottish critics believed that the Renton side was so much at the peak of their form at this time that no team in England could have held them. It was certainly true that even the waterlogged pitch had not diminished the brilliance of their passing.

Youngest
Albert Geldard is believed to have been the youngest player to appear in a Football League match. He was 15 years 156 days old when he made his debut for Bradford Park Avenue against Millwall on 16 September 1929, a Division Two match.

He had attended Whiteley Lane School and won schoolboy international honours for England and joined the Bradford club from Manningham Mills as an amateur in 1928.

Later he played for Everton and Bolton Wanderers, where he ended his career in 1947. He played four times for England at outside-right. In November 1949 he made a brief come-back with Darwen.

Ronnie Dix is believed to have been the youngest player to score in a Football League match. He was 15 years 180 days old when he scored for Bristol Rovers against Norwich City on 3 March 1928 in a Division Three (Southern Section) game.

He had attended South Central School, Bristol, and joined the Bristol club before making his League debut just seven days before his first League goal.

Later he played for Blackburn Rovers, Aston Villa, Derby County, Tottenham Hotspur and Reading in a career which spanned the war years. He made one appearance for England.

Terry Neill captained his club Arsenal when only 20 years old, the Northern Ireland international side when 21 and at 25 he was the youngest Players Union chairman appointed to the position. He became player-manager of Hull City at 28 and had a similar appointment with Ireland when 29. With Tottenham Hotspur he came the youngest manager in Division One at 32 before taking a similar position with Arsenal.

Robbie James, born in March 1957, became the youngest player to complete 100 Football League appearances when he played for Swansea City against Torquay United on 14 February 1976.

Youth tournaments

The International Youth Tournament was first contested in 1948 and is open to members of UEFA for youths under 18 years of age. Eight countries competed in the initial competition but a qualifying tournament now reduces the entries for this annual event to sixteen teams in the final stages played in one country.

England has been the most successful team with victories in 1948, 1963, 1964, 1971, 1972, 1973 and 1975. In 1955 and 1956 there was no final as such, with the tournament being played in groups only.

The World Youth Tournament was first contested in 1977 and organised under the auspices of FIFA for players between 16 and 18 years of age on 1 January of the year of the tournament. Sixteen teams were included in the final stages held in Tunisia and the USSR won the title.

The South American Youth Tournament was first contested in 1954 with the original intention of holding it every four years. But it has been held rather irregularly since and of the seven tournaments completed Uruguay, the first winners, have won it four times.

Yo-yo effect

Shildon-born goalkeeper, John Hope, played in all four divisions of the Football League in the course of only seven consecutive games. In the 1966–67 season he was with Darlington in Division Three and they were relegated that term. He played four games in Division Four before his transfer to Newcastle United in March 1969 and then made one appearance for them in Division One. His next League appearance was with Sheffield United in Division Two in 1970–71.

Liverpool rank as the only club ever to have finished first, last and first in that sequence in the table in successive seasons. They were Division Two champions in 1893–94, at the bottom of Division One a year later, and champions of Division Two again in 1895–96.

A study of the ups and downs of the League clubs in the last two decades makes out Colchester United to be easily Soccer's champion yo-yo. Since the 1960s they have now descended from Division Three four times and have risen from the Fourth just as often.

There are few contemporary players who have had as much of an up-and-down career in a strictly literal sense as Cambridge United and ex-Rotherham United and Doncaster Rovers midfield player Graham Watson. He has had four promotions and three relegations. Watson went down with Rotherham (1967–68), up with Doncaster (1968–69) and down with them (1970–71), up with Cambridge (1972–73), down with them (1973–74), and up with them (1976–77) and (1977–78).

Rodney Johnson has figured in promotion or relegation with all the four clubs for whom he has played in his native Yorkshire. He was with Leeds United when they took the Division One title in season 1963–64, Doncaster Rovers when they were Division Four champions in 1968–69, with Rotherham United when they descended from Division Three in 1972–73, and with Bradford City when they rose from Division Four in 1976–77 and down again the following season.

Don McEvoy was a centre-half with two Yorkshire clubs when both in turn were relegated one season and promoted the next. With Huddersfield Town he went down in 1952 and up in 1953; with Sheffield Wednesday he went down in 1955 and up in 1956.

WORLD CUP

The 11th World Cup final tournament was held in Argentina in June 1978 in five cities and on six grounds. Cordoba, Mendoza, Rosario and Mar del Plata provided one venue each while two were used in the capital of Buenos Aires at the River Plate and Velez Sarsfield stadiums.

Brazil is the only country to have appeared in all 11 final stages and of the 16 teams in 1978 only Iran and Tunisia had never previously reached the finals, thus becoming the 46th and 47th different countries to achieve this honour.

The World Cup trophy itself is now the second in the lifetime of the competition. The first was named after Jules Rimet, the late Honorary President of FIFA from 1921 to 1954. Brazil won this Cup outright in 1970.

A new trophy of solid gold 36 cm high known as the FIFA World Cup and designed by an Italian from an entry of some 53 submitted for selection was used in 1974 for the first time.

Of the five different previous winners of the competition: Brazil, Italy, West Germany, Uruguay and England, only the last two named did not qualify in 1978.

Argentina became the sixth winners, beating Holland 3–1 after extra-time.

CÓRDOBA

ROSARIO

PARAGUAY

CHILE

ARGENTINA

MENDOZA

BUENOS AIRES
RIVER PLATE/VELEZ SARSFIELD

MAR DEL PLATA

The first goal scored in the World Cup was credited to Louis Laurent for France against Mexico on 13 July 1930 in Montevideo. France won 4–1. It was Bastille Day.

The fastest goal scored in a World Cup final tournament was probably attributed to Olle Nyberg of Sweden against Hungary on 16 June 1938 in Paris, after approximately 30 seconds of play. Bernard Lacombe scored for France against Italy in 31 seconds during the 1978 tournament.

Vava (real name Edwaldo Izidio Neto) of Brazil is the only player to have scored in successive World Cup finals. He did so against Sweden in 1958 (scoring twice) and against Czechoslovakia in 1962. Pele is the only other to score in 1958 and once against Italy in 1970.

WORLD CUP APPEARANCES

Antonio Carbajal (Mexico) is the only player to have appeared in five World Cup final tournaments. He kept goal for Mexico in 1950, 1954, 1958, 1962 and 1966, making 11 appearances in all.

Uwe Seeler (West Germany) established a record of appearances in World Cup final tournaments by making a total 21 appearances in 1958, 1962, 1966 and 1970 as a centre-forward.

Antonio Carbajal of Mexico, the only player to appear in five different World Cup final tournaments.

Pele (Brazil) is the only player to have been with three World Cup winning teams, though he missed the final of the 1962 competition because of injury. He made four appearances in the 1958 final tournament, two in 1962 before injury and six in 1970. He also appeared in two matches in 1966 for a total of 14 appearances in all.

Mario Zagalo is the only man who has won a World Cup winners medal and managed a World Cup winning team. He played in the 1958 and 1962 World Cup winning teams of Brazil and was manager when they achieved their third success in 1970.

Goalscoring

Just Fontaine (France) scored a record 13 goals in six matches of the 1958 World Cup final tournament. Gerd Muller (West Germany) scored 10 goals in 1970 and four in 1974 for the highest aggregate of 14 goals. Fontaine and Jairzinho (Brazil) are the only two players to have scored in every match in a final series, as Jairzinho scored seven goals in six matches in 1970.

Including World Cup qualifying matches in the 1970 series, Muller scored a total of 19 goals with nine coming six preliminary games and ten in the final stages.

Pele is the third highest scorer in World Cup final tournaments, having registered 12 goals in his four competitions.

Geoff Hurst (England) is the only player to have scored a hat-trick in a final when he registered three of his side's goals in their 4–2 win over West Germany in 1966.

The first player to score as many as four goals in any World Cup match was Paddy Moore who registered all the Republic of Ireland's goals in the 4–4 draw with Belgium in Dublin during a World Cup qualifying match on 25 February 1934.

Robbie Rensenbrink (Holland) scored the 1,000th goal in World Cup finals when he converted a penalty against Scotland in the 1978 tournament.

1978 WORLD CUP QUALIFYING COMPETITION

EUROPE (West Germany already qualified as holders)

GROUP 1
Poland, Portugal, Denmark, Cyprus.

23–5–76	Cyprus (1) 1	Denmark (3) 5
16–10–76	Portugal (0) 0	Poland (0) 2
27–10–76	Denmark (0) 5	Cyprus (0) 0
31–10–76	Poland (3) 5	Cyprus (0) 0
17–11–76	Portugal (0) 1	Denmark (0) 0
5–12–76	Cyprus (0) 1	Portugal (1) 2
1–5–77	Denmark (0) 1	Poland (1) 2
15–5–77	Cyprus (1) 1	Poland (2) 3
21–9–77	Poland (2) 4	Denmark (0) 1
9–10–77	Denmark (1) 2	Portugal (2) 4
29–10–77	Poland (1) 1	Portugal (0) 1
16–11–77	Portugal (2) 4	Cyprus (0) 0

	P	W	D	L	F	A	Pts
Poland	6	5	1	0	17	4	11
Portugal	6	4	1	1	12	6	9
Denmark	6	2	0	4	14	12	4
Cyprus	6	0	0	6	3	24	0

GROUP 2
Italy, England, Finland, Luxembourg.

13–6–76	Finland (1) 1	England (2) 4
22–9–76	Finland (3) 7	Luxembourg (0) 1
13–10–76	England (1) 2	Finland (0) 1
16–10–76	Luxembourg (0) 1	Italy (2) 4
17–11–76	Italy (1) 2	England (0) 0
30–3–77	England (1) 5	Luxembourg (0) 0
26–5–77	Luxembourg (0) 0	Finland (0) 1
8–6–77	Finland (0) 0	Italy (1) 3
12–10–77	Luxembourg (0) 0	England (1) 2
15–10–77	Italy (3) 6	Finland (0) 1
16–11–77	England (1) 2	Italy (0) 0
3–12–77	Italy (2) 3	Luxembourg (0) 0

	P	W	D	L	F	A	Pts
Italy	6	5	0	1	18	4	10
England	6	5	0	1	15	4	10
Finland	6	2	0	4	11	16	4
Luxembourg	6	0	0	6	2	22	0

GROUP 3
East Germany, Austria, Turkey, Malta.

31–10–76	Turkey (1) 4	Malta (0) 0
17–11–76	East Germany (1) 1	Turkey (1) 1
5–12–76	Malta (0) 0	Austria (0) 1
2–4–77	Malta (0) 0	East Germany (0) 1
17–4–77	Austria (1) 1	Turkey (0) 0
30–4–77	Austria (4) 9	Malta (0) 0
24–9–77	Austria (1) 1	East Germany (1) 1
12–10–77	East Germany (0) 1	Austria (1) 1
29–10–77	East Germany (3) 9	Malta (0) 0
30–10–77	Turkey (0) 0	Austria (0) 1
16–11–77	Turkey (0) 1	East Germany (1) 2
27–11–77	Malta (0) 0	Turkey (2) 3

	P	W	D	L	F	A	Pts
Austria	6	4	2	0	14	2	10
East Germany	6	3	3	0	15	4	9
Turkey	6	2	1	3	9	5	5
Malta	6	0	0	6	0	27	0

GROUP 4
Netherlands, Belgium, Northern Ireland, Iceland.

5–9–76	Iceland (0) 0	Belgium (0) 1
8–9–76	Iceland (0) 0	Netherlands (1) 1
13–10–76	Netherlands (0) 2	Northern Ireland (1) 2
10–11–76	Begium (1) 2	Northern Ireland (0) 0
26–3–77	Belgium (0) 0	Netherlands (1) 2
11–6–77	Iceland (1) 1	Northern Ireland (0) 0
31–8–77	Netherlands (3) 4	Iceland (0) 1
4–9–77	Belgium (2) 4	Iceland (0) 0
21–9–77	Northern Ireland (0) 2	Iceland (0) 0
12–10–77	Northern Ireland (0) 0	Netherlands (0) 1
26–10–77	Netherlands (1) 1	Belgium (0) 0
16–11–77	Northern Ireland (1) 3	Belgium (0) 0

	P	W	D	L	F	A	Pts
Holland	6	5	1	0	11	3	11
Belgium	6	3	0	3	7	6	6
Northern Ireland	6	2	1	3	7	6	5
Iceland	6	1	0	5	2	12	2

GROUP 5
Bulgaria, France, Eire.

9–10–76	Bulgaria (1) 2	France (2) 2
17–11–76	France (0) 2	Eire (0) 0
30–3–77	Eire (1) 1	France (0) 0
1–6–77	Bulgaria (1) 2	Eire (0) 1
12–10–77	Eire (0) 0	Bulgaria (0) 0
16–11–77	France (1) 3	Bulgaria (0) 1

	P	W	D	L	F	A	Pts
France	4	2	1	1	7	4	5
Bulgaria	4	1	2	1	5	6	4
Eire	4	1	1	2	2	4	3

GROUP 6
Sweden, Switzerland, Norway.

16–6–76	Sweden (2) 2	Norway (0) 0
8–9–76	Norway (0) 1	Switzerland (0) 0
9–10–76	Switzerland (1) 1	Sweden (1) 2
8–6–77	Sweden (0) 2	Switzerland (0) 1
7–9–77	Norway (1) 2	Sweden (0) 1
30–10–77	Switzerland (1) 1	Norway (0) 0

	P	W	D	L	F	A	Pts
Sweden	4	3	0	1	7	4	6
Norway	4	2	0	2	3	4	4
Switzerland	4	1	0	3	3	5	2

GROUP 7
Scotland, Czechoslovakia, Wales.

13–10–76	Czechoslovakia (0) 2	Scotland (0) 0
17–11–76	Scotland (1) 1	Wales (0) 0
30–3–77	Wales (1) 3	Czechoslovakia (0) 0
21–9–77	Scotland (2) 3	Czechoslovakia (0) 1
12–10–77	Wales (0) 0	Scotland (0) 2
16–11–77	Czechoslovakia (1) 1	Wales (0) 0

	P	W	D	L	F	A	Pts
Scotland	4	3	0	1	6	3	6
Czechoslovakia	4	2	0	2	4	6	4
Wales	4	1	0	3	3	4	2

GROUP 8
Yugoslavia, Spain, Rumania.

10–10–76	Spain (0) 1	Yugoslavia (0) 0
6–4–77	Rumania (1) 1	Spain (0) 0
8–5–77	Yugoslavia (0) 0	Rumania (2) 2
26–10–77	Spain (0) 2	Rumania (0) 0
3–11–77	Rumania (3) 4	Yugoslavia (2) 6
30–11–77	Yugoslavia (0) 0	Spain (0) 1

	P	W	D	L	F	A	Pts
Spain	4	3	0	1	4	1	6
Rumania	4	2	0	2	7	8	4
Yugoslavia	4	1	0	3	6	8	2

GROUP 9
USSR, Hungary, Greece.
9–10–76	Greece (0) 1	Hungary (0) 1
24–4–77	USSR (1) 2	Greece (0) 0
30–4–77	Hungary (1) 2	USSR (0) 1
10–5–77	Greece (0) 1	USSR (0) 0
18–5–77	USSR (2) 2	Hungary (0) 0
25–5–77	Hungary (2) 3	Greece (0) 0

	P	W	D	L	F	A	Pts
Hungary	4	2	1	1	6	4	5
USSR	4	2	0	2	5	3	4
Greece	4	1	1	2	2	6	3

SOUTH AMERICA (Argentina already qualified as host nation)

GROUP 1
Brazil, Paraguay, Colombia.
20–2–77	Colombia (0) 0	Brazil (0) 0
24–2–77	Colombia (0) 0	Paraguay (1) 1
6–3–77	Paraguay (0) 1	Colombia (0) 1
9–3–77	Brazil (4) 6	Colombia (0) 0
13–3–77	Paraguay (0) 0	Brazil (0) 1
20–3–77	Brazil (1) 1	Paraguay (0) 1

	P	W	D	L	F	A	Pts
Brazil	4	2	2	0	8	1	6
Paraguay	4	1	2	1	3	3	4
Colombia	4	0	2	2	1	8	2

GROUP 2
Uruguay, Venezuela, Bolivia.
9–2–77	Venezuela (0) 1	Uruguay (1) 1
27–2–77	Bolivia (0) 1	Uruguay (0) 0
6–3–77	Venezuela (0) 1	Bolivia (1) 3
13–3–77	Bolivia (2) 2	Venezuela (0) 0
17–3–77	Uruguay (1) 2	Venezuela (0) 0
27–3–77	Uruguay (1) 2	Bolivia (1) 2

	P	W	D	L	F	A	Pts
Bolivia	4	3	1	0	8	3	7
Uruguay	4	1	2	1	5	4	4
Venezuela	4	0	1	3	2	8	1

GROUP 3
Chile, Peru, Ecuador.
20–2–77	Ecuador (0) 1	Peru (1) 1
27–2–77	Ecuador (0) 0	Chile (1) 1
6–3–77	Chile (1) 1	Peru (0) 1
12–3–77	Peru (1) 4	Ecuador (0) 0
20–3–77	Chile (2) 3	Ecuador (0) 0
26–3–77	Peru (0) 2	Chile (0) 0

	P	W	D	L	F	A	Pts
Peru	4	2	2	0	8	2	6
Chile	4	2	1	1	5	3	5
Ecuador	4	0	1	3	1	9	1

SOUTH AMERICAN PLAY-OFF
10–7–77	Brazil (0) 1	Peru (0) 0
14–7–77	Brazil (4) 8	Bolivia (0) 0
17–7–77	Peru (2) 5	Bolivia (0) 0

	P	W	D	L	F	A	Pts
Brazil	2	2	0	0	9	0	4
Peru	2	1	0	1	5	1	2
Bolivia	2	0	0	2	0	13	0

Brazil and Peru qualified, Bolivia had to play-off against the European Group 9 winner, Hungary.

EUROPEAN/SOUTH AMERICAN PLAY-OFF
29–10–77	Hungary (5) 6	Bolivia (0) 0
30–11–77	Bolivia (1) 2	Hungary (2) 3

CONCACAF

GROUP 1 (northern)
Canada, USA, Mexico.
24–9–76	Canada (0) 1	USA (1) 1
3–10–76	USA (0) 0	Mexico (0) 0
10–10–76	Canada (1) 1	Mexico (0) 0
15–10–76	Mexico (2) 3	USA (0) 0
20–10–76	USA (0) 2	Canada (0) 0
27–10–76	Mexico (0) 0	Canada (0) 0

	P	W	D	L	F	A	Pts
Mexico	4	1	2	1	3	1	4
USA	4	1	2	1	3	4	4
Canada	4	1	2	1	2	3	4

Play-off for second place:
22–12–76 Canada (1) 3 USA (0) 0
Mexico and Canada qualified for six-nation play-off.

GROUP 2 (central)
Guatemala, El Salvador, Costa Rica, Panama.
4–4–76	Panama (0) 3	Costa Rica (1) 2
2–5–76	Panama (0) 1	El Salvador (1) 1
11–7–76	Costa Rica (3) 3	Panama (0) 0
1–8–76	El Salvador (2) 4	Panama (0) 1
17–9–76	Panama (2) 2	Guatemala (0) 4
26–9–76	Guatemala (3) 7	Panama (0) 0
1–12–76	El Salvador (1) 1	Costa Rica (0) 1
5–12–76	Costa Rica (0) 0	Guatemala (1) 0
8–12–76	Guatemala (2) 3	El Salvador (1) 1
12–12–76	Guatemala (0) 1	Costa Rica (0) 1
17–12–76	Costa Rica (1) 1	El Salvador (0) 1
19–12–76	El Salvador (1) 2	Guatemala (0) 0

	P	W	D	L	F	A	Pts
Guatemala	6	3	2	1	15	6	8
El Salvador	6	2	3	1	10	7	7
Costa Rica	6	1	4	1	8	6	6
Panama	6	1	1	4	7	21	3

Guatemala and El Salvador qualified for six-nation play-off.

GROUP 3 (Caribbean)
Netherlands Antilles, Barbados, Cuba, Guyana, Haiti, Jamaica, Surinam, Trinidad-Tobago, Dominican Republic.
Extra Preliminary Round
2–4–76	Dominican Republic (0) 0	Haiti (3) 3
17–4–76	Haiti (2) 3	Dominican Republic (0) 0

Preliminary Round
4–7–76	Guyana (1) 2	Surinam (0) 0
29–7–76	Surinam (2) 3	Guyana (0) 0
31–7–76	Netherlands Antilles (0) 1	Haiti (2) 2
14–8–76	Haiti (4) 7	Netherlands Antilles (0) 0
15–8–76	Jamaica (0) 1	Cuba (1) 3
29–8–76	Cuba (1) 2	Jamaica (0) 0
15–8–76	Barbados (0) 2	Trinidad-Tobago (0) 1
31–8–76	Trinidad-Tobago (0) 1	Barbados (0) 0

Play-off
14–9–76 Trinidad-Tobago (1) 3 Barbados (1) 1

Final Preliminary Round
14–11–76	Surinam (1) 1	Trinidad-Tobago (1) 1
28–11–76	Trinidad-Tobago (1) 2	Surinam (1) 2

Play-off
18–12–76	Surinam (2) 3	Trinidad-Tobago (1) 2
28–11–76	Cuba (1) 1	Haiti (0) 1
11–12–76	Haiti (0) 1	Cuba (0) 0

Play-off
29–12–76   Cuba (0) 0   Haiti (0) 2

Haiti and Surinam qualify for six-nation play-off.

Six-Nation Play-Off (in Mexico)
8–10–77   Guatemala (2) 3   Surinam (1) 2
8–10–77   Canada (0) 1   El Salvador (1) 2
9–10–77   Mexico (1) 4   Haiti (0) 1
12–10–77   Canada (1) 2   Surinam (1) 1
12–10–77   Mexico (1) 3   El Salvador (0) 1
12–10–77   Guatemala (0) 1   Haiti (2) 2
15–10–77   Mexico (3) 8   Surinam (1) 1
16–10–77   El Salvador (0) 0   Haiti (1) 1
16–10–77   Canada (2) 2   Guatemala (0) 1
19–10–77   Mexico (1) 2   Guatemala (1) 1
20–10–77   El Salvador (1) 3   Surinam (0) 2
20–10–77   Canada (0) 1   Haiti (0) 1
22–10–77   Mexico (2) 3   Canada (1) 1
23–10–77   Haiti (1) 1   Surinam (0) 0
23–10–77   Guatemala (0) 2   El Salvador (1) 2

	P	W	D	L	F	A	Pts
Mexico	5	5	0	0	20	5	10
Haiti	5	3	1	1	6	6	7
Canada	5	2	1	2	7	8	5
El Salvador	5	2	1	2	8	9	5
Guatemala	5	1	1	3	8	10	3
Surinam	5	0	0	5	6	17	0

Mexico qualified.

AFRICA
Extra Preliminary Round.
7–3–76   Sierra Leone (1) 5   Niger (1) 1
21–3–76   Niger (1) 2   Sierra Leone (1) 1
13–3–76   Upper Volta (0) 1   Mauritania (1) 1
28–3–76   Mauritania (0) 0   Upper Volta (1) 2
Sierra Leone and Upper Volta qualified for First Round Proper in Africa.
First Round
1–4–76   Algeria (0) 1   Libya (0) 0
16–4–76   Libya (0) 0   Algeria (0) 0
12–12–76   Morocco (1) 1   Tunisia (0) 1
9–1–77   Tunisia (1) 1   Morocco (0) 1
Tunisia qualified 4–2 on penalties.
17–10–76   Togo (0) 1   Senegal (0) 0
10–10–76   Ghana (0) 2   Guinea (0) 1
24–10–76   Guinea (0) 2   Ghana (0) 1
Play-off
16–1–77   Guinea (2) 2   Ghana (0) 0
Zaire (bye) Central Africa (withdrew)
16–10–76   Sierra Leone (0) 0   Nigeria (0) 0
30–10–76   Nigeria (4) 6   Sierra Leone (0) 2
17–10–76   Congo (0) 2   Cameroon (2) 2
31–10–76   Cameroon (1) 1   Congo (1) 2
Congo had originally withdrawn, but re-entered.
4–9–76   Upper Volta (0) 1   Ivory Coast (1) 1
25–9–76   Ivory Coast (2) 2   Upper Volta (0) 0
29–10–76   Egypt (2) 3   Ethiopia (0) 0
14–11–76   Ethiopia (1) 1   Egypt (1) 2
Sudan (withdrew) Kenya (bye).
Uganda (bye) Tanzania (withdrew).
9–5–76   Zambia (2) 4   Malawi (0) 0
30–5–65   Malawi (0) 0   Zambia (0) 1

Second Round
6–2–77   Tunisia (0) 2   Algeria (0) 0
28–2–77   Algeria (1) 1   Tunisia (0) 1
13–2–77   Togo (0) 0   Guinea (1) 2
27–2–77   Guinea (2) 2   Togo (0) 1

Nigeria (bye)
13–2–77   Ivory Coast (2) 3   Congo (1) 2
27–2–77   Congo (0) 1   Ivory Coast (1) 3
6–2–77   Kenya (0) 0   Egypt (0) 0
27–2–77   Egypt (1) 1   Kenya (0) 0
13–2–77   Uganda (0) 1   Zambia (0) 0
27–2–77   Zambia (2) 2   Uganda (1) 1
Zambia won 4–2 after extra time.
Third Round
5–6–77   Guinea (0) 1   Tunisia (0) 0
19–6–77   Tunisia (1) 3   Guinea (1) 1
10–7–77   Nigeria (3) 4   Ivory Coast (0) 0
24–7–77   Ivory Coast (1) 2   Nigeria (0) 2
15–7–77   Egypt (1) 2   Zambia (0) 0
31–7–77   Zambia (0) 0   Egypt (0) 0
Final Round
25–9–77   Tunisia (0) 0   Nigeria (0) 0
8–10–77   Nigeria (1) 4   Egypt (0) 0
21–10–77   Egypt (2) 3   Nigeria (0) 1
12–11–77   Nigeria (0) 0   Tunisia (0) 1
25–11–77   Egypt (1) 3   Tunisia (0) 2
11–12–77   Tunisia (2) 4   Egypt (0) 1

	P	W	D	L	F	A	Pts
Tunisia	4	2	1	1	7	4	5
Egypt	4	2	0	2	7	11	4
Nigeria	4	1	1	2	5	4	3

ASIA/OCEANIA

OCEANIA
Australia, New Zealand, Taiwan (Republic of China).
13–3–77   Australia (2) 3   Taiwan (0) 0 (in Fiji)
16–3–77   Taiwan (1) 1   Australia (1) 2 (in Fiji)
20–3–77   New Zealand (4) 6   Taiwan (0) 0
23–3–77   Taiwan (0) 0   New Zealand (2) 6 (in New Zealand)
27–3–77   Australia (0) 3   New Zealand (1) 1
30–3–77   New Zealand (1) 1   Australia (1) 1

	P	W	D	L	F	A	Pts
Australia	4	3	1	0	9	3	7
New Zealand	4	2	1	1	14	4	5
Taiwan	4	0	0	4	1	17	0

ASIA GROUP 1
Hong Kong, Indonesia, Malaysia, Thailand, Singapore.
Tournament held in Singapore.
27–2–77   Singapore (0) 2   Thailand (0) 0
28–2–77   Hong Kong (0) 4   Indonesia (1) 1
1–3–77   Malaysia (4) 6   Thailand (1) 4
2–3–77   Hong Kong (1) 2   Singapore (1) 2
3–3–77   Indonesia (0) 0   Malaysia (0) 0
5–3–77   Thailand (0) 1   Hong Kong (1) 2
6–3–77   Singapore (1) 1   Malaysia (0) 0
7–3–77   Thailand (3) 3   Indonesia (1) 2
8–3–77   Malaysia (1) 1   Hong Kong (1) 1
9–3–77   Indonesia (3) 4   Singapore (0) 0

	P	W	D	L	F	A	Pts
Hong Kong	4	2	2	0	9	5	6
Singapore	4	2	1	1	5	6	5
Malaysia	4	1	2	1	7	6	4
Indonesia	4	1	1	2	7	7	3
Thailand	4	1	0	3	8	12	2

Final:
12–3–77   Singapore (0) 0   Hong Kong (1) 1

ASIA GROUP 2
Israel, Japan, Republic of Korea (DPR Korea withdrew).
27–2–77   Israel (0) 0   Korea Rep. (0) 0
6–3–77   Israel (1) 2   Japan (0) 0
10–3–77   Japan (0) 0   Israel (1) 2 (in Israel)

20–3–77	Korea Rep. (1) 3	Israel (0) 1				
26–3–77	Japan (0) 0	Korea Rep. (0) 0				
3–4–77	Korea Rep. (0) 1	Japan (0) 0				

	P	W	D	L	F	A	Pts
Korea Rep.	4	2	2	0	4	1	6
Israel	4	2	1	1	5	3	5
Japan	4	0	1	3	0	5	1

ASIA GROUP 3

Iran, Saudi Arabia (Syria withdrew 4–3–77)

12–11–76	Saudi Arabia (1) 2	Syria (0) 0
26–11–77	Syria (1) 2	Saudi Arabia (1) 1
7–1–77	Saudi Arabia (0) 0	Iran (1) 3
28–1–77	Syria (0) 0	Iran (1) 1
8–4–77	Iran 2	Syria 0 (forfeit)
22–4–77	Iran (1) 2	Saudi Arabia (0) 0

	P	W	D	L	F	A	Pts
Iran	4	4	0	0	8	0	8
Saudi Arabia	4	1	0	3	3	7	2
Syria	4	1	0	3	2	6	2

ASIA GROUP 4

Bahrain, Kuwait, Qatar (United Arab Emirates withdrew).
Tournament held in Doha, Qatar.

11–3–77	Bahrain (0) 0	Kuwait (2) 2
13–3–77	Bahrain (0) 0	Qatar (1) 2
15–3–77	Qatar (0) 0	Kuwait (1) 2
17–3–77	Bahrain (0) 1	Kuwait (1) 2
19–3–77	Qatar (0) 0	Bahrain (1) 3
21–3–77	Qatar (0) 1	Kuwait (3) 4

	P	W	D	L	F	A	Pts
Kuwait	4	4	0	0	10	2	8
Qatar	4	1	0	3	3	9	2
Bahrain	4	1	0	3	4	6	2

ASIA FINAL ROUND

19–6–77	Hong Kong (0) 0	Iran (1) 2
26–6–77	Hong Kong (0) 0	Korea Rep. (0) 1
3–7–77	Korea Rep. (0) 0	Iran (0) 0
10–7–77	Australia (1) 3	Hong Kong (0) 0
14–8–77	Australia (0) 0	Iran (0) 1
27–8–77	Australia (0) 2	Korea Rep. (1) 1
2–10–77	Hong Kong (1) 1	Kuwait (1) 3
9–10–77	Korea Rep. (0) 1	Kuwait (0) 0
16–10–77	Australia (0) 1	Kuwait (1) 2
23–10–77	Korea Rep. (0) 0	Australia (0) 0
28–10–77	Iran (0) 1	Kuwait (0) 0
30–10–77	Hong Kong (0) 2	Australia (3) 5
5–11–77	Kuwait (0) 2	Korea Rep. (1) 2
11–11–77	Iran (0) 2	Korea Rep. (1) 2
12–11–77	Kuwait (3) 4	Hong Kong (0) 0
18–11–77	Iran (3) 3	Hong Kong (0) 0
19–11–77	Kuwait (0) 1	Australia (0) 0
25–11–77	Iran (1) 1	Australia (0) 0
3–12–77	Kuwait (1) 1	Iran (0) 2
4–12–77	Korea Rep. (2) 5	Hong Kong (0) 2

	P	W	D	L	F	A	Pts
Iran	8	6	2	0	12	3	14
Korea Rep.	8	3	4	1	12	8	10
Kuwait	8	4	1	3	13	8	9
Australia	8	3	1	4	11	8	7
Hong Kong	8	0	0	8	5	26	0

Summary of Matches in World Cup Finals 1930-78

		P	W	D	L	F	A
1.	Brazil	52	33	10	9	119	56
2.	West Germany*	47	28	9	10	110	68
3.	Italy	36	20	6	10	62	40
4.	Uruguay	29	14	5	10	57	39
5.	Argentina	29	14	5	10	55	43
6.	Hungary	26	13	2	11	73	42
7.	Sweden	28	11	6	11	48	46
8.	England	24	10	6	8	34	28
9.	Yugoslavia	25	10	5	10	45	34
10.	USSR	19	10	3	6	30	21
11.	Holland (Netherlands)	16	8	3	5	32	19
12.	Poland	14	9	1	4	27	17
13.	Austria	18	9	1	8	33	36
14.	Czechoslovakia	22	8	3	11	32	36
15.	France	20	8	1	11	43	38
16.	Chile	18	7	3	8	23	24
17.	Spain	18	7	3	8	22	25
18.	Switzerland	18	5	2	11	28	44
19.	Portugal	6	5	0	1	17	8
20.	Mexico	24	3	4	17	21	62
21.	Peru	12	4	1	7	17	25
22.	Scotland	11	2	4	5	12	21
23.	East Germany	6	2	2	2	5	5
24.	Paraguay	7	2	2	3	12	19
25.	United States of America	7	3	0	4	12	21
26.	Wales	5	1	3	1	4	4
27.	Northern Ireland	5	2	1	2	6	10
28.	Rumania	8	2	1	5	12	17
29.	Bulgaria	12	0	4	8	9	29
30.	Tunisia	3	1	1	1	3	2
31.	North Korea	4	1	1	2	5	9
32.	Cuba	3	1	1	1	5	12
33.	Belgium	9	1	1	7	12	25
34.	Turkey	3	1	0	2	10	11
35.	Israel	3	0	2	1	1	3
36.	Morocco	3	0	1	2	2	6
37.	Australia	3	0	1	2	0	5
38.	Iran	3	0	1	2	2	8
39.	Colombia	3	0	1	2	5	11
40.	Norway	1	0	0	1	1	2
41.	Egypt	1	0	0	1	2	4
42.	Dutch East Indies	1	0	0	1	0	6
43.	El Salvador	3	0	0	3	0	9
44.	South Korea	2	0	0	2	0	16
45.	Haiti	3	0	0	3	2	14
46.	Zaire	3	0	0	3	0	14
47.	Bolivia	3	0	0	3	0	16

*including Germany 1934-1938

WORLD CUP 1978 — Teams, players, appearances and goals.

Argentina

1.	Norberto Alonso	Hs	Fs			Bs		
2.	Osvaldo Ardiles	H	F	IT	PL	B		Ho
3.	Hector Baley							
4.	Daniel Bertoni	H¹s		IT	PL	B	P	Ho¹
5.	Ubaldo Fillol	H	F	IT	PL	B	P	Ho
6.	Americo Gallego	H	F	IT	PL	B	P	Ho
7.	Luis Galvan	H	F	IT	PL	B	P	Ho
8.	Ruben Galvan							
9.	Rene Houseman	H	F	ITs	PL		Ps¹	Hos
10.	Mario Kempes	H	F	IT	PL²	B	P²	Ho²
11.	Daniel Killer							
12.	Omar Larrosa						P	Hos
13.	Ricardo Lavolpe							
14.	Leopoldo Luque	H¹	F¹			B	P²	Ho
15.	Jorge Olguin	H	F	IT	PL	B	P	Ho
16.	Oscar Ortiz		Fs	IT	PLs	B	P	Ho
17.	Miguel Oviedo						Ps	
18.	Ruben Pagnanini							
19.	Daniel Passarella	H	F	IT	PL	B	P	Ho
20.	Alberto Tarantini	H	F	IT	PL	B	P¹	Ho
21.	Daniel Valencia	H	F	IT	PL			
22.	Ricardo Villa				PLs	Bs		

Manager: Cesar Luis Menotti

Austria

1.	Friedl Koncilia	Sp	Sw	B	Ho	IT	WG
2.	Robert Sara	Sp	Sw	B	Ho	IT	WG
3.	Erich Obermayer	Sp	Sw	B	Ho¹	IT	WG
4.	Gerhard Breitenberger	Sp	Sw	B	Ho		
5.	Bruno Pezzey	Sp	Sw	B	Ho	IT	WG
6.	Roland Hattenberger						
7.	Josef Hickersberger	Sp	Sw	B	Ho	IT	WG
8.	Herbert Prohaska	Sp	Sw	B	Ho	IT	WG
9.	Hans Krankl	Sp¹	Swᵖ	B	Ho	IT	WG²
10.	Willy Kreuz	Sp	Sw	B	Ho	IT	WG
11.	Kurt Jara	Sp	Sw	B	Ho		
12.	Eduard Krieger		Sw	B	Ho	IT	WG
13.	Gunther Happich			Bs			
14.	Heinrich Strasser					IT	WG
15.	Heribert Weber	Sps	Sws	Bs			
16.	Peter Persidis						
17.	Franz Oberacher						WGs
18.	Walter Schachner	Sp¹				IT	WG
19.	Hans Pirkner	Sps				ITs	
20.	Ernst Baumeister						
21.	Erwin Fuchsbichler						
22.	Hubert Baumgartner						

Manager: Helmut Senekowitsch   og¹

Brazil

1.	Leao	Sw	Sp		Au	P	A	PL	IT
2.	Toninho	Sw	Sp		Au	P	A	PL	
3.	Oscar	Sw	Sp		Au	P	A	PL	IT
4.	Amaral	Sw	Sp		Au	P	A	PL	IT
5.	Cerezo	Sw	Sp		Au	P		PL	IT
6.	Edinho	Sw	Sp				As		
7.	Ze Sergio								
8.	Zico	Sw	Sp		Aus	Psᵖ	As	PL	
9.	Reinaldo	Sw¹	Sp						ITs
10.	Rivelino	Sw						PLs	ITs
11.	Dirceu	Sws	Sp		Au	P²	A	PL	IT¹
12.	Carlos								
13.	Nelinho	Sws	Sp					PL¹	IT¹
14.	Abel								
15.	Polozi								
16.	Rodriques Neto				Au	P	A		IT
17.	Batista	Sw	Sp		Au	P	A	PL	IT
18.	Gil	Sw	Sp	Sps	Au	P	A	PL	IT
19.	Jorge Mendonca			Sps	Au	P	A	PLs	IT
20.	Roberto				Au¹	P	A	PL²	IT
21.	Chicao				Aus	Ps	A		
22.	Valdir Peres								

Manager: Claudio Coutinho

France

1.	Dominique Baratelli		As	
2.	Patrick Battiston		A	
3.	Maxime Bossis	IT	A	
4.	Gerard Janvion	IT	A	H
5.	Francois Bracci			H
6.	Christian Lopez		A	H¹
7.	Patrick Rio	IT		
8.	Marius Tresor	IT	A	H
9.	Dominique Bathenay		A	H
10.	Jean-Marc Guillou	IT		
11.	Henri Nichel	IT	A	
12.	Clade Papi			H
13.	Jean Petit			H
14.	Marc Berdoll	ITs		H¹
15.	Michel Platini	IT	A¹	Hs
16.	Christian Dalger	IT		
17.	Bernard Lacombe	IT¹	A	
18.	Dominique Rocheteau		A	H¹
19.	Didier Six	IT	A	Hs
20.	Olivier Rouyer	ITs		H
21.	Jean-Paul Bertrand-Demanes	IT	A	
22.	Dominique Dropsy			H

Manager: Michel Hidalgo

Holland

1.	Piet Schrijvers				Au	WG	IT	
2.	Jan Poortvliet		P	S	Au	WG	IT	A
3.	Dirk Schoenaker				Aus			
4.	Adri Van Kraay				Aus		ITs	
5.	Rudi Krol	I	P	S	Au	WG	IT	A
6.	Wim Jansen	I	P	S	Au	WG	IT	A
7.	Piet Wildschut			Ss	Au	WG		
8.	Jan Jongbloed	I	P	S			ITs	A
9.	Arie Haan	I	P		Au	WG¹	IT¹	A
10.	Rene Van der Kerkhof	I	P	S	Au	WG¹	IT	A
11.	Willy Van der Kerkhof	I	P	S	Au¹	WG¹	IT	A
12.	Robby Rensenbrink	I³(²p)	P	Sᵖ	Auᵖ	WG	IT	A
13.	Johan Neeskens	I	P	S			IT	A
14.	Jan Boskamp			Ss				
15.	Hugo Hovenkamp							
16.	Johnny Rep	I	Ps	S¹	Au²	WG	IT	A
17.	Wim Rijsbergen	I	P	S				
18.	Dick Nanninga	1s	Ps			WGs		As¹
19.	Wim Doesburg							
20.	Wim Suurbier	I	P	S				As
21.	Harry Lubse							
22.	Ernie Brandts				Au¹	WG	IT¹	A

Manager: Ernst Happel

The Van der Kerkhof twins each scored in the 83rd minute of matches against W. Germany and Austria.

Hungary

1.	Sandor Gujdar	A		F
2.	Peter Torok	A		
3.	Istvan Kocsis	A	IT	
4.	Jozsef Toth	A	IT	F
5.	Sandor Zombori	A	IT	F¹
6.	Zoltan Kereki	A	IT	F
7.	Laszlo Fazekas		IT	
8.	Tibor Nyilasi	A		F
9.	Andras Torocsik	A		F
10.	Sandor Pinter	A	IT	F
11.	Bela Varadi			
12.	Gyozo Martos	As	IT	F
13.	Karoly Csapo	A¹	IT	Fs
14.	Laszlo Balint			F
15.	Tibor Rab			
16.	Istvan Halasz		ITs	
17.	Laszlo Pusztai		IT	F
18.	Laszlo Nagy	A	IT	F
19.	Andras Toth		ITᵖs	
20.	Ferenc Fulop			
21.	Ferenc Meszaros		IT	
22.	Laszlo Kovacs			

Manager: Lajos Baroti

Key: s = substitute; ¹ goals; ᵖ penalties

Iran

1.	Nasser Hejazi	Ho	S	P
2.	Bahram Mavadat			
3.	Mohammad Reza Karbandi			
4.	Hassan Nazari	Ho	S	P
5.	Alireza Ghashghaian			
6.	Andranik Eskandarian	Ho	S	
7.	Hossein Kazerani	Ho	S	P
8.	Nassrullah Abdollahi	Ho	S	P
9.	Ali Shoja'i			
10.	Hassan Nayebagha	Ho	Ss	
11.	Ali Parvin	Ho	S	P
12.	Javad Allahverdi			P
13.	Iraj Danaiifar		S¹	P
14.	Ebrahim Ghassempoor	Ho	S	P
15.	Behtash Fariba			Ps
16.	Mohammed Sadeghi	Ho	S	P
17.	Hassan Rowshan	Hos	Ss	P¹
18.	Hossein Faraki	Ho	S	P
19.	Ghafoor Jahani	Ho	S	Ps
20.	Majid Beshkar			
21.	Naser Nooraii			
22.	Hamid Majdtaymoori			

Manager: Heshmat Mohajerani

Peru

#	Player	S	Ho	I	B	PL	A
1.	Ottorino Sartor						
2.	Jaime Duarte	S	Ho	I	B	PL	A
3.	Rodulfo Manzo	S	Ho	I	B	PL	A
4.	Hector Chumpitaz	S	Ho	I	B	PL	A
5.	Toribio Diaz	S	Ho	I	B		
6.	Jose Velasquez	S	Ho	I¹	B		A
7.	Juan Munante	S	Ho	I	B	PL	A
8.	Cesar Cueto	S¹	Ho	I	B	PL	A
9.	Percy Rojas	Ss			Bs	PLs	
10.	Teofilo Cubillas	S²	Ho	I³(²P)	B	PL	A
11.	Juan Oblitas	S	Ho	I	B	PL	A
12.	Roberto Mosquera						
13.	Juan Caceres						
14.	Jose Navarro				Bs	PL	
15.	German Leguia			Is			
16.	Raul Gorriti						As
17.	Alfredo Quesada					PL	A
18.	Ernesto Labarthe						
19.	Guillermo La Rosa	S	Ho	I	B	PL	
20.	Hugo Sotil	Ss	Hos	Is		PLs	
21.	Ramon Quiroga	S	Ho	I	B	PL	A
22.	Roberto Rojas						

Manager: Marcos Calderon

Italy

1.	Dino Zoff	F	H	A	WG	Au	Ho	B
2.	Mauro Bellugi	F	H	A	WG	Au		
3.	Antonio Cabrini	F	H	A	WG	Au	Ho	B
4.	Antonello Cuccureddu		Hs	As		Aus	Ho	B
5.	Claudio Gentile	F	H	A	WG	Au	Ho	B
6.	Aldo Maldera							B
7.	Lionello Manfredonia							
8.	Gaetano Scirea	F	H	A	WG	Au	Ho	B
9.	Giancarlo Antognoni	F	H	A	WG			B
10.	Romeo Benetti	F	H¹	A	WG	Au	Ho	
11.	Eraldo Pecci							
12.	Paolo Conti							
13.	Patrizio Sala							B
14.	Marco Tardelli	F	H	A	WG	Au	Ho	
15.	Renato Zaccarelli	F¹s		As	WGs	Au	Ho	
16.	Franco Causio	F	H	A	WG	Au	Ho	B¹
17.	Claudio Sala						Hos	Bs
18.	Roberto Bettega	F	H¹	A¹	WG	Au	Ho	B
19.	Francesco Graziani		Hs			Aus	Hos	
20.	Paolino Pulici							
21.	Paolo Rossi	F¹	H¹	A	WG	Au¹	Ho	B
22.	Ivano Bordon							

Manager: Enzo Bearzot   og¹

Poland

#	Player	WG	T	M	A	P	B
1.	Jan Tomaszewski	WG	T	M	A		
2.	Wlodzimierz Mazur				As		
3.	Henryk Maculewicz	WG	T	Ms	A	P	B
4.	Antoni Szymanowski	WG	T	M	A	P	B
5.	Adam Nawalka	WG	T		A	P	B
6.	Jerzy Gorgon	WG	T	M		P	B
7.	Andrzej Iwan		Ts	M			
8.	Henryk Kasperczak	WGs	T	M	A	Ps	B
9.	Wladyslaw Zmuda	WG	T	M	A	P	B
10.	Wojciech Rudy			M			
11.	Bohdan Masztaler	WG		M	A	P	
12.	Kazimierz Deyna	WG	T	M¹	A	P	B
13.	Janusz Kupcewicz						
14.	Mioroslaw Justek						
15.	Makre Kusto						
16.	Grzegorz Lato	WG	T¹	M	A	P	B¹
17.	Andrzej Szarmach	WG	T		A	P¹	B
18.	Zbigniew Boniek	WGs	Ts	M²	A	P	B
19.	Wlodzimierz Lubanski	WG	T	Ms		Ps	Bs
20.	Roman Wojcicki						
21.	Zygmunt Kukla					P	B
22.	Zdzislaw Kostrzewa						

Manager: Jacek Gmoch

Mexico

#	Player	T	WG	PL
1.	Pilar Reyes	T	WG	
2.	Manuel Najera			
3.	Alfredo Tena	T	WG	
4.	Eduardo Ramos	T	WG	
5.	Arturo Vazquez Ayala	T^p	WG	PL
6.	Guillermo Mendizabal	T	WG	PLs
7.	Antonio De la Torre	T	WG	PL
8.	Enrique Lopez Zarsa		WG	
9.	Victor Rangel	T	WG	PL¹
10.	Cristobal Ortega			PL
11.	Hugo Sanchez	T	WG	PL
12.	Jesus Martinez	T	WG	
13.	Rigoberto Cisneros			PL
14.	Carlos Gomez			PL
15.	Ignacio Flores			PL
16.	Javier Cardenas			PL
17.	Leonardo Cuellar	T	WG	PL
18.	Gerardo Lugo	Ts	WGs	
19.	Hugo Rene Rodriguez			
20.	Mario Medina			
21.	Paul Isiordia	T		
22.	Pedro Soto		WGs	PL

Manager: Jose Antonio Roca

Scotland

1.	Alan Rough	P	I	Ho
2.	Sandy Jardine		I	
3.	Willie Donachie		I	Ho
4.	Martin Buchan	P	I	Ho
5.	Gordon McQueen			
6.	Bruce Rioch	P		Ho
7.	Don Masson	P		
8.	Kenny Dalglish	P	I	Ho¹
9.	Joe Jordan	P¹	I	Ho
10.	Asa Hartford	P	I	Ho
11.	Willie Johnston	P		
12.	Jim Blyth			
13.	Stuart Kennedy	P		Ho
14.	Tom Forsyth	P	Is	Ho
15.	Archie Gemmill	Ps	I	Ho²(¹P)
16.	Lou Macari	Ps	I	
17.	Derek Johnstone			
18.	Graeme Souness			Ho
19.	John Robertson		I	
20.	Bobby Clark			
21.	Joe Harper		Is	
22.	Kenny Burns	P	I	

Manager: Ally MacLeod   og¹

Key: s = substitute; ¹ goals; ^{P} penalties

Spain
1. Arconada
2. De la Cruz — Au
3. Uria — B Sw
4. Asensi — Au B Sw[1]
5. Migueli — Au B
6. Biosca — Bs Sw
7. Dani — Au[1]
8. Juanito — B Sw
9. Quini — Aus
10. Santillana — B Sw
11. Cardenosa — Au B Sw
12. Guzman — Bs
13. Miguel Angel — Au B Sw
14. Leal — Aus B Sw
15. Maranon
16. Olmo — B Sw
17. Marcelino — Au B Sw
18. Pirri — Au Sws
19. Rexach — Au
20. Ruben Cano — Au
21. San Jose — Au B Sw
22. Urruticoechea
Manager: Ladislao Kubala

Tunisia
1. Attouga
2. Mokhtar Dhouib — M[1] PL WG
3. Ali Kaabi — M[1] PL WG
4. Khaled Gasmi — PL WG
5. Mohsen Jendoubi — M PL WG
6. Nejib Gommidh — M[1] PL WG
7. Temime Lahzami — M PL WG
8. Mohamed Agrebi — M PL WG
9. Mohamed Ali Akid — M PL WG
10. Tarek Dhiab — M PL WG
11. Raouf Ben Aziza — M WGs
12. Khemais Labidi — Ms
13. Moahmed Najib Limam
14. Slah Karoui — Ms
15. Mohamed Ali Moussa
16. Othman Chehaibi
17. Ridha Ellouze
18. Kamel Chebli
19. Kokhtar Hasni
20. Amor Jebali — M PL WG
21. Lamine Ben Aziza
22. Mokhtar Naili — M PL WG
Manager: Majid Chetali

Sweden
1. Ronnie Hellstrom — B Au Sp
2. Hasse Borg — B Au Sp
3. Roy Andersson — B Au Sp
4. Bjorn Nordqvist — B Au Sp
5. Ingemar Erlandsson — B Au Sp
6. Staffan Tapper — B Au
7. Anders Linderoth — B Au Sps
8. Bo Larsson — B Au Sp
9. Lennart Larsson — B Au Sp
10. Thomas Sjoberg — B[1] Au Sp
11. Benny Wendt — B Au Sps
12. Goran Hagberg
13. Magnus Andersson
14. Ronald Aman
15. Torbjorn Nilsson — Sp
16. Conny Torstensson — Aus
17. Jan Moller
18. Olle Nordin — Sp
19. Ken Karlsson
20. Roland Andersson
21. Sanny Aslund
22. Ralf Edstrom — Bs Aus Sp
Manager: Georg Ericsson

West Germany
1. Sepp Maier — PL M T IT Ho A
2. Berti Vogts — PL M T IT Ho A
3. Bernard Dietz — M T IT Ho A
4. Rolf Russmann — PL M T IT Ho A
5. Manfred Kaltz — PL M T IT Ho A
6. Rainer Bonhof — PL M T IT Ho A
7. Rudiger Abramczik — PL Ho[1] A
8. Herbert Zimmermann — PL IT
9. Klaus Fischer — PL M T IT As
10. Heinz Flohe — PL M[2] T IT
11. Karl-Heinz Rummenigge — M[2] T IT Ho A[1]
12. Georg Schwarzenbeck
13. Harald Konopka — ITs
14. Dieter Muller — M[1] T Ho[1] A
15. Erich Beer — PL ITs Ho A
16. Bernd Cullmann
17. Bernd Holzenbein — IT Ho A[1]
18. Gerd Zewe
19. Ronald Worm
20. Hans Muller — PL M[1] T As
21. Rudi Kargus
22. Dieter Burdenski
Manager: Helmut Schoen

Key: s = substitute; [1] goals; [P] penalties

World Cup Attendances 1930-1978 - Goals - Average

Year	Venue	Attendances	Average	Matches	Goals	Average
1930	Uruguay	434,500	24,139	18	70	3.88
1934	Italy	395,000	23,235	17	70	4.11
1938	France	483,000	26,833	18	84	4.66
1950	Brazil	1,337,000	60,772	22	88	4.00
1954	Switzerland	943,000	36,270	26	140	5.38
1958	Sweden	868,000	24,800	35	126	3.60
1962	Chile	776,000	24,250	32	89	2.78
1966	England	1,614,677	50,458	32	89	2.78
1970	Mexico	1,673,975	52,312	32	95	2.96
1974	West Germany	1,774,022	46,685	38	97	2.55
1978	Argentina	1,610,215	42,374	38	102	2.68

Helmut Schoen who retired as West Germany's team manager after the 1978 World Cup finals was the most successful international coach. In 1966 his team finished runners-up in the World Cup, were third in 1970 and became European Championship winners in 1972. They won the World Cup in 1974 and were runners-up in the European Championship in 1976. Schoen had been in charge for 14 years.

Making his 100th international appearance for Poland, Kazimierz Deyna had a penalty kick saved by the Argentine goalkeeper Ubaldo Fillol in the 1978 tournament.

The longest period that a goal keeper has kept his charge intact during a World Cup final tournament is 475 minutes. Josef 'Sepp' Maier of West Germany conceded a penalty to Holland in the first minute of the 1974 World Cup Final itself and was not beaten again until Holland scored against him in the 1978 tournament.

WORLD CUP FINAL SERIES 1930–1978
(List of participating countries and results)

Key: W=Winners; 2nd=Runners-up; 3rd=Won match for third place; 4th=Lost match for third place; SF=Semi-final; p-o=play-off; r=replay

	1930	1934	1938	1950	1954
ARGENTINA	France 1–0 Mexico 6–3 Chile 3–1 USA 6–1 (SF) Uruguay 2–4 (2nd)	Sweden 2–3			
AUSTRALIA					
AUSTRIA		France 3–2 Hungary 2–1 Italy 0–1 (SF) Germany 2–3 (4th)			Scotland 1–0 Czechoslovakia 5–0 Switzerland 7–5 West Germany 1–6 (SF) Uruguay 3–1 (3rd)
BELGIUM	USA 0–3 Paraguay 0–1	Germany 2–5	France 1–3		England 4–4 Italy 1–4
BOLIVIA	Yugoslavia 0–4 Brazil 0–4			Uruguay 0–8	
BRAZIL	Yugoslavia 1–2 Bolivia 4–0	Spain 1–3	Poland 6–5 Czechoslovakia 1–1 Czechoslovakia (r) 2–1 Italy 1–2 (SF) Sweden 4–2 (3rd)	Mexico 4–0 Switzerland 2–2 Yugoslavia 2–0 Sweden 7–1 Spain 6–1 Uruguay 1–2 (2nd)	Mexico 5–0 Yugoslavia 1–1 Hungary 2–4
BULGARIA					
CHILE	Mexico 3–0 France 1–0 Argentina 1–3			England 0–2 Spain 0–2 USA 5–2	
COLOMBIA					
CUBA			Rumania 3–3 Rumania (r) 2–1 Sweden 0–8		

...ding World Cup scorers (final tournament)

...ar	Name	Country	Goals
...0	Guillermo Stabile	Argentina	8
...4	Angelo Schiavio	Italy	4
	Oldrich Nejedly	Czechoslovakia	4
	Edmund Conen	Germany	4
...8	Leonidas da Silva	Brazil	8
...0	Ademir	Brazil	7
...4	Sandor Kocsis	Hungary	11
...8	Just Fontaine	France	13
...2	Drazen Jerkovic	Yugoslavia	5
...6	Eusebio	Portugal	9
...0	Gerd Muller	West Germany	10
...4	Grzegorz Lato	Poland	7
...8	Mario Kempes	Argentina	6

The record individual score in a World Cup final tournament is four goals, a feat which has been achieved on eight occasions:

Name	For	Against
Gustav Wetterstroem	Sweden	v. Cuba 1938
Leonidas de Silva	Brazil	v. Poland 1938
Ernest Willimowski	Poland	v. Brazil 1938
Ademir	Brazil	v. Sweden 1950
Juan Schiaffino	Uruguay	v. Bolivia 1950
Sandor Kocsis	Hungary	v. W. Germany 1954
Just Fontaine	France	v. W. Germany 1958
Eusebio	Portugal	v. North Korea 1966

...8	1962	1966	1970	1974	1978
...st Germany 1–3	Bulgaria 1–0	Spain 2–1		Poland 2–3	Hungary 2–1
...rthern Ireland 3–1	England 1–3	West Germany 0–0		Italy 1–1	France 2–1
...choslovakia 1–6	Hungary 0–0	Switzerland 2–0		Haiti 4–1	Italy 0–1
		England 0–1		Netherlands 0–4	Poland 2–0
				Brazil 1–2	Brazil 0–0
				East Germany 1–1	Peru 6–0
					Netherlands 3–1 (W)
				East Germany 0–2	
				West Germany 0–3	
				Chile 0–0	
...zil 0–3				Spain 2–1	
...SR 0–2				Sweden 1–0	
...land 2–2				Brazil 0–1	
				Netherlands 1–5	
				Italy 0–1	
				West Germany 3–2	
			El Salvador 3–0		
			USSR 1–4		
			Mexico 0–1		
...tria 3–0	Mexico 2–0	Bulgaria 2–0	Czechoslovakia 4–1	Yugoslavia 0–0	Sweden 1–1
...land 0–0	Czechoslovakia 0–0	Hungary 1–3	England 1–0	Scotland 0–0	Spain 0–0
...SR 2–0	Spain 2–1	Portugal 1–3	Rumania 3–2	Zaire 3–0	Austria 1–0
...es 1–0	England 3–1		Peru 4–2	East Germany 1–0	Peru 3–0
...ce 5–2	Chile 4–2		Uruguay 3–1	Argentina 2–1	Argentina 0–0
...den 5–2 (W)	Czechoslovakia 3–1 (W)		Italy 4–1 (W)	Netherlands 0–2	Poland 3–1
				Poland 0–1 (4th)	Italy 2–1 (3rd)
	Argentina 0–1	Brazil 0–2	Peru 2–3	Sweden 0–0	
	Hungary 1–6	Portugal 0–3	West Germany 2–5	Uruguay 1–1	
	England 0–0	Hungary 1–3	Morocco 1–1	Netherlands 1–4	
	Switzerland 3–1	Italy 0–2		West Germany 0–1	
	Italy 2–0	North Korea 1–1		East Germany 1–1	
	West Germany 0–2	USSR 1–2		Australia 0–0	
	USSR 2–1				
	Brazil 2–4 (SF)				
	Yugoslavia 1–0 (3rd)				
	Uruguay 1–2				
	USSR 4–4				
	Yugoslavia 0–5				

	1930	1934	1938	1950	1954
CZECHOSLOVAKIA		Rumania 2–1 Switzerland 3–2 Germany 3–1 Italy 1–2 (2nd)	Netherlands 3–0 Brazil 1–1 Brazil (r) 1–2		Uruguay 0–2 Austria 0–5
DUTCH EAST INDIES			Hungary 0–6		
EAST GERMANY					
EGYPT		Hungary 2–4			
ENGLAND				Chile 2–0 USA 0–1 Spain 0–1	Belgium 4–4 Switzerland 2–0 Uruguay 2–4
EL SALVADOR					
FRANCE	Mexico 4–1 Argentina 0–1 Chile 0–1	Austria 2–3	Belgium 3–1 Italy 1–3		Yugoslavia 0–1 Mexico 3–2
GERMANY		Belgium 5–2 Sweden 2–1 Czechoslovakia 1–3 (SF) Austria 3–2 (3rd)	Switzerland 1–1 Switzerland (r) 2–4		
HAITI					
HUNGARY		Egypt 4–2 Austria 1–2	Dutch East Indies 6–0 Switzerland 2–0 Sweden 5–1 Italy 2–4		South Korea 9–0 West Germany 8–3 Brazil 4–2 Uruguay 4–2 West Germany 2–3 (2nd)
IRAN					
ISRAEL					
ITALY		USA 7–1 Spain 1–1 Spain (r) 1–0 Austria 1–0 Czechoslovakia 2–1 (W)	Norway 2–1 France 3–1 Brazil 2–1 Hungary 4–2 (W)	Sweden 2–3 Paraguay 2–0	Switzerland 1–2 Belgium 4–1 Switzerland 1–4 (p-o)
SOUTH KOREA					Hungary 0–9 Turkey 0–7
MEXICO	France 1–4 Chile 0–3 Argentina 3–6			Brazil 0–4 Yugoslavia 1–4 Switzerland 1–2	Brazil 0–5 France 2–3
MOROCCO					

8	1962	1966	1970	1974	1978
thern Ireland 0–1 ..t Germany 2–2 ..entina 6–1 ..h Ireland 1–2 (p-o)	Spain 1–0 Brazil 0–0 Mexico 1–3 Hungary 1–0 Yugoslavia 3–1 Brazil 1–3 (2nd)		Brazil 1–4 Rumania 1–2 England 0–1		
				Australia 2–0 Chile 1–1 West Germany 1–0 Brazil 0–1 Netherlands 0–2 Argentina 1–1	
..R 2–2 ..il 0–0 ..ria 2–2 ..R 0–1 (p-o)	Hungary 1–2 Argentina 3–1 Bulgaria 0–0 Brazil 1–3	Uruguay 0–0 Mexico 2–0 France 2–0 Argentina 1–0 Portugal 2–1 West Germany 4–2 (W)	Rumania 1–0 Brazil 0–1 Czechoslovakia 1–0 West Germany 2–3		
			Belgium 0–3 Mexico 0–4 USSR 0–2		
..guay 7–3 ..oslavia 2–3 ..tland 2–1 ..thern Ireland 4–0 ..il 2–5 (SF) ..t Germany 6–3 (3rd)		Mexico 1–1 Uruguay 1–2 England 0–2			Italy 1–2 Argentina 1–2 Hungary 3–1
				Italy 1–3 Poland 0–7 Argentina 1–4	
..es 1–1 ..den 1–2 ..ico 4–0 ..es 1–2 (p-o)	England 2–1 Bulgaria 6–1 Argentina 0–0 Czechoslovakia 0–1	Portugal 1–3 Brazil 3–1 Bulgaria 3–1 USSR 1–2			Argentina 1–2 Italy 1–3 France 1–3
					Netherlands 0–3 Scotland 1–1 Peru 1–4
			Uruguay 0–2 Sweden 1–1 Italy 0–0		
	West Germany 0–0 Chile 0–2 Switzerland 3–0	Chile 2–0 USSR 0–1 North Korea 0–1	Sweden 1–0 Uruguay 0–0 Israel 0–0 Mexico 4–1 West Germany 4–3 Brazil 1–4 (2nd)	Haiti 3–1 Argentina 1–1 Poland 1–2	France 2–1 Hungary 3–1 Argentina 1–0 West Germany 0–0 Austria 1–0 Netherlands 1–2 Brazil 1–2 (4th)
..eden 0–3 ..es 1–1 ..gary 0–4	Brazil 0–2 Spain 0–1 Czechoslovakia 3–1	France 1–1 England 0–2 Uruguay 0–0	USSR 0–0 El Salvador 4–0 Belgium 1–0 Italy 1–4		Tunisia 1–3 West Germany 0–6 Poland 1–3
			West Germany 1–2 Peru 0–3 Bulgaria 1–1		

	1930	1934	1938	1950	1954
NETHERLANDS (HOLLAND)		Switzerland 2–3	Czechoslovakia 0–3		
NORTHERN IRELAND					
NORTH KOREA					
NORWAY			Italy 1–2		
PARAGUAY	USA 0–3 Belgium 1–0			Sweden 2–2 Italy 0–2	
PERU	Rumania 1–3 Uruguay 0–1				
POLAND			Brazil 5–6		
PORTUGAL					
RUMANIA	Peru 3–1 Uruguay 0–4	Czechoslovakia 1–2	Cuba 3–3 Cuba (r) 1–2		
SCOTLAND					Austria 0–1 Uruguay 0–7
SPAIN		Brazil 3–1 Italy 1–1 Italy (r) 0–1		USA 3–1 Chile 2–0 England 1–0 Uruguay 2–2 Brazil 1–6 Sweden 1–3 (4th)	
SWEDEN		Argentina 3–2 Germany 1–2	Cuba 8–0 Hungary 1–5 Brazil 2–4 (4th)	Italy 3–2 Paraguay 2–2 Brazil 1–7 Uruguay 2–3 Spain 3–1 (3rd)	
SWITZERLAND		Netherlands 3–2 Czechoslovakia 2–3	Germany 1–1 Germany (r) 4–2 Hungary 0–2	Yugoslavia 0–3 Brazil 2–2 Mexico 2–1	England 0–2 Italy 2–1 Italy 4–1 (p-o) Austria 5–7
TUNISIA					
TURKEY					West Germany 1–4 South Korea 7–0 West Germany 2–7 (p-o)

3	1962	1966	1970	1974	1978
				Uruguay 2–0 Sweden 0–0 Bulgaria 4–1 Argentina 4–0 East Germany 2–0 Brazil 2–0 West Germany 1–2 (2nd)	Iran 3–0 Peru 0–0 Scotland 2–3 Austria 5–1 West Germany 2–2 Italy 2–1 Argentina 1–3 (2nd)
choslovakia 1–0 entina 1–3 st Germany 2–2 choslovakia 2–1 (p-o) nce 0–4					
		USSR 0–3 Chile 1–1 Italy 1–0 Portugal 3–5			
nce 3–7 tland 3–2 goslavia 3–3					
			Bulgaria 3–2 Morocco 3–0 West Germany 1–3 Brazil 2–4		Scotland 3–1 Netherlands 0–0 Iran 4–1 Brazil 0–3 Poland 0–1 Argentina 0–6
				Argentina 3–2 Haiti 7–0 Italy 2–1 Sweden 1–0 Yugoslavia 2–1 West Germany 0–1 Brazil 1–0 (3rd)	West Germany 0–0 Tunisia 1–0 Mexico 3–1 Argentina 0–2 Peru 1–0 Brazil 1–3
		Hungary 3–1 Bulgaria 3–0 Brazil 3–1 North Korea 5–3 England 1–2 (SF) USSR 2–1 (3rd)			
			England 0–1 Czechoslovakia 2–1 Brazil 2–3		
goslavia 1–1 aguay 2–3 nce 1–2				Zaire 2–0 Brazil 0–0 Yugoslavia 1–1	Peru 1–3 Iran 1–1 Netherlands 3–2
	Czechoslovakia 0–1 Mexico 1–0 Brazil 1–2	Argentina 1–2 Switzerland 2–1 West Germany 1–2			Austria 1–2 Brazil 0–0 Sweden 1–0
xico 3–0 ngary 2–1 les 0–0 SR 2–0 st Germany 3–1 azil 2–5 (2nd)			Italy 0–1 Israel 1–1 Uruguay 1–0	Bulgaria 0–0 Netherlands 0–0 Uruguay 3–0 Poland 0–1 West Germany 2–4 Yugoslavia 2–1	Brazil 1–1 Austria 0–1 Spain 0–1
	Chile 1–3 West Germany 1–2 Italy 0–3	West Germany 0–5 Spain 1–2 Argentina 0–2			
					Mexico 3–1 Poland 0–1 West Germany 0–0

	1930	1934	1938	1950	1954
UNITED STATES of AMERICA	Belgium 3–0 Paraguay 3–0 Argentina 1–6 (SF)	Italy 1–7		Spain 1–3 England 1–0 Chile 2–5	
URUGUAY	Peru 1–0 Rumania 4–0 Yugoslavia 6–1 (SF) Argentina 4–2 (W)			Bolivia 8–0 Spain 2–2 Sweden 3–2 Brazil 2–1 (W)	Czechoslovakia 2–0 Scotland 7–0 England 4–2 Hungary 2–4 (SF) Austria 1–3 (4th)
USSR					
WALES					
WEST GERMANY					Turkey 4–1 Hungary 3–8 Turkey 7–2 (p-o) Yugoslavia 2–0 Austria 6–1 Hungary 3–2 (W)
YUGOSLAVIA	Brazil 2–1 Bolivia 4–0 Uruguay 1–6 (SF)			Switzerland 3–0 Mexico 4–1 Brazil 0–2	France 1–0 Brazil 1–1 West Germany 0–2
ZAIRE					

WORLD CUP WINNERS ANALYSIS (Final tournaments)

Year	Winners	Matches P	W	D	L	Goals F	A	Players used	Appearances (goals)
1930	**Uruguay**	4	4	0	0	15	3	15	Ballesteros, Nasazzi, Cea (5), Andrade (J), Fernandez, Gestido, Iriarte (2) 4 each; Dorado (2), Mascheroni, Scarone (1) 3 each; Castro (2), Anselmo (3) 2 each; Tejera, Urdinaran, Petrone 1 each.
	Final: Uruguay 4 Argentina 2 90,000 Montevideo								
1934	**Italy**	5	4	1	0	12	3	17	Combi, Allmandi, Monti, Meazza (2), Orsi (3) 5 each; Monzeglio, Bertolini, Schiavio (4), Ferrari (2), Guaita (1) 4 each; Ferraris IV 3; Pizziolo 2; Rosetta, Guarisi, Castellazzi, Borel, Demaria 1 each.
	Final: Italy 2 Czechoslovakia 1 50,000 Rome (after extra time)								
1938	**Italy**	4	4	0	0	11	5	14	Olivieri, Rava, Serantoni, Andreolo, Locatelli, Meazza (1), Piola (5), Ferrari (1) 4 each; Foni, Biavati, Colaussi (4) 3 each; Monzeglio, Pasinati, Ferraris II 1 each.
	Final: Italy 4 Hungary 2 45,000 Paris								
1950	**Uruguay**	4	3	1	0	15	5	14	Gonzales (M), Tejera, Varela (1), Andrade (R), Ghiggia (4), Perez, Miguez (4), Schiaffino (5) 4 each; Maspoli, Vidal (1) 3 each; Gonzales (W), Gambetta 2 each; Paz, Moran 1 each.
	Deciding match: Uruguay 2 Brazil 1 199,850 Rio de Janeiro								
1954	**West Germany**	6	5	0	1	25	14	18	Eckel, Walter (F) (3), 6 each; Turek, Kohlmeyer, Posipal, Mai, Morlock (6), Walter (O) (4), Schafer (4) 5 each; Liebrich, Rahn (4) 4 each; Laband 3; Klodt (1), Bauer 2 each; Herrmann (1), Mebus, Kwaitowski, Pfaff (1) 1 each. (own goal 1).
	Final: West Germany 3 Hungary 2 60,000 Berne								
1958	**Brazil**	6	5	1	0	16	4	16	Gilmar, Nilton Santos (1), Bellini, Orlando, Didi (1), Zagalo (1), 6 each; De Sordi 5; Vava (5), Zito, Garrincha, Pele (6), 4 each; Mazzola (2) 3; Dino, Joel 2 each; Djalma Santos, Dida 1 each.
	Final: Brazil 5 Sweden 2 49,737 Stockholm								

8	1962	1966	1970	1974	1978
	Colombia 2–1 Yugoslavia 1–3 USSR 1–2	England 0–0 France 2–1 Mexico 0–0 West Germany 0–4	Israel 2–0 Italy 0–0 Sweden 0–1 USSR 1–0 Brazil 1–3(SF) West Germany 0–1 (4th)	Netherlands 0–2 Bulgaria 1–1 Sweden 0–3	
gland 2–2 stria 2–0 zil 0–2 gland 1–0 (p-o) eden 0–2	Yugoslavia 2–0 Colombia 4–4 Uruguay 2–1 Chile 1–2	North Korea 3–0 Italy 1–0 Chile 2–1 Hungary 2–1 West Germany 1–2 (SF) Portugal 1–2 (4th)	Mexico 0–0 Belgium 4–1 El Salvador 2–0 Uruguay 0–1		
ngary 1–1 xico 1–1 eden 0–0 ngary 2–1 (p-o) zil 0–1					
gentina 3–1 echoslovakia 2–2 rthern Ireland 2–2 goslavia 1–0 eden 1–3 (SF) nce 3–6 (4th)	Italy 0–0 Switzerland 2–1 Chile 2–0 Yugoslavia 0–1	Switzerland 5–0 Argentina 0–0 Spain 2–1 Uruguay 4–0 USSR 2–1 England 2–4 (2nd)	Morocco 2–1 Bulgaria 5–2 Peru 3–1 England 3–2 Italy 3–4 (SF) Uruguay 1–0 (3rd)	Chile 1–0 Australia 3–0 East Germany 0–1 Yugoslavia 2–0 Sweden 4–2 Poland 1–0 Netherlands 2–1 (W)	Poland 0–0 Mexico 6–0 Tunisia 0–0 Italy 0–0 Netherlands 2–2 Austria 2–3
otland 1–1 nce 3–2 aguay 3–3 st Germany 0–1	USSR 0–2 Uruguay 3–1 Colombia 5–0 West Germany 1–0 Czechoslovakia 1–3 (SF) Chile 0–1 (4th)			Brazil 0–0 Zaire 9–0 Scotland 1–1 West Germany 0–2 Poland 1–2 Sweden 1–2	
				Scotland 0–2 Yugoslavia 0–9 Brazil 0–3	

1962	**Brazil**	6	5	1	0	14	5	12	Gilmar, Djalma Santos, Mauro, Zozimo, Nilton Santos, Zito (1), Didi, Garrincha (4), Vara (4), Zagalo (1), 6 each; Amarildo (3) 4; Pele (1) 2.

Final: Brazil 3 Czechoslovakia 1   68,679 Santiago

1966	**England**	6	5	1	0	11	3	15	Banks, Cohen, Wilson, Stiles, Charlton (J), Moore, Charlton (R) (3), Hunt (3), 6 each; Peters (1) 5; Ball 4; Greaves, Hurst (4) 3; Paine, Callaghan, Connelly 1 each.

Final: England 4 West Germany 2   93,802 Wembley
(after extra time)

1970	**Brazil**	6	6	0	0	19	7	15	Felix, Carlos Alberto (1), Piazza, Brito, Clodoaldo (1), Jairzinho (7), Tostao (2), Pele (4), 6 each; Everaldo, Rivelino (3), 5; Gerson (1) 4; Paulo Cesar 2+2 subs; Marco Antonio 1+1 sub; Roberto 2 subs; Fontana 1; Edu 1 sub.

Final: Brazil 4 Italy 1   107,412 Mexico City

1974	**West Germany**	7	6	0	1	13	4	18	Maier, Vogts, Breitner (3), Schwarzenbeck, Beckenbauer, Muller (4), Overath (2), 7 each; Hoeness (1) 6+1 sub; Grabowski (1) 5+1 sub; Holzenbein 4+2 subs; Bonhof (1) 4; Cullmann (1) 3; Flohe 1+2 subs; Heynckes, Herzog 2 each; Wimmer 1+1 sub; Netzer, Hottges 1 sub each.

Final: West Germany 2 Holland 1   77,833 Munich

1978	**Argentina**	7	5	1	1	15	4	17	Fillol, Luis Galvan, Olguin, Passarella, Tarantini (1), Gallego, Kempes (6) 7 each; Ardiles 6; Bertoni 5+1 sub; Ortiz 4+2 subs; (2) Luque (4) 5; Houseman (1) 3+3 subs; Valencia 4; Larrosa 1+1 sub; Alonso 3 subs; Villa 2 subs; Oviedo 1 sub.

Final: Argentina 3 Holland 1   77,000 Buenos Aires
(after extra time)

Uruguay (1930), Italy (1938) and Brazil (1970) have been the only winners with 100% records in one final series. They are also three of the four countries who have won the competition more than once, along with West Germany who have been the highest scorers in one tournament. They scored 25 in six matches (1954) which produced the highest average of 4.16 goals per game. England had the best defensive record in 1966 with only three goals conceded in six matches. Their 11 goals in these games was the lowest average.

INDEX

CODE FOR COUNTRIES ON PAGES 125, 126, 127

A, Austria; Alb, Albania; Bel, Belgium; Bul, Bulgaria;
Cy, Cyprus; Cz, Czechoslovakia; D, Denmark; E, England;
Ei, Eire; EG, East Germany; F, France; Fi, Finland; Gr,
Greece; H, Hungary; Ho, Holland; I, Italy; L, Luxembourg;
Ma, Malta; N. Norway; Ni, Northern Ireland; P, Portugal;
Pol, Poland; R, Rumania; S, Scotland; Se, Sweden;
Sp, Spain; Sw, Switzerland; T, Turkey; USSR, Russia;
W, Wales; WG, West Germany; Y, Yugoslavia.

Year	Value
1871–72	15
1872–73	16
1873–74	28
1874–75	29
1875–76	32
1876–77	37
1877–78	43
1878–79	43
1879–80	54
1880–81	63
1881–82	73
1882–83	84
1883–84	100
1884–85	116
1885–86	130
1886–87	126
1887–88	149
1888–89	149
1889–90	132
1890–91	161
1891–92	163
1892–93	183
1893–94	155
1894–95	179
1895–96	210
1896–97	244
1897–98	213
1898–99	235
1899–1900	242
1900–01	220
1901–02	226
1902–03	223
1903–04	252
1904–05	274
1905–06	280
1906–07	305
1907–08	348
1908–09	361
1909–10	424
1910–11	403
1911–12	410
1912–13	457
1913–14	476
1914–15	454
1919–20	445
1920–21	674